T0295900

Risk Factors and Contagion in
**Commodity Markets and
Stocks Markets**

Risk Factors and Contagion in
Commodity Markets and Stocks Markets

Stéphane Goutte

CEMOTEV, UVSQ Paris-Saclay, France

Khaled Guesmi

Climate Change (CRECC) - Paris School of Business
& Telfer School of Management, University of Ottawa, Canada.

World Scientific

NEW JERSEY · LONDON · SINGAPORE · BEIJING · SHANGHAI · HONG KONG · TAIPEI · CHENNAI · TOKYO

Published by

World Scientific Publishing Co. Pte. Ltd.

5 Toh Tuck Link, Singapore 596224

USA office: 27 Warren Street, Suite 401-402, Hackensack, NJ 07601

UK office: 57 Shelton Street, Covent Garden, London WC2H 9HE

Library of Congress Cataloging-in-Publication Data

Names: Goutte, Stéphane, editor. | Guesmi, Khaled, editor.
Title: Risk factors and contagion in commodity markets and stocks markets /
　　[edited by] Stéphane Goutte, CEMOTEV, UVSQ Paris-Saclay, France,
　　Khaled Guesmi, Climate Change (CRECC) - Paris School of Business &
　　Telfer School of Management, University of Ottawa, Canada.
Description: USA : World Scientific, 2020. | Includes bibliographical references and index.
Identifiers: LCCN 2020001808 | ISBN 9789811210235 (hardcover) |
　　ISBN 9789811210242 (ebook)
Subjects: LCSH: Commodity exchanges. | Stock exchanges. | Risk management. |
　　Contagion (Social psychology)
Classification: LCC HG6046 .R577 2020 | DDC 332.64--dc23
LC record available at https://lccn.loc.gov/2020001808

British Library Cataloguing-in-Publication Data
A catalogue record for this book is available from the British Library.

For any available supplementary material, please visit
https://www.worldscientific.com/worldscibooks/10.1142/11549#t=suppl

Desk Editors: Aanand Jayaraman/Karimah Samsudin

Typeset by Stallion Press
Email: enquiries@stallionpress.com

Preface

The relationship between economies and commodity prices, including domestic, macroeconomic and financial variables, has often been debated in the literature. To measure the impact of commodities on the economy, one can distinguish different modeling approaches. First, commodities can be represented as the pinnacle of cross-sectional financial asset prices. Second, price fluctuations due to seasonal variations, dramatic market changes, political and regulatory decisions or technological shocks may adversely impact producers who use commodities as input. This latter effect creates the so-called "commodities risk".

Furthermore, commodities price fluctuations may spread off to other sectors in the economy, via contagion effects. Besides, stronger investor interest in commodities may create closer integration with conventional asset markets; as a result, the financialization process also enhances the correlation between commodity markets and financial markets. Our objective lies in answering the following research questions: What are the interactions between commodities and stock market sentiment? Do some of these markets move together over-time? Did the financialization in energy commodities occur after the 2008 global financial crisis? These questions are essential to understanding whether commodities are driven only by their fundamentals or whether there is also a systemic component influenced by the volatility present within the stock markets.

The main contributions of our book to the literature on contagion effects are as follows: firstly, we consider the dynamics of commodities, which is crucial in the case of international portfolio choice. Secondly, we make clear the difference between simple correlations due to fundamentals, and finally, we consider asymmetric effects and enable stock markets to vary through time. Besides, we introduce commodities risks as an additional channel of contagion in the category of global/macro risks that have not been covered.

Besides these fundamental drivers of financial markets cited in this handbook, commodities are also impacted by a context of progressive financialization of raw materials, which implies a comovement between commodities and financial markets. Hence, if fundamentals would tend to foster market integration, commodities financialization could bias this trend. Moreover, both market integration and commodities financialization are very dynamic phenomena, changing over time, therefore *a priori* each of these forces can counteract the other one depending on their relative strength. The objective of our book is therefore two-fold: first, to test financial market integration, and secondly to analyze how the commodity markets reinforce or weaken this macroeconomic phenomenon in a time horizon which encompasses some important macroeconomic events such as the financial and economic crisis. To this end, we bring together two streams of literature: on the one hand, works on capital asset pricing, and on the other, models on the relationship between oil price and stock markets.

About the Editors

 **Stéphane Goutte** has two PhDs, one in Mathematics and one in Economics. He received his Habilitation for Supervising Scientific Research (HDR) degree in 2017 from the University Paris Dauphine. He is Full Professor at CEMOTEV, Université Versailles St Quentin en Yveline, France. He teaches mathematics and related topics in MSc and BSc. He is also a Senior Editor of *Finance Research Letters*; an Associate Editor of *International Review of Financial Analysis* (IRFA) and *Research in International Business and Finance*; a Subject Editor of *Journal of International Financial Markets, Institutions and Money* (JIFMIM) and an Editorial member of *European Management Review* (EMR). His interests lie in the area of mathematical finance and econometrics applied in energy and commodities. He has published more than 40 research papers in internationally reviewed journals. He has also been Guest Editor for various special issues of internationally peer-reviewed journals and Editor for many handbooks.

Dr. Khaled Guesmi is a Full Professor of Finance at Paris School of Business, and Head, Center of Research for Energy and Climate Change (CRECC). He is also Adjunct Professor at Telfer School of Management, University of Canada. He undertakes research and lectures on empirical finance, applied time-series econometrics and commodity markets. Dr Guesmi obtained his Habilitation for Supervising Doctoral Research (HDR) degree in July 2015. He holds his PhD in Economics from the University Paris Nanterre (2011) and his MSc in Finance from Paris I University of Sorbonne (2005). Previously, he served as Professor of Finance and Head of Environment, Climate Change, and Energy Transition Chair at IPAG Business School and held associate research positions at "EconomiX" laboratory at the University of Paris Ouest La Défense and "ERF" Economic Research Forum, Egypt as well. In 2003, Dr Guesmi joined the UNESCO as a Research Manager, and in 2008, he joined *Caisse de Dépôts et Consignations* as a Financial Analyst.

Dr. Guesmi has published more than 70 articles in leading refereed journals, including the *Energy Journal*; *International Review of Financial Analysis*; *Journal of International Financial Markets, Institutions & Money*; *Annals of Operations Research*; *Energy Economics* and *Energy Policy*.

Dr. Guesmi currently serves as an Associate Editor at *Finance Research Letters* and on the international advisory board of *The International Spectator*. In addition, Dr Guesmi is the founder of the *International Symposium on Energy and Finance Issues* and the Project Manager of European Commission's Horizon 2020 Program for Research and Innovation. This program has focused on new models of cooperation between EU and the south-eastern Mediterranean region, which are expected to promote a radical re-design of the energy strategies of these countries, focusing on sustainability and efficiency policies. Cooperation, for instance, could be applied to various aspects of the energy sector, including the development of renewables, energy efficiency technologies and demand-side policies. Sustainability and efficiency are certainly the domains where EU support for these countries could bring added value.

About the Contributors

Abdulnasser Hatemi-J is a Professor of Finance at the UAE University. He received his PhD degree from Jonkoping University, Sweden, in 2001. Hatemi-J has developed tests for cointegration with two unknown breaks, tests for asymmetric causality, a new approach for portfolio diversification, hidden panel cointegration, asymmetric impulse responses, and a new formula for option pricing during financial crisis, among others.

Adil Oran is an Associate Professor of Business Administration and the Director of the GIMER Entrepreneurship Center at the Middle East Technical University (METU), Turkey. He teaches a wide array of courses including must and elective courses in finance, financial accounting, entreprepreneurship, business, investment valuation, and interdisciplinary problem solving. He greatly enjoys teaching, research, consulting, and mentoring.

Anupam Dutta is working as an Assistant Professor in the School of Accounting and Finance, Vaasa University, Finland. He has a number of publications in the area of financial economics. His other research interests include energy market volatility, financial market integration, asset pricing, and tourism management. He has recently published in top-tier Business journals including *Journal of Empirical Finance, Economics Letters, Tourism Management, Annals of*

Tourism Research, Journal of Cleaner Production, Resources Policy and many others.

Beyza Mina Ordu-Akkaya is working as an Assistant Professor in the Department of Business Administration at the Social Sciences University of Ankara. Her research interests include but are not limited to commodity markets, energy finance/economics, and contagion. She has publications in journals such as *Journal of Banking & Finance, Resources Policy, and Emerging Markets Finance and Trade*.

Dominique Guegan is currently an Emeritus Professor of Mathematics at the University Paris 1 Panthéon-Sorbonne and associate Professor at University Ca'Foscari in Venezia. Her domains of research are: Financial regulation, Fintech technology (Blockchain, big data, HFT), nonlinear econometrics modeling, Extreme value theory and risk measures in finance, pricing theory in incomplete markets and Deterministic dynamical systems. She has already published 11 books in statistics theory, time series and finance, contributed chapters in 30 books, and published more than 130 academic papers and supervised 30 PhD students. She has participated in several European projects and collaborated with French, European, Chinese, and North American universities on innovation fields including Blockchain and Artificial intelligence.

El Mehdi Ferrouhi, PhD, is a professor of finance and economics at Ibn Tofail University. His research focuses on finance, banking and stock markets, financial markets microstructure, and risk management.

Fatih Pınarbaşı is a Research Assistant in İstanbul Medipol University. He graduated from the department of Business Administration in Marmara University. After that, he acquired two different Master's degrees. One of them was taken from the marketing program of Marmara University. The second degree is related to the management program of Yıldız Technical University. He is a PhD candidate in business administration program of Yıldız Technical University. His research interests lie in digital marketing and data mining.

Hasan Dinçer is an Associate Professor of finance at Istanbul Medipol University, Faculty of Economics and Administrative Sciences, Istanbul, Turkey. Dincer has BAs in Financial Markets and Investment Management at Marmara University. He received PhD in Finance and Banking with his thesis entitled "The Effect of Changes on the Competitive Strategies of New Service Development in the Banking Sector". He has work experience in the finance sector as a portfolio specialist and his major academic studies focuses on financial instruments, performance evaluation, and economics. He has to his credit more than 150 studies and some of them are indexed in SSCI, SCI, and Scopus.

Ibrahim Jamali is an Associate Professor of Finance at the Olayan School of Business of the American University of Beirut. He completed his Bachelor of Arts in Economics at the American University of Beirut. He then earned his M.A. and PhD in economics at Concordia University in Montreal, Canada. Jamali's research centers on futures (and forwards) markets and predictability in asset markets. His research appeared in journals such as the *Journal of Empirical Finance, Journal of Futures Markets*, and *European Financial Management*. Dr. Jamali's research has also been featured in the *Wall Street Journal* and on *Risk.net* (centralbanking.com).

Jamel Boukhatem is currently an Associate Professor of Financial and Monetary Economics at the College of Islamic Economics and Finance, UQU Saudi Arabia. He was affiliated previously with the High School of Management, the High Business School, the High School of Business and Economic Sciences and the Faculty of Economic Sciences and Management (Tunisia). Jamel Boukhatem holds a Master's degree in Money Banking and Finance (University of Tunis El Manar) and a PhD in Financial Economics (University of Paris West Nanterre la Defense). He has published several papers in ranked journals such as *Annals of Operations Research, Finance Research Letters, Journal of Applied Business Research, Annals of*

Financial Economics. His current research interest revolves around Islamic economics, applied econometrics, and monetary and financial macroeconomics.

Jussi Nikkinen is a Professor of Finance as the University of Vaasa, Finland. His research interests include financial markets and risk management. Nikkinen has published over 40 scientific research papers in respectable international journals including *Applied Energy, European Financial Management, Journal of Empirical Finance, Journal of Futures Markets,* and *Quantitative Finance.* His research papers have received international and domestic Outstanding Paper awards.

Leila Dagher is an Associate Professor of Economics and the Director of the Institute of Financial Economics at the American University of Beirut (AUB). She previously chaired the Department of Economics at AUB, and has been an adjunct lecturer at the George Washington University since 2016. Dagher's research is at the nexus of energy, environment, and economics. Using econometrics tools and especially time-series econometrics, she studies various aspects of the environmental and energy sectors and their relationship to the economy. Her research is frequently presented at international conferences such as the ASSA and the WEAI annual conferences, and has appeared in The *Energy Journal, Energy Policy, Energy Economics,* and other leading peer-reviewed journals. Leila has been a visiting scholar at Harvard's Kennedy School of Government, GWU, Virginia Tech, UCLA, and the National Renewable Energy Lab in Golden, Colorado. Dagher holds a Bachelor of Engineering from the American University of Beirut and a Ph.D. in Mineral Economics from the Colorado School of Mines.

Marius-Cristian Frunza is a Director with Schwarzthal Kapital, a London-based advisory firm, and collaborates as Senior Researcher with the Ural Federal University in Yekaterinburg, Russian Federation. He lectures on alternative finance courses at the Dauphine University in Paris. His professional activity in the banking industry allowed him to specialize in risk management and financial crime.

His research activity encompasses topics in the area of alternative finance including environmental markets, cryptocurrencies, commodities, and sports betting.

Mazin A. M. Al Janabi is a Full Professor of Finance at EGADE Business School, Tecnologico de Monterrey, Mexico. Al Janabi holds a PhD degree from the University of London, UK, and has over 30 years of real-world experience in academic institutions and financial markets. He published in:*European Journal of Operational Research, International Review of Financial Analysis, Physica A, Journal of Forecasting, Annals of Operations Research, Applied Economics, Economic Modelling, Review of Financial Economics*, among others.

Mehmet Ali Alhan is a PhD candidate in İstanbul Medipol University. He has a BS in Business Administration (in English) from Çankaya University, 2005. After that, he acquired the Master's degree from Işık University in 2012. He is currently working on his PhD in the program of Management and Strategy in İstanbul Medipol University. His thesis is related to the analysis of social movements with artificial intelligence applications within the framework of strategic management.

Mouldi Djelassi is a Professor of Money and Banking, Umm ElQura University, Makka, Saudi Arabia. He holds a PhD in Economics from the University of Orléans, France. Djelassi's research passion revolves around Islamic Economics, Monetary, and Financial economics.

Nasser Badra is currently working as Associate Economic Officer at UN-ESCWA, EDID, Regional Integration Section, since July 2019. He also worked for the same department as Research Assistant between August 2017 through May 2018, where he contributed to the regional trade report, operated on large datasets including data analysis, using economic software such as STATA and MATLAB. He also worked for the modeling and forecasting section at EDID, UN-ESCWA analyzing sources of exchange rate misalignment in the MENA region. He gained his Masters in Economics from the American University of Beirut with best thesis of the 2013 graduating class and has a history of publication at peer reviewed double-blinded journals such as *Journal of Quantitative Economics* and *Journal of Research in International business & Finance*. Before joining ESCWA, Nasser has worked as full-time Research Assistant at the American university of Beirut, Institute of Financial Economics where he contributed to the publication agenda through econometric analysis and drafting reports based on findings that address monetary, fiscal, and development topics that have been published in international journals or as working papers. Also, he has been engaged in short-term constancy assignments analyzing food insecurity determinants using multilevel models.

Olfa Kaabia is an Assistant Professor of Finance at INSEEC School of Business and Economics. She received her MSc in Risk Management from the ENS Cachan and a PhD in Economics from the Paris West University in 2013. Before joining INSEEC Business School, she worked as Research Manager at Banque de France and AXA. She published many papers in ranked journals such as *Annals of Operations Research, Economic Modelling, Journal of Quantitative Economics* and so on. Her current research areas cover topics such as: Financial contagion, crises transmission channels, energy and financial market interactions, and cryptocurrencies.

Rostislav Haliplii was a commodity derivatives trader in the past, Rostislav is now advising top financial institutions in quantitative trading and risk management. He graduated in Financial Engineering at Imperial College London and is undergoing PhD in Economics from Paris-Sorbonne University. Rostislav is an avid promoter of innovative trading solutions and is the founder of darqube.io, a platform focusing on market analytics and algorithmic trading.

Serhat Yüksel is an Associate Professor of finance in İstanbul Medipol University. Before this position, he worked as a senior internal auditor for seven years in Finansbank, Istanbul, Turkey, and 1 year in Konya Food and Agriculture University as an assistant professor. Yüksel has a BS in Business Administration (in English) from Yeditepe University (2006) with full scholarship. He got his Master's degree from the economics department in Boğaziçi University (2008). He also has a PhD in Banking from Marmara University (2015). His research interests lie in banking, finance, and financial crisis. He has to his credit more than 130 studies and some of them are indexed in SSCI, SCI, and Scopus.

Timo Rothovius is a Professor at the School of Accounting and Finance, University of Vaasa, Finland. He has published in various areas of Finance (*European Financial Management, Applied Financial Economics, Global Finance Journal, European Journal of Operational Research*, and *Journal of Housing Research*) as well as energy economics (*Applied Energy, Energy, Journal of Commodity Markets*). At the moment, his main research interests include market microstructure and energy markets.

Uğur Soytaş is a Professor in the Department of Business Administration and Earth System Science Graduate Program at the Middle East Technical University (METU), Turkey. He is the co-editor of *Energy Economics* journal and the lead editor of *Routledge Handbook of Energy Economics*. He has an h-index of 25, i10 index of 33, and more than 6600 citations according to Google Scholar.

Youssef El-Khatib is an Associate Professor of Mathematics at the United Arab Emirates University. He received his PhD degree from La Rochelle University, France, in 2003. His research is on stochastic calculus applied to finance with emphasis on Malliavin calculus and applications to pricing, hedging, and sensitivities computations of financial derivatives.

Contents

Preface   v

About the Editors   vii

About the Contributors   xi

1. Bubbles on Bitcoin Price: The Bitcoin Rush   1
    Dominique Guegan and Marius-Cristian Frunza

2. Investigating the Association between Oil VIX and
    Equity VIX: Evidence from China   25
    Anupam Dutta, Timo Rothovius and Jussi Nikkinen

3. The Predictive Power of Oil and Commodity Prices
    for Equity Markets   47
    Leila Dagher, Ibrahim Jamali and Nasser Badra

4. Time-Varying Linkage between Equities and Oil   83
    Beyza Mina Ordu-Akkaya, Adil Oran and Uğur Soytaş

5. Has the Causal Nexus of Oil Prices and Consumer
    Prices Been Asymmetric in the US during the Last
    Fifteen Decades?   121

    Abdulnasser Hatemi-J and Youssef El-Khatib

6. Risky Financial Assets in Financial Integration and
    the Impacts of Derivatives on Banking Returns   133

    Hasan Dinçer, Serhat Yüksel, Fatih Pınarbaşı and
    Mehmet Ali Alhan

7. The Risk-Sharing Paradigm in Islamic Financial
    System: Myth or Reality?   161

    Jamel Boukhatem and Mouldi Djelassi

8. Commodity Markets' Asset Allocation with Robust
    Liquidity Risk Management Optimization Parameters   197

    Mazin A. M. Al Janabi

9. Comovements and Integration in African Stock Markets   237

    El Mehdi Ferrouhi

10. Interdependence or Contagion in Equity Markets?
    Evidence from Past Crises   257

    Olfa Kaabia

11. Impact of Contagion on Proxy-Hedging in
    Jet-Fuel Markets   291

    Dominique Guegan, Marius-Cristian Frunza and
    Rostislav Haliplii

Index   323

Chapter 1

Bubbles on Bitcoin Price: The Bitcoin Rush

Dominique Guegan[*,‡,§,¶] and Marius-Cristian Frunza[†,‡,∥]

*Paris-1 Panthéon-Sorbonne, 106 bd de l'Hopital, 75013, Paris, France
† Ural Federal University (UrFU), Ekaterinburg, Russia
‡ LABEX ReFi, Paris, France
§ University Ca'Foscari, Venezia, Italy
¶ dominique.guegan@univ-paris1.fr
∥ mfrunza@urfu.ru

1. Introduction

In 2014, *Fortune* magazine published an igniting article on Jeffrey Robinson,[1] one of the world's biggest financial crime authors who tackled cryptocurrencies, in a harsh way especially Bitcoin. The article made a very pessimistic forecast for Bitcoin's legacy. The French journal *Marianne* was even more direct, qualifying Bitcoin as the new scam *à-la-mode* on the Internet.[2] Despite a negative and reluctant reception from part of the public, cryptocurrencies are without any doubt the main financial innovation since the credit derivatives. Many libertarian economists see this new "virtual" currency as the new Holy Grail of a 21st century global economy trapped in a long

---

[1] Jeffrey Robinson argues that the Bitcoin movement will end in tears for the little guy. http://fortune.com/2014/10/24/bitcoin-fraud-scam/.

[2] Marianne, Bitcoin, The giant scam on Internet. http://www.marianne.net/Bitcoin-l-arnaque-geante-sur-internet_a231609.html.

recovery post-crisis scenario. Its advocates pledge for its advantages as sources of progress in the electronic economy and also for democratizing global trade and the access to currencies.

Bitcoin, by far the most popular, surfaced in 2013 (Figure 1) when its exchange rate with the US dollar rallied from almost nothing to 1,000 dollars for one Bitcoin, thereby leading most likely to the first virtual financial bubble.

Looking back at the history, it appears that alternative payment methods are not new and many solutions like PayPal, Apple Pay, and Google Wallet, which are still based on fiat currency, represent viable solutions mainly for e-commerce. Beyond these digital ways of using fiat money, new digital currencies have risen over the past two decades, cryptocurrencies being only a subcategory of digital currencies (Lee, 2015).

Attempts to create a distributed digital currency date from 1990 with DigiCash Inc., founded by David Chaum (Chaum *et al.*, 1990). DigiCash introduced eCash as probably the first cryptocurrency. Despite some initial popularity, eCash did not survive the 2000 Internet bubble (Frunza, 2015).

In 1971, when the Nixon administration liberated the US dollar from the Breton Woods' covenant, which implied a monetary mass backed by gold, many economists predicted the beginning of the country's economic decline. Nixon's idea that the dollar is backed by confidence remained one of America's fundamental doctrines. And yet investors had an appetite for a currency backed by gold and the opportunity came with the Internet era in early 2000, when digital gold currencies surfaced. Most of those second-generation digital currencies like iGolder, gbullion, and e-gold were in fact electronic money backed by one ounce of gold, which was stored for a fee. Their legacy was short as the companies that ran those currencies were either shut down by the Federal Government for various offenses or faded away due to heavy regulatory burdens (Frunza, 2015).

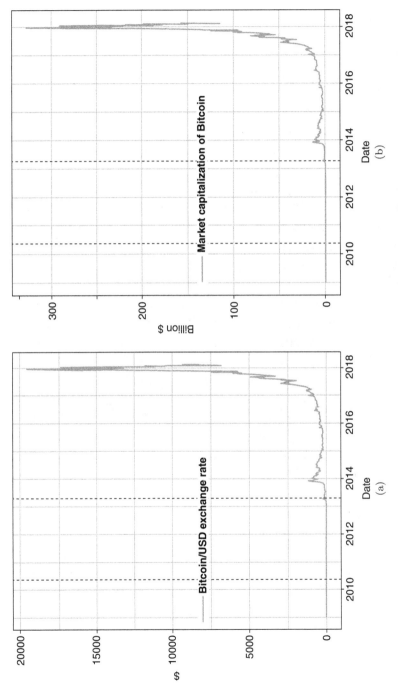

Figure 1: Bitcoin market price evolution. (a) Bitcoin–USD exchange rate reached the 1,000 dollars level toward the end of 2013 and 19,000 dollars in December 2017. (b) Bitcoin market capitalization in million US dollars is mainly driven by the exchange rate.

The main motivation, however, behind this study is to assess the sharp explosions in Bitcoin's price that occurred in 2014 and 2017. The econometric features and the price efficiency are channeling consistent facts on the economic nature of the Bitcoin in relation to other investments.

These aspects were explored by previous researches including MacDonell (2014) who used auto-regressive moving average functions to explain trading values, then applied log-periodic power law models in an attempt to predict crashes. Bouoiyour *et al.* (2016) used empirical mode decomposition and showed that despite the fact that Bitcoin is usually labeled as a purely speculative asset, it is extremely driven by long-term fundamentals (above 1 year). Dyhrberg (2016) tested the hedging capabilities of Bitcoin by applying the asymmetric GARCH methodology showing that Bitcoin can clearly be used as a hedge against stocks in the Financial Times Stock Exchange Index.

Another crucial issue related to the efficiency of the Bitcoin price is the role of speculation. Blau (2017) tested whether the unusual level of Bitcoin's volatility is attributable to speculative trading. Dwyer (2015) explained how the use of these technologies and limitations on the quantity produced can create an equilibrium in which a digital currency has a positive value and also summarizes the rise of 24/7 trading on computerized markets in Bitcoin in which there are no brokers or other agents.

This chapter enriches the literature related to Bitcoin's econometric features and explores these features. When looking at its statistical features, Bitcoin seems closer in nature to a commodity than to classic currency. The efficiency tests support this finding. The main results are focused on the presence and around the timing of bubbles in the Bitcoin–USD rates. The chapter is organized as follows: Section 2 discusses the nature of Bitcoin from a qualitative point of view, Section 3 explains the particularities of Bitcoin prices and explores the market efficiency test, Section 4 describes the methodology for bubble testing introduced by Phillips *et al.* (2013), Section 5 presents the results of bubbles tests and Section 6 concludes with a brief summary.

2. Bitcoin: Is Bitcoin a New Currency?

A first particularity of Bitcoin compared to other digital currencies is in the fact that it uses open source software, which is not owned by any one company, and there is no legal entity behind it (Lee, 2015). Nevertheless, a dedicated team that does the maintenance of the software does exist. The software that allows the interface with the Bitcoin universe can be downloaded freely, and the system runs through a decentralized and fully distributed peer-to-peer network.

This implies that all hardware terminals involved are connected to each other and each terminal can leave and rejoin the network at its convenience, and will later accept the information supplied by other terminals as the authoritative record. The basic idea in this way of functioning revolves around the concept of *blocks*, which incorporate the information about the previous validated transactions. In the world of physical currency, this would mean that the holder of a coin or a note would be able to trace all the previous owners of the money since its inception as well as all the transactions. The complete history of transactions is stored such that anyone can verify who the owner is of a particular group of coins. The blocks are aggregated in historical order in a blockchain. The number of transactions in a block is limited in size at 1,000,000 bytes to support quick propagation and reduce anomalies. The size of each transaction is determined by the number of inputs and outputs of that transaction. The transaction information is included in the body of a block. When a Bitcoin holder is connected to the system and reads the inputs from the blockchain, they have available the history of what happened previously in terms of transactions. The blockchain is thus like a general ledger, carrying the track of transactions, and is available to everybody at any given time.

Few studies including that of Burniske and White (2017) assessed Bitcoin's and generally cryptocurrencies's economic nature. When looking at the historical time series of Bitcoin–USD exchange rate, it can be easily observed that Bitcoin appreciated massively since 2013 as shown in Figure 1. The currency exhibits jump and regime-change, due to a multitude of factors, like technology advances, new arrivals in the mining arena, and changes in the confidence for both crypto- and real currencies. At the dusk of the financial crisis, cryptocurrencies appeared as a solution in order to provide an alternative tool to the failing classic financial system. The increasing lack of confidence in the banking system that culminated with the Lehman default in September 2008, and the perspective of deposit holders of their losing economies, inflamed the speculation around cryptocurrencies. They are perceived by some as a *deus-ex-machina* able to deal with the current situation. Cryptocurrency bypasses not only the financial system but also the governmental authority related to the financial system. For these reasons, Bitcoin and the similar underlyings represent more than a simple currency.

Scholars seem to find consensus (Selgin, 2013) in considering Bitcoin and generally virtual currencies as a "synthetic" commodity because they share features with both commodity money and fiat money. Bitcoin offers its owner an alternative that carries value in the same way stamps or art objects do. Thus, Bitcoin is more like a digital commodity that has a circumstantial intrinsic value, related to investor propensity toward it. The only difference from commodities is that it does not carry any physical/real value (besides the value of the hardware used for mining). Bitcoin could be perceived as virtual good or service used for transactions as simple as electricity or gas that is used for functioning houses and industries. This argument, juxtaposed with the econometric features discussed further in Table 1, makes Bitcoin move a commodity than a currency.

Bitcoin also offers its owner a unique right to exert financial activities at the international level, without passing through the classic system. In this new-system, there are or there should be no issues related to the country of residence of the parties and the regulation specific to those jurisdictions. The new Matrix is libertarian and is equal in terms of rights to trade or transfer money despite the embargo or sanctions that a country, corporation or group of individuals could face. At this point, the *Matrix* has no *Mr. Smith* to deal with the less compliant miners. This point gives Bitcoin a similar right-to-transfer-freely value in the same way that CO_2 or SO_2 allowances give their owners the right to pollute.

2.1. *Econometric models*

Statistics of the Bitcoin–USD rate (Table 1) underline that the returns exhibit strong kurtosis and high variance. Also, the time series show a positive significant asymmetry. The Jarque–Bera test indicates non-Gaussian features. In terms of distribution fit, the Normal Inverse Gaussian looks like the best candidate, as shown in Figure 2.

When looking at the annualized volatility of the Bitcoin–USD exchange rate exhibited in Figure 3, it appears that the cryptocurrency has more fluctuations than other forex markets. Even the US dollar to Russian ruble rate, since the Donbass crisis, has lower volatility levels (arround 50%) than Bitcoin–USD. European CO_2 pollution rights and British power prices have volatility levels comparable to Bitcoin–USD rate, reinforcing the above-mentioned hypothesis about, Bitcoin's nature.

The analysis of the persistence in returns with the auto-correlation function reveals a strong effect of volatility clustering (Figure 4), similar to what can be observed in many commodities markets from the energy complex.

Table 1: Descriptive statistics for the daily returns on Bitcoin–USD exchange rate.

Metric	Value
Mean	0.004289975
Maximum	0.6418539
Minimum	−0.4783052
Standard deviation	0.05841347
Skewness	1.485072
Kurtosis	21.60493
Jarque–Bera test	54327 (p-value $= 0.00$)

Notes: The series exhibit strong kurtosis and high variance. The Jarque–Bera test indicates non-Gaussian features (January 2010– February 2018).

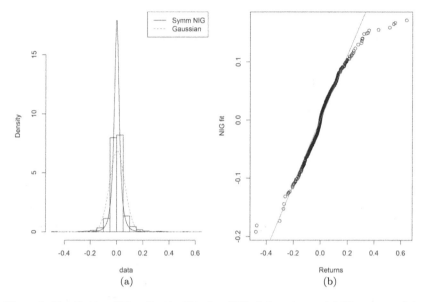

Figure 2: Distribution fitting for the Bitcoins–USD daily returns. (a) Histogram of the fit for the Normal Inverse Gaussian compared to the Gaussian distribution. (b) QQ plot for the observed returns against the NIG fit.

Table 2 shows the results of fitting GARCH models with various innovations to the daily returns of the Bitcoin–USD rate. The best fit in terms of Bayesian Information criteria (BIC) corresponds to the GARCH model with NIG innovations, thereby underlining the fat-tails effects.

A deposit holder in a specific currency bears in mind many of the aspects related to this very basic investment. First, the perspective of the currency and of the underlying economy, second the interest rate, and last but not the least the creditworthiness of the banks taking the deposit if the bank is located in the currency domestic country. The strengthening of the American dollar during 2014 compared to the European currency is a very good example to underline the first point. Since the Eurozone crisis, the American economy observed a faster and stronger recovery relative to the European Union and many analysts forecasted the US dollar going toward, parity with the Euro. Thus, based on this appreciation one could expect to see deposit flight toward the US currency.

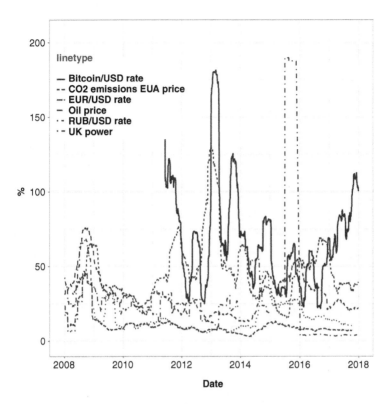

Figure 3: Volatility of the Bitcoin–USD exchange rate: Benchmark with other underlyings.

In the case of a cryptocurrency, it would be very difficult or almost impossible to make any judgments regarding the economy that backs the currency. In fact the only reasoning would be linked to the degree of confidence merchants have toward that particular currency. Interest rates are another argument for holding deposits in fiat currency, but in the case of crytpocurrencies, the interest rate seems to be a very complex topic. Currently, a Bitcoin account holder does not receive interest in the same way a Yen deposit holder does.

The point of the deposit guarantee scheme which is proposed for almost all developed countries for deposits lower than 100,000 dollars (euros) is out of scope in the case of the cryptocurrencies, at least until banks will adopt one of them.

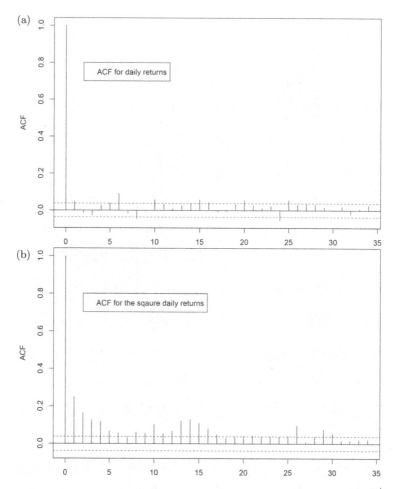

Figure 4: Autocorrelation in the Bitcoin–USD rates. (a) ACF for the daily returns. (b) ACF for the squared daily returns.

So the question relative to the true nature of Bitcoin (or other virtual/cryptocurrencies) is crucial before entering into further discussions about the Bitcoin–USD rates. Looking at its pure econometric features, it can be observed that Bitcoin is as different from a classic currency as can be.

The presence of persistence in returns, clustering in volatility, and fat tails in Bitcoin–USD exchange rate underline the fact that

Table 2: GARCH fit parameters.

Parameter	GARCH			GARCH-NIG			GARCH-STD		
	Value	Std	p-value	Value	Std	p-value	Value	Std	p-value
ω	0.000068	0.000037	0.066	0.000052	0.000023	0.025	0.000047	0.000022	0.03
α	0.158890	0.027404	0.00	0.196502	0.023891	0.00	0.198569	0.022786	0.00
β	0.838407	0.027757	0.00	0.802498	0.032198	0.00	0.800431	0.032863	0.00
ν							3.111196	0.119759	0.00
ζ				0.185832	0.033286	0.00			
ξ				0.324860	0.040720	0.00			
LL	4688.52			5241.528			5195.99		
BIC	−3.4186			−3.8171			−3.7867		

Notes: Successful fitting of GARCH model to the daily returns of Bitcoin–USD rate underlines the existence of clustering in volatility. GARCH(1,1) model with Normal Inverse Gaussian innovation provides the best results.

Bitcoin should be regarded differently from others currencies. From its features, Bitcoin has a lot in common with commodities, with sudden disruptures in the supply demand equilibrium. A first similarity would be with commodities from the energy complex (electricity, gas, emissions). Jumps and spikes in energy (electricity) prices are explained by the fact that small increases in demand can inflate the price rapidly and vice versa. Oversupplies can push prices very low if there is no need for that commodity. As revealed in Figure 1, the Bitcoin–USD rate exploded in 2013 and once again in 2017. This would be very uncommon for a real currency even in a fast growing emerging economy. The shock observed over 2014 and 2018, when Bitcoin lost almost 50% of its value to the US dollar, would have catastrophic consequences if it would happen for a real currency. Nevertheless, in the commodities world these kinds of variations are very frequent as regime changes in price equilibrium operate often.

2.2. *Bitcoin and market efficiency*

As the Bitcoin becomes more popular and the flows grow in volume and frequency, the question on market efficiency rises naturally. The EUR–USD exchange is one of the most liquid markets across the globe and given its features it could be a good candidate for market efficiency. In the case of Bitcoin, the dialectic is different from what one can experience in the classic markets. A Bitcoin deposit owner is generally a Bitcoin generator if he is also involved in the mining process. The mining process induces a lot of particularities that impact the market efficiency. In a classic efficient market, all investors have homogeneous access to information and the ability to buy and sell a fraction of the available stock. If classic currency faces high and sudden depreciation, the central bank can try to address the issues by buying back currencies or altering the interest rates. Obviously, in the case of the cryptocurrency these aspects are not applicable. The concept of mining that currencies create an asymmetry among "investors" is due to the fact that not all miners have access to the same mining tools, in terms of computation speed.

Thus, some have more advantages than the others given the features of their gear. Obviously, those with stronger mining tools have a comparative advantage in price discovery. Also, each technological jump creates new sources of asymmetry among miners. In theory, this heterogeneity due to technological aspects should be attenuated with times, when the total Bitcoin monetary mass will become stable, due to the fact that mining will become more and more cost-intensive.

If technology does represent a first source of behavioral asymmetry, another source of inefficiency is the breakdown of memory and computational capacity among miners. From this point of view, miner profiles vary strongly from a solo miner to pool mining and farms. A solo miner might use some classic technology like a central processing unit, a graphical unit, or application specific Integrated Circuit (ASIC) for generating Bitcoins on a standalone basis. In theory, the average time of a solo miner using a standalone computer to solve a block is around 2,000 years. Thus, the only economically feasible solutions are either massive inflation of the mining capacity or joining mining pools. Mining farms started becoming a trend in countries where the cost of electricity and rent were cheap, energy consumption being the main variable cost in the mining process.

Certainly, a mining farm or mining pool would have a net informational advantage compared to solo miners or smaller pools. Higher capacity of solving the cryptographic game implies a higher rate of block solving, thereby giving a better view on the Bitcoin inflows. If a Bitcoin pool trades forex against a real currency, they will have more information on the volume of Bitcoin that would enter the market. Structurally, they are better and more informed than a solo miner. This is a crucial source of market inefficiency, as a pool can generate bearish or bullish momentum on the market depending on the circumstances. Power market has similar issues in countries where there are big producers or quasi-monopolies. For example, in Germany the main energy producer RWE has obviously more information on the electricity market than a small broker, due to the position of the underlying main supplier and trader.

Table 3: Tests for assessing the efficient market hypothesis (weak-form).

Test name	Statistic	Critical value (95%)
Portmanteau	0.8522142	3.8
Chow and Denning	2.115319	1.959964
Wright (R1 statistics)	5.266816	1.917136
Wright (R2 statistics)	4.338164	1.903357
Wright (S1 statistics)	4.569499	1.930746
Lo and Mackinlay test	2.115319	1.95
Wald	4.474573	3.84

Notes: The tests are performed on the time series of daily returns of the Bitcoin–USD exchange rate from July 22, 2010, to February 21, 2018, assuming a holding period of 10 trading days.

Table 3 exhibits a series of tests for market efficiency (weak-form). All test statistics computed over a holding period of 10 trading days are higher than the 95% confidence level value, thereby rejecting the efficiency of the Bitcoin–USD rate from the following perspectives.

We recall the Lo and MacKinlay (1988) test for the random walk process, where they used stock-market returns. This involves the use of specification tests based on variance estimates. In particular, the method exploits the fact that the variance of the increments in a random walk is linear in the sampling interval, a hypothesis rejected in the case of the Bitcoin–USD rate in the Chow and Denning (1993) test, a generalization of the Lo and Mackinlay test, obtained from the maximum absolute value of the individual which statistics which confirms the results. Wright's (2000) alternative nonparametric test using signs and ranks is complementary to Lo's test. Both signs (R1 and R2) and ranks (S1) statistics reject the hypothesis of random walk. The Richardson and Smith (1991) version of the Wald test and the portmanteau test by Escanciano and Lobato (2009) for auto-correlation also confirm these findings. Markets do not become efficient automatically from their origin.

It is the actions of investors and various traders, sensing arbitrage opportunities and putting into effect schemes to generate profits from the markets, that make markets efficient.

From another point of view, bringing efficiency in the Bitcoin system is related to the mining capacity. Not all miners possess the same mining capacity and the mining capacity needs to increase much faster compared to the Bitcoin transactions. A double-edge effect can occur. On the one hand, there could be a massive increase in the number of new investors that purchase and trade Bitcoins, without mining. On the other hand, the mining capacity remains constant or progresses at a much lower level. This could be the reason why

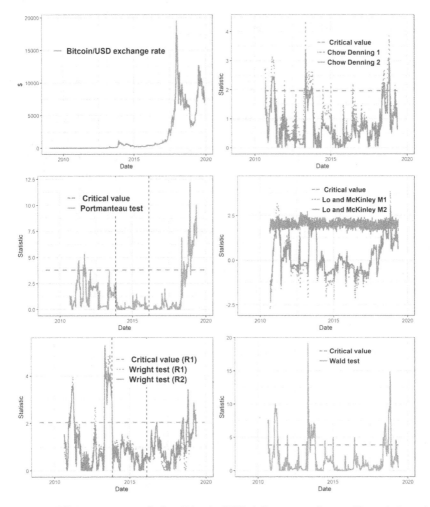

Figure 5: Efficiency tests applied to Bitcoin–USD daily returns for a rolling window of 200 days: Portmanteau test, Wright test, Wald test, Lo and MacKinlay test and Chow–Denning test.

the Bitcoin–USD became massively inefficient during 2013, when a massive inflow of demand was followed in an asymmetric manner in terms of mining ability. Figure 5 exhibits the random walk test applied over a rolling window of 200 days for a holding period of 10 trading days. The nonparametric Wright test underlines the non-random walk effect that occurred in 2013.

3. Testing for Bubbles

Since the South Sea Company frenzy in the early 18th century, financial markets faced many bubbles and as many crashes, the Black Tuesday from 1929 being one of the most dramatic ones.

The features of financial bubbles are explored in the academic literature. Zhao (2014) studied the unusual and puzzling stock price performance of USEC Inc., a company specialized in producing enriched uranium for nuclear plants. In July 2013, the stock price surged as much as 10 times over a mere 16 day trading period without apparent value-changing information being released and the hypotheses of market manipulation and speculative bubbles were analyzed.

Geng and Lu (2017) studied bubble-creating stock attacks, an interesting form of market fraud which is a mixture of manipulation and speculative bubbles in which speculators implicitly coordinate to pump up the stock price without any significant fundamental news and exploit behavioral-biased investors. The research provided empirical evidence in the Chinese stock market, underlining that stocks with low mutual fund ownership and stocks with high average purchase costs of existing shareholders are more likely to be attacked.

Johansen *et al.* (1999) presented a synthesis of all the available empirical evidence in the light of recent theoretical developments for the existence of characteristic log-periodic signatures of growing bubbles in a variety of markets.

Few straightforward methods for testing a market for bubbles are proposed by the recent works of Peter Phillips (Phillips *et al.*,

2011, 2013). These approaches come with enhanced versions of the augmented Dickey–Fuller (ADF) test (Dickey and Fuller, 1979 and Said and Dickey, 1984): sup ADF test and generalized sup ADF (GSADF) test.

The testing procedure for the ADF test for a unit root in time-series is based on the model as follows:

$$y_t = \alpha + \beta y_{t-1} + \gamma_1 \Delta y_{t-1} + \cdots + \gamma_p \Delta y_{t-p} + \varepsilon_t, \qquad (1)$$

where p is the lag order and $\varepsilon_t \propto N(0, \sigma_t)$.

Phillips *et al.* (2013) improved the basic version of the ADF test with a recursive approach that involves a rolling window with the implementation of the ADF style regression. If the rolling window regression sample starts from the r_1^{th} fraction of the total sample and ends at the r_2^{th} fraction of the sample, where $r_2 = r_1 + r_w$ and r_w is the fractional window size of the regression, the empirical regression model can then be written as follows:

$$y_t = \alpha_{r_1,r_2} + \beta_{r_1,r_2} y_{t-1} + \gamma_{r_1,r_2}^1 \Delta y_{t-1} + \cdots + \gamma_{r_1,r_2}^p \Delta y_{t-p} + \varepsilon_t, \quad (2)$$

where α_{r_1,r_2} is the intercept, β_{r_1,r_2} the coefficient on a time trend, and p the lag order of the auto-regressive process computed on the window $r_1 T$, $r_2 T$. Under these circumstances, the unit root null hypothesis is $\mathbf{H}_0 : \beta = 1$ and the explosive root right-tailed alternative hypothesis is $\mathbf{H}_a : \beta > 1$. The ADF statistic (based on this regression is denoted by $\mathrm{ADF}_{r_1}^{r_2}$ Phillips *et al.* (2011) where ADF_0^1 is the ADF statistics for the full sample. Right-sided unit root tests provide information about explosive or submartingale behavior[3] in the time series and can be used in speculative bubble detection.

The sup ADF test introduced (Phillips *et al.*, 2011) for single bubble detection searches for the maximum value of the test, for all forward looking windows for a given sample. The window size r_w

---

[3]It should be recalled that a discrete-time submartingale is a price time series $y_1, y_2, y_3, \ldots$ satisfying $\mathbf{E}[y_{n+1} | \Phi_n] \geq y_n$, Φ_n being the filtration with all information at the moment when the price is y_n.

varies from the smallest sample window noted r_0 to the maximum value of 1. In terms of the formalism in equation (2), the starting point r_1 is 0; and the end point of r_2 is chosen in such a way that the statistic $\text{ADF}_0^{r_2}$ is maximized, and the fact can be written as

$$\text{SADF}(r_0) = \underbrace{\sup}_{r_2 \in [r_0,1]} \text{ADF}_0^{r_2}. \tag{3}$$

A further improvement of the sup ADF test is the GSADF leveraging the idea of repeatedly running the ADF test regression on subsamples of the data in a recursive fashion. Thus, in addition to varying the end point of the regression r_2 from r_0 to 1, the GSADF test allows the starting point r_1 to change from 0 to $r_2 - r_0$. The GSADF statistic searches for the biggest ADF statistic over all possible starting points and possible window lengths,

$$\text{GSADF}(r_0) = \underbrace{\sup}_{r_2 \in [r_0,1], r_1 \in [0, r_2 - r_0]} \text{ADF}_{r_1}^{r_2}. \tag{4}$$

The bottom line of this test is to search for a period where the prices exhibit consistently increasing exponential trajectories.

4.   The Bitcoin Rush

Gold miners have been attracted throughout history to regions rich in gold and silver. From Dacia in antiquity, to California and Alaska in the early years of the industrial revolution, to Sierra Leone and Kirghistan in the present days, the perspective of generating quick profits from mining ignited the spirit of many generations. Similarly,

Table 4: Testing for bubbles.

Test name	Statistic	Critical value (95%)
sup ADF test	27.56	0.99
GSADF test	27.56	1.92

Note: Sup ADF and GSADF have both statistics above the 95% critical value, thereby rejecting the null hypothesis of a no-bubble-episode in the considered Bitcoin–USD time series.

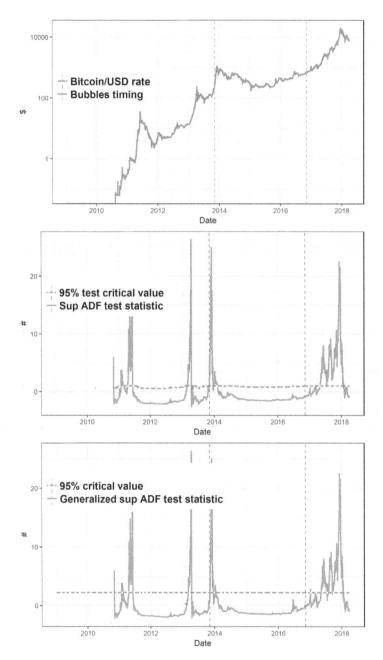

Figure 6: Bubble detection tests on Bitcoin prices. The sup ADF test indicates two bubbles during 2013. The GSADF test indicates also another mini bubble during 2012.

the foreseeable gains that the cryptocurrency world seems to generate through a new Bitcoin rush translated not only in a high number of new comers in the crypto-world but also a bubble of Bitcoin's value. As of 2017, the number of Bitcoin wallet users is around 10 million, compared to only 80,000 in early 2013.

The assessment of the formation and propagation of bubbles in markets can be utilized in many ways. The results obtained from applying this bubble detection approach to the Bitcoin–USD rate daily returns is shown in Table 4. The critical values from a 95% confidence level are the asymptotic values communicated in Phillips *et al.* (2013).

Figure 6 shows the evolution over time for the statistics of two tests and indicates the corresponding timing of the bubbles. The sup AGF test indicates two bubbles during 2013 and one in 2017. The GSADF test indicates also another mini bubble formed during 2011.

Bubbles are periods when markets change their features dramatically and also give a positive and biased signal to behavioral investors. During bubble periods, market prices are far removed from the fundamentals and investors may take irrational decisions. Bitcoin is no exception.

The episodes of the Bitcoin bubble resulting from the Phillips test are shown in Table 5. The main bubble episodes are from November 2013 to January 2014, when Bitcoin peaked at USD 1,151, and from May 2017 to January 2018 when Bitcoin peaked at USD 19,498.68. The 2013 bubble ended after the MtGox event (Frunza, 2015) that

Table 5: Timeline of Bitcoin bubbles.

Bubble timeline	Initial price (USD)	Peak price (USD)
2011-02-01/2011-02-18	0.95	1.1
2011-04-23/2011-06-13	1.7	35
2013-03-05/2013-03-05	40.04	237
2013-11-06/2014-01-11	258.23	1,151
2017-05-07/2018-01-21	1,560.41	19,498.68

Note: The main bubble episodes are from November 2013 to January 2014 and from May 2017 to January 2018.

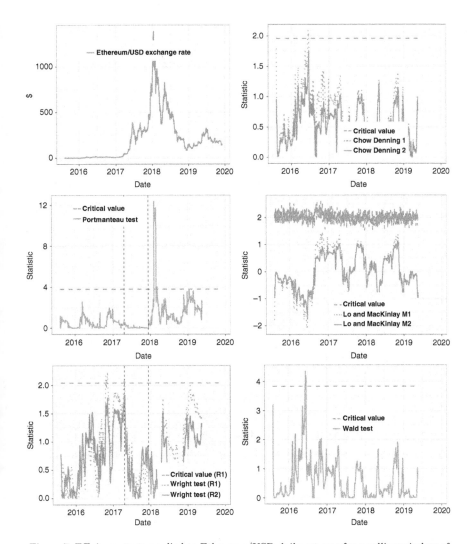

Figure 7: Efficiency tests applied to Ethereum/USD daily returns for a rolling window of 200 days: Portmanteau test, Wright test, Wald test, Lo and MacKinley test and Chow–Denning test.

led to the theft of 10% of all available Bitcoins at the time. The 2017 bubble ended when Bitcoin futures where listed on the Chicago Mercantile Exchange.

The same tests applied to Ethereum prices (Figure 7) showed no bubble effect as presented in Table 6. Thus, the price inflation of

Table 6: Testing for bubbles.

Test name	Statistic	Critical value (95%)
sup ADF test	−0.78	0.99
GSADF test	−0.15	1.92

Note: sup ADF and GSADF have both statistics above the 95% critical value, thereby rejecting the null hypothesis of a no-bubble episode in the considered Ethereum USD time series.

Bitcoins was not reflected with the same amplitude on Ethereum markets. An extended study on the presence of bubbles on altcoins will be addressed in a future research.

5. Conclusions

This chapter explores the occurrence and the timing of bubbles in the Bitcoin–USD rates. Being a very new and innovative currency, Bitcoin exhibits unique features that makes it different from other currencies. The problem is studied in two steps: first, the econometric features and the efficiency hypothesis are assessed and second, a bubble test procedure is developed and tested on Bitcoin prices.

The results from the first part indicate that Bitcoin's econometric features include volatility clustering and heavy tails. The weak efficiency hypothesis was breached on few occasions, during the 2013 price inflation.

The second part shows that bubble episodes occurred in 2013 and in 2017. The bubble effect on other altercoins will be addressed in a future study.

References

Blau, B. M. (2017). Price dynamics and speculative trading in bitcoin, *Research in International Business and Finance*, 41, 493–499.
Bouoiyour, J., Selmi, R., Tiwari, A. K., Olayeni, O. R., *et al.* (2016). What drives bitcoin price, *Economics Bulletin*, 36(2), 843–850.
Burniske, C., and White, A. (2017). Bitcoin: Ringing the bell for a new asset class. Ark Invest (January 2017) https://research.ark-invest.

com/hubfs/1_Download_Files_ARK-Invest/White_Papers/Bitcoin-Ri nging-The-Bell-For-A-New-Asset-Class.pdf.

Chaum, D., Fiat, A., and Naor, M. (1990). Untraceable electronic cash. In: *Proceedings on Advances in Cryptology*, New York: Springer-Verlag New York, Inc., pp. 319–327.

Chow, K. V., and Denning, K. C. (1993). A simple multiple variance ratio test, *Journal of Econometrics*, 58(3), 385–401.

Dickey, D. A., and Fuller, W. A. (1979). Distribution of the estimators for autoregressive time series with a unit root, *Journal of the American statistical association*, 74(366a), 427–431.

Dwyer, G. P. (2015). The economics of bitcoin and similar private digital currencies, *Journal of Financial Stability*, 17, 81–91.

Dyhrberg, A. H. (2016). Hedging capabilities of bitcoin. is it the virtual gold? *Finance Research Letters*, 16, 139–144.

Escanciano, J. C., and Lobato, I. N. (2009). An automatic portman-teau test for serial correlation, *Journal of Econometrics*, 151(2), 140–149.

Frunza, M. C. (2015). *Solving Modern Crime in Financial Markets: Analytics and Case Studies*. Academic Press, United Kingdom.

Geng, Z., and Lu, X. (2017). Bubble-Creating Stock Market Attacks: Widespread Evidence from the Chinese Stock Market, Available at SSRN 2897378.

Johansen, A., Sornette, D., and Ledoit, O. (1999). Predicting finan-cial crashes using discrete scale invariance.arXiv preprint cond-mat/9903321.

Lee, D. (2015). *Handbook of Digital Currency: Bitcoin, Innovation, Financial Instruments, and Big Data*. Academic Press, United Kingdom.

Lo, A. W., and MacKinlay, A. C. (1988). Stock market prices do not follow random walks: Evidence from a simple specification test, *Review of Financial Studies*, 1(1), 41–66.

MacDonell, A. (2014). Popping the bitcoin bubble: An application of log-periodic power law modeling to digital currency. Working paper, University of Notre Dame.

Phillips, P. C., Shi, S. P., and Yu, J. (2015). Testing for multiple bubbles: Historical episodes of exuberance and collapse in the S&P 500, *International Economic Review*, 56(4), 1043–1078.

Phillips, P. C., Wu, Y., and Yu, J., (2011). Explosive behavior in the 1990s nasdaq: When did exuberance escalate asset values? *International Economic Review*, 52(1), 201–226.

Richardson, M., and Smith, T. (1991). Tests of financial models in the presence of overlapping observations, *Review of Financial Studies*, 4(2), 227–254.

Said, S. E., and Dickey, D. A. (1984). Testing for unit roots in autoregressive-moving average models of unknown order, *Biometrika*, 71(3), 599–607.

Selgin, G. (2013). *Synthetic Commodity Money*, University of Georgia Economics.

Wright, J. H. (2000). Alternative variance-ratio tests using ranks and signs, *Journal of Business & Economic Statistics*, 18(1), 1–9.

Zhao, X. (2014). Trade-based manipulation or speculative bubble: A case study, *International Business & Economics Research Journal* (*IBER*), 13(4), 841–852.

Chapter 2

Investigating the Association between Oil VIX and Equity VIX: Evidence from China

Anupam Dutta[*], Timo Rothovius[†] and Jussi Nikkinen[‡]

School of Accounting and Finance, University of Vaasa, Finland
[*] *adutta@uwasa.fi*
[†] *tr@uwasa.fi*
[‡] *jn@uwasa.fi*

1. Introduction

Although the associations between oil and equity markets have been extensively explored over the last few decades, there is no consensus about such relationships among the researchers and economists. To be specific, the results of previous studies are somewhat mixed. While some papers (e.g. Hammoudeh and Li, 2005; Basher and Sadorsky, 2006; Hammoudeh and Choi, 2007; Nandha and Faff, 2008; Kilian and Park, 2009) find a negative link between oil and stock returns, several others (e.g. Sadorsky, 2001; El-Sharif *et al.*, 2005; Narayan and Narayan, 2010; Zhang and Chen, 2011; Arouri and Rault, 2012; Bouri, 2015a, 2015b) document a positive association between these markets. In addition, few studies (Chen *et al.*, 1986; Huang *et al.*, 1996; Apergis and Miller, 2009; Fowowe, 2013; Zhu *et al.*, 2014; Fang and You, 2014) even conclude that the markets under consideration do not move together.

Investigating the oil–stock link is vital, since variations in oil prices may have substantial impacts on the stock market as well as the overall economy. Ciner (2013), for instance, argues that variations in oil prices exert an impact on stock markets in two major ways. Firstly, uncertainty in oil market leads to a change in expected cash flows by affecting the whole economy. Secondly, such fluctuations in oil prices could have a significant influence on the discount rate used to value the stocks by altering inflationary expectations. Moreover, Vo (2011) contends that rising oil prices can have either a positive or a negative effect on the future cash flows of a company, depending on whether it is producing or consuming oil. Chiou and Lee (2009) also add that if variations in oil prices impact real output, rising oil prices will depress aggregate equity prices, indicating a significant linkage between oil and stock returns.

However, a central feature of all the studies cited above is that they have examined the association between oil and equity markets using the traditional price series and, to date, very little is known about the connection between the implied volatility indices of these markets. In fact, such studies are almost non-existent. The only exceptions include Liu *et al.* (2013) and Maghyereh *et al.* (2016). Each of these papers sheds light on the importance of using the information content of implied volatility indices. Liu *et al.* (2013), for instance, recommend crude oil volatility index (OVX) to be a better indicator of oil price uncertainty arguing that implied volatilities not only contain historical volatility information but also investors' expectation of future market conditions. The authors further add that the application of implied volatility indices, as measures of investor sentiment or risk aversion, could reveal more information than the historical price series. In addition, Maghyereh *et al.* (2016) argue that implied volatilities appear to be more accurate indicators in comparison to realized volatilities.

With a view to expanding this limited literature, we investigate the volatility transmission relationship between OVX and Chinese equity market volatility index (VXFXI). It is noteworthy that this study could not be possible without the introduction of VXFXI.

The Chinese volatility index has been recently published by the Chicago Board Options Exchange (CBOE). We choose China for a number of reasons. First, China was the second-largest oil consumer surpassing Japan in 2003.[1] Moreover, the consumption of crude oil in China has significantly increased over the last decade. For example, its oil consumption amounts to 272.74 million tons in 2003, reaching 507.40 million tons in 2013, implying an increase of 86.04%. Second, it is currently the leading oil-importing nation as well. In 2003, China imported 91.02 million tons crude oil and this figure turns out to be 281.92 million tons in 2013, increasing by 209.73%. Third, its economy is prominently stirred by the agricultural sector, which is highly sensitive to oil price volatility. Fourth, China's metal market is also highly oil-intensive. Zhang and Tu (2016), for instance, document that changes in oil prices will affect the costs of the production process directly, further resulting in the changes of metal prices. Finally, China's oil import dependency exceeds 50%, and the country's oil sector is greatly affected by the changes in international oil prices (Li *et al.*, 2016). Due to this high external dependency on oil, the global oil price fluctuations inevitably impact relevant industries in China and further affect its overall economic activity. Nonetheless, there is surprisingly little literature investigating the association between the Chinese stock market and the global oil market (Chen and Lv, 2015). Our study aims to fill this void.

This chapter adds to the prior works of Liu *et al.* (2013) and Maghyereh *et al.* (2016) in several aspects. First, our study mainly concentrates on an emerging equity market. Based on the recent statistics, emerging economies are the main consumers of energy-related products (58.1% of global energy consumption[2]). In addition, Basher and Sadorsky (2006) also document that compared to the developed economies, emerging markets are more sensitive to energy price uncertainty. Nevertheless, the existing literature is mostly focused on the developed markets and regions. The study

---

[1] *Source*: US Energy Information Administration (2014).

[2] *Source*: www.bp.com.

thus makes a contribution by furthering the evidence on the impact of oil volatility shocks on emerging equity markets.

Second, unlike Liu *et al.* (2013) and Maghyereh *et al.* (2016), we have adopted two sophisticated bivariate GARCH approaches to examine the volatility transmission relationship between stock and oil VIX. Such methods are popularly known as VAR–GARCH and VAR–AGARCH developed by Ling and McAleer (2003) and McAleer *et al.* (2009), respectively. By doing so, we also contribute to the limited literature dealing with oil–stock volatility linkages. This can be considered as a major contribution, since the volatility of an asset is associated with the rate of information flow to a market and hence volatilities from different financial markets could affect each other. Arouri *et al.* (2011) also argue that understanding the volatility spillover between oil and equity markets provides efficient means of generating precise asset-pricing models and accurate forecasts of the volatility of both markets. Such analyses can help investors as well for choosing appropriate portfolio management strategies during periods of uncertainty in order to mitigate risk (Caporale *et al.*, 2015).

Third, we examine whether OVX can be used as a hedging tool for the Chinese equity market option prices. Thus, our findings could help investors to hedge downside risk in oil markets and make appropriate investment decisions. In addition, the results could also be helpful to understanding the dynamics between OVX and VXFXI to construct volatility related portfolio containing OVX and VXFXI from the perspective of diversifying the risk of the resultant portfolio (Liu *et al.*, 2013).

Our findings, in short, suggest that volatility significantly runs from global oil to China's equity options. That is, the Chinese equity options are highly sensitive to oil volatility shocks. Such volatility linkages indicate that any turmoil in the oil markets could bring uncertainty to the Chinese economic development and growth. Therefore, the government in China should adopt appropriate measures to reduce the impact of oil price uncertainty. For instance, increasing the use of biofuels could comprehensively minimize the dependency on imported oil. The findings further document that although China, as one of the major oil consumers, plays an important role in the international oil market, we do not find any significant volatility transmission from its stock market to the global oil market. Besides, the results also support the usefulness of including crude oil in the equity option portfolio for risk management purposes. Thus, the findings have important implications for traders and investors in terms of portfolio diversification benefits. The outcomes of our empirical analysis are robust, in that the employed methodologies lead to similar conclusions.

The rest of our study is structured as follows. Section 2 reviews the related literature. Section 3 includes a brief description of the data. Section 4 outlines the bivariate GARCH methodologies. Results are discussed in Section 5. Section 6 concludes the paper.

2.   A Brief Review of Related Literature

This section briefly reviews the previous literature focusing on the relationship between oil and Chinese stock markets. Although such literature is very limited, there are still some important scholarly works to be discussed. We begin with the study by Cong *et al.* (2008) who investigate the interactive relationships between oil price shocks and Chinese stock market using multivariate vector auto-regression. The authors find that oil price shocks do not show statistically significant impact on the real stock returns of most Chinese stock market indices, except for manufacturing index and some oil companies. Zhang and Chen (2011) assess the impact of global oil price shocks on China's stock market, using the ARJI($-h_t$)–EGARCH model. Separating the volatilities into expected, unexpected, and negatively unexpected ones, the study reports that there are jumps varying in time in China's stock market, and that China's stock returns are correlated only with expected volatilities in world oil prices.

Moreover, Broadstock *et al.* (2012) examine how the dynamics of international oil prices affect energy-related stock returns in China. To do so, the authors use the time-varying conditional correlation and asset pricing models. The results suggest that the underlying stock market has a positive and significant reaction to the oil shocks, especially after the 2008 financial crisis. Besides, Li *et al.* (2012) explore the relationship between oil prices and the Chinese stock market at the sector level using a panel cointegration and Granger causality framework. Considering the effects of cross-sectional dependence and multiple structural breaks, the results indicate some evidence of structural breaks in the interaction between oil prices and Chinese sectoral stocks. When investigating the effects of oil price shocks on China's stock market returns, Wang *et al.* (2013) document that the Chinese stock market positively and strongly responds to oil-specific precautionary demand shocks.

Furthermore, Caporale *et al.* (2015) inspect the time-varying impact of oil price uncertainty on stock prices in China using a bivariate VAR–GARCH-in-mean model. The study reveals that oil price volatility affects stock returns positively during periods characterized by demand-side shocks in all cases except the Consumer Services, Financials, and Oil and Gas sectors. Chen and Lv (2015) examine the asymptotic dependence between the Chinese stock market and the world crude oil market based on the extreme value theory (EVT) and find a positive extremal dependence. The study also investigates the contagion effect and shows that the dependence level tends to increase dramatically during the crisis period, but that the simultaneous booms between these two markets decrease considerably after the crisis.

A recent study by Zhu *et al.* (2016) explores the dependence between real crude oil price changes and Chinese real industry stock market returns using the quantile regression approach. Empirical results reveal that the reaction of market returns to crude oil is highly heterogeneous across conditional distribution of industry stock returns. Additionally, adopting a structural vector auto-regression (SVAR) model, Li *et al.* (2016) decompose oil price changes into four components: oil supply shocks, global demand shocks, domestic demand shocks, and precautionary demand shocks and then investigate the impacts of these oil price shocks on the stock returns of

China's listed companies in the oil industrial chain. The study reports that the returns of the listed companies in the whole oil industrial chain benefit from appreciation in the oil price, the impacts of oil supply shocks and precautionary demand shocks are the most significant; and there was a structural change in the impacts of oil price shocks in 2012.

Reviewing the existing literature, we find only a single study by Luo and Qin (2016) that considers OVX to investigate the impact of implied oil volatility shocks on the Chinese stock market index and five sector returns. The empirical results suggest that oil volatility shocks positively affect the Chinese stock returns. More importantly, evidence indicates that the OVX shocks have significant and negative effects on the Chinese stock market while the impact of realized volatility shocks is negligible, especially after the recent financial crisis.

3. Data

In this chapter, we investigate the uncertainty transmission relationship between the implied volatility indices OVX and VXFXI. The use of implied volatilities is beneficial, since such indices can reflect markets' expectation for future near-term volatility. In addition, they are also considered as direct measures of market uncertainty.

The CBOE publishes OVX index, from the middle of 2007, as a measure of expected 30-day volatility of crude oil prices. The OVX considers real-time bid/ask quotes of nearby and second nearby options with at least 8 days to expiration, and weights these options to derive a constant, a 30-day estimate of the expected volatility (Liu *et al.*, 2013).

Our sample starts in March 16, 2011, and ends in June 30, 2016, providing a total of 1382 observations. We pick this period because the VXFXI data are available from the commencing date of our sample. We collect the information on OVX and VXFXI from the Thomson Reuters DataStream database.

Table 1: Descriptive statistics.

Index	Mean	Standard deviation	Skewness	Kurtosis	Jarque–Bera test
Panel A: Levels					
VXFXI	27.81	7.21	1.55	5.84	1025.26***
OVX	34.01	12.51	0.59	2.83	82.10***
Panel B: Logarithmic change					
VXFXI	−0.009	2.19	1.16	8.25	1899.09***
OVX	−0.003	2.11	1.07	16.52	10785.80***

Notes: This table reports the main descriptive statistics for different indices studied. *** indicates statistical significance at 1% level.

Table 1 displays the descriptive statistics for VXFXI and OVX (Panel A) along with their logarithmic change (Panel B). Now Panel A shows that OVX is more volatile than VXFXI, while the results of Panel B report the opposite. In addition, both these indices are positively skewed. We further report that the indices usually have kurtosis higher than 3, implying that these volatility series have leptokurtic distribution with asymmetric tails. The overall results thus imply that the volatility indices do not follow a standard normal distribution. Additionally, the Jarque–Bera test also rejects the null hypothesis of normality.

Figure 1 exhibits both OVX and VXFXI for the whole sample period. The figure illustrates that these volatility indices move closely together across time. In addition, several common spikes are observed in both indices and it is interesting to note that such spikes are the consequences of either economic or political events. For instance, the spike arising during the beginning of 2011 can be accredited to the sovereign debt and banking problems in Italy and Spain for which the uncertainty in equity and oil markets increases evidently.

Table 2 reports the unit root tests for the indices. We conduct three different tests including augmented Dickey–Fuller (ADF) test, the Phillips–Perron (PP) test and the Kwiatkowski–Phillips–Schmidt–Shin (KPSS) test to investigate the stationary condition. The ADF test and PP test have a null hypothesis of a unit root,

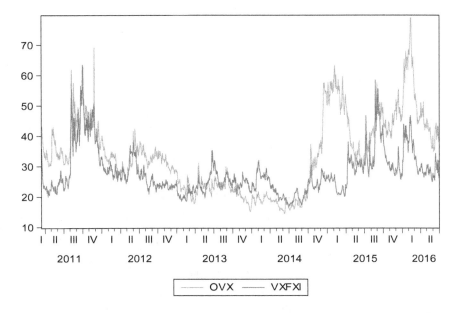

Figure 1: OVX and VXFXI for the whole sample period.

Table 2: Results of unit root tests.

	ADF tests		PP tests		KPSS tests	
Index	Level	1st difference	Level	1st difference	Level	1st difference
VXFXI	−4.67***	−36.60***	−4.31***	−37.69***	0.44	0.03
OVX	−2.75*	−39.10***	−2.51	−40.45***	1.01***	0.11

Notes: This table shows the results for the ADF, PP, and KPSS tests. *** and * indicate statistical significance at 1% and 10% levels, respectively.

while the KPSS test has a null hypothesis of no unit root. Observing these unit-root tests, we document that mainly the first-order differenced series are stationary for OVX, while for VXFXI we find stationarity even at the levels. Thus, the unit root tests are somewhat mixed. However, it is at least established that both OVX and VXFXI are stationary when the first-order differenced series are considered.

4.   Methodology

4.1.   *The VAR–GARCH approach*

Previous studies use multivariate GARCH models (such as BEKK or DCC) for the purpose of assessing the volatility transmission linkages among different financial markets. Some of the important studies include Malik and Hammoudeh (2007), Malik and Ewing (2009), Kang *et al.* (2009), and several others. Note that the BEKK specification is not free from limitations as it has issues related to convergence (Arouri *et al.*, 2012; Bouri, 2015a). In order to deal with such problems, we employ the VAR–GARCH model proposed by Ling and McAleer (2003). Chang *et al.* (2011), Arouri *et al.* (2011), and Bouri (2015a) have also considered this model to estimate the volatility cross-effects between oil and stock markets.

The initial step in the bivariate VAR(1)–GARCH (1,1) methodology is to specify the following mean equation:

$$R_t = D + \gamma R_{t-1} + \epsilon_t,$$
$$\epsilon_t = A_t^{1/2} \eta_t. \tag{1}$$

In Equation (1), R_t is a 2×1 vector of daily returns on oil and equity market implied volatility indices at time t, D defines a 2×1 vector of constants, γ denotes a 2×2 matrix of parameters measuring the effects of own lagged and cross-mean transmissions between two markets, ϵ_t is the residual of the mean equation for the oil and stock options at time t, η_t indicates a 2×1 vector of independently and identically distributed innovations, and $A_t^{1/2} = \mathrm{diag}(\sqrt{h_t^s}, \sqrt{h_t^o})$, where h_t^s and h_t^o, which indicate the conditional variances of stock and oil volatility index returns, respectively, are given as

$$h_t^s = d_s^2 + b_{11}^2 h_{t-1}^s + b_{21}^2 h_{t-1}^o + a_{11}^2 \varepsilon_{s,t-1}^2 + a_{21}^2 \varepsilon_{o,t-1}^2, \tag{2}$$

$$h_t^o = d_o^2 + b_{12}^2 h_{t-1}^s + b_{22}^2 h_{t-1}^o + a_{12}^2 \varepsilon_{s,t-1}^2 + a_{22}^2 \varepsilon_{o,t-1}^2. \tag{3}$$

Equations (2) and (3) allow us to explore how shocks and volatility are transmitted over time and across different indices. Now, the conditional covariance between oil and equity option returns is estimated as follows:

$$h_t^{so} = \rho_t \sqrt{h_t^s} \sqrt{h_t^o}, \tag{4}$$

where ρ_t is the conditional correlation between oil and stock returns at time t.

In order to capture the non-normality associated with oil and equity market indices, we employ the quasi-maximum likelihood estimation method to achieve the estimates of the parameters of our bivariate VAR(1)–GARCH (1,1) model. Later, we utilize such estimates to compute the optimal weights and hedge ratios.

4.2. *The VAR–AGARCH approach*

For the purpose of assessing the robustness of the results obtained from the VAR–GARCH approach, we now apply the bivariate VAR–AGARCH model proposed by McAleer *et al.* (2009). The advantage of using such a specification is that it is capable of capturing the asymmetric relationships between returns (Lin *et al.*, 2014). The bivariate VAR–AGARCH model assumes the following form:

$$h_t^s = d_s^2 + b_{11}^2 h_{t-1}^s + b_{21}^2 h_{t-1}^o + a_{11}^2 A(\varepsilon_{s,t-1})^2 + a_{21}^2 A(\varepsilon_{o,t-1})^2$$
$$+ B[(\varepsilon_{s,t-1}) \times ((\varepsilon_{s,t-1}) < 0)], \tag{5}$$
$$h_t^o = d_o^2 + b_{12}^2 h_{t-1}^s + b_{22}^2 h_{t-1}^o + a_{12}^2 A(\varepsilon_{s,t-1})^2 + a_{22}^2 A(\varepsilon_{o,t-1})^2$$
$$+ B[(\varepsilon_{o,t-1}) \times ((\varepsilon_{o,t-1}) < 0)]. \tag{6}$$

Within this framework, $A(\varepsilon_{s,t-1})^2$ and $B[(\varepsilon_{s,t-1}) \times ((\varepsilon_{s,t-1}) < 0)]$ along with $A(\varepsilon_{o,t-1})^2$ and $B[(\varepsilon_{o,t-1}) \times ((\varepsilon_{o,t-1}) < 0)]$ signify the relationship between a market's volatility and own lagged positive as well as negative returns, respectively.

5.   Empirical Results

5.1.   *Spillover effects*

The estimated results of our bivariate GARCH models have been reported in Tables 3 and 4. Table 3 shows the findings obtained from the VAR–GARCH model, while the outcomes of the VAR–AGARCH approach are presented in Table 4. In these two tables, h^o_{t-1} is a measure of oil market volatility at time $t-1$ and h^s_{t-1} refers to the conditional variance of the Chinese stock market at time $t-1$. Additionally, $\varepsilon^2_{s,t-1}$ and $\varepsilon^2_{o,t-1}$ measure the impact of shocks in stock and oil markets, respectively.

It is evident from Table 3 that in each market lagged returns do not impact the present returns, indicating the non-existence of short-term predictability in these markets. We further observe that OVX affects VXFXI returns negatively, albeit the corresponding parameter appears to be statistically insignificant. Such an outcome suggests

Table 3: Results of the VAR–GARCH model.

Independent variable	VXFXI	OVX
r^s_{t-1}	−0.0002 (0.99)	−0.0356 (0.18)
r^o_{t-1}	0.0357 (0.15)	−0.0361 (0.24)
$\varepsilon^2_{s,t-1}$	0.1419 (0.00)***	0.0118 (0.50)
$\varepsilon^2_{o,t-1}$	−0.0272 (0.00)***	0.0726 (0.00)***
h^s_{t-1}	0.7327 (0.00)***	0.0489 (0.85)
h^o_{t-1}	0.5220 (0.00)***	0.6404 (0.00)***
CCC		
VXFXI	1.000	
OVX	0.4569 (0.00)***	1.000
Log likelihood	−5670.98	

Notes: This table reports the outcomes for the VAR–GARCH model. r^s_{t-1} refers to the return on the Chinese equity options at time $t-1$ and r^o_{t-1} denotes the same for the oil market. In addition, h^o_{t-1} measures the conditional variance of the oil market option returns at time $t-1$ and h^s_{t-1} indicates the conditional variance of stock market option returns at time $t-1$. The squared error terms $\varepsilon^2_{s,t-1}$ and $\varepsilon^2_{o,t-1}$ measure the effects of unexpected news or shocks in stock and oil markets, respectively. CCC denotes the constant conditional correlation between VXFXI and OVX. ***indicates statistical significance at 1% level. Values in parentheses indicate *p*-values.

Table 4: Results of the VAR–AGARCH model.

Independent variable	VXFXI	OVX
r^s_{t-1}	−0.0079 (0.78)	0.0412 (0.13)
r^o_{t-1}	0.0438 (0.12)	−0.0069 (0.82)
$A(\varepsilon_{s,t-1})^2$	0.0270 (0.00)***	0.0024 (70)
$A(\varepsilon_{o,t-1})^2$	−0.0218 (0.00)***	0.0115 (0.00)***
$B[(\varepsilon_{s,t-1}) \times ((\varepsilon_{s,t-1}) < 0)]$	0.0339 (0.00)***	
$B[(\varepsilon_{o,t-1}) \times ((\varepsilon_{o,t-1}) < 0)]$		0.0359 (0.00)***
h^s_{t-1}	0.8320 (0.00)***	0.0054 (0.87)
h^o_{t-1}	0.1053 (0.00)***	0.7298 (0.00)***
CCC		
VXFXI	1.000	
OVX	0.4493 (0.00)***	1.000
Log likelihood	−5627.94	

Notes: This table reports the outcomes for the VAR–AGARCH model. r^s_{t-1} refers to the return on the Chinese equity options at time $t-1$ and r^o_{t-1} denotes the same for the oil market. In addition, h^o_{t-1} measures the conditional variance of the oil market option returns at time $t-1$ and h^s_{t-1} indicates the conditional variance of stock market option returns at time $t-1$. The squared error terms $\varepsilon^2_{s,t-1}$ and $\varepsilon^2_{o,t-1}$ measure the effects of unexpected news or shocks in stock and oil markets, respectively. CCC denotes the constant conditional correlation between VXFXI and OVX. ***indicates statistical significance at 1% level. Values in parentheses indicate *p*-values.

that there is no price spillover between these two volatility indices. This result is consistent with Fang and You (2014) who also document, using traditional price indices, an insignificant relationship between global oil and the Chinese stock market returns.

When turning to the estimates of the variance equations, our analysis further suggests that the Chinese implied volatility index does receive volatility from the international oil market volatility index. Thus, the uncertainty caused by the global oil price volatility may have an impact on China's equity market. This result is expected due to the fact that China has to rely heavily on foreign oil, as its domestic production fails to meet the country's net oil demand. Moreover, oil remains the dominant fuel in China's industrial and transport sectors. In addition, over the last decade, China has been the most important driver of crude oil market due to its exponentially growing economy. The oil consumption in China has also substantially increased in recent years. Since China's economic growth is largely dependent on the global oil market, its financial markets seem to be highly susceptible to changes in world oil prices. Not surprisingly, there is no evidence of risk spillover from the underlying stock market to the energy market. The possible reason could be that China is a leading oil-importing country, not an oil-exporting one, even though the increasing oil demand in China could exert an impact on the international oil market. Maghyereh *et al.* (2016) also document similar results while studying the association among implied volatility indices of global oil and different oil-importing markets. The authors show that the connection is largely dominated by the transmissions from the oil market to equity markets and not the other way around.

The results presented in Table 3 further show that the Chinese stock market is also affected by the shock and news emanating from the crude oil market, while the reverse effect is not found to be statistically significant. Furthermore, we find a strong positive correlation between OVX and VXFXI returns suggesting that maintaining a portfolio using these assets would not be highly beneficial.

Next the findings, shown in Table 4, mirror those reposted in Table 3. The results for this model coincide with those of the VAR–GARCH model due to the evidence of strong ARCH and GARCH effects and significant volatility spillover between oil and equity markets. Like the VAR–GARCH approach, the VAR–AGARCH method also confirms that the volatility spillover effect runs only from the oil to the stock markets. As mentioned earlier, this finding is not unexpected since China is one of the largest oil-consuming nations and, consequently, oil volatility shocks are likely to affect its equity market and hence the real economic activity. Li and Leung (2011) also contend that China is now an active participant in the world oil market, showing that oil prices in China are statistically maintaining a long-run relationship with major world oil prices. Therefore, dynamics in the global oil price could affect the overall economic performance in China. Our findings further indicate the significance of the multivariate asymmetric effects for both market returns. The positive association between negative returns and volatility specifies that "bad news" increases volatility in the markets while "good news", despite being significant, does not have the same effect on volatility, as documented by the size of the coefficients.

On the whole, our findings reveal that causality significantly runs from oil implied volatility to stock implied volatility. That is, the direction of causality between implied volatilities of equity and crude oil markets is dominated by oil. Thus, China is evidently affected by the international oil price shocks. Previous literature explains the origins of this significant uncertainty transmission from the oil market to the equity market. Maghyereh *et al.* (2016), for instance, argue that oil price volatility may create comparable uncertainties regarding business cost, disposable income, and consumer spending on energy using durable goods. In addition, volatile oil markets may also convey information on future global economic uncertainty. As a result, they can influence the volatility in global equity markets.

It is worth mentioning that the results of the bivariate GARCH models are consistent with a large number of existing studies (e.g. Malik and Ewing, 2009; Arouri *et al.*, 2011, 2012; Bouri, 2015a, 2015b and others) that report significant linkages between the oil and equity volatilities. However, we differ from the existing literature, in that our analysis is based on the implied volatilities of the oil and equity markets.

Moreover, the findings of our empirical analysis suggest that China should adopt appropriate policies to deal with oil market volatility. One possible policy could be the improvement of China's strategic oil reserves system to stabilize its oil price as the oil reserve is essential for those countries which are highly dependent on imported oil. Earlier studies such as Wang and Zhang (2014) and Zhang and Tu (2016) also argue that the oil reserve system reduces the impacts of oil supply shocks by stabilizing prices and eliminating the risk of oil supply by changing the oil inventory during the period of uncertainty. Additionally, the industrial sectors in China could make use of other energies, for example, biofuels and solar energy, in order to minimize the oil dependency. Such renewable and environmental friendly energies should be exploited so as to diversify the energy structure and moderate the dependence on overseas oil (Wang and Zhang, 2014).

5.2.   *Economic implications of the results*

We now utilize the estimates of our bivariate VAR–GARCH and VAR–AGARCH models to analyze how oil price risk can be hedged effectively. Lets' suppose an investor is holding options in the Chinese equity market and he would like to hedge his exposure against the adverse movements in oil option prices. Following Kroner and Ng (1998), the optimal portfolio weight can be constructed as follows:

$$\omega_t^{so} = \frac{h_t^s - h_t^{so}}{h_t^o - 2h_t^{so} + h_t^s}, \tag{7}$$

where ω_t^{so} refers to the weight of oil in a \$1 portfolio consisting of oil and equity options at time t, h_t^s and h_t^o indicate the conditional covariances of stock and oil options, respectively, and h_t^{so} denotes the covariance term between these two markets at time t. The weight for the equity option is then given by $(1 - \omega_t^{so})$.

Additionally, our results could also be exercised for computing optimal hedge ratios for the portfolio considered. Kroner and Sultan (1993) show that in order to minimize the risk of a portfolio, an investor should short β_t dollar in the equity market which is one dollar long in the oil market, where β_t is given by

$$\beta_t^{so} = \frac{h_t^{so}}{h_t^s}. \tag{8}$$

The values of optimum portfolio weights ω_t^{so} and hedge ratios β_t^{so} are presented in Table 5. These numbers reveal that the optimal weights provided by the VAR–GARCH approach are equal to 0.54 and 0.46, respectively, suggesting that for a \$1 portfolio, on average 54 cents should be invested in the oil market and the remaining 46 cents should be utilized on equity option. The corresponding weights produced by the VAR–AGARCH model are 53% and 47%, respectively. Thus, the overall outcomes suggest that investors holding assets in oil and Chinese equity options should invest more in oil than in stock

Table 5: Portfolio optimum weights and Hedge ratios.

Model ↓	ω_t^{so}	β_t^{so}
VAR–GARCH	0.54	0.44
VAR–AGARCH	0.53	0.42

Notes: This table shows the average optimal weights along with hedge ratios for the oil–stock portfolio. The crude oil volatility index is considered as the oil asset, while the Chines equity market volatility index is employed to represent the stock market.

in order to reduce the portfolio risk without impacting the expected return.

When turning to the hedge ratio results, we observe that the estimated risk minimizing hedge ratio for our VAR(1)–GARCH(1,1) model is 0.44 between oil and China's equity options. This finding shows that while holding a long position for \$1 in the oil market, investors should short 44 cents on the Chinese volatility index. The corresponding hedge ratio found from the VAR–AGARCH model amounts to 0.42.

Following Ku *et al.* (2007), we also obtain the hedging effectiveness (HE) for our oil–stock portfolio. This can be determined by examining the realized hedging errors given as

$$\text{HE} = \frac{\text{Var}_{\text{unhedged}} - \text{Var}_{\text{hedged}}}{\text{Var}_{\text{unhedged}}}, \tag{9}$$

where $\text{Var}_{\text{unhedged}}$ refers to the variance of the returns on VXFXI and $\text{Var}_{\text{hedged}}$ indicates the variance of returns on the OVX–VXFXI portfolios. Note that a higher HE of a given portfolio results in greater portfolio risk reduction, implying that the underlying investment policy is reckoned as a superior hedging scheme (Arouri *et al.*, 2011). The outcomes of Table 6 indicate that hedging strategies comprising oil and stock assets significantly minimize the portfolio risk. We further document that the reduction in variance due to the inclusion of oil in an optimal portfolio ranges from 30.27% for VAR–GARCH approach

Table 6: Hedging effectiveness.

Model ↓	Variance (unhedged)	Variance (hedged)	HE (%)
VAR–GARCH	4.79	3.34	30.27
VAR–AGARCH	4.79	3.26	31.94

Notes: This table presents the hedging effectiveness for the oil–stock portfolio. $\text{Var}_{\text{unhedged}}$ indicates the variance of the returns on the portfolio of equity option and $\text{Var}_{\text{hedged}}$ denotes the variance of returns of the oil–stock portfolio. HE implies the hedging effectiveness.

to 31.94% for VAR–AGARCH model. We thus conclude that significant portfolio diversification benefits are possible if investors hold options in both the oil and equity markets.

6. Conclusion

Although a strand of literature has investigated the associations between oil and stock markets over the years, examining of such links using implied volatility indices has been rare. In order to conceal this gap, the present study makes an attempt to focus on the linkages of implied volatilities that are used to price global oil and Chinese equity options. In particular, we explore the return and volatility transmission relationship between crude oil OVX and the Chinese VXFXI. In order to serve our purpose, we employ the VAR–GARCH as well as the VAR–AGARCH methodologies. The findings of our empirical analyses are robust, in that both approaches yield similar results. Below are the summaries of our major findings.

First, we document strong evidence of ARCH and GARCH effects in global oil and China's equity option markets. The sum of GARCH parameters also indicates high degree of persistence in the return fluctuations. Second, we do not find any evidence of return spillover between these two markets. Third, there exists a unidirectional volatility spillover running from oil implied volatility to equity implied volatility. The results thus suggest that the global oil market embodies a crucial role in predicting the Chinese stock market trends. It is not surprising that the Chinese economy is very sensitive to oil volatility shocks. Oil consumption in China has remarkably increased over the years and accordingly its important industries (e.g. agriculture and metal) have become highly oil-intensive. Since China is heavily dependent on imported oil, its overall economy significantly reacts to the variations in global oil prices. Finally, the portfolio risk analysis shows that if investors diversify their portfolios by holding options in both global oil and the Chinese equity markets, the resulting portfolios would significantly improve on the original a great deal in terms of reducing market risk or increasing long-term benefits. That is, such investments could generate remarkable long-run gains in portfolio diversification.

The findings of our empirical analysis have important implication for investors and policymakers who are interested in derivative pricing, portfolio rebalancing, and risk management practices. Investors, for example, could use our results to have better understanding of the cross-market linkages in terms of asset return and volatility transmission for building efficient business strategies and designing optimal portfolios. Policymakers, on the other hand, could implement effective measures during periods of uncertainty in order to reduce the oil price risk. Adopting such policies will then help to ensure a country's economy from global oil price shocks.

Acknowledgments

Jussi Nikkinen gratefully acknowledges the generous financial support from the Niilo Helander Foundation. The chapter has greatly benefited from the comments of discussants and participants at the 2017 European Financial Management Symposium.

References

Apergis, N. and Miller, S. (2009). Do structural oil-market shocks affect stock prices? *Energy Economics*, 31, 569–575.
Arouri, M., Jouini, J. and Nguyen, D. (2011). Volatility spillovers between oil prices and stock sector returns: Implications for portfolio management, *Journal of International Money and Finance*, 30, 1387–1405.

Arouri, M., Jouini, J. and Nguyen, D. (2012). On the impacts of oil price fluctuations on European equity markets: Volatility spillover and hedging effectiveness, *Energy Economics*, 34, 611–617.

Arouri, M. and Rault, C. (2012). Oil prices and stock markets in GCC countries: Empirical evidence from panel analysis, *International Journal of Finance and Economics*, 17, 242–253.

Basher, S. and Sadorsky, P. (2006). Oil price risk and emerging stock markets, *Global Finance Journal*, 17, 224–251.

Bouri, E. (2015a). Return and volatility linkages between oil prices and the Lebanese stock market in crisis periods, *Energy*, 89, 365–371.

Bouri, E. (2015b). Oil volatility shocks and the stock markets of oil-importing MENA economies: A tale from the financial crisis, *Energy Economics*, 51, 590–598.

Broadstock, D. C., Cao, H. and Zhang, D. Y. (2012). Oil shocks and their impact on energy related stocks in China, *Energy Economics*, 34, 1888–1895.

Caporale, G. M., Ali, F. M. and Spagnolo, N. (2015). Oil price uncertainty and sectoral stock return in China: A time varying approach, *China Economic Review*, 34, 311–321.

Chang, C.-L., Khamkaew, T., Tansuchat, R. and McAleer, M. (2011). Interdependence of international tourism demand and volatility in leading ASEAN destinations, *Tourism Economics*, 17, 481–507.

Chen, Q. and Lv, X. (2015). The extreme-value dependence between the crude oil price and Chinese stock markets, *International Review of Economics and Finance*, 39, 121–132.

Chen, N., Roll, R. and Ross, S. (1986). Economic forces and the stock market, *Journal of Business*, 59, 383–403.

Chiou, J. S. and Lee, Y. H. (2009). Jump dynamics and volatility: Oil and the stock markets, *Energy*, 34, 788–796.

Ciner, C. (2013). Oil and stock returns: Frequency domain evidence, *Journal of International Financial Markets Institutions and Money*, 23, 1–11.

Cong, R. G., Wei, Y. M., Jiao, J. L. and Fan, Y. (2008). Relationships between oil price shocks and stock market: An empirical analysis from China, *Energy Policy*, 36, 3544–3553.

El-Sharif, I., Brown, D., Nixon, B. and Russel, A. (2005). Evidence on the nature and extent of the relationship between oil prices and equity values in the UK, *Energy Economics*, 27, 819–930.

Fang, C. R. and You, S. Y. (2014). The impact of oil price shocks on the large emerging countries' stock prices: Evidence from China, India and Russia, *International Review of Economics and Finance*, 29, 330–338.

Fowowe, B. (2013). Jump dynamics in the relationship between oil prices and the stock market: Evidence from Nigeria, *Energy*, 56, 31–38.

Hammoudeh, S. and Choi, K. (2007). Characteristics of permanent and transitory returns in oil-sensitive emerging stock markets: The case of GCC countries, *Journal of International Financial Markets Institutions and Money*, 17, 231–245.

Hammoudeh, S. and Li, H. (2005). Oil sensitivity and systematic risk in oil-sensitive stock indices, *Journal of Economics and Business*, 57, 1–21.

Huang, R., Masulis, R. and Stoll, H. (1996). Energy shocks and financial markets, *Journal of Futures Markets*, 16, 1–27.

Kang, S. H., Kang, S. M. and Yoon, S. M. (2009). Forecating volatility of crude oil markets, *Energy Economics*, 31, 119–125.

Kilian, L. and Park, C. (2009). The impact of oil price shocks on the U.S. stock market, *International Economic Review*, 50, 1267–1287.

Kroner, K. F. and Ng, V. K. (1998). Modeling asymmetric movements of asset prices, *Review of Financial Studies*, 11, 844–871.

Kroner, K. F. and Sultan, J. (1993). Time dynamic varying distributions and dynamic hedging with foreign currency futures, *Journal of Financial and Quantitative Analysis*, 28, 535–551.

Ku, Y. H. H., Chen, H. C. and Chen, K. H. (2007). On the application of the dynamic conditional correlation model in estimating optimal time-varying hedge ratios, *Applied Economics Letters*, 14, 503–509.

Li, Q. M., Cheng, K. and Yang, X. G. (2017). Response pattern of stock returns to international oil price shocks: From the perspective of China's oil industrial chain, *Applied Energy*, 185, 1821–1831.

Li, R. and Leung, G. C. K. (2011). The integration of China into the world crude oil market since 1998, *Energy Policy*, 39, 5159–5166.

Li, S. F., Zhu, H. M. and Yu, K. (2012). Oil prices and stock market in China: A sector analysis using panel cointegration with multiple breaks, *Energy Economics*, 34, 1951–1958.

Lin, B., Wesseh Jr, P. K. and Appiah, M. O. (2014). Oil price fluctuation, volatility spillover and the Ghanaian equity market: Implication for portfolio management and hedging effectiveness, *Energy Economics*, 42, 172–182.

Ling, S. and McAleer, M. (2003). Asymptotic theory for a vector ARMA-GARCH model, *Econometric Theory*, 19, 278–308.

Liu, M. L., Ji, Q. and Fan, Y. (2013). How does oil market uncertainty interact with other markets: An empirical analysis of implied volatility index? *Energy*, 55, 860–868.

Luo, X. and Qin, S. (2016). Oil price uncertainty and Chinese stock returns: New evidence from the oil volatility index, *Finance Research letters*, 20, 29–34.

Maghyereh, A. I., Awartani, B. and Bouri, E. (2016). The directional volatility connectedness between crude oil and equity markets: New evidence from implied volatility indexes, *Energy Economics*, 57, 78–93.

Malik, F. and Ewing, B. T. (2009). Volatility transmission between oil prices and equity sector returns, *International Review of Financial Analysis*, 18, 95–100.

Malik, S. and Hammoudeh, S. (2007). Shock and volatility transmission in the oil, US and Gulf equity markets, *International Review of Economics and Finance*, 17, 357–368.

McAleer, M., Hoti, S. and Chan, F. (2009). Structure and asymptotic theory for multivariate asymmetric conditional volatility, *Econometric Reviews*, 28, 422–440.

Nandha, M. and Faff, R. (2008). Does oil move equity prices? A global view, *Energy Economics*, 30, 986–997.

Narayan, P. and Narayan, S. (2010). Modelling the impact of oil prices on Vietnam's stock prices, *Applied Energy*, 87, 356–361.

Sadorsky, P. (2001). Risk factors in stocks returns of Canadian oil and gas companies, *Energy Economics*, 23, 17–28.

Vo, M. T. (2011). Oil and stock market volatility: A multivariate stochastic volatility perspective, *Energy Economics*, 33, 956–965.

Wang, Y., Wu, C. and Yang, L. (2013). Oil price shocks and stock market activities: Evidence from oil-importing and oil-exporting countries, *Journal of Comparative Economics*, 41, 1220–1239.

Wang, X. and Zhang, C. (2014). The impacts of global oil price shocks on China's fundamental industries, *Energy Policy*, 68, 394–402.

Zhang, C. G. and Chen, X. Q. (2011). The impact of global oil price shocks on China's stock returns: Evidence from the ARJI $(-ht)$-EGARCH model, *Energy*, 36, 6627–6633.

Zhang, C. and Tu, X. (2016). The effect of global oil price shocks on China's metal markets, *Energy Policy*, 90, 131–139.

Zhu, H., Guo, Y., You, W. and Xu, Y. (2016). The heterogeneity dependence between crude oil price changes and industry stock market returns in China: Evidence from a quantile regression approach, *Energy Economics*, 55, 30–41.

Zhu, H. M., Li, R. and Li, S. F. (2014). Modeling dynamic dependence between crude oil prices and Asia-Pacific stock market returns, *International Review of Economics and Finance*, 29, 208–223.

Chapter 3

The Predictive Power of Oil and Commodity Prices for Equity Markets

Leila Dagher[*,§], Ibrahim Jamali[†,¶] and Nasser Badra[‡,‖]

*Department of Economics and Director of Institute of Financial Economics, American University of Beirut, P.O. Box 11-0236, Riad El-Solh, Beirut 1107 2020, Lebanon
†Department of Finance, Accounting and Managerial Economics, Olayan School of Business, American University of Beirut, Beirut 1107 2020, P.O. Box 11-0236, Riad El-Solh Street, Lebanon
‡Institute of Financial Economics, American University of Beirut, P.O. Box 11-0236, Riad El-Solh, Beirut 1107 2020, Lebanon
§ld08@aub.edu.lb
¶ij08@aub.edu.lb
‖nbb03@mail.aub.edu

1. Introduction

Understanding the relation between equity markets and oil price movements is a subject of intense academic scrutiny. Starting with the seminal papers of Kling (1985) and Jones and Kaul (1996), a sizeable literature has explored the linkages between the stock and oil markets.[1] A relatively newer strand of the literature examines

---

[1]An excellent review of the literature on interaction between oil price movements and stock returns is provided in Degiannakis *et al.* (2017). In general, studies that examine the interdependence between oil and stock price movements employ multivariate time

the predictive ability of oil market information on stock returns. For example, Liu *et al.* (2015) find that including oil market variables yields better stock market return forecasts.

The goal of this study is to examine the predictive ability of oil and commodity (metals) price changes on the equity markets of four countries using causality tests. With the possible financialization of commodity markets, commodity and oil price changes might possess predictive ability for stock returns.[2] One of our contributions is that we straddle three separate strands of the literature on the interlinkages between equity and oil prices, between equity and commodity prices, as well as the literature on the relation between equity markets and exchange rates.

We employ a multivariate vector auto-regressive (VAR) model to undertake the analysis. This choice is motivated by the cautionary notes echoed in a number of studies regarding bivariate VAR models especially in the context of Granger causality testing.[3] In fact, existing research (Caporale and Pittis, 1997; Lütkepohl, 1983, 2006) demonstrates that the omission of an important variable may lead to invalid inferences about causality in a bivariate system.

Our VAR model comprises seven variables, which are: market returns, Brent oil price changes, gold price changes, copper price changes, silver price changes, exchange rate changes, and changes in the Baltic Dry Index. We conduct causality tests using a rolling

---

series models (Hammoudeh and Choi, 2006; Sadorsky, 1999 among others) while those examining the volatility transmission between equity and oil markets use multivariate generalized auto-regressive conditional heteroscedasticity models (Arouri *et al.*, 2011; Guesmi and Fattoum, 2014 among others).

[2]The "financialization debate" garnered significantly more academic attention following the testimony of Masters (2008) before Congress, in which he attributes the increase in commodity prices to the participation of long-only commodity index traders in commodity investing. Academics have largely been skeptical of the financialization view. For an excellent review of the literature, see Fattouh *et al.* (2013).

[3]For instance, Tang and Yao (2017) consider bivariate Granger causality studies as "incomplete systems" due to the omission of important variables, while Phylaktis and Ravazzolo (2015) caution against the use of bivariate VARs to test for Granger causality. Our decision to employ a seven variable VAR stems, in part, from being mindful of the prior cautionary notes regarding bivariate studies.

window approach for two main reasons: (i) Causality may be time-varying and studies that treat the whole sample as one fixed period will not detect such time variation, and (ii) traditional causality tests are not valid in the presence of structural breaks within a sample period.[4] The analysis is conducted for France, Italy, Kingdom of Saudi Arabia, and the United Arab Emirates, which are, respectively, two oil importers and two oil exporters.

Our chapter differs from existing studies by assessing the predictive power of oil price movements while accounting for the changes in the prices of other important commodities as well as changes in the exchange rate. As a by-product of our analysis, the predictive power of the exchange rate, copper, gold, and silver price changes for equity returns can also be assessed.

We complement existing work (Broadstock and Filis, 2014; Kang and Ratti, 2013; Cuando and de Garcia, 2014) by providing evidence that oil and, to a lesser extent, copper price changes are useful predictors of the stock returns of the two oil exporters in the post-2014 period. The strong predictive ability of oil price changes in the post-2014 period is possibly related to the declining oil price regime prevailing over that period. Contrary to the latter contributions, we do not disentangle oil supply and demand shocks using the methodology of Kilian (2009) and Kilian and Park (2009), given that our primary concern is to examine the predictive ability of the oil price changes on equity returns at high frequencies. Our study also differs from the prior contributions by focusing squarely on two oil-importing and two oil-exporting countries to assess oil price changes' predictive ability for the equity markets of oil exporters and importers.

Our findings also suggest that copper price changes are, to a lesser extent, useful predictors of equity returns for Saudi Arabia and the United Arab Emirates. We argue that our results are of interest to local authorities in the studied countries, but even more so to national and international investors, forecasters, and portfolio

---

[4]The rolling window approach is used by a number of studies. See, for example, Swanson (1998).

managers. For forecasters, our findings may imply that the use of oil price changes is essential when predicting the equity returns of oil exporters after 2014. Because oil (and copper) price changes are not ubiquitous predictors of the equity returns of the four countries, we view our findings as not consistent with the financialization view but rather indicative of oil's importance for the economies of the two oil exporters. Indeed, the financialization of commodity markets would suggest an important predictive role for oil in predicting equity returns for the four countries.

The rest of the chapter proceeds as follows. Section 2 provides a review of the related literature. Section 3 discusses the data and variables used in our empirical analysis while Section 4 outlines our econometric methodology and tests. The empirical results are provided and discussed in Section 5 while Section 6 offers some concluding remarks.

2.   Literature Review

Under market efficiency, prices quickly impound all the available information. That is, in an efficient market, stock prices cannot be predicted using variables that are in investors' information set at time t. Conversely, evidence that a variable that is part of the information set at time t has predictive ability for stock returns implies either that markets are inefficient or that there is a time-varying risk premium. As noted earlier, causality tests are tests of predictive ability. Therefore, finding that a variable causes stock returns indicates inefficiency or the existence of a time-varying risk premium.

The consensus emerging from existing studies which examine Granger causality from oil price changes to stock returns is somewhat mixed. Using monthly data for the period 1973–1982, Kling (1985) finds causality running from the S&P500 to crude oil prices, but not in the opposite direction. In contrast to those findings, Jones and Kaul (1996) provide empirical evidence that oil price changes Granger-cause aggregate real stock returns in the United States,

Japan, and Canada but not the United Kingdom. Using daily data for the period October 9, 1979–March 16, 1990, Huang *et al.* (1996) do not detect causality running in any direction between crude oil prices and the S&P 500 index. However, they find evidence of Granger causality running from oil futures price changes to the returns of individual oil companies.

Another strand of literature that investigates causality between foreign exchange rates and stock market returns has also reached somewhat inconclusive results. Bahmani-Oskooee and Sohrabian (1992) find bidirectional causality between stock prices measured by the S&P 500 index and the effective exchange rate of the dollar for the period July 1973–December 1988, while Ajayi *et al.* (1998) find unidirectional causality from stock returns to exchange rates for six developed countries (Canada, Germany, France, Italy, Japan, UK, and USA) using daily data from between April 1985–August 1991. Using monthly data for the period 1993–1998, Hatemi and Irandoust's (2002) findings for Sweden agree with those of Ajayi *et al.* (1998), but the authors do not detect consistent causal relations between these two markets in the case of emerging economies. Smyth and Nandha (2003) find unidirectional causality that runs from exchange rates to stock prices for India and Sri Lanka, but do not detect causality in either direction for Bangladesh and Pakistan.

Very few papers have combined the former two strands of the literature and even fewer have explored the predictive power of commodity prices for equity returns, after evidence of a higher correlation between equities and commodities emerged from the "financialization" literature. Among these is the paper by Basher *et al.* (2012), which investigates very thoroughly the relationship between oil prices, exchange rates, and stock prices using a structural VAR, impulse response analysis, and variance decompositions. However, Basher *et al.*'s (2012) study does not include the price of non-energy commodities and the authors do not conduct any causality testing. Another paper by Choi and Hammoudeh (2010) uses a GARCH model to analyze volatility spillovers between WTI oil prices, Brent oil prices, gold, silver, and copper prices as well as the US S&P

500 index. The authors estimate dynamic conditional correlation models with weekly data over the period January 2, 1990–May 1, 2006, and their results point to increasing correlations among all the commodities since the 2003 Iraq war. They also find that the correlation between commodities and equities is decreasing over the same period. Choi and Hammoudeh (2010) do not, however, conduct any causality testing.

Even though it is widely known that causality results are sensitive to the sample period being studied, only a few attempts at investigating time-varying relationships in the causality between equity returns and commodities price or exchange rate changes have been made. In order to account for time-varying causality, one can split the sample into multiple subsamples. However, this requires *a priori* knowledge of the dates at which the causality relationship changes, which could be difficult to obtain. An example is Tsai (2015), who divides his sample into pre-, post-, and during a financial crisis, while another example is El Charif *et al.* (2005) who divide their sample into six periods. Umer *et al.* (2015) divide their sample into two periods, the tranquil and the crisis periods, and find the results to be divergent across the two subsamples.

Using a rolling window approach allows researchers to examine all possible subsamples and to avoid *ad hoc* sample splitting. The rolling window approach may also shed light on the reasons underlying the divergence in the results reported in the literature. Time-varying causality tests using a fixed size rolling window have already been used by researchers to examine the relation between output and economic growth in the US (Inglesi-Lotz *et al.*, 2014), money and real output (Swanson, 1998), money stock and disposable income (Hill, 2007), money and aggregate prices (Tang, 2010), economic growth and energy consumption (Balcilar *et al.*, 2010), economic growth and electricity consumption (Dlamini *et al.*, 2015), export and GDP (Balcilar and Ozdemir, 2013), house price index and GDP (Nyakabawo *et al.*, 2015), tourism receipts and GDP (Arslanturk *et al.*, 2011), and stock market returns of different markets (Smith *et al.*, 1993).

A single study in the literature we are interested in uses the rolling window approach. Smiech and Papiez (2013) use a 3-year rolling window with weekly data to investigate the dynamics of causality between each pair of the following variables: oil prices, coal prices, German stock market index, and the exchange rate USD/EUR. However, the study is only concerned with the German stock market and the authors' modeling strategy differs significantly from ours.

3. Data and Variables

We collect data on the nearest Brent crude oil (OIL), gold (GLD), silver (SIL), and copper (CPR) futures, denominated in US Dollar (USD), from Datastream. Our data span the period May 31, 2005–April 27, 2018, for a total of 3,369 observations. We construct a continuous futures price series by rolling over from the nearest (or front) to the next-to-nearest (or second) contract on the first day of the expiration month.[5] Following existing studies (Fama and French, 1987; Gospodinov and Ng, 2013), we employ the nearest futures prices as a proxy for the spot (or cash) prices. The prior studies argue that the spot prices in commodity markets are not accurate and opt for using the nearest futures price instead of the spot price. Recent contributions to the literature (Baumeister and Kilian, 2017; Kilian, 2016) also indicate that, following the US shale oil revolution, the price of Brent oil is a better proxy of the global price of oil. Therefore, we employ Brent prices as the main proxy for the price of oil in our empirical analysis.

Our cross-section of countries comprises two oil exporting countries, the Kingdom of Saudi Arabia (KSA) and the United Arab Emirates, as well as two oil importing countries, which are France and Italy. The UAE and KSA have pegged exchange rates, while the exchange rates of France and Italy are floating. We obtain data on

---

[5]Existing studies commonly employ this rollover strategy. See, for example, Bessembinder (1992), de Roon *et al.* (2000), and Gorton and Rouwenhorst (2006).

the exchange rate (XR), expressed in units of the foreign currency per USD, for each of the countries included in our sample. The investible MSCI index, expressed in USD, is used as a measure of aggregate equity prices for each of the countries. Data on the MSCI index as well as the exchange rate for each of the countries are obtained from Datastream.

We control for global economic activity using the Baltic Dry Index (BDI).[6] The BDI, which is constructed and disseminated by the Baltic Dry Exchange, measures the cost of shipping major raw materials by sea (Dbouk and Jamali, 2018; Schinas *et al.*, 2015). The use of the BDI as a measure of global economic activity stems from the insight, articulated in detail by Kilian (2009), that economic activity is possibly the most important determinant of transport services (Klovland, 2004). Kilian (2009) provides compelling arguments that an increase in freight rates is an indicator of strong cumulative global demand pressures.[7] The BDI, and freight rates in general, have also been widely used by practitioners to assess the degree of global demand pressures (Kilian, 2009). Bakshi *et al.* (2011) provide empirical evidence of the predictive ability of the BDI for global economic activity as well as for equity and commodity returns.

We test for a unit root in the levels of each of the series using the augmented Dickey–Fuller (ADF) (1979), Phillips and Perron (PP) (1988), and the Kwiatkowski, Phillips, Schmidt, and Shin (KPSS) (1992) test. The null hypothesis for the ADF and PP tests is that the series contains a unit root. The KPSS test, whose null is that the series is (trend-) stationary, is employed for confirmatory analysis. The ADF test is known to exhibit low power when the alternative is near unit root behavior (Elliot *et al.*, 1996). Therefore, we also

---

[6]Not controlling for global economic activity may lead to omitted variable bias. Lütkepohl (2005) demonstrates that the omission of an important variable leads to invalid inferences about the causality structure in a bivariate system.

[7]In fact, Kilian (2009) constructs a monthly measure of global economic activity whose underlying nominal data are identical to those used in constructing the BDI (Alquist *et al.*, 2013). Given that we require a daily measure of global economic activity, we cannot employ Kilian's (2009) index and we rely instead on the BDI, which is available daily.

employ the ADF test with GLS detrending of Elliot *et al.* (1996).
The existing literature shows that the ADF–GLS test has good power
properties against near unit root behavior.

The results, presented in Table 1, show that the null of a unit root
in the level of each of the series cannot be rejected. Based on the unit

Table 1: Unit root tests.

	ADF	ADF-GLS	PP	KPSS
Panel A: Unit root tests for variables in log levels				
Commodities				
Brent oil (OIL)	−1.97	−1.37	−2.06	1.02***
Copper (CPR)	−2.89	−1.11	−2.92	0.59***
Gold (GLD)	−2.03	−0.65	−2.02	1.67***
Silver (SIL)	−2.02	−1.09	−2.00	1.36***
BDI	−2.63	−2.51	−2.99	0.37***
Stock market				
KSA	−1.81	−1.44	−1.95	0.86***
UAE	−1.50	−1.08	−1.52	1.32***
France	−2.37	−2.25	−2.37	0.64***
Italy	−1.82	−1.90	−1.71	0.83***
Exchange rates				
EUR/USD (XR)	−2.42	−1.70	−2.44	0.87***
Panel B: Unit root tests for variables in log changes				
Commodities				
Brent oil (OIL)	−61.88***	−2.53	−61.87***	0.08
Copper (CPR)	−62.56***	−7.34***	−62.41***	0.08
Gold (GLD)	−58.03***	−57.89***	−58.05***	0.05
Silver (SIL)	−59.49***	−56.89***	−59.49***	0.04
BDI	−23.62***	−17.80***	−21.57***	0.03
Stock market				
KSA	−56.75***	−2.70	−56.84***	0.04
UAE	−37.20***	−35.34***	−53.65***	0.09
France	−59.13***	−56.61***	−59.22***	0.05
Italy	−58.45***	−57.84***	−58.53***	0.07
Exchange rates				
EUR/USD (EX)	−57.67***	−5.26***	−57.67***	0.05

Notes: All unit root tests are performed with an intercept and a trend in the
test equation. The optimal lag length is selected using the BIC. ADF refers to
the augmented Dickey and Fuller (1979) test. ADF–GLS refers to the ADF with
GLS detrending of Elliott *et al.* (1996). PP is the Phillips and Perron (1988)
test. KPSS is the Kwiatkowski, Phillips *et al.* (1992) test. With the exception of
the KPSS test whose null is trend stationarity, the null for all the tests is one
of a unit root. *, **, *** denote statistical significance at the 10%, 5% and 1%
levels, respectively.

root test results, we proceed with testing for a cointegrating relationship among the variables using the Johansen (1988) approach.[8] The trace and maximum eigenvalue tests both suggest the absence of cointegrating relationships between the variables and our results are consistent with those of Granger *et al.* (2000), Nieh and Lee (2001), Yang and Doong (2004) Aloui (2007) and Le and Chang (2015).

Based on the discussion above, our empirical analysis is conducted with log changes in the variables. Using log changes in the variables is also consistent with our goal of examining the *short-run* predictive power of crude oil price changes and other variables for stock returns using causality tests. In fact, log changes in the MSCI index and exchange rates are continuously compounded returns and several studies (Bessembinder, 1992; de Roon *et al.*, 2000; Gorton and Rouwenhorst, 2006) refer to log changes in the nearest futures prices for oil, gold, and copper as the returns on the futures contracts.[9]

The time series dynamics of the commodity and oil prices (in levels) are displayed in Figure 1. Figure 2 presents the time series dynamics of log changes in the prices of copper, gold, silver, oil, and the BDI, while Figure 3 shows the continuously compounded returns on the investible MSCI index for KSA, UAE, France, and Italy.

As can be seen in Figure 1, oil prices were on an upward trend over the period 2005–2008. The sharp increase in oil prices corresponded to a run-up in commodity prices during the same period. Oil prices exhibited a sharp decline since 2014 (that lasted until 2016). The time series dynamics in Figure 1 suggest the presence of different price regimes (especially in oil prices) which can potentially induce shifts in the dynamic relationships between the variables. To account for the possible presence of structural breaks or regime shifts, it is important to employ a rolling window approach when testing for causality.

---

[8]The results are available from the authors upon request.

[9]Some studies refer to changes in the nearest futures price simply as price changes. We prefer the former terminology when using commodity futures prices. However, we henceforth use the terms "price changes" and "returns" interchangeably.

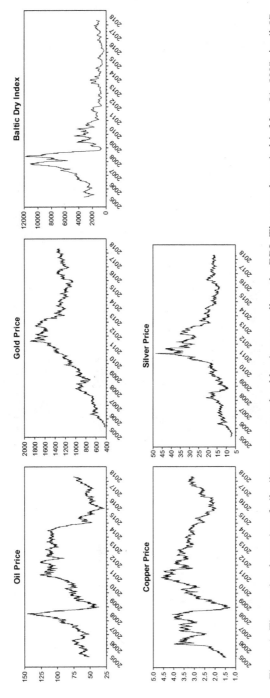

Figure 1: Time series dynamics of oil, silver, copper and gold prices as well as the BDI. The sample period is May 31, 2005–April 27, 2018.

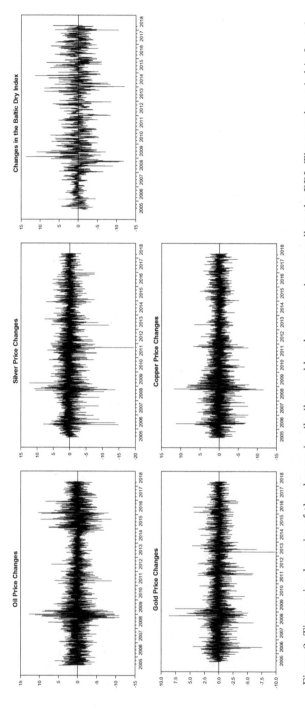

Figure 2: Time series dynamics of the changes in oil, silver, gold and copper prices as well as the BDI. The sample period is June 1, 2005–April 27, 2018.

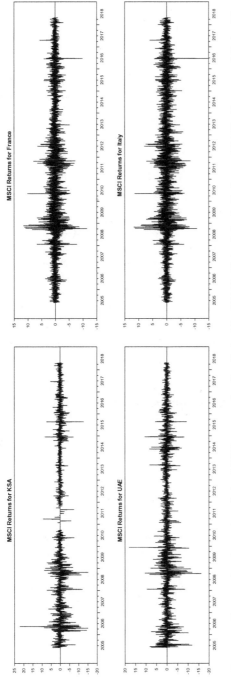

Figure 3: Time series dynamics of the MSCI returns for Saudi Arabia (KSA), United Arab Emirates (UAE), France and Italy. The sample period is June 1, 2005–April 27, 2018.

Table 2: Descriptive statistics.

	Mean	Std. dev.	Skewness	Kurtosis	AC(1)
Commodities					
$\Delta\ln$(OIL)	0.011	2.096	0.013	3.460	−0.063
$\Delta\ln$(CPR)	0.020	1.815	−0.092	3.911	−0.075
$\Delta\ln$(GLD)	0.034	1.178	−0.347	5.580	0.000
$\Delta\ln$(SIL)	0.023	2.097	−0.893	7.188	−0.024
$\Delta\ln$(BDI)	−0.025	2.226	0.078	3.545	0.757
Stock market returns					
KSA	−0.009	1.657	−0.988	25.104	0.023
UAE	−0.016	1.768	−0.584	12.659	0.086
France	0.012	1.568	−0.084	7.535	−0.019
Italy	−0.008	1.735	−0.254	6.323	−0.007
Exchange rate returns					
EUR/USD (XR)	−0.000	0.607	0.136	3.38	0.005

Note: The table provides the summary statistics of the variables used in the empirical analysis. Std. dev. refers to the standard deviation, while AC(1) denotes the first-order auto-correlation.

Table 2 provides the descriptive statistics of the variables used in our empirical analysis.

The summary statistics show that the returns on the KSA, UAE, and Italian MSCI investible indexes are, on average, negative, while the return on the French MSCI is, on average, positive over our sample period. The average commodity price change for the four commodities is also positive over our sample period, suggesting that investors who held a long position in one of the commodity futures contracts earned a positive risk premium over the sample period.[10] The descriptive statistics in Table 2 show very little persistence in the variables as evidenced by the low first-order auto-correlation coefficient. Commodity prices appear to be slightly more volatile than the equity index returns of the four countries that we consider, while exchange rate returns exhibit the lowest volatility. As widely documented in the literature, the equity index return distributions are leptokurtic, as evidenced by a kurtosis coefficient that is much larger than three. While gold and silver price changes appear to also have

---

[10]This positive risk premium induces investors to hold a long position in the futures contract.

Table 3: Cross-correlations among variables.

	OIL	CPR	GLD	SIL	BDI	XR	KSA	UAE	France	Italy
Panel A: Cross-correlations in levels										
OIL	1.00									
CPR	0.41	1.00								
GLD	0.25	0.36	1.00							
SIL	0.32	0.46	0.81	1.00						
BDI	0.04	0.01	0.03	0.04	1.00					
XR	0.20	0.28	0.34	0.36	0.02	1.00				
KSA	0.06	0.06	−0.10	−0.00	0.01	0.01	1.00			
UAE	0.10	0.09	−0.00	0.06	0.05	0.06	0.40	1.00		
FRANCE	0.37	0.48	0.15	0.30	0.02	0.56	0.12	0.19	1.00	
ITALY	0.36	0.44	0.12	0.27	0.01	0.54	0.13	0.18	0.92	1.00
Panel B: Cross-correlations in log changes										
OIL	1.00									
CPR	0.41	1.00								
GLD	0.25	0.36	1.00							
SIL	0.32	0.46	0.81	1.00						
BDI	0.04	0.01	0.03	0.04	1.00					
XR	0.20	0.28	0.34	0.36	0.02	1.00				
KSA	0.06	0.06	−0.06	−0.01	0.01	0.01	1.00			
UAE	0.10	0.09	−0.01	0.06	0.05	0.06	0.40	1.00		
FRANCE	0.37	0.48	0.15	0.30	0.02	0.56	0.12	0.19	1.00	
ITALY	0.36	0.44	0.12	0.27	0.01	0.54	0.13	0.18	0.92	1.00

Note: The table provides the cross-correlations between the variables used in VAR analysis in levels and log changes.

leptokurtic distributions, the other commodity price changes do not exhibit excess kurtosis.

The cross-correlations between the variables in levels, reported in Panel A of Table 3, show that the highest correlation of 0.86 is between gold and silver prices. The cross-correlation between the variables in log changes are reported in Panel B of Table 3.

Just as in the results with the levels of the variables, the largest cross-correlation in log changes of 0.81 is also between gold and silver.

4.   Econometric Methodology

In an important contribution to the literature, Granger (1969) introduced a concept of causality which closely ties to the predictive power of one variable for another variable. Let y_{1t} and y_{2t} denote two time series.[11] The variable y_{2t} is said to Granger-cause y_{1t} when accounting for the information in y_{2t} lowers the mean square prediction error (MSPE) in y_{1t}.

More formally, let Ω_t denote the information set at time t and $y_{1,t+h,\Omega_t}$ denote the optimal (i.e. lowest mean square error) h-step prediction of y_{1t}. Let $\sigma_{y_1}^2(h/\Omega_t)$ denote the MSPE of the variable y_{1t}. Kilian and Lütkepohl (2017) note that the process y_{2t} is said to Granger-cause the process y_{1t} if:

$$\sigma_{y_1}^2(h/\Omega_t) < \sigma_{y_1}^2(h/\Omega_t\{y_{2s}|s \leq t\}),$$

where $\Omega_t y_{2s}|s \leq t$ denotes the information set excluding past and present information regarding the series y_{2t}. In other words, the process y_{2t} is said to Granger-cause the process y_{1t} if exploiting information on the past and contemporaneous values of y_{2t} lowers the prediction error of the process y_{1t} at some horizon h.

Tests of Granger causality are performed by placing restrictions on the coefficients of a VAR. Denote by Y_t a vector of variables of interest. A VAR relates Y_t to p of its lags. A test of Granger causality amounts to zero restrictions on a subset of the coefficients of the VAR.

We follow the exposition in Lütkepohl and Kratzig (2004) to demonstrate testing for causality within the context of a trivariate VAR. A trivariate VAR(p) is given by

$$\begin{bmatrix} y_{1t} \\ y_{2t} \\ y_{3t} \end{bmatrix} = \begin{bmatrix} \mu_1 \\ \mu_2 \\ \mu_3 \end{bmatrix} + \sum_{i=1}^{p} \begin{bmatrix} \alpha_{11,i} & \alpha_{12,i} & \alpha_{13,i} \\ \alpha_{21,i} & \alpha_{22,i} & \alpha_{23,i} \\ \alpha_{31,i} & \alpha_{32,i} & \alpha_{33,i} \end{bmatrix} \begin{bmatrix} y_{1,t-i} \\ y_{2,t-i} \\ y_{3,t-i} \end{bmatrix} + \begin{bmatrix} u_{1t} \\ u_{2t} \\ u_{3t} \end{bmatrix}.$$

In the above VAR, $Y_t = (y_{1t} \quad y_{2t} \quad y_{3t})'$. As noted in Lütkepohl and Kratzig (2004), checking for causality of y_{2t} for y_{1t} by testing $H_0 : \alpha_{12,i} = 0$, $i = 1, \ldots, p$ is equivalent to equality of the one-step forecasts $y_{1,t+1/\Omega_t} = y_{1,t+1/\Omega_t \backslash \{y_{2,s}|s \leq t\}}$. The latter restriction can be tested using a Wald (F-) test but is not strictly a test of Granger

---

[11]Our exposition in this section follows Kilian and Lütkepohl (2017) and Lütkepohl (2006).

causality in the general sense first introduced in this section. If this restriction is rejected by the data, then the variable y_{2t} causes y_{1t}, in the sense that it possesses predictive power for the *one-step-ahead* forecast of y_{1t}.

In our empirical application, the horizon of interest is $h = 1$. We restrict the forecast horizon to one, given that Dufour and Renault (1998) caution against using multivariate VAR models for testing for causality at multiple steps ahead. Our VAR contains seven variables and is given by $Y_t = \{\Delta Brent_t, \Delta MSCI_t, \Delta Gold_t \Delta Silver_t, \Delta Copper_t, \Delta Exchange\ Rate_t, \Delta BDI\}'$. Despite the larger VAR model that we employ, testing for causality from Brent oil price changes to stock returns, for example, still amounts to testing zero restrictions on the lags of the oil price changes in the stock return equation of the VAR.

Having differenced the data, our sample consists of a total of 3,368 observations. When testing for causality, we use a fixed rolling window of size 600, resulting in 2,769 windows. That is, the first test of causality is conducted with a VAR estimated over the period June 1, 2005–September 18, 2007. The window is then shifted by one observation and the next test of causality is conducted with a VAR estimated over the sample June 2, 2005–September 19, 2007. The last causality test is performed using a VAR estimated over the period January 11, 2016–April 27, 2018.

In every window, the lag length of the VAR is selected based on the Akaike information criterion (AIC) and the maximum lag length is selected using Schwert's (1989) criterion $p_{\max} = 12 * (\frac{T}{100})^{0.25}$, where T is the window size.[12]

5.   Results and Discussion

We start by estimating the VAR over the full sample for the four countries and testing for auto-correlation and heteroscedasticity in

---

[12]In our case, $T = 600$ which implies that the maximum lag length is 19.

the residuals of the VAR. We also test for stability of the covariance matrix of the VAR. We employ the Hosking (1981) variant of the multivariate Q statistic to test for auto-correlation and test for the presence of conditional heteroscedasticity in the VAR's residuals using a multivariate test for auto-regressive conditional heteroscedasticity (ARCH). We assess the stability of the VAR's covariance matrix using the Nyblom (1989) test.

The results, reported in Panel A of Table 4, overwhelmingly reject the null hypotheses of no auto-correlation, homoscedasticity and covariance matrix stability.

In view of the evidence of auto-correlation and conditional heteroscedasticity in the VAR's residuals, we employ the heteroscedasticity and auto-correlation consistent (HAC) standard errors of Newey and West (1987) for inference. The Nyblom (1989) stability test provides preliminary evidence of instability in the VARs. We proceed to a more thorough assessment of the stability of the VAR parameters. To test for parameter stability, we apply the Chow (1960) breakpoint test and the Quandt–Andrews (Quandt, 1960;

Table 4: VAR diagnostic tests.

	KSA	UAE	France	Italy
Panel A: Autocorrelation, heteroscedasticity and stability tests				
Multivariate Q	3004.13	3044.43	3045.45	3034.00
p-value	0.00	0.00	0.00	0.00
Multivariate ARCH	48655.06	44964.48	68620.47	64653.34
p-value	0.00	0.00	0.00	0.00
Nyblom test for covariance matrix	37.13	35.29	36.73	39.82
p-value	0.00	0.00	0.00	0.00
Panel B: Quandt–Andrews breakpoint test				
Max LR (F-statistic)	3.50	4.30	4.89	3.40
p-value	0.00	0.01	0.02	0.03
Dates	10/28/2008	10/7/2008	10/14/2008	10/14/2008

Notes: Panel A provides the Hosking (1981) variate of the multivariate Q statistics for serial correlation in the VAR's residuals. The table also provides multivariate tests for ARCH in the VAR's residuals as well as the Nyblom (1989) test for stability of the estimated VAR's covariance matrix. Panel B provides the Quandt (1960) and Andrews (1993) breakpoint tests applied to the VAR's equation with stock returns as a dependent variable. The asymptotic p-values of the Quandt–Andrews test are computed using Hansen (1987)'s approach.

Andrews, 1993) tests to the VAR equation with stock returns as a dependent variable. The Chow test rejects the null of stability for multiple dates, while the Quandt–Andrews breakpoint test, whose results are reported in Panel B of Table 4, detects the date associated with the highest likelihood of having a break. In addition to the latter tests, we employ the CUSUM of squares, reported in Figure 4, to test for instability. The CUSUM of squares test relies on the cumulative sum of the squared residuals to detect structural instability in the VAR's equation with stock returns as a dependent variable.

Figure 4 clearly shows evidence of instability given that the CUSUM of squares test statistic lies outside of the 95% confidence interval. Overall, we find compelling evidence of structural breaks as well as parameter and covariance matrix instability, which justifies the use of a rolling window estimation scheme. In fact, Rossi (2013) emphasizes the fact that causality tests are inconsistent in the presence of instabilities. Therefore, the use of a rolling window estimation scheme that accounts for instabilities is critical.

The results of the rolling window causality tests are displayed in Figures 5–10 while the results of the bi-directional causality tests are provided in Table 5. When interpreting the results, we combine information from the table and from the graphs. The numbers presented in Table 5 represent the number of windows out of a total of 2,769 rolling windows in which a variable is found to cause the other. The p-value of the causality test as well as a horizontal line indicating the 5% level of significance are displayed in each of the figures. We view the information from the graphs and Table 5 as complementary and essential in interpreting the results.

We begin by examining bidirectional causality from exchange rate returns to stock returns. Figure 5 shows no causality running from exchange rate changes to stock returns. However, Panel B of Table 3 provides evidence of causality running from stock returns to the exchange rate for France and Italy. Our results regarding the direction of causality are consistent with those of Ajayi *et al.* (1998) and Aloui (2007) who find unidirectional causality from stock to exchange rate returns for both France and Italy using daily data from 1985 to

66   *Risk Factors and Contagion in Commodity Markets and Stocks Markets*

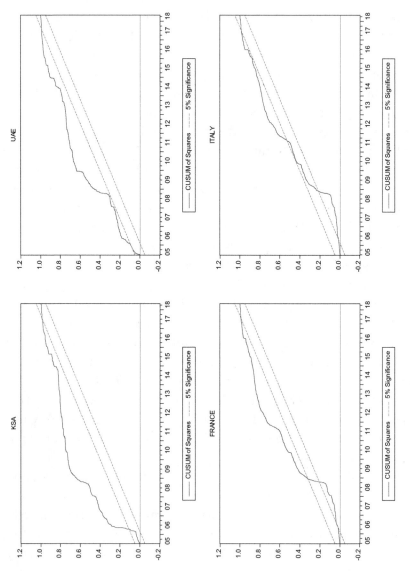

Figure 4: CUSUM of squares plots for the regressions where the stock market returns is the dependent variable.

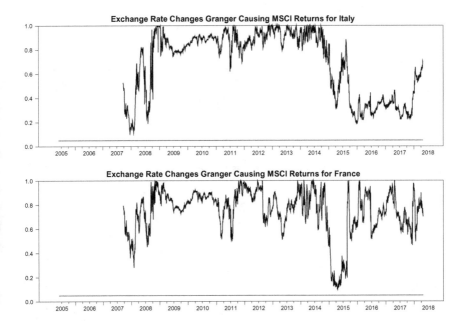

Figure 5: *p*-Values of causality tests from exchange rate changes to stock returns. The null is one of no causality and the horizontal line indicates the 5% level of significance.

1991 and from 1990 to 2005, respectively. One might conclude that the stock market has maintained its predictive ability for exchange rates that were present since the 1980s in the case of France and Italy.

We turn next to examining the causality between gold price changes and stock returns. Our results also show that there is sparse evidence of gold price changes causing stock returns for KSA, and similarly scant evidence of UAE and KSA stock market returns causing gold price changes. These results are consistent with those of Al Janabi *et al.* (2010) who do not find any significant causality between gold and stock returns in KSA and UAE for the period 2006–2008. Miyazaki and Hamori (2013) find a unidirectional causality from stock returns to gold prices for the US during the period 2000–2011.

The results in Figure 7 and Table 5 provide very weak evidence of silver price changes causing the stock index returns for

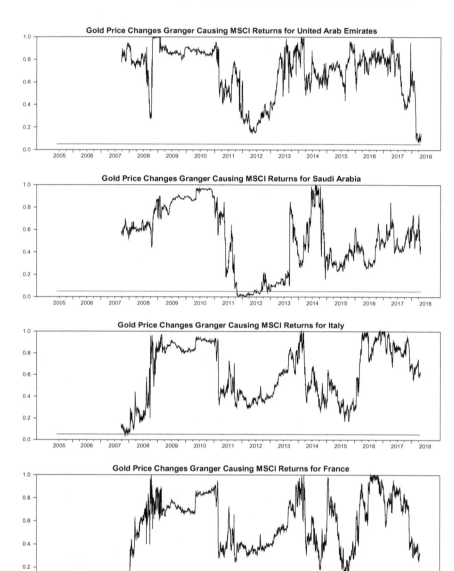

Figure 6: *p*-Values of causality tests from gold price changes to stock returns. The null is one of no causality and the horizontal line indicate the 5% level of significance.

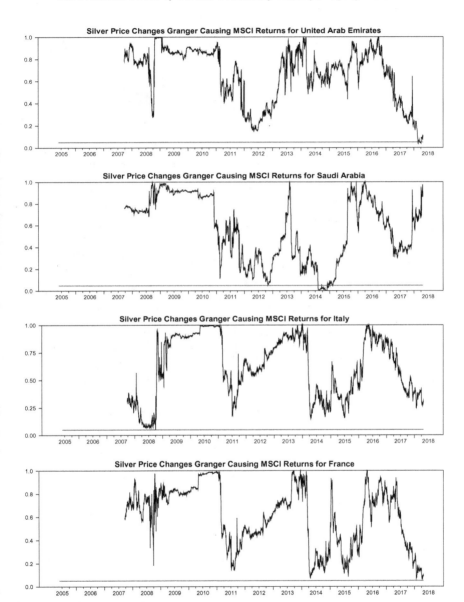

Figure 7: *p*-Values of causality tests from silver price changes to stock returns. The null is one of no causality and the horizontal line indicate the 5% level of significance.

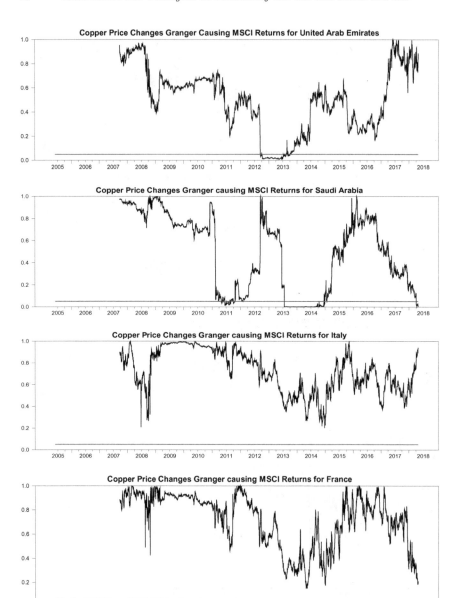

Figure 8: p-Values of causality tests from copper price changes to stock returns. The null is one of no causality and the horizontal line indicate the 5% level of significance.

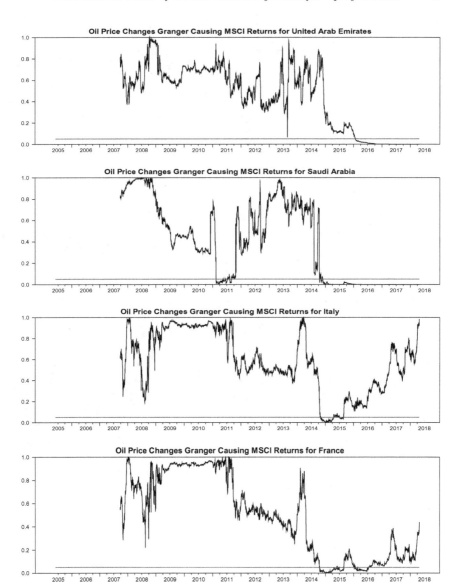

Figure 9: *p*-Values of causality tests from oil price changes to stock returns. The null is one of no causality and the horizontal line indicate the 5% level of significance.

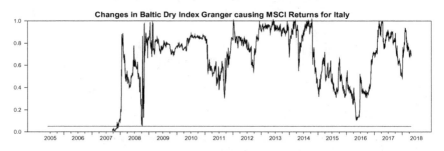

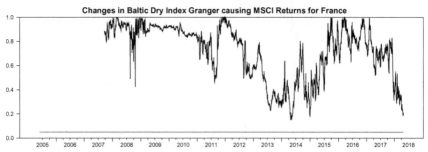

Figure 10: p-Values of causality tests from changes in the BDI to stock returns. The null is one of no causality and the horizontal line indicate the 5% level of significance.

Table 5: Rolling window causality test results.

	Oil	Gold	Silver	Copper	Exchange rate	BDI
Panel A: Causality from Commodity Price Changes, Exchange Rates and Baltic Dry Index Changes to Stock Returns						
Italy	590	5	1	0	0	48
France	347	0	0	0	0	0
KSA	1013	203	99	474	—	203
UAE	590	0	14	259	—	0
Panel B: Causality from Stock Returns to Commodity Price Changes, Exchange Rates and Baltic Index Price Changes						
Italy	0	0	0	0	489	252
France	0	8	0	0	1344	179
KSA	0	331	0	0	—	130
UAE	0	281	0	108	—	21

Note: The table provides the number of significant causality tests (at the 5% level) in 2769 windows.

KSA and UAE. Furthermore, there is no evidence of stock returns causing silver price changes.

These results are in line with our *ex ante* expectations. In fact, existing studies (Baur and Lucey, 2010; Baur and McDermott, 2010; Ciner *et al.*, 2013; Lucey and Li, 2015) provide empirical evidence that the precious metals, and in particular gold and silver, act as safe havens and hedges to equity markets. As such, it is unlikely for the precious metals' price changes to cause equity returns.

Figure 8 and Table 5 show that copper price changes cause the returns on the KSA and UAE returns, but not the equity returns of Italy and France. With the exception of meager evidence for the UAE, we also find that stock returns do not cause copper price changes. These results have an intuitive explanation. Former Federal Reserve Chairman Bernanke (2016) notes that the price of industrial metals commodities act as a gauge of global economic activity and reflect investors' perceptions of global demand. Other important contributions (Pindyck and Rotemberg, 1990; Labys *et al.*, 1999; Lombardi *et al.*, 2012) also document a relation between global economic activity and metals prices.[13] Starting from the premise that

---

[13]Caldara *et al.* (2016) provide a lengthier discussion of the literature on the role of metals prices as indicators of global economic activity. The financial press also

copper prices are high-frequency indicators of global economic activity, our results which indicate that causality runs from copper prices to the returns on the UAE and KSA market highlights the latter two equity markets' sensitivity to global economic conditions. To our knowledge, no existing study has examined the causality between copper price changes and stock returns.

We turn next to assessing the predictive ability of the BDI. Figure 10 suggests that changes in the BDI caused the returns on the KSA market for a short period in 2011 and 2012. Changes in the BDI do not appear to have caused the returns on the equity indexes of any of the other countries that we consider. This latter finding might be attributable to copper prices embedding similar information as the BDI as a gauge of global economic activity. The returns on the four equity markets appear to cause the changes in the BDI, but the evidence is rather sparse.

Our strongest causality results are obtained when we examine the relation between oil price changes and stock returns. In fact, Figure 9 shows that oil price changes caused UAE and KSA's stock returns for extended periods of time and France's equity returns to a lesser extent. Panel A of Table 5 clearly shows that the most frequent occurrences of causality in our sample pertain to oil price changes causing stock returns. In contrast, Panel B of Table 3 shows no causality running from equity returns to oil price changes. Notably, the evidence in favor of causality running from oil price changes to equity returns coincides with a period of declining oil prices. While there could be other contributing factors, our findings show hardly any causality during the period when oil prices are on an increasing trend, while the causality is significant when the trend reverses. From the results, we can conclude that evidence of oil price changes causing equity returns is more pronounced and persistent for the oil-exporting countries relative to the oil-importing countries.

---

views copper prices as a leading indicator of global economic activity. See, for example, *The Economist* article: https://www.economist.com/blogs/buttonwood/2014/03/commodities-and-economy.

As a robustness check for our results, we examine the sensitivity to: (i) employing the West Texas Intermediate (WTI) prices instead of Brent prices, (ii) the length of the fixed window by experimenting with two alternative window sizes (300 and 900), and (iii) replacing the investible MSCI index with each country's main stock index. All robustness checks yield very similar results (available from the authors upon request).

6. Concluding Remarks

The aim of this chapter is to investigate causality between oil price changes, commodity (metals) price changes, exchange rates, and equity returns. We examine causality within the framework of a multivariate VAR model that includes stock market returns, Brent oil price changes, gold price changes, copper price changes, silver price changes and exchange rate returns and control for global economic activity using the BDI. The empirical analysis is carried out at the daily frequency for Saudi Arabia, the United Arab Emirates, Italy, and France, which are, respectively, two oil-exporting and two oil-importing countries.

Due to the expected time-varying nature of causality as well as evidence of parameter and covariance matrix instability, we employ a rolling window methodology for the period June 1, 2005–April 27, 2018. Fortunately, this sample period includes all possible oil price trends (rising, declining, and stable).

We provide strong empirical evidence that oil price changes caused equity returns for Saudi Arabia and United Arab Emirates since 2014. Given that the post-2014 period is one of declining oil prices, our findings may suggest that causality depends on the prevailing oil price regime. Our findings also suggest that copper price changes are, to a lesser extent, useful predictors of the equity returns of Saudi Arabia and the United Arab Emirates.

Because oil (and copper) price changes are not pervasive predictors of the equity returns of the four countries, we view our findings as not consistent with the financialization view, but rather indicative of oil's importance for the economies of the two oil exporters.

Acknowledgments

The authors would like to thank the participants in the 2nd International Conference of the Hellenic Association for Energy Economics, the WEAI 14th International Conference, seminar participants in UC Dublin as well as in the 2018 International Conference on Energy Finance in Beijing, China, for numerous insightful comments and suggestions. We gratefully acknowledge support in funding conference travel from the Institute of Financial Economics at the American University of Beirut and from the American University of Beirut's University Research Board. This research did not receive any specific grant from funding agencies in the public, commercial, or not-for-profit sectors.

References

Ajayi, R., Friedman, J. and Mehdian, S. (1998). On the relationship between stock returns and exchange rates: Tests of Granger causality, *Global Finance Journal*, 9, 241–251.

Al-Janabi, M. A. M., Hatemi. A. J. and Irandoust, M. (2010). An empirical investigation of the informational efficiency of the GCC equity markets: Evidence from bootstrap simulation, *International Review of Financial Analysis*, 19, 47–54.

Aloui, C. (2007). Price and volatility spillovers between exchange rates and stock indexes for the pre-and post-euro period, *Quantitative Finance*, 7, 669–685.

Alquist, R., Kilian, L. and Vigfusson, R. J. (2013). Forecasting the price of oil, in *Handbook of Economic Forecasting*, Vol. 2, Elsevier, pp. 427–507.

Andrews, D. W. (1993). Tests for parameter instability and structural change with unknown change point, *Econometrica*, 61, 821–856.

Arouri, M. E. H., Jouini, J. and Nguyen, D. K. (2011). Volatility spillovers between oil prices and stock sector returns: Implications for portfolio management, *Journal of International Money and Finance*, 30, 1387–1405.

Arslanturk, Y., Balcilar, M. and Ozdemir, Z. A. (2011). Time-varying linkages between tourism receipts and economic growth in a small open economy, *Economic Modelling*, 28, 664–671.

Bahmani-Oskooee, M. and Sohrabian, A. (1992). Stock prices and the effective change rate of the dollar, *Applied Economics*, 24, 459–464.

Bakshi, G., Panayotov, G. and Skoulakis, G. (2011). The baltic dry index as a predictor of global stock returns, commodity returns, and global economic activity, Working Paper, University of Maryland.

Balcilar, M. and Ozdemir, Z. A. (2013). The export-output growth nexus in Japan: a bootstrap rolling window approach, *Empirical Economics*, 44, 1–22.

Balcilar, M., Ozdemir, Z. A. and Arslanturk, Y. (2010). Economic growth and energy consumption causal nexus viewed through a bootstrap rolling window, *Energy Economics*, 32, 1398–1410.

Basher, S. A., Haug, A. A. and Sadorsky, P. (2012). Oil prices, exchange rates and emerging stock markets, *Energy Economics*, 34, 227–240.

Baumeister, C. and Kilian, L. (2017). A general approach to recovering market expectations from futures prices with an application to crude oil, Working Paper, University of Notre Dame.

Baur, D. G. and Lucey, B. M. (2010). Is gold a hedge or a safe haven? An analysis of stocks, bonds and gold, *Financial Review*, 45, 217–229.

Baur, D. G. and McDermott, T. K. (2010). Is gold a safe haven? International evidence, *Journal of Banking and Finance*, 34, 1886–1898.

Bernanke, B. S. (2016). The relationship between stocks and oil prices. http://www.brookings.edu/blogs/ben-bernanke/posts/2016/02/19-stocks-and-oil-prices? cid=00900015020089101US0001-02201.

Bessembinder, H. (1992). Systematic risk, hedging pressure, and risk premiums in futures markets, *Review of Financial Studies*, 5, 637–667.

Black, A. J., Klinkowska, O., McMillan, D. G. and McMillan, F. J. (2014). Forecasting stock returns: do commodity prices help? *Journal of Forecasting*, 33, 627–639.

British Petroleum Statistical Review of World Energy (2017). Available at https://www.bp.com/content/dam/bp/en/corporate/pdf/energy-economics/statistical-review-2017/bp-statistical-review-of-world-energy-2017-full-report.pdf. Last accessed on 8/14/2017.

Broadstock, D. C. and Filis, G. (2014). Oil price shocks and stock market returns: New evidence from the United States and China, *Journal of International Financial Markets, Institutions and Money*, 33, 417–433.

Caporale, G. M. and Pittis, N. (1997). Causality and forecasting in incomplete systems, *Journal of Forecasting*, 16, 425–437.

Choi, K. and Hammoudeh, S. (2010). Volatility behavior of oil, industrial commodity and stock markets in a regime-switching environment, *Energy Policy*, 38, 4388–4399.

Chow, G. C. (1960). Tests of equality between sets of coefficients in two linear regressions, *Econometrica*, 28, 591–605.

Ciner, C., Gurdgiev, C. and Lucey, B. M. (2013). Hedges and safe havens: An examination of stocks, bonds, gold, oil and exchange rates, *International Review of Financial Analysis*, 29, 202–211.

Cunado, J. and de Gracia, F. P. (2014). Oil price shocks and stock market returns: Evidence for some European countries, *Energy Economics*, 42, 365–377.

Dbouk, W. and Jamali, I. (2018). Predicting daily oil prices: Linear and non-linear models, *Research in International Business and Finance*, 46, 149–165.

De Roon, F. A., Nijman, T. E. and Veld, C. (2000). Hedging pressure effects in futures markets, *Journal of Finance*, 55, 1437–1456.

Dickey, D. A. and Fuller, W. A. (1979). Distribution of the estimators for autoregressive time series with a unit root, *Journal of the American Statistical Association*, 74, 427–431.

Dlamini, J., Balcilar, M., Gupta, R. and Inglesi-Lotz, R. (2015). Revisiting the causality between electricity consumption and economic growth in South Africa: a bootstrap rolling-window approach, *International Journal of Economic Policy in Emerging Economies*, 8, 169–190.

Dufour, J. M. and Renault, E. (1998). Short run and long run causality in time series: Theory, *Econometrica*, 66, 1099–1125.

Elliott, G., Rothenberg, T. and Stock, J. (1996). Efficient tests for an autoregressive unit root, *Econometrica*, 64, 813–836.

El-Sharif, I., Brown, D., Burton, B., Nixon, B. and Russell, A. (2005). Evidence on the nature and extent of the relationship between oil prices and equity values in the UK, *Energy Economics*, 27, 819–830.

Fattouh, B., Kilian, L. and Mahadeva, L. (2013). The role of speculation in oil markets: What have we learned so far? *Energy Journal*, 34, 7–33.

Fama, E. F. and French, K. R. (1987). Commodity futures prices: Some evidence on forecast power, premiums, and the theory of storage, *Journal of Business*, 60, 55–73.

Gorton, G. and Rouwenhorst, K. G. (2006). Facts and fantasies about commodity futures, *Financial Analysts Journal*, 62, 47–68.

Granger, C. W. (1969). Investigating causal relations by econometric models and cross-spectral methods, *Econometrica*, 37, 424–438.

Guesmi, K. and Fattoum, S. (2014). The relationship between oil price and OECD stock markets: A multivariate approach, *Economics Bulletin*, 34, 510–519.

Hatemi–J, A. and Irandoust, M. (2002). On the causality between exchange rates and stock prices: A note, *Bulletin of Economic Research*, 54, 197–203.

Hammoudeh, S. and Choi, K. (2006). Behavior of GCC stock markets and impacts of US oil and financial markets, *Research in International Business and Finance*, 20, 22–44.

Hansen, B. E. (1997). Approximate asymptotic P values for structural-change tests, *Journal of Business and Economic Statistics*, 15, 60–67.

Hill, J. B. (2007). Efficient tests of long-run causation in trivariate VAR processes with a rolling window study of the money–income relationship, *Journal of Applied Econometrics*, 22, 747–765.

Hosking, J. R. M. (1981). Equivalent forms of the multivariate portmanteau statistic, *Journal of the Royal Statistical Society. Series B (Methodological)*, 261–262.

Huang, R. D., Masulis, R. W. and Stoll, H. R. (1996). Energy shocks and financial markets, *Journal of Futures Markets*, 16, 1–27.

Inglesi-Lotz, R., Balcilar, M. and Gupta, R. (2014). Time-varying causality between research output and economic growth in US, *Scientometrics*, 100, 203–216.

Jones, C. M. and Kaul, G. (1996). Oil and the stock markets, *Journal of Finance*, 51, 463–491.

Johansen, S. (1988). Statistical analysis of cointegration vectors, *Journal of Economic Dynamics and Control*, 12, 231–254.

KAMCO Research (2017). GCC Equity Markets: 2016-The year that was... Available at https://www.islamicbanker.com/publications/gcc-equity-markets-report-2016. Last accessed on 8/14/2017.

Kang, W. and Ratti, R. A. (2013). Oil shocks, policy uncertainty and stock market return, *Journal of International Financial Markets, Institutions and Money*, 26, 305–318.

Kilian, L. (2009). Not all oil price shocks are alike: Disentangling demand and supply shocks in the crude oil market, *American Economic Review*, 99, 1053–1069.

Kilian, L. and Park, C. (2009). The impact of oil price shocks on the US stock market, *International Economic Review*, 50, 1267–1287.

Kilian, L. (2016). The Impact of the shale oil revolution on U.S. oil and gas prices, *Review of Environmental Economics and Policy*, 10, 185–205.

Kilian, L. and Lütkepohl, H. (2017). *Structural Vector Autoregressive Analysis*, Cambridge University Press.

Kling, J. L. (1985). Oil price shocks and stock market behavior, *Journal of Portfolio Management*, 12, 34–39.

Klovland, J. T. (2004). Business cycles, commodity prices and shipping freight rates: Some evidence from the pre-WWI Period, in Paper presented at *Workshop on Market Performance and the Welfare Gains of Market Integration in History*, Florence, Italy.

Kwiatkowski, D., Phillips, P. C., Schmidt, P. and Shin, Y. (1992). Testing the null hypothesis of stationarity against the alternative of a unit root: How sure are we that economic time series have a unit root? *Journal of Econometrics*, 54, 159–178.

Labys, W., Achouch, A. and Terraza, M. (1999). Metal prices and the business cycle, *Resources Policy*, 25, 229–238.

Le, T-H. and Chang, Y. (2015). Effects of oil price shocks on the stock market performance: Do nature of the shocks and economies matter? *Energy Economics*, 51, 261–274.

Liu, L., Feng M. and Wang, Y. (2015). Forecasting excess stock returns with crude oil market data, *Energy Economics*, 48, 316–324.

Lombardi, M. J., Osbat, C. and Schnatz, B. (2012). Global commodity cycles and linkages: A FAVAR approach, *Empirical Economics*, 55, 541–565.

Lucey, B. M. and Li, S. (2015). What precious metals act as safe havens, and when? Some US evidence, *Applied Economics Letters*, 22, 35–45.

Lütkepohl, H. (1983). Non-causality due to omitted variables, *Journal of Econometrics*, 19, 367–378.

Lütkepohl, H. (2005). *New Introduction to Multiple Time Series Analysis*, Springer.

Lütkepohl, H. and Krätzig, M. (2004). *Applied Time Series Econometrics*, Cambridge University Press.

Masters, M. W. (2008). Testimony before the committee on homeland security and governmental affairs, United States Senate, May 20.

Miyazaki, T. and Hamori, S. (2016). Asymmetric correlations in gold and other financial markets, *Applied Economics*, 48, 4419–4425.

Moore, T. and Wang, P. (2014). Dynamic linkage between real exchange rates and stock markets: Evidence from developed and Asian markets, *International Review of Economics and Finance*, 29, 1–11.

Newey, W. K. and West, K. (1987). A simple, positive semi-definite, heteroskedasticity and auto-correlation consistent covariance matrix, *Econometrica*, 55, 703–708.

Nieh, C-C. and Lee, C-F. (2001). Dynamic relationship between stock prices and exchange rates for G-7 countries, *Quarterly Review for Economics and Finance*, 41, 477–900.

Nyakabawo, W., Miller, S. M., Balcilar, M., Das, S. and Gupta, R. (2015). Temporal causality between house prices and output in the US: A bootstrap rolling-window approach, *The North American Journal of Economics and Finance*, 33, 55–73.

Nyblom, J. (1989). Testing for the constancy of parameters over time, *Journal of the American Statistical Association*, 84, 223–230.

OPEC Annual Statistical Bulletin (2016). Organization of the Petroleum Exporting Countries, Vienna, Austria. Available at https://www.opec.org/opec_web/static_files_project/media/downloads/publications/ASB2016.pdf. Last accessed on 8/14/2017.

Phylaktis, K. and Ravazollo, F. (2005). Stock prices and exchange rate dynamics, *Journal of International Money and Finance*, 24, 1031–1053.

Phillips, P. C. and Perron, P. (1988). Testing for a unit root in time series regression, *Biometrika*, 75, 335–346.

Pindyck, R. S. and Rotemberg, J. J. (1990). The excess co-movement of commodity prices, *Economic Journal*, 100, 1173–1189.

Rossi, B. (2013). Advances in forecasting under instabilities, in Elliott, G. and Timmermann, A. (eds.), *Handbook of Economic Forecasting*, Vol. 2, Elsevier, Amsterdam, pp. 1203–1324.

Quandt, R. E. (1960). Tests of the hypothesis that a linear regression system obeys two separate regimes, *Journal of the American statistical Association*, 55, 324–330.

Sadorsky, P. (1999). Oil price shocks and stock market activity, *Energy Economics*, 21, 449–469.

Schinas, O., Grau, C. and Johns, M. (2015). *HSBA Handbook on Ship Finance*, Springer Berlin Heidelberg.

Schwert, W. G. (1989). Why does stock market volatility change over time? *Journal of Finance*, 44, 1115–1153.

Śmiech, S. and Papież, M. (2013). Fossil fuel prices, exchange rate, and stock market: A dynamic causality analysis on the European market, *Economics Letters*, 118, 199–202.

Smith, K. L., Brocato, J. and Rogers, J. E. (1993). Regularities in the data between major equity markets: Evidence from Granger causality tests, *Applied Financial Economics*, 3, 55–60.

Smyth, R. and Nandha, M. (2003). Bivariate causality between exchange rate and stock prices in South Asia, *Applied Economic Letters*, 10(11), 699–704.

Swanson, N. R. (1998). Money and output viewed through a rolling window, *Journal of Monetary Economics*, 41, 455–474.

Swanson, N. R., Ozyildrim, A. and Pisu, M. (2003). A comparison of alternative causality and predictive accuracy tests in the presence of integrated and co-integrated economic variables, in Giles, D. E. A. (ed.), *Computer-Aided Econometrics*, Routledge, London.

Tang, C. F. (2010). The money-prices nexus for Malaysia: New empirical evidence from the time-varying cointegration and causality tests, *Global Economic Review*, 39, 383–403.

Tsai, C. L. (2015). How do US stock returns respond differently to oil price shocks pre-crisis, within the financial crisis, and post-crisis? *Energy Economics*, 50, 47–62.

Tang, X. and Yao, X. (2017). Do financial structures affect exchange rate and stock price interaction? Evidence from emerging markets, *Emerging Markets Review*, 34, 64–76.

Umer, M. U., Sevil, G. and Kamisli, S. (2015). The dynamic linkages between exchange rates and stock prices: Evidence from emerging markets, *Journal of Finance and Investment Analysis*, 4, 17–32.

Walid, C., Chaker, A., Masood, O. and Fry, J. (2011). Stock market volatility and exchange rates in emerging countries: A Markov-state switching approach, *Emerging Markets Review*, 12, 272–292.

Yang, S. Y. and Doong, S. C. (2004). Price and volatility spillovers between stock prices and exchange rates: Empirical evidence from the G-7 countries, *International Journal of Business and Economics*, 3, 139.

Chapter 4

Time-Varying Linkage between Equities and Oil

Beyza Mina Ordu-Akkaya[*,†,§], Adil Oran[†] and Uğur Soytaş[†,‡]

[*]*Social Sciences University of Ankara, Department of Management,*
Hükümet Meydanı No. 2, Altındağ, Ulus, 06050, Ankara, Turkey
[†]*Middle East Technical University, Department of Business*
Administration, 06531 Ankara, Turkey
[‡]*Middle East Technical University, Department of*
Earth System Science, 06531 Ankara, Turkey
[§]*beyza.akkaya@asbu.edu.tr*

1. Introduction

Global and local financial crises throughout history push investors to search for potential hedging instruments. One of the fundamental arguments of finance is that diversification is beneficial because they may diversify away risk. Unfortunately, the benefits of diversification seem to be the lowest when needed the most, that is, during crisis periods. Previous studies have shown that during financial stress periods, correlation between different countries (Longin and Solnik, 1995) and asset classes seem to rise (Forbes and Rigobon, 2002; Ciner et al., 2013; Creti et al., 2013). It is important to understand whether these observed changes in correlations are short term or long term in nature, as they have strong bearing on risk management strategies. Chiang et al. (2007) examine nine Asian markets and find evidence of contagion between those markets and high correlations which, they argue, may be due to the herding behavior of investors.

Roll (2013) states that when well-diversified portfolios are also formed so as to include assets from different classes, these portfolios tend to have lower correlations. This is interpreted as being consistent with the existence of several systematic factors. In light of these facts, Roll indicates that the diversification benefits should be quite high across asset classes (e.g. commodities and equities). The major investment tool for most investors is the equity market; however, commodities are some of the leading tools of diversification due to their relatively low correlations with equities as pointed out in the literature (Gorton and Rouwenhorst, 2006; Erb and Harvey, 2006; Arouri *et al.*, 2014; Buyuksahin and Robe, 2014). This low correlation has led to the financialization of commodities, which is a term used to describe what happens to commodity prices when institutional investors begin to play larger roles in these markets and prices are no longer determined by only supply and demand conditions in these markets. According to the Commodity Futures Trading Commission (CFTC), commodity futures positions of institutional investors increased from USD15 billion in 2003 to USD200 billion in 2008 (CFTC, 2008). Furthermore, as Basak and Pavlova (2016) show, 11–17% of the exceptionally high commodity prices in 2008 are attributable to the financialization of commodities.

Oil continues to be the chief commodity in the global economy, despite displaying exceptional volatility over the years, which can be seen in Figure 1. Even in a relatively stagnant world economy, global oil consumption continued to increase by 1.9% in 2015 (BP, 2016). Volatility is not something desired by most investors, since high volatility in oil prices creates some doubt about its diversification benefits as an investment. Furthermore, an oil shock creates a chain reaction in the prices of traditional financial assets, due to the financialization phenomenon. Hence, the correlation between

Figure 1: S&P 500 and WTI 1-month futures oil prices.

these two major asset classes, oil and US equities, is of significant importance.

The movements of US equity and energy commodity markets over the last two decades can be seen in Figure 1. An overview of the figure allows us to see that the volatilities seem to have increased over time and if there is a relationship between oil prices and US equities, it seems to be a dynamic rather than a constant relation. There may also be a strengthening of the linkage between the commodity and financial markets after the crisis. Basak and Pavlova (2016) argue that the introduction of institutional investors increases the correlation between commodities and equities. As a result, financialization may increase prices and push correlations higher, thus lowering diversification benefits. In this environment, understanding how correlations are affected by changes in the business cycle or the macroeconomic environment becomes a point of significant interest.

In this study, we investigate the dynamic asymmetric link between oil and the S&P 500. Particularly, we place emphasis on whether correlation changes are short term or long term in nature. This is important since it will have significant effects on risk management strategies. Furthermore, our time frame allows us to analyze a number of shocks both in the commodity and financial markets and discern how each shock shapes the correlation structure. Events such as the 9/11 attack, the 2001 dot.com bubble, the 1997 Asian economic crisis, the 2003 Iraq war, the 2008 global financial crisis, and others incorporate valuable information into the dataset. From a methodological point of view, we utilize the asymmetric DCC (A-DCC) GARCH method, introduced by Engle (2002) and further improved by Cappiello *et al.* (2006). The A-DCC method not only captures the time-varying nature of correlation but also takes into account the asymmetric impact of negative and positive shocks on the correlation.

In order to better understand the relation between the oil and US stock markets, we also examine how other factors affect the correlation between oil prices and US equity returns. Our analysis includes five additional factors, each representing one market including the USD/EUR parity from foreign exchange market, the 3-month T-bill rates from the US sovereign bond market, gold prices from the precious metals, copper prices from the metals commodity markets, and finally, the Cleveland Financial Stress Index (CFSI) which measures the common systematic risk in the market. By including these factors, we would like to better understand how the relationship between equities and oil is affected.

The contribution of this study to the literature is three-fold. First, it examines the asymmetric time-varying correlation between oil and equity markets, which is expected to have a relatively low correlation and carry diversification benefits. In addition to the initial analysis being carried out on the equity market as a whole by using the S&P 500, the analysis is also repeated for different industries to see whether the correlation dynamics change at the disaggregated level. Second, it distinguishes between the short-term and long-term changes in correlation, as this may affect the diversification benefits and risk management actions of investors. Third, it examines how the correlation between oil prices and US equity is affected by particular factors. To the best of our knowledge, this study is the first to examine the effects of additional market factors on the correlation between oil and equity prices, which we believe will be of significant interest to those involved in portfolio management strategies.

Our findings support previous findings that oil and equity correlation is dynamic in nature (Chang *et al.*, 2013; Sadorsky, 2012; Degiannakis *et al.*, 2013). Furthermore, correlations also possess an asymmetric nature, showing that negative shocks have a stronger impact on correlations compared to positive shocks. This has strong implications for portfolio diversification strategies. More importantly, we show that during financial distress periods, correlations tend to increase, though some are short-term effects while others endure longer term. We find that the 2008 global financial crisis is an interesting episode such that pre-2008 correlation increases tend to be short term while those post-2008 appear to be longer-term changes. The CFSI seems to do a good job at differentiating the longer-term correlation increase horizons, implying that it should be closely followed for risk management strategies.

The remainder of this study is organized as follows. Section 2 presents an overview of the relevant empirical literature. Section 3 discusses the data and Section 4 describes the methodology. Section 5 analyzes the empirical results. Finally, Section 6 concludes.

2. Literature Review

The portfolio management and diversification literature examines which investment tools help investors to lower their risk levels and how financial distress periods can affect risk management strategies. One strand of the literature examines safe-haven assets, which are especially important during crisis times. For instance, Ranaldo and Soderlind (2010) indicate that the Swiss Franc appreciates when the S&P 500 is falling, bond prices are rising, and currency markets are volatile. Baur and McDermott (2010) find gold to play a safe-haven role in 7 of 13 countries included in their sample due to its stabilizing role. Upper (2000) looks into a different asset class and indicates that the German bonds were liquid during the 1998 crisis and hence they are good investment tools during turmoil periods. Ciner *et al.* (2013), among other studies, analyze oil–bond and oil–stock relationships for the US and UK and find that the correlations for the oil–bond pair are low to negative, whereas for the oil–stock pair, they are not significantly different from zero. This supports the argument that oil can be a useful hedge for bonds. These findings push us to examine the relationship between equity and oil prices in more detail.

The roots of interest in the relationship between oil and other economic factors go back to at least the 1970s when oil shocks started to create serious problems in economies. Among others, Hamilton (1983, 1996), Bernanke (2006), and Gisser and Goodwin (1986) provide findings on the impacts of oil prices on the macroeconomy. In their seminal paper, Chen *et al.* (1986) include oil prices into a multifactor model to explain stock returns. Even though their results suggest insignificance of oil prices, the following studies yield different evidence. Besides others, Papapetrou (2001), Park and Ratti (2008), and Jones and Kaul (1996) indicate increasing oil prices have a negative impact on equity returns. The rationale behind this negative relationship is consistent with the economic theory (Fisher, 1930; Williams, 1938). Since oil prices generally cause input prices to increase, they create an inflationary pressure and increase the cost base of the firms and can decrease profitability if they are not able to pass along the price increases to their customers. Moreover, inflation may also result in higher discount rates which directly lowers the intrinsic value of the company and may result in a selling behavior for stocks (Huang *et al.*, 1996). As a result, equity returns are generally expected to be negatively affected by rising oil prices.

However, findings of some recent price spillovers propose that the relationship could actually depend on whether the country is an oil-importer or exporter (Aloui *et al.*, 2012), or is economically developed or developing (Ramos and Veiga, 2011). Even the disaggregated indices in a country can display diverse characteristics; hence, many recent studies examine how oil prices affect major industry returns instead of the aggregate index (Degiannakis *et al.*, 2013; Sadorsky, 2001). However, the relationship could actually be time-varying for the same sector or the same country, depending upon the economic conditions the country is experiencing.

Arouri *et al.* (2012) show that there is a significant volatility transmission and the spillover is even more obvious from oil to the DJ Stoxx Europe 600 Index. Degiannakis *et al.* (2013) also examine the European market and find time-variation, but additionally they show that correlations are affected by whether the oil shocks are supply shocks, precautionary demand, or aggregate demand shocks. Given the findings showing that the sensitivity of the stock markets to oil prices is very much dependent upon the country being an oil importer or exporter, Filis *et al.* (2011) investigate six emerging and developed oil-importer and exporter countries. They find that correlation is affected positively by aggregate demand shocks, such as the Asian economic crisis, and negatively by precautionary demand shocks, such as the Iraq wars. Furthermore, they find supply shocks to have no impact on the correlations. However, these findings are not much in line with Degiannakis *et al.* (2013) who argue that a precautionary demand pushes correlations to zero and that supply shocks lead to low levels of positive correlation.

Salisu and Oloko (2015) study the volatility spillover between the S&P 500 and oil and find that volatility transmission of oil after the recent global financial crisis has risen. Chang *et al.* (2013) demonstrate that the relationship between oil and equity markets including the Dow Jones, FTSE100, NYSE, and S&P 500 with oil is dynamic in nature. Creti *et al.* (2013) analyze the correlation of 25 major commodities with US equity market, and show that the 2008 global financial crisis has bolstered the linkages between commodity and financial markets, supporting the financialization of commodities. Mollick and Asefa (2013) investigate the interrelationship of the US stocks with gold, oil, USD/EUR exchange rate, and short- and long-term interest rates. They find that the financial turmoil in 2008 reshapes the correlation between oil and the S&P 500. Before the crisis, the linkage was not strong, whereas following the crisis, oil prices and weaker

USD/EUR rate have a positive impact on stock returns. Turhan *et al.*
(2014) also find that the correlation between oil and stock returns
strengthens after the 2008 crisis and has stayed at relatively high
levels.

Thus, it seems there is a critical threshold in recent findings which
clearly affects the correlation level between asset classes. This phenomenon of increasing comovements during stress periods opens up
a new strand of the literature, which is contagion. However, the consensus on a discrete definition of contagion has not been reached
yet (Bekaert *et al.*, 2005), and nuances between researchers' definitions of contagion result in significant differences in findings. Calvo
and Reinhart (1996) indicate that the cross-market correlation coefficients for Latin American countries increased during the Mexican
crisis, and thus contagion occurred. However, Forbes and Rigobon
(2002) state the correlation coefficient is a biased and inaccurate measure since during the financial stress periods volatility would increase
and cross-market correlations would be biased upwards. Therefore,
they conclude that neither the Mexican nor the Asian crisis should
be considered as a contagion. Further, Bekaert *et al.* (2005) take the
time-varying nature of volatility into account and show that the 1997
Asian crisis displayed significant contagion characteristics.

In the last decade, the global financial crisis opened up a new
research area in the contagion literature. Rose and Spiegel (2010)
find no evidence of contagion for 85 countries during specific financial turmoil periods, whereas Longstaff (2010) finds strong evidence
of contagion through the liquidity channel during 2008. The majority
of the above findings focus on linkages between geographically separate financial markets, whereas in the current study we consider contagion in terms of different asset classes. Contagion might be present
not only between different regional markets but also between different
asset classes. Therefore, the diversification advantages of commodity markets (Gorton and Rouwenhorst, 2006) could be severely hurt
during contagion across asset classes.

Financialization of commodities is a relatively recent phenomenon that has taken place with the increased role of institutional investors in commodity markets. Nazlioglu *et al.* (2015) study whether financialization affects volatility spillover dynamics between financial markets and oil. Increasing participation of financial investors in commodity markets strengthens the link between oil and financial markets (Tang and Xiong, 2012). Hence, financial stress might spillover to commodity markets, which is thought to have a negative correlation with traditional financial markets (Gorton and Rouwenhorst, 2006). Nazlioglu *et al.* (2015) employ CFSI to proxy for financial stress and find that risk was transferred from oil to financial stress before the recent global financial crisis and from financial stress to oil after the crisis. Buyuksahin and Robe (2014) state that increasing hedge funds' participation in commodity and equity markets resulted in much higher correlations between these two asset classes. Tang and Xiong (2012) also indicate that institutional investors' presence in commodity markets has led to correlation increases also across commodities.

As previously mentioned, some theories argue that the correlation between commodities and equities may be negative. However, we see that correlations seem to be changing during periods of financial distress (Forbes and Rigobon, 2002; Bekaert *et al.*, 2005; Markwat *et al.*, 2009; Mollick and Assefa, 2013; Turhan *et al.*, 2014; Creti *et al.*, 2013). The relationship of commodities and in particular oil with equity markets is of great interest to investors, so we examine how the time-varying correlation between oil and US equity returns changes through time and investigate which factors influence this correlation.

In order to shed more light on the relationships between commodities and equity markets, we focus on the relationship between oil and equity markets. We attempt to capture the asymmetric time-varying nature of correlations both at aggregated and disaggregated levels and examine whether changes in correlations are short term or long term in nature. To the best of our knowledge, the factors driving the A-DCCs have not been studied yet. This study attempts to contribute by filling this gap.

3. Data

All variables employed in this study are of daily frequency and are available for the sample period between June 6, 1995, and May 28, 2015, except the USD/EUR exchange rate since the euro came into existence on January 1, 1999. All price series are in US dollars. Table 1 lists the variable abbreviations, descriptions, and data sources.

We tried to choose a relatively long-time period in order to attempt to capture the time-varying nature of correlation between oil prices and US equity returns. This time period includes a number of shocks such as the 1997 Asian crisis, the 9/11 New York attack, the 2003 Iraq war, the 2008 global financial crisis, etc. Hence, crucial information on different macroeconomic environments and shock types are inserted into the correlation indirectly. Moreover, the study

Table 1: The variables' notations and sources.

Variable	Description	Source
SP500	SP500 composite index	Datastream
OIL	WTI Cushing 1 month forward Oil prices	EIA
SP5ECOD	SP500 Consumer Discretionary	Datastream
SP5EENE	SP500 Energy	Datastream
SP5EFIN	SP500 Financials	Datastream
SP5EHCR	SP500 Health Care	Datastream
SP5EIND	SP500 Industrials	Datastream
SP5EINT	SP500 Information Technology	Datastream
SP5EMAT	SP500 Materials	Datastream
SP5EUTL	SP500 Utilities	Datastream
SP5ETEL	SP500 Telecommunication	Datastream
CFSI	Daily Cleveland Financial Stress Index	Cleveland Fed website
3MTB	3-month Treasury Bill rates	FRED
USDEUR	USD/EUR exchange rate	FRED
GOLD	COMEX 1 month forward gold prices	Quandl
COPPER	COMEX 1 month forward copper prices	Quandl

is implemented in daily frequency to account for the pace of movement in financial markets and capture, to the extent possible, all information embedded in volatilities.

Our equity return variables are based on the S&P 500 composite index together with nine industry level indices (Materials, Industrials, Information Technology, Telecommunication Services, Utilities, Consumer Discretionary, Energy, Financials, and Healthcare). The S&P 500 is the major representative used in the literature for the US equity market and covers around 80% of the total US market capitalization. Industry level indices have been included to analyze whether the asymmetric time-varying correlation of oil and stocks differ at disaggregated levels.

The other major variable is the West Texas Intermediate (WTI) Cushing oil 1-month forward price. Sadorsky (2001) states that spot prices carry more irrelevant information, compared to futures prices, thus we use 1-month futures prices. Moreover, WTI as a benchmark is closely followed by other crude oil baskets such as Brent, Dubai, and OPEC.

Next, we discuss potential factors that may affect the dynamic correlation between oil and equity markets. The CFSI obtained from the Federal Reserve Bank of Cleveland is available as daily data, as opposed to other financial stress indices such as the corresponding Kansas, Chicago, or St. Louis Federal Reserve bank indices. Readers interested in further information on the construction of this index should refer to Oet *et al.* (2011). We use this measure of stress in the US economy in order to observe whether high distress periods have effects on the relationships. A historical graph for the CFSI is presented in Figure 2.

The shaded areas in this figure denote US recession periods. In addition to the specified US recession periods, the world economy has experienced severe political and economic distress periods in the last 20 years. Hence, we observe quite high levels of CFSI, for instance, during the Asian or Eurozone crisis, as well.

Long-term interest rate is one of the key indicators of the US bond market and is closely followed by policymakers and investors.

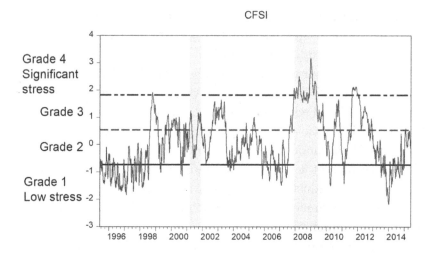

Figure 2: Historical CFSI.

This factor has been used in many multifactor models to investigate whether interest rates are helpful in explaining stock returns. The proxy used for the interest rate is either the spread between the long- and short-term interest rates (Sadorsky, 2008; Mollick and Assefa, 2013) or the short-term interest rate (Henriques and Sadorsky, 2008; Huang *et al.*, 1996; Sadorsky, 1999; Cong *et al.*, 2008), and the interest rate is usually found to be significant.

Since gold is considered to be a safe haven for investors, particularly in the recent 2008 financial crisis, its nominal price increased by 42% over the period between July 2007 and March 2009. Even though it plummeted later, it is still seen as a worldwide major investment tool. Hence, we include gold prices to see how precious metals affect the dynamic correlation between stocks and oil.

The major industrial metal commodity, copper, is sometimes referred to as "Dr. Copper" due to its success in predicting economic activity (Sadorsky, 2014). As a result, we include copper in our analysis to further examine the relationship between the equity and commodity markets.

Last but not least, we include the USD/EUR exchange rate, which is the major parity between two reserve currencies. Lizardo

Table 2: Descriptive statistics (levels).

	Mean	Median	Max.	Min.	Std. dev.	Skewness	Kurtosis
SP500	1219.45	1208.14	2130.82	527.94	328.25	0.43	3.43
OIL	54.01	48.68	145.29	10.72	31.82	0.42	1.88
SP5ECOD	269.24	253.48	615.58	109.89	106.69	1.26	4.53
SP5ECST	263.93	238.98	516.45	113.30	85.30	1.09	3.85
SP5EENE	353.21	338.41	737.09	110.27	170.37	0.35	1.73
SP5EFIN	297.55	306.56	509.55	81.74	94.32	0.06	2.19
SP5EHCR	375.85	361.64	867.54	116.97	135.21	1.33	5.81
SP5EIND	273.75	267.36	498.14	114.95	81.57	0.64	3.40
SP5EINT	386.41	350.49	988.49	126.09	158.15	0.99	3.83
SP5EMAT	183.77	165.28	326.60	102.55	56.74	0.69	2.40
SP5ETEL	153.75	136.79	339.28	79.00	53.59	1.63	5.15
SP5EUTL	159.46	157.73	251.40	77.27	33.97	0.15	2.35
CFSI	0.12	−0.01	3.18	−2.18	1.02	0.36	2.43
_3MTB	2.50	1.81	6.24	0.00	2.17	0.15	1.34
USDEUR	1.22	1.27	1.60	0.83	0.18	−0.49	2.36
GOLD	721.63	439.00	1889.70	253.70	474.20	0.79	2.19
COPPER	2.04	1.49	4.62	0.60	1.22	0.31	1.48

and Mollick (2010) find that oil price increases induce USD to depreciate against oil-exporting economies' currencies, and Mollick and Assefa (2013) find that, following the recent global financial crisis, a weaker USD/EUR positively affects stock returns. Hence, we include this parity to capture the intertwining nature of commodity–stock returns–foreign exchange.

Tables 2 and 3 present the descriptive statistics for the entire sample period. The natural logarithms of all variables except the 3-month T-bill and CFSI are arranged on a 5-working-day basis and the returns are computed by taking first differences. In our analysis, we include CFSI in levels and the 3-month T-bill in first differences. As one can note, D3MTB is the most volatile series compared to those of the commodity, equities, and foreign exchange markets. The S&P 500 mean return exceeded the returns of both oil and USD/EUR, and specifically the Health Care industry is the winner between all price series with its 9.7% average annual return. As can be seen, all variables display non-normality according to the Jarque–Bera tests, which is partially due to high kurtosis of the variables. We also present the Ljung–Box and Ljung–Box-squared statistics, which

Table 3: Descriptive statistics (returns).

	Mean	Median	Max.	Min.	Std. dev.	Skewness	Kurtosis	LB-Q prob.	LB-Q2 prob.
DLSP500	0.0003	0.0003	0.1096	−0.0947	0.0120	−0.2416	11.4	0.00	0.00
DLOIL	0.0002	0.0000	0.1641	−0.1654	0.0232	−0.1195	7.5	0.00	0.00
DLSP5ECOD	0.0003	0.0002	0.1231	−0.1033	0.0136	−0.1074	10.1	0.00	0.00
DLSP5ECST	0.0003	0.0002	0.0884	−0.0930	0.0096	−0.1275	11.7	0.00	0.00
DLSP5EENE	0.0003	0.0000	0.1696	−0.1688	0.0159	−0.3017	13.7	0.00	0.00
DLSP5EFIN	0.0002	0.0000	0.1720	−0.1864	0.0190	−0.0978	18.4	0.00	0.00
DLSP5EHCR	0.0004	0.0003	0.1171	−0.0917	0.0118	−0.1292	9.5	0.00	0.00
DLSP5EIND	0.0003	0.0002	0.0952	−0.0960	0.0132	−0.3376	8.8	0.00	0.00
DLSP5EINT	0.0003	0.0006	0.1608	−0.1001	0.0180	0.1588	7.9	0.00	0.00
DLSP5EMAT	0.0002	0.0000	0.1247	−0.1293	0.0150	−0.2438	9.7	0.00	0.00
DLSP5ETEL	0.0001	0.0000	0.1293	−0.1032	0.0141	0.0585	9.7	0.00	0.00
DLSP5EUTL	0.0001	0.0002	0.1268	−0.0900	0.0116	−0.0249	13.3	0.00	0.00
CFSI	0.1189	−0.0094	3.1821	−2.1812	1.0229	0.3560	2.4	0.00	0.00
D3MTB	−0.0011	0.0000	0.7400	−0.8100	0.0492	−0.9446	57.7	0.00	0.00
DLUSDEUR	0.0000	0.0000	0.0420	−0.0474	0.0064	−0.0035	5.9	0.00	0.00
DLGOLD	0.0002	0.0000	0.0883	−0.0981	0.0110	−0.1151	11.2	0.00	0.00
DLCOPPER	0.0001	0.0000	0.1817	−0.1450	0.0183	−0.1754	11.2	0.00	0.00

test the null hypothesis of no auto-correlation. Tables 2 and 3 show that both auto-correlation and ARCH effects are found in all series, and hence employing the GARCH methodology is appropriate.

4. Methodology

The study utilizes a two-stage analysis. In the first stage, we investigate the correlation between US equities and oil prices by utilizing the A-DCC model. This method allows us to compute the dynamic conditional correlation series (hereafter referred to as Rho). In the second stage, we examine the factors that affect Rho by using the Generalized Impulse Response functions.

4.1. *Asymmetric DCC*

The A-DCC method is an extension of the dynamic conditional correlation method of the GARCH family introduced by Engle (2002). Later, Cappiello *et al.* (2006) extended the DCC to capture the conditional asymmetric portion:

$$H_t = D_t R_t D_t, \tag{1}$$

where D_t is the $k \times k$ diagonal matrix of time-varying standard deviations gathered from the estimation process of the univariate GARCH [1,1] process. So $\sqrt{h_{it}}$ is extant on the ith diagonals and R_t is the correlation matrix.

EGARCH models are found to be more suitable for financial analysis due to the leverage effect therefore we employ EGARCH models.

The estimation of the A-DCC model is a two-stage method, and in the first stage the univariate EGARCH models are estimated for both S&P 500 and oil returns

$$\log(h_t) = \alpha_0 + \alpha_1 \bar{\varepsilon}_{t-1} + \beta_1 \log(h_{t-1}) + \gamma_1 \left[\bar{\varepsilon}_{t-1} - \sqrt{\frac{2}{\pi}} \right]. \tag{2}$$

The second step involves computing the standardized residuals

$$\bar{\varepsilon}_t = \frac{\varepsilon_t}{\sqrt{h_t}}, \tag{3}$$

which helps to compute the conditional correlation in the DCC model as follows:

$$Q_t = (1 - a - b)\bar{R} + a\bar{\varepsilon}_{t-1}\bar{\varepsilon}'_{t-1} + bQ_{t-1}. \tag{4}$$

However, we would like to include the asymmetric impact, and therefore the standardized negative residuals are defined as

$$\bar{\nu}_t = \begin{cases} \bar{\varepsilon}_t & \text{if and only if} \\ \bar{\varepsilon}_t < 0. \end{cases} \tag{5}$$

Thus, the A-DCC is given by the following equation:

$$Q_t = (1 - a - b)\bar{R} - c\bar{S} + a\bar{\varepsilon}_{t-1}\bar{\varepsilon}'_{t-1} + c\bar{\nu}_{t-1}\bar{\nu}'_{t-1} + bQ_{t-1}, \tag{6}$$

$$\bar{R} = Q_t^{*-1} Q_t Q_t^{*-1}, \tag{7}$$

where $\bar{R} = E[\bar{\varepsilon}_t\bar{\varepsilon}'_t]$ and $\bar{S} = E[\bar{\nu}_t\bar{\nu}'_t]$

Q_t should be positive definite and therefore the following constraint should be satisfied:

$$a + b + \delta c < 1, \tag{8}$$

where $\delta = $ maximum eigenvalue $[\bar{R}^{-1/2}\bar{S}\bar{R}^{-1/2}]$.

If θ is the parameter in D_t and R_t, the log-likelihood is as follows:

$$L(\theta) = -\frac{1}{2}\sum_{t=1}^{T}(n\log(2\pi) + 2\log|D_t| + \varepsilon'_t D_t^{-1} D_t^{-1}\varepsilon_t)$$

$$-\frac{1}{2}\sum_{t=1}^{T}[\log|(R_t)| + \bar{\varepsilon}'_t R_t^{-1}\bar{\varepsilon}_t - \bar{\varepsilon}'_t\bar{\varepsilon}_t]. \tag{9}$$

Here, T and n are the number of series, which is 2 in our case, since we estimate the dynamic correlation between the S&P 500 and oil. As a result, we calculate Rho, which is the off-diagonal element of R_t and is the time-varying correlation for the selected asset classes.

4.2. Generalized impulse responses and Granger-causality results

To generate GIRs, we first need to determine a VAR system with seven variables including DLSP500, DLOIL, DLGOLD, DLCOPPER, DLUSD/EUR, D3MTB, and CFSI. Initially, we run the VAR system for the whole sample period and the lag length criterion is determined by the information criteria LR, FPE, AIC, SC, and HQ. If all these criteria point to a consistent lag, the lag length will be chosen, but if there are inconsistencies, then the highest lag length will be chosen. For the entire sample period, lag 4 is chosen, as supported by AIC and SC. The stability of VAR is also assured. As one would expect, we encounter serial auto-correlation and heteroscedasticity and solve the problem by reestimating the standard errors with the Newey–West and White adjustments.

$$Y_t = \sum_{n=1}^{4} X_{i,t-1} + \cdots + X_{i,t-4},$$

where $i = 1, 2, \ldots, 7$ and each represents one variable.

We also provide the GIRs for subperiods which are determined by the multiple breakpoint Bai and Perron (2003) test. A similar lag selection method is used for each subset, as well.

Next, we perform GIRs which were developed by Pesaran and Shin (1998). This method has important advantages over the orthogonalized method since the results are not affected by the order of integration of the variables. Moreover, to better estimate confidence intervals, we bootstrap the standard errors via 1,000 repetitions. In addition to the VARs which display auto-correlated and heteroscedastic characteristics, we also present the Granger-causality test results.

The Granger-causality method is a modified Wald test. The unit root tests offer stationarity for the seven variables RHO_SP5OIL, CFSI, DLOIL, DLSP500, D3MTB, DLCOPPER, DLGOLD, and DLUSDEUR. The results on the unit root tests are available in the appendix. We run a VAR for each subperiod, as well as for full sample period. If the null hypothesis of the lagged variables' coefficients being equal to zero is rejected, we are able to conclude that the specific variable Granger-causes the dependent variable.

5. Results

The estimation results for the A-DCC EGARCH [1,1] model are presented in Table 4.

We apply the Ljung–Box and ARCH tests for the remaining auto-correlation and conditional heteroscedasticity. The EGARCH models for the industries as well as the S&P 500 composite index appear to be free of auto-correlation and heteroscedasticity at the 5% significance level. The results of diagnostic tests are not tabulated here to conserve space but are available upon request.

In Table 4, a represents the impact of the lagged standardized shock — which is $\bar{\varepsilon}_{t-1}\bar{\varepsilon}'_{t-1}$ — and b represents the impact of the lagged time-varying conditional correlations — which is Q_{t-1}. Finally, c indicates the asymmetric impact of negative innovations, compared to positive innovations. The important condition for a stable and healthy A-DCC is: $a + b < 1$ which means the correlation is wandering around a constant level and is mean-reverting

Table 4: Asymmetric DCC estimation results.

	SP500	SP5 ECOD	SP5 EENE	SP5 EFIN	SP5 EHCR
a	0.02083***	0.02686***	0.01509***	0.01715***	0.01985***
b	0.97467***	0.96384***	0.98355***	0.97915***	0.97420***
c	0.00334*	0.00575**	0.00040	0.00325**	0.00672***
$a+b$	0.99551	0.99070	0.99864	0.99630	0.99405
	SP5 EIND	SP5 EINT	SP5 EMAT	SP5 EUTL	SP5 ETEL
a	0.021789***	0.019616***	0.014352***	0.010697***	0.016036***
b	0.972285***	0.976648***	0.983577***	0.986846***	0.978381***
c	0.005708***	0.00449***	0.001676	0.002035*	0.003654*
$a+b$	0.99407	0.99626	0.99793	0.99754	0.99442

Note: *, **, *** represent 10%, 5% and 1% significance, respectively.

(Lehkonen and Heimonen, 2014). If $a + b = 0$, the model can be simplified into a constant conditional correlation. As can be seen, the $a + b < 1$ condition is met for all models. Moreover, b's are all higher than 0.97, which implies the correlation between S&P 500 (as well as industry level indices) and oil is time-varying and is highly persistent (e.g. Creti *et al.*, 2013; Lehkonen and Heimonen, 2014). The third component is c, which captures the asymmetric portion and if it is significant, then it shows that the correlation is affected asymmetrically more from a negative shock compared to a positive shock. The findings in Table 4 show that the asymmetric component is significant for all industries, except Energy and Materials. Therefore, this means that the comovement of oil with all sector stocks, excluding Energy and Materials, gets stronger with a decrease (bad news) in those sectors. The absence of a significant asymmetric component for the Energy and Materials sectors indicates that good and bad news seem to have a similar impact on the correlation of oil with Energy and Materials stocks. This interesting finding might be attributable to Energy stocks' high association with oil. Moreover, the Materials sector includes firms which either discover or process raw materials, such as metals and chemicals; therefore, oil plays a key input role in their businesses. In summary, the results seem to indicate that good news is as important as bad news to the comovement of Energy and Materials stocks with oil.

The time-varying correlation between the S&P 500 and oil is provided in Figure 3. At first glance, there does not seem to be a dominant structure in the correlation levels prior to the global financial crisis of 2008. There is a movement around the zero value with periods of slightly higher correlations. However, post-2008, there seems to be a strong positive correlation, which may have recently declined. A finding worth pointing out is that the correlation levels seem to rise to high levels during the financial distress periods. As one can see in Figure 3, there are four major periods where the correlation between equities and oil has been relatively high. The first period labeled as A, is around the Mexican crisis and the runs on Japanese banks that occurred in 1995. The second period, B, occurs between

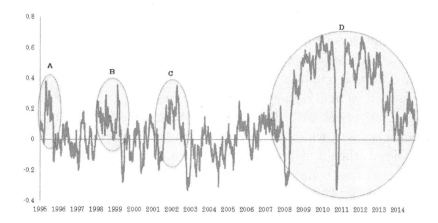

Figure 3: The A-DCC correlation of the S&P 500 and oil.

1998 and 1999, where the Asian crisis, LTCM crisis, and international aftershocks in Latin America and Asia were experienced. The third period, C, is the period of the 9/11 New York attack, followed by a huge stock market downturn, and lastly the Iraq war. The last period, D, is where the global economy went into crisis following the bankruptcy of Lehman Brothers. Severe problems in the US economy brought several other economies to the brink of financial crashes. By the end of 2009, the economies were trying to recover, but this time the Eurozone crisis impacted markets negatively. Not only Greece, but severe structural problems in Portugal, Spain, and Italy led to huge increases in the Credit Default Swap levels. Even though the problems in Greece at the time seemed to have been resolved by the European Central Bank, new problems have resurfaced.

Our results on the asymmetric dynamic correlation between oil and equities are generally consistent with those of Creti *et al.* (2013), which also report highly volatile and time-varying characteristics. However, the disaggregated sector correlations may provide information not apparent in the aggregated results. For example, while the dynamic correlation between oil and the S&P 500 (and for most sectors) displays asymmetric characteristics, the correlations of Energy and Materials stocks with oil do not show evidence of asymmetry. Figures for correlations between the industry level indices and oil are presented in Figure 4. It is worth noting that we have not presented the Consumer Staples industry since data showed erratic behavior. We were unable to resolve this problem, and the results are not robust to provide evidence on this industry.

To the best of our knowledge, there is no study that analyzes the asymmetric dynamic correlations on the disaggregated basis for the US market with oil.

When the correlations of US submarkets with oil are examined, we mostly see common patterns, however, there seem to be some peculiarities. First of all, the dynamic correlation of Utility and Energy stocks with oil is shifted upwards more into the positive side after 2003. The oil correlation with the Materials sector was very similar to correlation with the S&P 500 until 2008, but it has been consistently positive post-crisis, indicating a lower hedging potential between oil and materials stocks.

A visual overview of the data seems to indicate that during distress periods the correlation increases, but distinguishing between temporary and persistent effects is still important for choosing between alternative hedging strategies. We run a VAR system with the dynamic correlation (Rho), along with the CFSI, 3-month T-bill rate, oil, gold, copper, S&P 500, and USD/EUR exchange rate factors. Next, we calculate the generalized impulse responses (GIRs) which depict the response of Rho to generalized impulses in other factors in Figure 5. We also present the Granger-causality results in Table 5. The initial analysis is carried out for the entire period and the results start on January 1, 1999, since the EURO came into force in 1999, but will later be examined in subperiods.

When the findings for the entire sample period are examined, the GIRs indicate that while the shocks to the CFSI and the 3-month T-bill rate do not significantly affect the dynamic correlation (Rho) between the S&P 500 and oil, the shocks to the remaining variables (oil, gold, copper, S&P 500, and USD/EUR exchange rate)

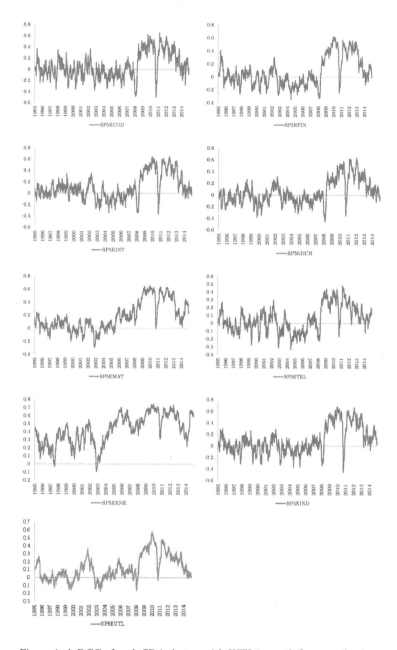

Figure 4: A-DCC of each SP industry with WTI 1-month futures oil prices.

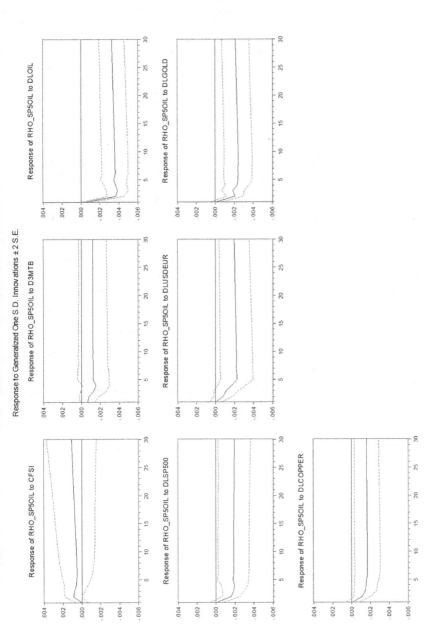

Figure 5: Generalized impulse responses (entire sample period).

Table 5: Granger-causality results (entire sample period).

	Granger-causality running from							
	DLRHO SP5OIL	CFSI	D3MTB	DL OIL	DL SP500	DL USDEUR	DL GOLD	DL COPPER
Granger-causality running to								
DLRHO_SP5OIL	—	0.6056	0.4948	**0.0167**	0.7441	0.1318	**0.0211**	0.7244
CFSI	0.4309	—	0.6605	0.1128	**0.0000**	0.4684	**0.003**	**0.0388**

have significant negative effects on Rho (the effect of the USD/EUR exchange rate seems to become significant after 3–4 days). On the other hand, the Granger-causality tests only find evidence of effects on Rho from oil and gold. The potential effect of CFSI on Rho is one of the focal points of this study. However, neither the GIRs nor Granger-causality tests for the entire sample are able to provide evidence of any significant effect. Furthermore, we have also checked for the potential effects of disaggregated risk measures in addition to the aggregated risk represented by CFSI by running a VAR system with each of the 15 components of CFSI with the oil-equity correlation. The impact of the CFSI subcomponents on the correlation is still insignificant for the entire sample period (not tabulated).

The relationships examined may be changing over time and under different regimes, so we obtain insignificant results for the aggregate sample period. However, there may still be significant effects in certain subsets. Rather than trying to arbitrarily identify the subsamples (as in Figure 3), we rely on the Bai–Perron multiple break point tests (Bai and Perron, 2003) to provide more objective results. The multiple change point detection tests that allow for heterogeneous error distributions across breaks are used. The maximum number of breaks is selected to be five and the test finds four breakpoints, which are presented in Table 6.

As the EURO came into force in 1999, the VAR system is available commencing from January 1, 1999. However, as one of the breakpoints is found to be on September 24, 1999, and the period before this would be too short to analyze, we choose to begin the subperiod analysis after this breakpoint.

Table 6: Bai–Perron multiple break-point test results.

Break test	F-statistic	Scaled F-statistic	Critical value**
0 vs. 1*	6,513.41	6,513.41	8.58
1 vs. 2*	424.27	424.27	10.13
2 vs. 3*	139.57	139.57	11.14
3 vs. 4*	23.14	23.14	11.83
4 vs. 5	0.00	0.00	12.25

Notes: * Significant at the 0.05 level.
** Bai–Perron (*Econometric Journal*, 2003) critical values.
Break dates: 1 — 10/16/2008; 2 — 5/31/2012; 3 — 2/5/2003;
4 — 9/24/1999.

The initial subperiod analysis based on the most significant break-point (October 16, 2008) provides two major subperiods:

- September 27, 1999–October 16, 2008
- October 17, 2008–May 28, 2015

Next, we also provide the results based on all four breakpoints suggested using the aforementioned test. The subperiods are:

- September 27, 1999–February 5, 2003
- February 6, 2003–October 16, 2008
- October 17, 2008–May 31, 2012
- June 1, 2012–May 28, 2015

We present responses of Rho to impulses in CFSI in each subset in Figure 6. Moreover, the Granger-causality results for above-mentioned sub-periods are presented in Table 7.

Findings from GIRs and Granger-causality tests indicate that, pre-2008, CFSI does not seem to have significant impact on the oil-SP500 correlation. However, post-2008, we see that CFSI significantly affects Rho in both the GIRs and Granger-causality tests. Distress periods, post-2008, seem to have significantly positive and persistent effects on the correlation level.

When the subperiod analyses are expanded to four periods, the pre-2008 results remain basically unchanged. CFSI does not seem to significantly affect the correlation between the S&P 500 and oil. In

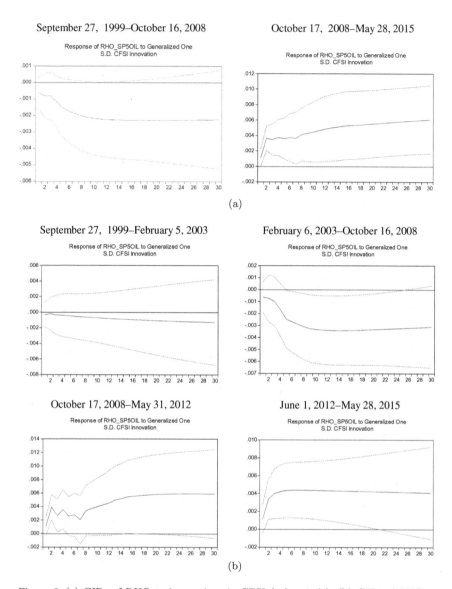

Figure 6: (a) GIRs of RHO to innovations in CFSI (subperiods). (b) GIRs of RHO to innovations in CFSI (subperiods).

Table 7: Subperiod Granger-causality results.

Granger-causality running to	Granger-causality running from							
	DLRHO_SP5OIL	CFSI	D3MTB	DLOIL	DLSP500	DLUSDEUR	DLGOLD	DLCOPPER
9/24/1999–10/17/2008								
DLRHO_SP5OIL	—	0.3377	0.5572	0.5701	0.6959	0.8895	0.3812	0.9106
CFSI	0.9616	—	0.5673	**0.0045**	**0.0014**	0.5484	**0.0198**	0.5814
10/17/2008–5/28/2015								
DLRHO_SP5OIL	—	**0.0001**	0.9313	**0.0073**	0.4621	**0.0520**	**0.0037**	0.1070
CFSI	0.2781	—	0.5864	0.7828	**0.0001**	**0.0892**	**0.6794**	0.4290
9/27/1999–2/5/2003								
DLRHO_SP5OIL	—	0.8343	0.5790	0.3940	0.5519	0.2148	**0.0663**	0.1526
CFSI	0.8590	—	0.2939	0.2795	0.2860	0.6212	0.1915	0.6858
2/6/2003–10/16/2008								
DLRHO_SP5OIL	—	0.3975	0.6180	0.8996	0.4931	0.6199	0.3616	0.9945
CFSI	0.8463	—	0.4333	**0.0160**	**0.0518**	0.3882	**0.0049**	0.1891
10/17/2008–5/31/2012								
DLRHO_SP5OIL	—	0.1113	**0.0920**	0.1648	0.8493	**0.0108**	0.1375	0.6174
CFSI	0.3854	—	0.7494	0.7984	0.2146	0.5003	0.4007	**0.0026**
6/1/2012–5/28/2015								
DLRHO_SP5OIL	—	**0.0766**	0.7023	**0.0297**	0.2630	0.3052	**0.0042**	**0.0979**
CFSI	0.4678	—	0.9416	0.6314	**0.0005**	**0.0490**	0.2524	0.8822

Note: Statistically significant findings are presented in bold.

the post-2008 periods, the GIRs seem to indicate that a shock to CFSI leads to a significant rise in the correlations between oil and S&P 500. However, the effect seems to be transitory for the October 17, 2008–May 31, 2012 subperiod while it is persistent for the June 1, 2012–May 28, 2015 subperiod. The Granger-causality tests are only able to find evidence of a significant relationship in the June 1, 2012–May 28, 2015 subperiod.

Therefore, both individual and professional investors should be thoroughly careful of their hedging strategies between commodity and equity markets. Even though the commodity markets are believed to be relatively good hedges against inflation and have a low correlation with stocks and bonds (Gorton and Rouwenhorst, 2006), this diversification benefit could vanish in stress episodes. Given that CFSI is a continuous measure of financial stress and is available in daily frequency, we believe investors would be wise to follow the CFSI closely. Investors observing high levels of CFSI should consider the potential increases in comovement and change their portfolio decisions accordingly.

The responses of Rho to impulses in other variables are summarized in Table 8.

As one can note, the full sample and subperiods show quite different results. In the pre-2008 subperiod, we see a very little role for any of the variables, so Rho is quite independently shaped. On the other hand, after 2008, the results provide evidence of changing financial dynamics in the global economy. GIRs propose that all variables except the 3-month T-bill rate have a significant impact on the correlation levels. When we check the subperiods, we observe that the 2008–2012 subperiod dominates the post-2008 results for the variables other than the CFSI. On the other hand, for the CFSI we observe that for both subperiods after 2008, one standard deviation shock in the CFSI leads to an increase in the correlation levels. Though, as one can note from Figure 6(b), the impact of the CFSI is longer-lived for the 2012–2015 subperiod. As a result, the findings indicate that oil could provide a good diversification opportunity for equity investors, though not during financial stress episodes; due to

Table 8: GIR result summary — Response of Rho to innovations in variables.

	CFSI	D3MTB	DLOIL	DLSP500	DLUSDEUR	DLGOLD	DLCOPPER
1999–2015[a]	—	—	[-]VE*	[-]VE	[-]VE	[-]VE* TEMP. [-]VE	[-]VE
9/24/1999–10/17/2008	[+]VE*	—	—	—	—	—	—
10/17/2008–5/28/2015	—	—	[-]VE* TEMP. [-]VE	[-]VE	[-]VE*	TEMP. [-]VE* [-]VE*	TEMP.[-]VE
9/27/1999–2/5/2003	TEMP [-]VE	—	—	—	—	—	—
2/6/2003–10/16/2008	TEMP. [+]VE	—	—	—	—	—	—
10/17/2008–5/31/2012	TEMP. [+]VE*	—	[-]VE	TEMP. [-]VE	[-]VE*	—	TEMP. [-]VE
6/1/2012–5/28/2015		—	[-]VE*	[-]VE			—

Notes: Temp. stands for "Temporarily" and indicates the significance of the respective GIR is not permanent.
[a]Since EUR came into force by 1999, full sample starts from 1/1/1999.
*Refer to significant findings in Granger-causality results. Please refer to Tables 5 and 7 for *p*-values.

increasing correlation levels. When diversification is needed the most, the correlation is highly affected from other markets, and hence the diversification benefits could vanish. Therefore, to pinpoint the contagion periods, investors would benefit from following the CFSI since this financial stress variable positively feeds Rho during structural changes in the financial landscape.

6. Conclusion

This paper examines the time-varying correlation between the US equities and oil prices by employing the A-DCC model in the GARCH family. We also investigate which variables may be linked to the changing correlation levels. We employ seven factors and run a VAR analysis to try to better understand the dynamic correlation relationships. The A-DCC results indicate that dynamic nature of the correlation is observed for the S&P 500, as well as all nine industries. Furthermore, the asymmetric responses of conditional variances and covariances to negative shocks are identified in most sectors. This suggests that the correlation level (Rho) responds asymmetrically more to bad news in the market, compared to good news. However, the exceptions are the Energy and Materials stocks which do not show evidence of a significant asymmetric effect, indicating a positive shock has as much an impact as a negative shock. This finding might be attributable to the Energy and Materials stocks being highly affected by oil prices both on the positive and negative sides.

Furthermore, when the correlation between oil and equities is depicted, subperiods of higher correlation levels are observed to be related to financial distress periods. Hence, this poses a new question of whether the change in the correlation is temporary or permanent. Therefore, to determine the factors that may be linked to these changes in correlations and their persistence, we utilize the daily CFSI, the USD/EUR parity and the 3-month T-bill rates, gold and copper prices on top of the WTI crude oil prices, and the S&P 500 to generate the generalized impulse responses of Rho and Granger-causality tests. The results indicate that in the pre-2008 subperiod,

Rho is quite independent and is not highly affected by other asset markets. On the other hand, in the post-2008 subperiod, exchange rate markets and safe-haven assets seem to be Granger-causing Rho. In the post-2008 subperiod, the CFSI positively feeds into Rho, indicating that severe distress periods have a strengthening and long-term impact on the correlation between oil and US equities. However, in the four subperiod analyses, the evidence of this strengthening effect is found to be permanent only for the last subperiod. Hence, investors should also take the CFSI into account while determining their hedging alternatives, portfolio allocation, or risk management strategies.

Appendix

Table A.1: Correlation matrix.

	DLSP500	DLOIL	DLSP5ECOD	DLSP5ECST	DLSP5EENE	DLSP5EFIN	DLSP5EHCR	DLSP5EIND
DLSP500	1.0000	0.1752	0.9063	0.7090	0.7061	0.8575	0.7519	0.9191
DLOIL		1.0000	0.0926	0.0478	0.4530	0.1190	0.0654	0.1435
DLSP5ECOD			1.0000	0.6586	0.5763	0.7836	0.6590	0.8627
DLSP5ECST				1.0000	0.5298	0.5984	0.7178	0.6650
DLSP5EENE					1.0000	0.5583	0.5423	0.6432
DLSP5EFIN						1.0000	0.6018	0.7927
DLSP5EHCR							1.0000	0.6735
DLSP5EIND								1.0000
DLSP5EINT								
DLSP5EMAT								
DLSP5ETEL								
DLSP5EUTL								
CFSI								
D3MTB								
DLUSDEUR								
DLGOLD								
DLCOPPER								

	DLSP5EINT	DLSP5EMAT	DLSP5ETEL	DLSP5EUTL	CFSI	D3MTB	DLUSDEUR	DLGOLD	DLCOPPER
DLSP500	0.8361	0.8000	0.7307	0.6334	-0.0075	0.1171	0.0703	-0.0143	0.2577
DLOIL	0.1069	0.2155	0.0848	0.1496	-0.0113	0.0487	0.1091	0.2244	0.2882
DLSP5ECOD	0.7259	0.7424	0.6491	0.5354	0.0012	0.0927	0.0464	-0.0585	0.2103
DLSP5ECST	0.4079	0.6097	0.5279	0.5727	-0.0140	0.0936	0.0789	-0.0378	0.1466
DLSP5EENE	0.4402	0.7151	0.4674	0.6049	-0.0152	0.1095	0.1278	0.1220	0.3096
DLSP5EFIN	0.5995	0.6828	0.5911	0.5137	-0.0150	0.0982	0.0528	-0.0545	0.2022
DLSP5EHCR	0.4857	0.5787	0.5327	0.5456	0.0011	0.0919	0.0624	-0.0368	0.1554
DLSP5EIND	0.7175	0.8101	0.6300	0.5723	-0.0150	0.0994	0.0770	-0.0157	0.2513
DLSP5EINT	1.0000	0.5620	0.6064	0.3984	0.0039	0.0795	0.0126	-0.0313	0.1897
DLSP5EMAT		1.0000	0.5343	0.5477	-0.0125	0.0931	0.1239	0.1176	0.3319
DLSP5ETEL			1.0000	0.4921	-0.0024	0.1096	0.0516	-0.0380	0.1638
DLSP5EUTL				1.0000	-0.0165	0.1255	0.0833	0.0116	0.1794
CFSI					1.0000	-0.0395	-0.0039	0.0016	-0.0140
D3MTB						1.0000	-0.0340	-0.0595	0.0813
DLUSDEUR							1.0000	0.2186	0.1492
DLGOLD								1.0000	0.2744
DLCOPPER									1.0000

Table A.2: Unit root test results.

	DF-GLS	PP	Ng-Perron
RHO_SP5OIL	−3.57***	−3.62***	−25.36***
CFSI	−2.46**	−4.14***	−12.39**
D3MTB	−14.43***	−62.53***	−759.48***
DLOIL	−6.47***	−73.75***	−22.33***
DLSP500	−77.43***	−78.37***	−2,593.25***
DLUSDEUR	−65.56***	−65.57***	−2,138.49***
DLGOLD	−73.47***	−73.46***	−2,605.20***
DLCOPPER	−3.22***	−80.86***	−10.53**

Note: *, **, *** represent the 10%, 5% and 1% significance levels, respectively.

References

Aloui, C., Nguyen, D. K. and Njeh, H. (2012). Assessing the impacts of oil price fluctuations on stock returns in emerging markets, *Economic Modelling*, 29(6), 2686–2695.

Arouri, M. E. H., Jouini, J. and Nguyen, D. K. (2012). On the impacts of oil price fluctuations on European equity markets: Volatility spillover and hedging effectiveness, *Energy Economics*, 34(2), 611–617.

Arouri, M. E. H., Nguyen, D. K. and Pukthuanthong, K. (2014). Diversification benefits and strategic portfolio allocation across asset classes: the case of the US markets, DEPOCEN Working Paper Series No. 2014/09.

Bai, J. and Perron, P. (2003). Computation and analysis of multiple structural change models, *Journal of Applied Econometrics*, 18(1), 1–22.

Basak, S. and Pavlova, A. (2016). A Model of Financialization of Commodities. *Journal of Finance*, 71(4), 1511–1556.

Basher, S. A. and Sadorsky, P. (2006). Oil price risk and emerging stock markets, *Global Finance Journal*, 17(2), 224–251.

Baur, D. G. and McDermott, T. K. (2010). Is gold a safe haven? International evidence, *Journal of Banking & Finance*, 34(8), 1886–1898.

Bekaert, G., Harvey, C. R. and Ng, A. (2005). Market integration and contagion, *Journal of Business*, 78(1).

Bernanke, S. B. (2006). *The Economic Outlook*, Remarks before the National Italian American Foundation New York, November 28.

BP (2016). BP statistical review of world energy. http://www.bp.com/content/dam/bp/pdf/energy-economics/statistical-review-2016/bp-statistical-review-of-world-energy-2016-full-report.pdf. Last accessed on 31 July 2016.

Büyükşahin, B. and Robe, M. A. (2014). Speculators, commodities and cross-market linkages, *Journal of International Money and Finance*, 42, 38–70.

Cappiello, L., Engle, R. F. and Sheppard, K. (2006). Asymmetric dynamics in the correlations of global equity and bond returns, *Journal of Financial econometrics*, 4(4), 537–572.

Calvo, S. G. and Reinhart, C. M. (1996). Capital flows to Latin America: Is there evidence of contagion effects? *World Bank Policy Research Working Paper* (1619).

Chang, C. L., McAleer, M. and Tansuchat, R. (2013). Conditional correlations and volatility spillovers between crude oil and stock index returns, *The North American Journal of Economics and Finance*, 25, 116–138.

Chen, N. F., Roll, R. and Ross, S. A. (1986). Economic forces and the stock market, *Journal of Business*, 383–403.

Chiang, T. C., Jeon, B. N. and Li, H. (2007). Dynamic correlation analysis of financial contagion: Evidence from Asian markets, *Journal of International Money and Finance*, 26(7), 1206–1228.

Choi, K. and Hammoudeh, S. (2010). Volatility behavior of oil, industrial commodity and stock markets in a regime-switching environment, *Energy Policy*, 38(8), 4388–4399.

Ciner, C., Gurdgiev, C. and Lucey, B. M. (2013). Hedges and safe havens: An examination of stocks, bonds, gold, oil and exchange rates, *International Review of Financial Analysis*, 29, 202–211.

CFTC (Commodity Futures Trading Commission). (2008). Staff Report on Commodity Swap Dealers & Index traders with Commission Recommendations. 2008. Available from URL: http://www.cftc.gov/st ellent/groups/public/@newsroom/documents/file/cftcstaffreportons wapdealers09.pdf. Last accessed on 1 February 2016.

Cong, R. G., Wei, Y. M., Jiao, J. L. and Fan, Y. (2008). Relationships between oil price shocks and stock market: An empirical analysis from China, *Energy Policy*, 36(9), 3544–3553.

Creti, A., Joëts, M. and Mignon, V. (2013). On the links between stock and commodity markets' volatility, *Energy Economics*, 37, 16–28.

Degiannakis, S., Filis, G. and Floros, C. (2013). Oil and stock returns: Evidence from European industrial sector indices in a time-varying environment, *Journal of International Financial Markets, Institutions and Money*, 26, 175–191.

Engle, R. (2002). Dynamic conditional correlation: A simple class of multivariate generalized auto-regressive conditional heteroskedasticity models, *Journal of Business & Economic Statistics*, 20(3), 339–350.

Erb, C. B. and Harvey, C. R. (2006). The strategic and tactical value of commodity futures, *Financial Analysts Journal*, 62(2), 69–97.

Filis, G., Degiannakis, S. and Floros, C. (2011). Dynamic correlation between stock market and oil prices: The case of oil-importing and oil-exporting countries, *International Review of Financial Analysis*, 20(3), 152–164.

Fisher, I. (1930). *The Theory of Interest as Determined By Impatience to Spend Income and Opportunity to Spend It*, MacMillian, New York.

Forbes, K. J. and Rigobon, R. (2002). No contagion, only interdependence: Measuring stock market comovements, *The Journal of Finance*, 57(5), 2223–2261.

Gisser, M. and Goodwin, T. H. (1986). Crude oil and the macroeconomy: Tests of some popular notions: Note, *Journal of Money, Credit and Banking*, 95–103.

Gorton, G. and Rouwenhorst, K. G. (2006). Facts and fantasies about commodity futures, *Financial Analysts Journal*, 62(2), 47–68.

Hamilton, J. D. (1983). Oil and the macroeconomy since World War II, *The Journal of Political Economy*, 91(2), 228–248.

Hamilton, J. D. (1996). This is what happened to the oil price-macroeconomy relationship, *Journal of Monetary Economics*, 38(2), 215–220.

Henriques, I. and Sadorsky, P. (2008). Oil prices and the stock prices of alternative energy companies, *Energy Economics*, 30(3), 998–1010.

Hirshleifer, D. and Hong Teoh, S. (2003). Herd behaviour and cascading in capital markets: A review and synthesis, *European Financial Management*, 9(1), 25–66.

Huang, R. D., Masulis, R. W. and Stoll, H. R. (1996). Energy shocks and financial markets, *Journal of Futures Markets*, 16(1), 1–27.

Jones, C. M. and Kaul, G. (1996). Oil and the stock markets, *The Journal of Finance*, 51(2), 463–491.

Lehkonen, H. and Heimonen, K. (2014). Timescale-dependent stock market comovement: BRICs vs. developed markets, *Journal of Empirical Finance*, 28, 90–103.

Lizardo, R. A. and Mollick, A. V. (2010). Oil price fluctuations and US dollar exchange rates, *Energy Economics*, 32(2), 399–408.

Longin, F. and Solnik, B. (1995). Is the correlation in international equity returns constant: 1960–1990? *Journal of international money and finance*, 14(1), 3–26.

Longstaff, F. A. (2010). The subprime credit crisis and contagion in financial markets, *Journal of Financial Economics*, 97(3), 436–450.

Markwat, T., Kole, E. and Van Dijk, D. (2009). Contagion as a domino effect in global stock markets, *Journal of Banking & Finance*, 33(11), 1996–2012.

Mohanty, S. K., Nandha, M., Turkistani, A. Q. and Alaitani, M. Y. (2011). Oil price movements and stock market returns: Evidence from Gulf Cooperation Council (GCC) countries, *Global Finance Journal*, 22(1), 42–55.

Mollick, A. V. and Assefa, T. A. (2013). US stock returns and oil prices: The tale from daily data and the 2008–2009 financial crisis, *Energy Economics*, 36, 1–18.

Nazlioglu, S., Soytas, U. and Gupta, R. (2015). Oil prices and financial stress: A volatility spillover analysis, *Energy Policy*, 82, 278–288.

Oet, M. V., Eiben, R., Bianco, T., Gramlich, D. and Ong, S. J. (2011). Financial stress index: Identification of systemic risk conditions, Federal Reserve Bank of Cleveland Working Paper 11–30.

Papapetrou, E. (2001). Oil price shocks, stock market, economic activity and employment in Greece, *Energy Economics*, 23(5), 511–532.

Park, J. and Ratti, R. A. (2008). Oil price shocks and stock markets in the US and 13 European countries, *Energy Economics*, 30(5), 2587–2608.

Pesaran, H. H. and Shin, Y. (1998). Generalized impulse response analysis in linear multivariate models, *Economics letters*, 58(1), 17–29.

Ramos, S. B. and Veiga, H. (2011). Risk factors in oil and gas industry returns: International evidence, *Energy Economics*, 33(3), 525–542.

Ranaldo, A. and Söderlind, P. (2010). Safe Haven Currencies, *Review of Finance*, 14(3), 385–407.

Roll, R. (2013). Volatility, Correlation, and Diversification in a Multi-Factor World, *The Journal of Portfolio Management*, 39(2), 11–18.

Rose, A. K. and Spiegel, M. M. (2010). Cross-country causes and consequences of the 2008 crisis: International linkages and American exposure, *Pacific Economic Review*, 15(3), 340–363.

Sadorsky, P. (1999). Oil price shocks and stock market activity, *Energy Economics*, 21(5), 449–469.

Sadorsky, P. (2001). Risk factors in stock returns of Canadian oil and gas companies, *Energy economics*, 23(1), 17–28.

Sadorsky, P. (2008). Assessing the impact of oil prices on firms of different sizes: Its tough being in the middle, *Energy Policy*, 36(10), 3854–3861.

Sadorsky, P. (2012). Correlations and volatility spillovers between oil prices and the stock prices of clean energy and technology companies, *Energy Economics*, 34(1), 248–255.

Sadorsky, P. (2014). Modeling volatility and correlations between emerging market stock prices and the prices of copper, oil and wheat, *Energy Economics*, 43, 72–81.

Salisu, A. A. and Oloko, T. F. (2015). Modeling oil price–US stock nexus: A VARMA–BEKK–AGARCH approach, *Energy Economics*, 50, 1–12.

Tang, K. and Xiong, W. (2012). Index investment and the financialization of commodities, *Financial Analysts Journal*, 68(5), 54–74.

Turhan, M. I., Sensoy, A., Ozturk, K. and Hacihasanoglu, E. (2014). A view to the long-run dynamic relationship between crude oil and the major asset classes, *International Review of Economics & Finance*, 33, 286–299.

Upper, C. (2000). How safe was the "Safe Haven"? Financial market liquidity during the 1998 turbulences. Discussion paper 1/00, Economic Research Group of the Deutsche Bundesbank.

Williams, B. J. (1938). *The Theory of Investment Value*, Harvard University Press, Cambridge.

Chapter 5

Has the Causal Nexus of Oil Prices and Consumer Prices Been Asymmetric in the US during the Last Fifteen Decades?

Abdulnasser Hatemi-J and Youssef El-Khatib

*United Arab Emirates University, Sheik Khalifa Bin Zayed St,
Abu Dhabi, UAE*

1. Introduction

Two major macroeconomic variables that affect the conducted economic policy and the behavior of consumers as well as producers are the oil prices along with the consumer prices. These two important variables are also pertinent to the investors worldwide because both oil prices and the inflation rate are two main factors in financial risk management. The interaction between these macroeconomic aggregates have been checked in the literature, among others by De Gregorio *et al.* (2007), Alvarez *et al.* (2011), Tiwari *et al.* (2019) and Zivkov *et al.* (2019). However, the potential asymmetric causal impacts between them have not been investigated to the best of our knowledge. Thus, the main goal of the current chapter is to fill this gap in the literature. Asymmetric-causality tests are implemented for this purpose in addition to estimating the asymmetric impulse response functions. The sample period covers the period 1871–2018 on a monthly basis for the US economy. Since this economy is the largest economy in the world, the results of this research might have important repercussions for other economies as well. In order to take into account the potential impact of the omitted variables, we also include the interest rate in the model.

The rest of this chapter is organized as follows: In Section 2, a brief literature review is provided. Section 3 describes the econometric methodology. Section 4 presents the data and the estimation results and the last section provides the conclusions.

2.   Literature Review

Studies such as Hamilton (1983, 1988), Mork (1989) and Hooker (1996) provide empirical evidence that oil prices impact the global economy significantly via a number of economic variables including inflation rates, while the robustness of this relationship is time-dependent. Blanchard and Gali (2007) investigate the potential impact of oil prices on inflation by making use of the structural vector auto-regressive model and also discover that the influence of an oil price shock has considerably varied across time. In addition, the published articles such as Kilian (2009) and Kilian and Park (2009) also show that the factors that cause oil price increases govern the impact of this variable on economic performance and the inflation level. Hooker (2002) makes use of tests for structural breaks and nonlinearities in the Phillips curve and finds that oil prices significantly impact the inflation until 1981 in the US. However, he also reports that the impact has decreased since then. In a comprehensive study that consists of nineteen countries and by making use of a time-varying method, Chen (2009) finds that the oil price impact on inflation rates tends to decrease across time. Choi *et al.* (2017) explore empirically the potential effect of oil prices on inflation by making use of a large panel consisting of 72 countries during the sample period of 1970–2015. Their results show that, on average, a 10% increase in the oil prices results in a 0.4% increase in the inflation rate under the *ceteris paribus* condition. Tiwari *et al.* (2019) investigate the relationship between the oil prices, the consumer prices, and the interest rate for the US during the same period as we are using. Their methodology is based on wavelet coherency analysis, which does not account for asymmetric impacts. Their results show that the relationship between oil prices and consumer prices has decreased across time and the impact is even weaker in the short run.

3. The Methodology

Since peoples' behavior is not the same depending on the situation they are in, that is they seem to be affected more by negative changes than by positive ones, we need to allow for asymmetric impacts in our empirical investigation in order to make the results representative and in accordance with reality. For this purpose, several methods are used. First, asymmetric-causality tests developed by Hatemi-J (2012) are implemented in the empirical investigation. Second, the asymmetric generalized impulse responses are estimated via the technique suggested by Hatemi-J (2014). The procedure developed by Hatemi-J and El-Khatib (2016) is used for transforming the data that has determinist trend components in addition to the stochastic parts. Let OP_t represent the oil prices expressed in logarithmic form at period t. Let us also assume that the data generating process for this variable is defined by the following equation:

$$OP_t = a + bt + OP_{t-1} + \varepsilon_{1t}, \tag{1}$$

where a and b are parametric constants and t is the deterministic trend. Via the application of the recursive method, the following solution to Equation (1) can be obtained:

$$OP_t = at + \frac{t(t+1)}{2}b + OP_0 + \sum_{i=1}^{t} \varepsilon_{1i}, \tag{2}$$

For the sample period, $t = 1, 2, \ldots, T$. The term OP_0 is the initial value and ε_{1t} represents a white noise random error. Positive and negative shocks based on the error term can be found via

$\varepsilon_{1i}^{+} := \max(\varepsilon_{1i}, 0)$ and $\varepsilon_{1i}^{-} := \min(\varepsilon_{1i}, 0)$. By making use of these partial components, the following can be expressed:

$$OP_t = a + bt + OP_{t-1} + \varepsilon_t = at + \frac{t(t+1)}{2}b + OP_0$$

$$+ \sum_{i=1}^{t} \varepsilon_{1i}^{+} + \sum_{i=1}^{t} \varepsilon_{1i}^{-}. \tag{3}$$

Now we are in the position of defining the negative and positive shocks of oil prices as follows:

$$OP_t^{+} = \frac{1}{2}[a + bt] + OP_{t-1}^{+} + \varepsilon_{1t}^{+}, \tag{4}$$

$$OP_t^{-} = \frac{1}{2}[a + bt] + OP_{t-1}^{-} + \varepsilon_{1t}^{-}. \tag{5}$$

Note that we also have $OP_0^{+} = OP_0^{-} := \frac{1}{2}OP_0$. Thus, the following solutions for partial cumulative sums of positive and negative components can be defined:

$$OP_t^{+} := \frac{at + \left[\frac{t(t+1)}{2}\right]b + OP_0}{2} + \sum_{i=1}^{t} \varepsilon_{1i}^{+}, \tag{6}$$

and

$$OP_t^{-} := \frac{at + \left[\frac{t(t+1)}{2}\right]b + OP_0}{2} + \sum_{i=1}^{t} \varepsilon_{1i}^{-}. \tag{7}$$

The other two variables, that is the consumer price index and the interest rate, can be decomposed into partial cumulative sums for negative and positive components similarly. The transformed data can then be used for implementing the asymmetric-causality tests as well as for estimating the asymmetric impulse response functions in order to capture the dynamic and asymmetric interaction between these three variables. In order to save space, these methods are not described here in detail. For a complete description of the asymmetric causality tests, see Hatemi-J (2012) and for details on the asymmetric generalized impulse response functions, the interested reader is referred to Hatemi-J (2014). It should be mentioned that the software for transforming the data is available in different languages. Hatemi-J (2011) has provided a statistical software component written in Gauss for this transformation of the data. Hatemi-J and El-Khatib (2017) have produced a code in C^{++} for this purpose. Hatemi-J and Mustafa (2016) have created an algorithm in Octave for this purpose.

4. The Data and the Estimation Results

The dataset that is used in the empirical investigation is on a monthly basis and it covers the period 1871–2018 for the US economy. The source of the data is as follows: The oil price index is obtained from the Global Financial Database; The consumer price index (CPI) is collected from the database that is provided by of the website of Robert J. Shiller, A measure of short-term interest rate (R) is

Table 1: Symmetric and asymmetric-causality test results.

Null hypothesis	Test value	p-Value	Null hypothesis	Test value	p-Value
$OP \nRightarrow CPI$	8.01743	0.0003	$CPI \nRightarrow OP$	12.8385	0.0003×10^{-2}
$R \nRightarrow CPI$	1.45135	0.2345	$CPI \nRightarrow R$	0.34101	0.7111
$R \nRightarrow OP$	0.11687	0.8897	$OP \nRightarrow R$	1.41724	0.2427
$OP^+ \nRightarrow CPI^+$	0.92765	0.3957	$CPI^+ \nRightarrow OP^+$	4.88044	0.0077
$R^+ \nRightarrow CPI^+$	0.18281	0.8329	$CPI^+ \nRightarrow R^+$	0.48394	0.6164
$R^+ \nRightarrow OP^+$	2.88442	0.0562	$OP^+ \nRightarrow R^+$	6.93931	0.0010
$OP^- \nRightarrow CPI^-$	8.01743	0.00002	$CPI^- \nRightarrow OP^-$	29.2658	0.0003×10^{-12}
$R^- \nRightarrow CPI^-$	10.9339	0.00002	$CPI^- \nRightarrow R^-$	4.87698	0.0077
$R^- \nRightarrow OP^-$	1.2407	0.2894	$OP^- \nRightarrow R^-$	18.4794	0.001×10^{-7}

Notes:

(1) OP represents oil prices, CPI is the consumer price index, and R is the interest rate.

(2) The optimal lag length in the VAR model is set.

(3) The symbol A $\nRightarrow$ B means that A does not cause B.

(4) The optimal lag is determined by minimizing the information criterion developed by Hatemi-J (2003, 2008). For a detailed application of this information criterion, see Mustafa and Hatemi-J (2019).

(5) An extra unrestricted lag is included in the model in order to account for the effect of one unit root as per suggestion of Toda and Yamamoto (1995).

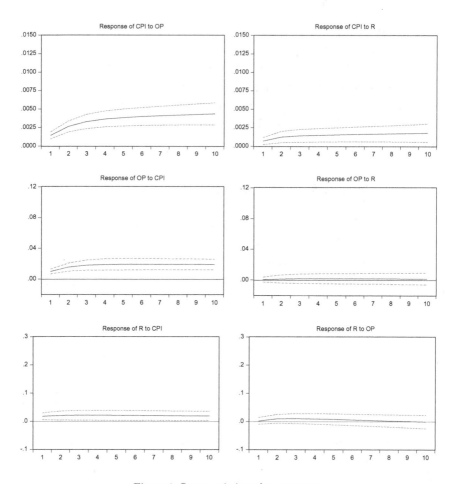

Figure 1: Symmetric impulse responses.

acquired from the website of Amit Goyal. The logarithmic value of each variable is used in all estimations.

The results of the asymmetric-causality tests are presented in Table 1. Symmetric as well as asymmetric-causality tests are implemented. The results of the symmetric causality tests show that both oil prices and consumer prices impact each other at the 1% significant level. However, no causal impacts are found between the interest rate and the oil prices. There are also no causal impacts between

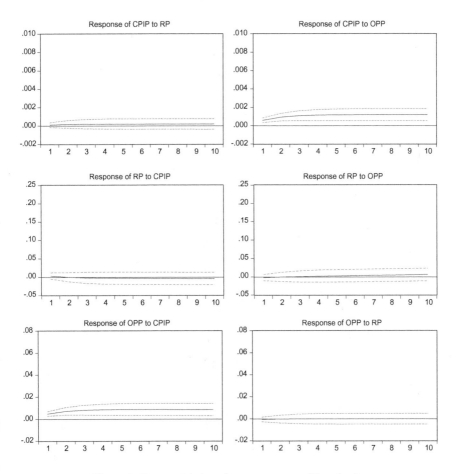

Figure 2: Asymmetric impulse responses, positive shocks.

the interest rate and consumer prices, which is surprising. Nevertheless, asymmetric-causality tests reveal the following. A positive shock in oil prices does not cause a positive shock in the consumer prices while the opposite causality prevails, which means a positive change in the consumer prices is causing a positive change in the oil prices. A positive shock in the interest rate is not causing a positive shock in the consumer prices and there is no reverse causality either in this particular case. There is a causal impact from a positive change in the interest rate on the oil prices and there is also a reverse

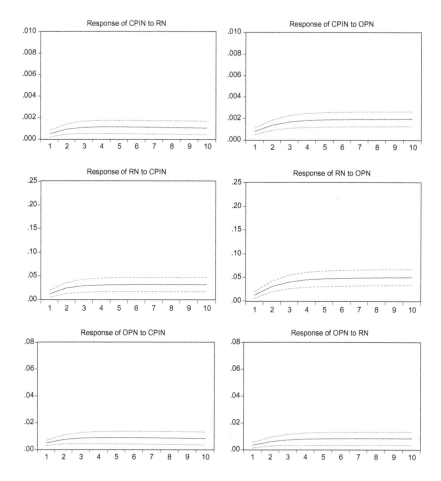

Figure 3: Asymmetric impulse responses, negative shocks.

causality between these two components. A negative shock in oil prices causes a negative shock in the consumer prices and *vice versa.* There is also a bi-directional causality between a negative interest rate shock and a negative consumer price shock. However, a negative shock in the interest rate does not have any significant causal impact on the oil prices, while a negative oil shock causes strongly a negative interest rate shock. These results are also confirmed more or less by the asymmetric impulse response functions that are presented in Figures 1–3.

5. Conclusions

The dynamic interaction between oil prices and consumer prices is of vital importance to policymakers, consumers, producers, and investors. A significant number of published papers have been dedicated to this issue. However, the asymmetric causal impact between these two important macroeconomic variables has not been investigated to the best of our knowledge. In order to fill this gap in the literature, we make use of the asymmetric-causality tests that explicitly separate the impact of positive changes from the negatives ones. It is widely agreed in the literature that allowing for asymmetry conforms well with the reality since economic agents tend to react more strongly to negative changes than to positive ones when they make an economic decision. We make use of a sample period for the US that covers around one and a half centuries, on a monthly basis. In order to account for the potential impact of the omitted variables, the interest rate is also included in the model as a control variable. Additionally, the asymmetric generalized impulse response functions are estimated in order to capture the dynamic interaction between these three variables. Especial attention is given to the stochastic as well as the deterministic trend properties of the data. The estimation output indicates clearly that asymmetric impacts prevail and separating the impact of positive changes from the negative ones has important empirical as well as policy repercussions.

References

Alvarez, L. J., Hurtado, S., Sánchez, I. and Thomas, S. (2011). The impact of oil price changes on Spanish and euro area consumer price inflation, *Economic Modelling*, 28, 422–431.

Blanchard, O. J. and Gali, J. (2007). The macroeconomic effects of oil shocks: Why are the 2000s so different from the 1970s? NBER Working Paper 13368.

Chen, S. S. (2009). Oil price pass-through into inflation, *Energy Economics*, 31, 126–133.

Clark, T. E. and Terry, S. J. (2010). Time variation in the inflation passthrough of energy prices, *Journal of Money, Credit and Banking*, 42, 1419–1433.

Choi, D. F., Loungani, P., Mishra, S. and Poplawski-Ribeiro, M. (2017). Oil prices and inflation dynamics: Evidence from advanced and developing economies, IMF Working Paper WP/17/196.

De Gregorio, J., Landerretche, O., Neilson, C., Broda, C. and Rigobon, R. (2007). Another pass-through bites the dust? Oil prices and inflation, *Economia*, 7, 155–208.

Hamilton, J. D. (1983). Oil and the macroeconomy since World War II, *Journal of Political Economy*, 91, 228–248.

Hamilton, J. D. (1988). A neoclassical model of unemployment and the business cycle, *Journal of Political Economy*, 96, 593–617.

Hamilton, J. D. and Herrera, A. M. (2004). Oil shocks and aggregate macroeconomic behaviour: The role of monetary policy: A comment, *Journal of Money, Credit and Banking*, 36, 265–286.

Hatemi-J, A. (2003). A new method to choose optimal lag order in stable and unstable VAR models, *Applied Economics Letters*, 10(3), 135–137.

Hatemi-J, A. (2008). Forecasting properties of a new method to choose optimal lag order in stable and unstable VAR models, *Applied Economics Letters*, 15(4), 239–243.

Hatemi-J, A. (2011). ACTEST: GAUSS module to Apply Asymmetric Causality Tests. Statistical Software Components G00012. Boston College Department of Economics. Available at: http://ideas.repec.org/c/boc/bocode/g00014.html.

Hatemi-J, A. (2012). Asymmetric causality tests with an application, *Empirical Economics*, 43(1), 447–456.

Hatemi-J, A. (2014). Asymmetric generalized impulse responses with an application in finance, *Economic Modelling*, 36, 18–22.

Hatemi-J, A. and El-Khatib, Y. (2016). An extension of the asymmetric causality tests for dealing with deterministic trend components, *Applied Economics*, 48(42), 4033–4041.

Hatemi-J, A. and El-Khatib, Y. (2017). ASYM_CAUS: C++ module for transforming an integrated variable with deterministic trend parts into negative and positive cumulative partial sums, Statistical Software Components CPP001, Boston College Department of Economics, Available online.

Hatemi-J, A. and Mustafa, A. (2016). TDICPS: OCTAVE module to transform an integrated variable into cumulative partial sums for negative and positive components with deterministic trend parts, Statistical Software Components OCT001, Boston College Department of Economics, Available online.

Hooker, M. A. (1996). What happened to the oil price-macroeconomy relationship? *Journal of Monetary Economics*, 38, 195–213.

Hooker, M. (2002). Are oil shocks inflationary? Asymmetric and nonlinear specifications versus changes in regime, *Journal of Money, Credit and Banking*, 34, 540–561.

Kilian, L. (2009). Not all oil price shocks are alike: Disentangling demand and supply shocks in the crude oil market, *American Economic Review*, 99, 1053–1069.

Kilian, L. and Park, C. (2009). The impact of oil price shocks on the US stock market, *International Economic Review*, 50, 1267–1287.

Mork, K. A. (1989). Oil and the macroeconomy when prices go up and down: An extension of Hamilton's results, *Journal of Political Economy*, 97, 740–744.

Mustafa, A. and Hatemi-J, A. (2019). A VBA module simulation for finding optimal lag order in time series models and its use on teaching financial data computation, *Applied Computing and Informatics*, forthcoming.

Tiwari, A. K., Cunado, J., Hatemi-J, A. and Gupta, R. (2019). Oil price-inflation pass-through in the United States over 1871 to 2018: A wavelet coherency analysis, *Structural Change and Economic Dynamics*, 50, 51–55.

Toda, H. Y. and Yamamoto, T. (1995). Statistical inference in vector autoregressions with possibly integrated processes, *Journal of Econometrics*, 66(1), 225–250.

Zivkov, D., -Ðuraskovic, J. and Manic, S. (2019). How do oil price changes affect inflation in Central and Eastern European countries? A wavelet-based Markov switching approach, *Baltic Journal of Economics*, 19(1), 84–104.

Chapter 6

Risky Financial Assets in Financial Integration and the Impacts of Derivatives on Banking Returns

Hasan Dinçer, Serhat Yüksel, Fatih Pınarbaşı
and Mehmet Ali Alhan

İstanbul Medipol University, Turkey

1. Introduction

The banking sector provides a lot of benefits for different parties. For example, investors can take loans from the banks and can increase their investments. Therefore, this situation makes an important contribution to the economic growth of countries. In addition, these companies, which have higher investments, prefer to employ new people, this leading to a decreasing effect of then unemployment problem. Moreover, the people who have some savings can give their money to the banks and get a chance to earn interest income (Yüksel *et al.*, 2017; Beck *et al.*, 2018).

However, banks are subject to many different risks while engaging in these operations. For instance, there is a risk that debtors may not pay their debts to the banks, which is named as credit risk (Shen *et al.*, 2018). Furthermore, banks may also have high amount of losses because of the volatility in the market. As an example, when there is a high amount of increase in currency exchange rate, the losses of the banks may increase if they have foreign debts (Huynh *et al.*, 2018). Moreover, natural disasters, hacking attacks and fraud of the employees may increase the losses of the banks, which is called operational risk (Mizgier and Wimmer, 2018).

Banks try to implement many different policies in order to minimize these risks (Suresh and Krishnan, 2018; Lundqvist and Vilhelmsson, 2018). For example, banks can follow the financial performance of the debtors periodically after giving the loans to them. This situation makes it possible for the banks to take action at an early stage. Furthermore, some banks do not give high amount of loans to the same sector to minimize losses if there is a problem is this sector. Another example for this aspect is that banks take out an insurance policy in order to control the risks which may be caused due to natural disasters, such as earthquakes and floods (Zengin and Yüksel, 2016).

Derivatives are the products which can also be used for this purpose (Yüksel, 2016a). They refer to the products in which there is a negotiation for the future date. In other words, although the price, quantity, and exchange time are defined at the beginning, the exchange of the money and the goods is performed on a future date. Owing to this situation, parties can have a chance to fix the prices of the products. Hence, this condition has a decreasing effect on the risks of the companies. There are mainly four different derivative products, which are forward, future, swap, and options (Oktar and Yüksel, 2015).

In addition to the risk management, derivative products are also used for speculative purposes (Norfield, 2012). It means that derivatives are preferred in order to increase the profitability of the companies. For example, although the company does not need to fix the prices of currency exchange rate for its operations, it prefers to purchase a derivative product to gain an income. As can be seen, despite the chance of gaining income, there is a significant risk of incurring losses while using derivative products for speculative purposes (Tanha and Dempsey, 2017).

Parallel to the aspects given above, the aim of this study is to understand the relationship between derivative products usage and profitability of Turkish banks. For this purpose, quarterly data of these banks for the periods between 2003 and 2016 is evaluated by using Toda–Yamamoto causality analysis method. As a result, it will be possible to understand the main purpose of Turkish banks behind the usage of derivative products. Thus, necessary recommendations can be presented according to the results of this analysis.

This study includes five different sections. After the introduction part, in Section 2, the studies in the literature, which focus on the derivative products, are analyzed. Thus, it will be possible to understand which subject in the literature is missing. Moreover, Section 3 gives information about the details of derivatives. In this section, some quantitative information about the derivatives is also shared. Additionally, Section 4 explains the applications on Turkish banking sector. Furthermore, Section 5 underlines the recommendations according to the analysis results.

2. Literature Review About the Derivative Usage of Companies

The popularity of the subject of derivative products has been increasing especially in the last decades. Therefore, there is an increase in the number of studies in the literature that have focused on this subject. Some of the featured studies are listed in Table 1.

Table 1 gives the information that most of the studies focused on the usage of derivatives for risk management purposes. Some of these studies identified that derivative products have a significant effect of decreasing the risks of the companies. For example, Hassan *et al.* (1994) made a study to understand this relationship in United States. With the help of regression analysis, it is concluded that derivative products are very important items to manage the risks of companies. Similarly, Angbazo (1997) also aimed to analyze this situation for 286 different banks. It is determined that the main purpose of the banks in derivative usage is to hedge the interest rate risk. Aydın (2000) and Göçmen (2004) focused on this aspect for Turkey and concluded that derivative products are mainly used to hedge the risks of companies. Altan and Parlakkaya (2004) also analyzed this situation with the

Table 1: Studies focused on derivatives.

Author	Scope	Method	Result
Hassan *et al.* (1994)	United States	Regression	It is defined that off-balance sheet items have a decreasing effect on the risks of the banks.
Jagtiani and Khanthavit (1996)	United States	Regression	There is a significant increase in the usage of derivatives, especially after 1980s.
Angbazo (1997)	286 Different Banks	Descriptive Statistics	It is seen that the main purpose of the banks in derivative usage is to hedge the interest rate risk.
Alp *et al.* (1997)	Turkey	Regression	One of the most important ways to increase the profitability for the banks is using derivatives.
Aydın (2000)	Turkey	Descriptive Statistics	Derivative products are very important to manage risks.
Göçmen (2004)	Turkey	Descriptive Statistics	The main purpose of using derivatives for the banks is to hedge the risks.
Altan and Parlakkaya (2004)	Turkey	Regression	Banks use derivatives mainly for the purpose of hedging interest rate and currency risks.
Casu and Girardone (2005)	European Union	Regression	There is a positive correlation between derivative usage and the profitability of the banks.
Selimler and Kale (2008)	Turkey	Descriptive Statistics	Especially after the 2008 global crisis, banks prefer to use derivative products to manage their risks.
Sayın (2008)	Turkey	Descriptive Statistics	Derivative products positively affect the financial performance of companies.
Pasiouras (2008)	Greece	Data Envelopment Analysis	There is no significant relationship between derivatives and profitability.
Calmès and Théoret (2010)	Canada	ARCH	There is no correlation between the derivative usage and the profitability of banks.
Oktar and Yüksel (2016)	Turkey	MARS	Turkish banks use derivatives for the purpose of hedging their credit risks.

(Continued)

Table 1: (*Continued*)

Author	Scope	Method	Result
Juhász (2016)	Hungary	Survey	It is identified that most of the managers do not know the details of derivative products.
Achugamonu *et al.* (2016)	Nigeria	Descriptive Statistics	Derivative products are very beneficial for the banks to manage risks and increase profitability.
Swain and Panda (2017)	India	Regression	Derivative products have an important influence on the financial performance of companies.
Badia *et al.* (2017)	Canada and United States	Regression	There is a direct relationship between derivative usage and profitability.
Venkatesh *et al.* (2017)	India	Data Envelopment Analysis	Derivative products play a key role in financial performance.
D'Avino (2017)	United States	Regression	It is determined that banks give importance to use of derivatives for speculative purposes.
Pushkala *et al.* (2017)	India	Descriptive Statistics	Private banks give more importance to derivatives in comparison with state banks.
Miao *et al.* (2018)	United States	Regression	Option prices are very effective to estimate oil prices.
Cheng *et al.* (2018)	United States	Regression	Derivatives are very effective to minimize the volatility in oil prices.
Chen and Hsu (2018)	China	Heath–Jarrow–Morton's (HJM) Model	They created a model to estimate the value of inflation indexed swaps.
Hsiao and Tsai (2018)	Taiwan	Logit	It is identified that household wealth is one of the most important factors that affect the usage of derivatives.
Akhigbe *et al.* (2018)	133 Different Banks	Regression	Investors face difficulty to predict future prices by looking at interest rate derivatives.

(*Continued*)

Table 1: (*Continued*)

Author	Scope	Method	Result
Evarest *et al.* (2018)	Sweden	Monte Carlo Simulation	They created a model to predict the future prices of weather derivatives.
Prasad and Suprabha (2018)	India	Descriptive Statistics	The forward contract to hedge currency risk is the most preferred derivative product.
Li (2018)	United States	Regression	The usage of interest rate derivatives does not have a decreasing effect on the risk.
Nguyen *et al.* (2018)	389 Different Companies	Regression	Derivatives are manly preferred to minimize the volatility in the market.

help of regression methodology and defined that banks use derivatives mainly for the purpose of hedging interest rate and currency risks. Selimler and Kale (2008) also identified that especially after the 2008 global crisis, banks prefer to use derivative products to manage their risks.

In addition to those studies, Oktar and Yüksel (2016) under took a study to understand the main indicators that affect the usage of derivatives for Turkish banks. For this situation, they used multivariate adaptive regression splines method. Consequently, they underlined that hedging credit risk is the main factor for Turkish banks to use derivatives. Achugamonu *et al.* (2016) also presented a study for Nigeria and identified that derivative products are very beneficial for the banks to manage risks. Moreover, Cheng *et al.* (2018) made a study to test this relationship for United States. By using the regression analysis, they reached the conclusion that derivatives are very effective to minimize the volatility in oil prices. Similar to this study, Prasad and Suprabha (2018) analyzed this situation for India and underlined that the forward contract to hedge currency risk is the most preferred derivative product. Nguyen *et al.* (2018) also considered 389 different companies to see the effects of derivatives on risk management. It is determined that derivatives are manly preferred to minimize the volatility in the market. In spite of all these studies, Li (2018) reached the conclusion that the usage of interest rate derivatives does not have a decreasing effect on risks.

Another important point in Table 1 is that the relationship between derivative usage and profitability is analyzed by many different researchers. For instance, Alp *et al.* (1997) made a study to evaluate whether derivative usage has an influence on the profitability of Turkish banks. For this evaluation, regression methodology is taken into consideration. In conclusion, it is identified that using derivatives is one of the most important ways to increase the profitability of the banks. In addition to this study, Casu and Girardone (2005) also undertook a similar study for the banks in the European Union. They concluded that there is a positive correlation between derivative usage and the profitability of the banks. Sayın (2008) also defined that derivative products positively affect the financial performance of companies. Moreover, Swain and Panda (2017) also focused on Indian companies and identified that derivative products have a significant effect on the financial performance of companies. Furthermore, Badia *et al.* (2017) and Venkatesh *et al.* (2017) determined that there is a direct relationship between derivative usage and profitability.

In spite of these studies, there are also some other studies which have reached the opposite conclusion. As an example, Pasiouras (2008) made a study to define whether derivative usage effects the profitability of the companies in Greece or not. Data Envelopment Analysis is considered in this analysis for this purpose. Consequently, it is determined that there is no significant relationship between derivatives and profitability. In addition to this study, Calmès and Théoret (2010) also focused on the same relationship for Canadian companies. ARCH methodology is used in this study in the analysis process. Similar to Pasiouras (2008), they also reached the conclusion that there is no correlation between the derivative usage and the financial performance of the banks.

In addition to the studies that focus on the relationship with risk management or profitability, the subject of derivative products also attracted the attention of many different researchers for different purposes. For example, Jagtiani and Khanthavit (1996) concluded that there is a significant increase in the usage of derivatives in United States, especially after 1980s. Moreover, D'Avino (2017) explained that banks in United States give importance to use of derivatives mainly for speculative purposes. Pushkala *et al.* (2017) also concluded that private banks give more importance to derivatives in comparison with the state banks in India. According to Miao *et al.* (2018), option prices are very effective to estimate oil prices. Furthermore, Chen and Hsu (2018), Evarest *et al.* (2018), and Akhigbe *et al.* (2018) created a model to estimate the value of some derivative products in the future. Parallel to this subject, Akhigbe *et al.* (2018) emphasized that it is very difficult for the investors to predict future prices by looking at interest rate derivatives. Additionally, Juhász (2016) underlined an important point in his study that most of the managers do not know the details of derivative products in Hungary.

By looking at similar studies in the literature, firstly, it is defined that the subject of derivatives is so popular that it has attracted the attention of many different researchers. It can also be seen that these studies mainly focused on the effects of derivative usage on risk management and profitability issues. There are also some other studies which try to create a model to create future prices or make a specific analysis, such as comparison of bank types regarding derivative usage. As a result, it is understood that there is a need for a new study which aims to evaluate the effect of profitability on the derivatives. In addition to this aspect, using an original study will also increase the originality of this study.

3. General Information about Derivatives and Derivative Usage in Turkish Banking Sector

3.1. *General information about derivatives*

In today's world, change and continuous development have become the most important factors of growth. Increasing technological developments, the development of communication networks, and the rapid change of resources around the world have influenced finance in many different ways (Capello and Lenzi, 2016; Salahuddin and Gow, 2017). In the 21st century, companies have to learn to act in markets and conditions by considering ever-changing dynamics. These changing dynamics have gained momentum in the years we left behind in the 20th century. One of the most important consequences of the continuous development and changes that take place is the uncertainty (Hsu *et al.*, 2014; Asongu *et al.*, 2017). Because companies do not like uncertainty in the market, they usually try to take actions to manage this problem.

The concept of derivatives is concerned with the point of dealing with this kind of problem. A derivative is a financial instrument which derives its performance from the performance of other underlying assets (Pirie, 2017; Miao *et al.*, 2018). Derivatives can be defined as a financial instrument whose value has a relationship with another asset which refers to "deriving". This type of financial instrument has a value and this value is tightly related to the price of underlying assets (Durbin, 2010). This underlying asset could be foreign exchange, equity, commodity, or bond (Hundman, 1999). The usage of derivative products has a very long history which goes back to the Hammurabi Law (Whaley, 2007).

After the definition and historic root of derivatives, the question of why people use derivative products comes to mind. It is mainly related to risk management and in other ways it can be summarized basically in two ways, first one is hedging and other one is speculating/speculation. Hedging is about managing uncertainty while speculating is about wagering (Popova and Simkins, 2015; Deng *et al.*, 2017). Before the section of types of derivatives, we have to touch on derivative markets. There are two types of derivative markets; over-the-counter (OTC) markets and organized markets. Over-the-counter market is the market where parties find, work, and transact with each other directly (Duffie and Stein, 2015; Hendershott and Madhavan, 2015). While organized market is the market where the opportunity to find potential buyers and sellers is provided for parties in an institution, such as stock exchange (Davidson, 2017).

3.2. *Type of derivatives*

Derivatives in the financial market can basically be grouped into four main categories. They are forward commitments, future commitments, options, and swaps.

- **Forward Commitments:** Forward commitment/contract is an agreement between two parties. One of them accepts to purchase a financial asset at a future date with a fixed price. Additionally, the other party agrees to deliver that asset according to the determined criteria. The main feature of forward commitment is that the contract between two parties can be customized very easily (Füss *et al.*, 2015; Chisholm, 2004). One of the parties can be named as long forward, who is the purchaser side of this agreement. The other party can be named as short forward, which is the seller side (Patrick, 2016; Gottesman, 2016). The main benefit of forward commitment is reduction of uncertainty. On the other hand, there can always be a loss for one of the two parties. If the price is different from the spot, the buyer may pay more money or the seller gets less payment (Brada, 2014; Kaunda, 2015). Furthermore, forward contract is not a usage right, it is an obligation. Foreign currency (FX), interest rate, and commodity forwards are different examples of the forward contracts.
- **Future Commitments:** Future commitment is similar to forward commitments but differentiates by way of agreement. In forward commitments, the agreement is between two parties directly, but future commitments are done through organized and regulated markets (Park, 2014). The exchange where the transaction takes place is called futures market (Chance and Brooks, 2015). Trading on exchanges makes future contracts standardized and regulated (Bhagwat and Maravi, 2016). The main advantage of future contracts in comparison with others is that there is a guarantee of the stock market for the operations. Therefore, parties feel themselves more secure while making future contracts. Owing to this aspect, the stock market wants the parties to fulfill extra obligations. For example, they must give an initial margin which

refers to an amount of guarantee for this operation. Additionally, the stock market controls the profit or loss situation of the parties daily and this process is named mark-to-market. Moreover, if the loss amount of one of the parties exceeds the limit defined in the contract, they have to increase this initial margin amount (Pandian, 2015).

- **Options:** Options are derivative types that are a form of agreement between two sides about transaction in future. There are mainly two different parts in an option, which are buyer and seller. The buyer of the option has the right to use this option or not (Blanco and Wehrheim, 2017; Maghrebi *et al.*, 2016). In other words, option is not an obligation for the buyer of this product. On the other side, seller has to complete his/her obligation when buyer decides to use this option. In order to have this right, buyer has to pay some amount of money to the seller, which is called as option premium. The buyer of the option cannot take this option premium back from the seller in any condition. While considering these aspects, it can be understood that the maximum loss of the buyer is the option premium, whereas this amount is infinite for the seller. In addition to this issue, the maximum profit of the seller is the option premium, but the buyer has a chance to gain infinite amount according to the market conditions (Carr and Wu, 2016; Munoz and Miranda, 2016).

- **Swap:** The word "swap" refers to the exchange as a meaning. A swap is an agreement about exchange of payments on a regular basis on future dates between two parties (Bavoso, 2016). According to another definition, swap is a contract about exchanging cash flows between two parties. The purposes of swaps are managing/hedging risks by volatile interest rates, commodity and share prices, and currency exchange rates (Rahman and Md Ramli, 2015).

3.3. *Purposes of derivatives*

The purposes can be summarized into two different categories; risk allocation and speculation.

- **Risk Allocation/Hedging:** One of the primary uses of derivatives relates to risk management. The main reason is that by using derivatives, people can have a chance to fix the price for the future. Although there is a risk for these people because of this situation, they can prevent high amount of losses owing to these products. In other words, if there were no derivatives, they would have high amount of losses because of the volatility in the market (Davis, 2016). Hedging is a specific form of risk management and it includes the action of recognizing and measuring an existing position in terms of financial risk. It takes action for a new position to protect itself from losses (Leoni *et al.*, 2014; Chambers, 2007).
- **Speculation:** In addition to these main benefits, derivatives also have speculation benefits for parties. For example, a speculator who is waiting for an increase in foreign exchange could use a derivative product. The purpose of this process is to provide a financial benefit, rather than being protected from a certain risk (Yüksel, 2016b; Aalbers *et al.*, 2017).

3.4. *General information about derivative usage in Turkish banking sector*

Turkey, along with the changes and developing economies experienced, is a country that is experiencing financial aspects of mobility. In this context, both in terms of financial management and risk management, it is useful to examine the development of derivative products in Turkey. Derivative products show a tendency to increase significantly in the Turkish banking sector.

When the data for the period 2003–2015 are examined, a derivative transaction volume of 200 million is noted between 2003 and 2007. As of 2008, this amount has exceeded the 200 million level and has started continued increase. The amount of derivative usage, which tended to rise until 2013, started to increase at a high pace in the third quarter of 2013. Following the fall in the first quarter of 2014, it continued to increase again in the period of 2014–2015.

Table 2: Derivative volume and sum of off-balance accounts by year.

Years	Derivatives	Sum of off-balance accounts	Ratio (%)
2002	25.423.868	228.477.512	11
2003	34.279.858	350.828.325	10
2004	38.973.539	513.231.630	8
2005	65.893.599	4.118.182.570	2
2006	106.125.271	4.716.660.310	2
2007	157.916.586	5.059.026.084	3
2008	192.575.682	6.832.863.775	3
2009	246.194.648	8.777.147.183	3
2010	384.521.033	11.863.769.624	3
2011	565.823.122	22.745.976.182	2
2012	609.229.676	7.049.497.062	9
2013	1.066.840.798	8.347.220.138	13
2014	1.207.129.674	9.812.006.750	12
2015	1.555.231.295	12.171.795.071	13
2016	1.935.205.146	15.198.735.892	13

Source: Turkish Banking Association.

Table 2 shows derivative volume and sum off off-balance accounts together. Ratio of derivatives/sum of off-balance account is also presented. When this ratio is examined according to the years, it is observed that the ratio which is close to 10% between 2002 and 2004 has decreased as of 2005. It can be interpreted that the increase in the amount of the off-balance calculations is more effective than the amount of the derivative in this apparent decrease. Along with the decline in off-balance accounts in 2012, this rate has reached 9%. In addition, the increase in the number of derivatives was realized in 2013.

4.   An Application on Turkish Banking Sector

4.1.   *Dataset and scope*

In this study, the causality relationship between derivative usage and profitability of Turkish banks is evaluated. Within this framework, the ratio of "net profits/total equity" is taken into consideration with respect to the profitability. On the other hand, regarding the variable of derivatives, the ratio of "total derivative amount/total assets" is used. Moreover, quarterly data of these variables for the years between 2003 and 2016 are evaluated. This data are derived from the website of Turkish Banking Association.

4.2. *Toda–Yamamoto causality analysis*

Toda–Yamamoto causality analysis is used to determine the causality relationship between the variables. It has some advantages in comparison with other causality analysis methods. First of all, there is no prior condition that variables be stationary. In other words, it is possible to make Toda–Yamamoto causality analysis when variables have unit roots or not. In the analysis process of this test, unit root and lag-order selection criteria tests should be performed. While making these analyses, optimal lag interval in VAR model (k) and maximum cointegration level (d) should be calculated. In order to make analysis by using Toda–Yamamoto causality test, the lag structure of the model should be estimated by using the sum of optimal lag interval in VAR model and maximum cointegration level $(k + d)$ (Toda and Yamamoto, 1995; Yüksel and Zengin, 2016; Yüksel and Özsarı, 2016).

Toda–Yamamoto causality analysis is so popular in the literature that it is used in many different subjects. For example, Manap *et al.* (2012), Alimi and Ofonyelu (2013), Burhop (2006), Abdul Manap *et al.* (2012), Sami (2013), Kassim and Abdul Manap (2008), Obradovic and Grbic (2015), Azouzi and Echchabi (2013), Majid and Hasin (2014), and Okuyan (2014) used this methodology to analyze the banking sector. In addition to those studies, Doğrul and Soytaş (2010), Gillani *et al.* (2009), Adriana (2014), Ahmad (2013), Alexandru *et al.* (2011), Torruam and Abur (2014), Strat *et al.* (2015), and Loganathan *et al.* (2011) considered this method in order to take action to decrease unemployment problem.

In addition to these studies, Altınay and Karagol (2005), Wolde-Rufael (2006), Soytas and Sari (2009), Chowdhury and Mavrotas (2006), Belke *et al.* (2011), Lotfalipour *et al.* (2010),

Deb and Mukherjee (2008), Awokuse (2003), Payne (2009), Kum *et al.* (2012), Amiri and Ventelou (2012), Awokuse (2006), Apergis and Payne (2010) and Duasa (2007) considered Toda–Yamamoto causality analysis to reach sustainable economic growth. Furthermore, Kelly (2008), Özdemir and Fisunoğlu (2008), Meidani *et al.* (2011), Conrad and Karanasos (2005), Akcay (2011), Nezhad and Zarea (2007), Umar and Dahalan (2015), and David and Ann (2014) made an analysis by using this approach to control high inflation problem.

4.3. *Analysis results*

In the first stage of the analysis, variables are subject to stationary analysis. For this purpose, augmented Dickey Fuller (ADF) unit root test is performed to see whether the variables are stationary or not. As it can be seen in Table A.1, the probability value of the variable of profitability is 0.88. Because this value is greater than 0.05, it is understood that this variable has a unit root. In other words, it is understood that it is not stationary on its level value. Hence, to see when this variable is stationary, the first difference of this variable is also tested by using ADF unit root test. Table A.2 shows that the probability value is 0.00. Since it is lower than 0.05, it can be said that the variable of profitability is stationary when the first difference is considered. On the other hard, Table A.3 gives information about the unit root test of the variable of derivatives. The probability value of this variable is 0.0139, which is lower than 0.05. Because of this aspect, it is identified that this variable does not have any unit root on its level value.

After stationary analysis, in the second stage, optimal lag interval should be selected. For this, vector auto-regression (VAR) analysis is performed. The details of this analysis are presented in Table A.4. It can be seen that "lag 4" is the optimal lag according to final prediction error (FPE), Akaike (AIC), Schwarz (SC), and Hannan-Quinn (HQ) information criteria. While looking at the results of these two analyses, it is identified that the model should be estimated by using fifth lag $(1+4)$ because maximum cointegration level is 1 and optimal lag interval in VAR model is 4. The details are shown in Table 3.

After that, Toda–Yamamoto causality analysis is performed. Within this framework, a new model was created for the condition where the lag is equal to 5. The details of this analysis are presented in Table 4.

Table 4 shows that when the dependent variable is "profitability", the probability value of the independent variable "derivatives" is 0.1402. Because it is higher than 0.05, it is understood that there is no a significant relationship. In other words, it is identified that the usage of derivatives does not have a significant influence on the profitability. This situation is similar in some studies in the literature. For example, Pasiouras (2008) and Calmès and Théoret (2010) also concluded that usage of derivative products does not lead to increase in the financial performance of the companies.

Table 3: Selection of the lag in Toda–Yamamoto causality analysis.

ADF unit root analysis			Optimal lag interval analysis		Lag used in Toda–Yamamoto analysis
Variable	Analysis result	Maximum cointegration level	Criteria	Optimal lag interval	
Profitability	It is stationary on the first difference		FPE	4	$4+1=5$
			AIC	4	
Derivative	It is stationary on the level value	1	SC	4	
			HQ	4	

Table 4: Details of Toda–Yamamoto-causality analysis results.

Excluded	Chi-sq	df	Prob.
Dependent variable: Profitability			
Derivatives	8.304334	5	0.1402
All	8.304334	5	0.1402
Dependent variable: Derivatives			
Profitability	17.52416	5	0.0036
All	17.52416	5	0.0036

In addition to this analysis, it is also determined that when the dependent variable is "derivatives", the independent variable's (profitability) probability is 0.0036. Since this value is less than 0.05, it can be defined that this causality relationship is significant. Hence, it is concluded that there is a causality relationship from the profitability to the derivatives. In other words, it can be said that profitability of Turkish banks is the main reason for using derivative products.

While considering these aspects, it can be seen that derivatives usage is not the main cause of profitability. This situation shows that Turkish banks do not use derivative products for speculative purposes. Nevertheless, it is also determined that higher financial performance has a significant influence on the usage of derivative products. It gives information that Turkish banks, which have higher profitability, give more importance to the derivative products. This condition gives information that these banks mainly prefer derivatives to manage their risks. Similar to this aspect, Hassan *et al.* (1994), Angbazo (1997), Aydın (2000), Göçmen (2004), Altan and Parlakkaya (2004), and Selimler and Kale (2008) also emphasized that companies use derivatives to control their risks.

5. Conclusion

Banks have to face a lot of different risks in their operations. For example, there is a risk that banks may not collect their receivables from. the customers. In addition to this risk, banks are also subject to the risk due to the volatility in the market, such as interest rate and currency exchange rate. Moreover, banks may have high amount of losses if they do not have enough liquidity when there is a need. Almost all banks make significant researches in order to minimize these risks. Otherwise, these banks may go bankrupt due to these problems.

Derivative products are also preferred by the banks for this purpose. Because it is possible to fix the prices in the market by using derivative products, they will have an important contribution to hedging of the risks. Nonetheless, these products may also be used for speculative purposes. This indicates that banks may prefer to use these products to get income. However, it can be seen that there is also the risk of getting losses when banks use these products for speculative expectations. Due to this situation, this kind of derivative usage is criticized by many researchers.

In this study, the relationship between derivative usage and profitability is analyzed. Within this scope, quarterly data for the years between 2003 and 2016 are evaluated. For this purpose, Toda–Yamamoto causality approach is taken into consideration. In the first step of this analysis, ADF unit root test is performed to see whether the variables are stationary or not. It is defined that profitability is not stationary, whereas there is no unit root in the variable of derivatives. Hence, the first difference of the variable of the profitability is considered.

After stationary analysis, VAR analysis is performed to see optimal lag interval. It is identified that "lag 4" is the optimal lag according to final prediction error (FPE), Akaike (AIC), Schwarz (SC), and Hannan-Quinn (HQ) information criteria. According to these results, it is determined that the model should be estimated by using fifth lag $(1 + 4)$. The main reason behind this aspect is that maximum cointegration level is 1 and optimal lag interval in VAR model is 4.

As a result of Toda–Yamamoto causality analysis, it is concluded that there is no significant causality relationship from derivative usage to the profitability. This situation gives information that derivative products cannot contribute to the financial performance of banks. On the other hand, it is identified that higher profitability is the main cause for Turkish banks to use more derivative products. These results explain that Turkish banks prefer to use derivative products mainly for risk management purposes instead of speculative expectations.

In this study, it is concluded that there is a causality relationship between profitability and derivatives usage. However, it is also defined that the opposite of the relationship is not identified. Because of this aspect, it can be said that Turkish banks use derivative products mainly for hedging in comparison with speculative purposes.

Therefore, it is recommended that speculative purposes of derivatives should be avoided for all banks. Because this usage has a significant amount of risks, it may cause important losses for the banks.

This study aims to evaluate the causality relationship between derivative usage and profitability of Turkish banks. In this study, the data of whole banking sector is analyzed by using Toda–Yamamoto causality analysis method. For future researches, Turkish banks may be evaluated separately by using panel causality analysis, such as Dumitrescu Hurlin methodology. Additionally, this panel data analysis may also be performed for many different countries. Moreover, this study may be performed for some companies in other sectors.

References

Aalbers, M. B., Loon, J. V. and Fernandez, R. (2017). The financialization of a social housing provider, *International Journal of Urban and Regional Research*, 41(4), 572–587.

Abdul Manap, T. A., Abduh, M. and Omar, M. A. (2012). Islamic banking growth nexus: Evidence from Toda–Yamamoto and bootstrap granger causality test, *Journal of Islamic Finance*, 176(813), 1–8.

Achugamonu, B. U., Osunkoya, M., Aiyepeku, D. A., Adetiloye, K. A. and Akinjare, V. A. (2016). Risk and profitability considerations in off-balance sheet engagements: A comparative analysis of deposit money banks in Nigeria.

Adriana, D. (2014). Revisiting the relationship between unemployment rates and shadow economy. A Toda–Yamamoto approach for the case of Romania, *Procedia Economics and Finance*, 10, 227–236.

Ahmad, F. (2013). The effect of oil prices on unemployment: Evidence from Pakistan, *Business and Economics Research Journal*, 4(1), 43.

Akcay, S. (2011). The causal relationship between producer price index and consumer price index: Empirical evidence from selected European countries, *International Journal of Economics and Finance*, 3(6), 227.

Akhigbe, A., Makar, S., Wang, L. and Whyte, A. M. (2018). Interest rate derivatives use in banking: Market pricing implications of cash flow hedges, *Journal of Banking and Finance*, 86, 113–126.

Alexandru, A. A., Dobre, I. and Ghinararu, C. C. (2011, July). The causal relationship between unemployment rate and US shadow economy. A Toda–Yamamoto approach, in *Proceedings of the 5th International Conference on Applied Mathematics, Simulation, Modelling,*

World Scientific and Engineering Academy and Society (WSEAS), pp. 100–105.

Alimi, S. R. and Ofonyelu, C. C. (2013). Toda–Yamamoto causality test between money market interest rate and expected inflation: the Fisher hypothesis revisited, *European Scientific Journal, ESJ*, 9(7).

Alp, C., Ekinci, D., Gültekin, M. S., Şentürk, M., Şahin, E. and Küfrevioğlu, Ö. İ. (2010). A novel and one-pot synthesis of new 1-tosyl pyrrol-2-one derivatives and analysis of carbonic anhydrase inhibitory potencies, *Bioorganic & medicinal chemistry*, 18(12), 4468–4474.

Altan, M. and Parlakkaya, R. (2004). *Bilanço Dışı İşlemlerin Banka Performansına Etkisi: Türk Bankacılık Sektörü Örneği, Iktisat Isletme ve Finans*, 19(219), 107–122.

Altinay, G. and Karagol, E. (2005). Electricity consumption and economic growth: Evidence from Turkey, *Energy Economics*, 27(6), 849–856.

Amiri, A. and Ventelou, B. (2012). Granger causality between total expenditure on health and GDP in OECD: Evidence from the Toda–Yamamoto approach, *Economics Letters*, 116(3), 541–544.

Angbazo, L. (1997). Commercial bank net interest margins, default risk, interest-rate risk, and off-balance sheet banking, *Journal of Banking & Finance*, 21(1), 55–87.

Apergis, N. and Payne, J. E. (2010). Coal consumption and economic growth: Evidence from a panel of OECD countries, *Energy Policy*, 38(3), 1353–1359.

Asongu, S. A., Koomson, I. and Tchamyou, V. S. (2017). Financial globalisation uncertainty/instability is good for financial development, *Research in International Business and Finance*, 41, 280–291.

Awokuse, T. O. (2003). Is the export-led growth hypothesis valid for Canada? *Canadian Journal of Economics/Revue canadienne d'économique*, 36(1), 126–136.

Awokuse, T. O. (2006). Export-led growth and the Japanese economy: Evidence from VAR and directed acyclic graphs, *Applied Economics*, 38(5), 593–602.

Aydın, A. (2000). *Bilanço Dışı İşlemler, Bankacılık Dergisi* (34).

Azouzi, D. and Echchabi, A. (2013). Islamic banking and economic growth: The Kuwait experience, *Middle East Journal of Management*, 1(2), 186–195.

Badia, M., Duro, M., Jorgensen, B. N. and Ormazabal, G. (2017). Market-wide Effects of Off-Balance Sheet Disclosures (No. 12152). CEPR Discussion Papers.

Bavoso, V. (2016). Financial innovation, derivatives and the UK and US interest rate swap scandals: Drawing new boundaries for the regulation of financial innovation, *Global Policy*, 7(2), 227–236.

Beck, T., Degryse, H., De Haas, R. and Van Horen, N. (2018). When arm's length is too far: Relationship banking over the credit cycle, *Journal of Financial Economics*, 127(1), 174–196.

Belke, A., Dobnik, F. and Dreger, C. (2011). Energy consumption and economic growth: New insights into the cointegration relationship, *Energy Economics*, 33(5), 782–789.

Bhagwat, S. and Maravi, A. S. (2016). An anlysis of past and present status of commodity derivatives market in India, *International Journal of Advanced Research in Management and Social Sciences (IJARMSS)*, ISSN, 2278–6236.

Blanco, I. and Wehrheim, D. (2017). The bright side of financial derivatives: Options trading and firm innovation, *Journal of Financial Economics*, 125(1), 99–119.

Brada, J. (2014). Use of forward interest rates and forward exchange rates for the valuation of currency-interest rate derivatives, *Český finanční a účetní časopis*, 2014(1), 6–18.

Burhop, C. (2006). Did banks cause the German industrialization? *Explorations in Economic History*, 43(1), 39–63.

Calmès, C. and Théoret, R. (2010). The impact of off-balance-sheet activities on banks returns: An application of the ARCH-M to Canadian data, *Journal of Banking & Finance*, 34(7), 1719–1728.

Capello, R. and Lenzi, C. (2016). Relevance and utility of European Union research, technological development and innovation policies for a smart growth, *Environment and Planning C: Government and Policy*, 34(1), 52–72.

Carr, P. and Wu, L. (2016). Analyzing volatility risk and risk premium in option contracts: A new theory, *Journal of Financial Economics*, 120(1), 1–20.

Casu, B. and Girardone, C. (2005). An analysis of the relevance of off-balance sheet items in explaining productivity change in European banking, *Applied Financial Economics*, 15(15), 1053–1061.

Chambers, N. (2007). *Türev Piyasaları, Beta Yayınları.*

Chance, D. M. and Brooks, R. (2015). *Introduction to Derivatives and Risk Management*, Cengage Learning.

Chen, S. N. and Hsu, P. P. (2018). Pricing inflation-indexed derivatives with default risk, *The European Journal of Finance*, 1–16.

Cheng, B., Nikitopoulos, C. S., and Schlögl, E. (2018). Pricing of long-dated commodity derivatives: Do stochastic interest rates matter? *Journal of Banking & Finance*, 95, 148–166.

Chisholm, A. M. (2004). *Derivatives Demystified: A Step-by-Step Guide to Forwards, Futures, Swaps and Options*, John Wiley & Sons.

Chowdhury, A. and Mavrotas, G. (2006). FDI and growth: What causes what? *The World Economy*, 29(1), 9–19.

Conrad, C. and Karanasos, M. (2005). Dual long memory in inflation dynamics across countries of the Euro area and the link between inflation uncertainty and macroeconomic performance, *Studies in Nonlinear Dynamics & Econometrics*, 9(4).

David, U. and Ann, T. N. (2014). Causality dynamics between money supply and inflation in Nigeria: A Toda–Yamamoto test and error correction analysis, *Journal of Empirical Economics*, 3(2), 63–75.

Davidson, P. (2017). The role of financial markets and liquidity, in *Who's Afraid of John Maynard Keynes?* Palgrave Macmillan, Cham, pp. 81–96.

D'Avino, C. (2017). Banking regulation and the changing geography of off-balance sheet activities, *Economics Letters*.

Davis, M. H. (2016). Model-free methods in valuation and hedging of derivative securities, in *The Handbook of Post Crisis Financial Modeling*, Palgrave Macmillan, London, pp. 168–189.

Deb, S. G. and Mukherjee, J. (2008). Does stock market development cause economic growth? A time series analysis for Indian economy, *International Research Journal of Finance and Economics*, 21(3), 142–149.

Deng, S., Elyasiani, E. and Mao, C. X. (2017). Derivatives-hedging, risk allocation and the cost of debt: Evidence from bank holding companies, *The Quarterly Review of Economics and Finance*, 65, 114–127.

Doğrul, H. G. and Soytas, U. (2010). Relationship between oil prices, interest rate, and unemployment: Evidence from an emerging market, *Energy Economics*, 32(6), 1523–1528.

Duasa, J. (2007). Malaysian foreign direct investment and growth: Does stability matter? *Journal of Economic Cooperation Among Islamic Countries*, 28(2).

Duffie, D. and Stein, J. C. (2015). Reforming LIBOR and other financial market benchmarks, *Journal of Economic Perspectives*, 29(2), 191–212.

Durbin, M. (2010). *All About Derivatives*, 2nd edn., McGraw Hill Professional.

Evarest, E., Berntsson, F., Singull, M. and Yang, X. (2018). Weather derivatives pricing using regime switching model, *Monte Carlo Methods and Applications*, 24(1), 13–27.

Füss, R., Mahringer, S. and Prokopczuk, M. (2015). Electricity derivatives pricing with forward-looking information, *Journal of Economic Dynamics and Control*, 58, 34–57.

Gillani, S. Y. M., Rehman, H. U. and Gill, A. R. (2009). Unemployment, poverty, inflation and crime nexus: Cointegration and causality analysis of Pakistan, *Pakistan Economic and Social Review*, 79, 79–98.

Gottesman, A. (2016). *Derivatives Essentials: An Introduction to Forwards, Futures, Options and Swaps*, John Wiley & Sons.

Göçmen, G. (2007). Türkiye'de Bankacılık Sektörünün Bilanço DışıFaaliyetlerindeki Gelişmeler. Dumlupınar Üniversitesi Sosyal Bilimler Dergisi, (17), 1–21.

Hassan, M. K., Karels, G. V. and Peterson, M. O. (1994). Deposit insurance, market discipline and off-balance sheet banking risk of large US commercial banks, *Journal of Banking & Finance*, 18(3), 575–593.

Hendershott, T. and Madhavan, A. (2015). Click or call? Auction versus search in the over-the-counter market, *The Journal of Finance*, 70(1), 419–447.

Hsiao, Y. J. and Tsai, W. C. (2018). Financial literacy and participation in the derivatives markets, *Journal of Banking & Finance*, 88, 15–29.

Hsu, P. H., Tian, X. and Xu, Y. (2014). Financial development and innovation: Cross-country evidence, *Journal of Financial Economics*, 112(1), 116–135.

Hundman, K. (1999). An analysis of the determinants of financial derivative use by commercial banks, *The Part Place Economists*, 7, 83–92.

Huynh, T. L. D., Nguyen, S. P. and Duong, D. (2018, January). Pricing assets with higher co-moments and value-at-risk by quantile regression approach: Evidence from Vietnam stock market, in *International Econometric Conference of Vietnam*, Springer, Cham, pp. 953–986.

Jagtiani, J. and Khanthavit, A. (1996). Scale and scope economies at large banks: Including off-balance sheet products and regulatory effects (1984–1991), *Journal of Banking & Finance*, 20(7), 1271–1287.

Juhász, P. (2016). Management under limited information–the measurement of off-balance sheet assets at hungarian firms, *Central European Business Review*, 5(4), 23–33.

Kassim, S. H. and Abdul Manap, T. A. (2008). The information content of the Islamic interbank money market rate in Malaysia, *International Journal of Islamic and Middle Eastern Finance and Management*, 1(4), 304–312.

Kaunda, M. A. (2015). Forward–backward-difference time-integrating schemes with higher order derivatives for non-linear finite element analysis of solids and structures, *Computers & Structures*, 153, 1–18.

Kelly, R. (2008). *The causal relationship between inflation and inflation expectations in the United Kingdom* (No. 24). External MPC Unit Discussion Paper.

Kum, H., Ocal, O. and Aslan, A. (2012). The relationship among natural gas energy consumption, capital and economic growth: Bootstrap-corrected causality tests from G-7 countries, *Renewable and Sustainable Energy Reviews*, 16(5), 2361–2365.

Leoni, P., Vandaele, N. and Vanmaele, M. (2014). Hedging strategies for energy derivatives, *Quantitative Finance*, 14(10), 1725–1737.

Li, S. (2018). The use of financial derivatives and risks of US bank holding companies, in *Financial Institutions in the Global Financial Crisis*, Springer, Singapore, pp. 9–67.

Loganathan, N., Sukemi, M. N. and Kogid, M. (2011). Dynamic causal relationship between trade balance and unemployment scenario in Malaysia: Granger non-causality analysis, *Economics and Finance Review*, 1(3), 13–20.

Lotfalipour, M. R., Falahi, M. A. and Ashena, M. (2010). Economic growth, CO2 emissions, and fossil fuels consumption in Iran, *Energy*, 35(12), 5115–5120.

Lundqvist, S. A. and Vilhelmsson, A. (2018). Enterprise risk management and default risk: Evidence from the banking industry, *Journal of Risk and Insurance*, 85(1), 127–157.

Majid, M. S. A. and Hasin, Z. (2014). Islamic banks and monetary transmission mechanism in Malaysia, *Journal of Economic Cooperation and Development*, 35(2), 137.

Maghrebi, N., Iqbal, Z. and Mirakhor, A. (2016). Scope of financial engineering and derivatives, *Intermediate Islamic Finance*, 12, 171–222.

Manap, T. A. A., Abduh, M. and Omar, M. A. (2012). Islamic banking-growth nexus: Evidence from Toda–Yamamoto and bootstrap granger causality test, *Journal of Islamic Finance*, 1(1).

Meidani, A. A. N., Zabihi, M. and Ashena, M. (2011). House prices, economic output, and inflation interactions in Iran, *Research in Applied Economics*, 3(1), 1.

Miao, H., Ramchander, S., Wang, T. and Yang, J. (2018). The impact of crude oil inventory announcements on prices: Evidence from derivatives markets, *Journal of Futures Markets*, 38(1), 38–65.

Mizgier, K. J. and Wimmer, M. (2018). Incorporating single and multiple losses in operational risk: A multi-period perspective, *Journal of the Operational Research Society*, 69(3), 1–14.

Munoz, M. and Miranda, E. (2016, July). A fuzzy system for estimating premium cost of option exchange using Mamdani inference: Derivates market of Mexico, in *2016 IEEE International Conference on Fuzzy Systems (FUZZ-IEEE)*, IEEE, pp. 888–895.

Nezhad, M. Z. and Zarea, R. (2007). Investigating the causality Granger relationship between the rates of interest and inflation in Iran, *Journal of Social Science*, 3(4), 237–244.

Nguyen, Q., Kim, T. and Papanastassiou, M. (2018). Policy uncertainty, derivatives use, and firm-level FDI, *Journal of International Business Studies*, 49(1), 96–126.

Norfield, T. (2012). Derivatives and capitalist markets: The speculative heart of capital, *Historical Materialism*, 20(1), 103–132.

Obradovic, S. and Grbic, M. (2015). Causality relationship between financial intermediation by banks and economic growth: Evidence from Serbia, *Prague Economic Papers*, 24(1), 60–72.

Oktar, S. and Yüksel, S. (2015). *Bankacilik Krizlerinin Erken Uyari Sinyalleri: Türkiye Üzerine Bir Uygulama, İstanbul Ticaret Üniversitesi Sosyal Bilimler Dergisi*, 14(28), 37.

Oktar, S. and Yüksel, S. (2016). *Bankalarin Türev Ürün Kullanimini Etkileyen Faktörler: Mars Yöntemi ile Bir Inceleme* (Determinants of the use derivatives in banking: An analysis with MARS model), *Finans Politik & Ekonomik Yorumlar*, 53(620), 31.

Okuyan, H. A. (2014). The effect of asymmetric information on Turkish banking sector and credit markets, *Revue économique*, 65(5), 699–708.

Özdemir, Z. A. and Fisunoğlu, M. (2008). On the inflation-uncertainty hypothesis in Jordan, Philippines and Turkey: A long memory approach, *International Review of Economics & Finance*, 17(1), 1–12.

Pandian, R. (2015). A study on financial derivatives (futures & options), *International Journal of Research in Business Management*, 3(3), 1–15.

Park, K. (2014). Controlled drug delivery systems: Past forward and future back, *Journal of Controlled Release*, 190, 3–8.

Pasiouras, F. (2008). Estimating the technical and scale efficiency of Greek commercial banks: The impact of credit risk, off-balance sheet activities, and international operations, *Research in International Business and Finance*, 22(3), 301–318.

Patrick, M. U. M. U. (2016). A comparison of prices generated by the derivative commodity model (Ornstein–Uhlenbeck process) with those obtained by the conventional arbitrage-free method of pricing forward derivatives with respect to tea in Nduti tea factory Kenya, *Journal of Statistics and Actuarial Research*, 1(1), 12–23.

Payne, J. E. (2009). On the dynamics of energy consumption and output in the US, *Applied Energy*, 86(4), 575–577.

Pirie, W. L. (2017). *Derivatives*, John Wiley & Sons.

Popova, I. and Simkins, B. (2015). OTC vs. exchange traded derivatives and their impact on hedging effectiveness and corporate capital requirements, *Journal of Applied Corporate Finance*, 27(1), 63–70.

Prasad, K. and Suprabha, K. R. (2018). Exchange rate exposure and usage of foreign currency derivatives by Indian nonfinancial firms, in *The Impact of Globalization on International Finance and Accounting*, Springer, Cham, pp. 71–80.

Pushkala, N., Mahamayi, J. and Venkatesh, K. A. (2017). Liquidity and off-balance sheet items: A comparative study of public and private sector banks in India, *SDMIMD Journal of Management*, 8(1), 47–54.

Rahman, A. A. and Md Ramli, R. (2015). Islamic cross currency swap (ICCS): Hedging against currency fluctuations, *Emerald Emerging Markets Case Studies*, 5(4), 1–12.

Salahuddin, M. and Gow, J. (2016). The effects of internet usage, financial development and trade openness on economic growth in South Africa: A time series analysis, *Telematics and Informatics*, 33(4), 1141–1154.

Sami, J. (2013). Remmittances, banking sector development and economic growth in Fiji, *International Journal of Economics and Financial Issues*, 3(2), 503.

Sayın, K. Ş. (2009). Türk Bankacılık Sisteminde Bilanço Dışı İşlemler Ve Risk Yönetimi Açısından Değerlendirilmesi. Dokuz Eylül Üniversitesi İktisadi İdari Bilimler Fakültesi Dergisi, 24(1), 15–41.

Selimler, H. and Kale, S. (2012). *Türk Bankacılık Sektöründe Bilanço Dışı İşlemlerin Risk Ve Karlılık Açısından Değerlendirilmesi* (Evaluation of the Off-Balance Sheet Activities of the Turkish Banking Sector with Risk and Profitability Approach, *Marmara Üniversitesi İİB Dergisi*, 33(2), 173–204.

Shen, F., Ma, X., Li, Z., Xu, Z. and Cai, D. (2018). An extended intuitionistic fuzzy TOPSIS method based on a new distance measure with an application to credit risk evaluation, *Information Sciences*, 428, 105–119.

Soytas, U. and Sari, R. (2009). Energy consumption, economic growth, and carbon emissions: challenges faced by an EU candidate member, *Ecological economics*, 68(6), 1667–1675.

Strat, V. A., Davidescu, A. and Paul, A. M. (2015). FDI and the unemployment-A causality analysis for the latest EU members, *Procedia Economics and Finance*, 23, 635–643.

Suresh, G. and Krishnan, P. A. (2018). Asset–liability management as a risk management tool in commercial banks in India, *IUP Journal of Bank Management*, 17(1), 21–49.

Swain, A. K. and Panda, G. P. (2017). Off balance sheet exposure of public sector banks in India: An empirical analysis, *Imperial Journal of Interdisciplinary Research*, 3(2).

Tanha H., and Dempsey, M. (2017). Derivatives usage in emerging markets following the GFC: Evidence from the GCC countries, *Emerging Markets Finance and Trade*, 53(1), 170–179.

Toda, H. Y. and Yamamoto, T. (1995). Statistical inference in vector autoregressions with possibly integrated processes, *Journal of Econometrics*, 66(1–2), 225–250.

Torruam, J. T. and Abur, C. (2014). The relationship between unemployment, inflation and crime: An application of cointegration and causality analysis in Nigeria, *Journal of Economics and Sustainable Development*, 5(4), 131–137.

Umar, M. and Dahalan, J. (2015). Evidence on real exchange rate-inflation causality: An application of Toda–Yamamoto dynamic granger causality test, *International Business Management*, 9(5), 666–675.

Venkatesh, K. A., Pushkala, N., and Mahamayi, J. (2017). Profit efficiency of foreign banks in India in the context of off-balance sheet items: A DEA approach. *International Journal of Engineering Technology Science and Research*, 4(9), 1379–1386.

Whaley, R. E. (2007). *Derivatives: Markets, Valuation, and Risk Management*, Vol. 345, John Wiley & Sons.

Wolde-Rufael, Y. (2006). Electricity consumption and economic growth: A time series experience for 17 African countries, *Energy Policy*, 34(10), 1106–1114.

Yüksel, S. (2016b). *Alternatif Finans Teknikleri ve Türev Ürünler*, in *Uluslararası Finans Teori ve Politika*, Orion Kitabevi, pp. 311–355.

Yüksel, S. and Özsarı, M. (2016). Impact of consumer loans on inflation and current account deficit: A Toda–Yamamoto causality test for Turkey, *World Journal of Applied Economics*, 2(2), 3–14.

Yüksel, S. and Zengin, S. (2016). Causality relationship between import, export and growth rate in developing countries, *International Journal of Commerce and Finance*, 2(1), 147.

Yüksel, S. (2016a). *Bankacılık Krizlerinin Erken Uyarı Sinyalleri: Türkiye Üzerine Bir Uygulama*, Akademisyen Yayınevi, Ankara.

Yüksel, S., Dinçer, H. and Emir, Ş. (2017). Comparing the performance of Turkish deposit banks by using DEMATEL, grey relational analysis (GRA) and MOORA approaches, *World Journal of Applied Economics*, 3(2), 26–47.

Zengin, S. and Yuksel, S. (2016). A comparison of the views of internal controllers/auditors and branch/call center personnel of the banks for operational risk: A case for Turkish banking sector, *International Journal of Finance & Banking Studies* (2147–4486), 5(4), 10–29.

Chapter 7

The Risk-Sharing Paradigm in Islamic Financial System: Myth or Reality?

Jamel Boukhatem[*,†,§] and Mouldi Djelassi[*,‡,¶]

*Department of Banking and Financial Markets, College of Islamic Economics and Finance, Umm al Qura University, Saudi Arabia
†Department of Economics, Faculty of Economic sciences and Management FSEGT, University of Tunis el Manar, Tunisia
‡High school of Economic and Business Sciences ESSECT, University of Tunis, Tunisia
§jeboukhatem@uqu.edu.sa, jboukhatem@yahoo.com
¶madjelassi@uqu.edu.sa, jelassi19631963@gmail.com

1. Introduction

The present chapter discusses the evolution of the role of banks in the allocation of risks in an Islamic economy. Concern about this issue arises from the following four observations: (1) At the end of the 19th century, Islamic and non-Islamic scholars imagine an Islamic financial system based on Islamic values and principles as an alternative to the western financial system (Rosly, 1999). They envisioned banks as a change agent, which will promote values like cooperation, welfare, risk, and profit-sharing relationships, while promoting development, growth, and financial inclusion, (2) in practice,

Islamic banks over the world operate in dual banking system that competes with conventional banks; they have been undergoing substantial changes compared to the original business model. Some of the changes involve quite drastic reallocations of both resources and certain risks. For instance, Islamic banks have oriented their financing activities more to debt instruments and they moved from risk-sharing paradigm to risk transfer.[1] (3) The 2007 and 2008 years have seen a recurrence of banking crises in several countries, raising the spectrum that debt-based system with risk transfer mechanism may be a substantial source of risks for the rest of the economy. According to some authors, equity-based system with risk-sharing principal may be a substantial source of stability and constitute an adequate solution for the debt crisis. (4) Economic theory has yet little to say about this gap between theory and practice of Islamic banking. Theories of risk allocation in an Islamic environment are typically presented in a context of equity contract and 100% reserve system; in this system, there is no room for credit and liquidity risk. Theories of Islamic financial intermediation are typically presented in a setting of markets in which no gain without risk and skin in the game principles resolve the problems of agency problems and lead to efficient allocation of business risk. Finally, theories of risk-sharing in Islamic banking system are typically presented in a setting in which the financial intermediary and depositor play an active monitoring role and are not considered simply as ordinary agents.

Given these observations, we see a need for a systematic theoretical assessment on the role of Islamic financial intermediation in allocating risks in the economy including the role of risk-taking by Islamic financial intermediaries themselves in dual banking system. This chapter makes a start towards such an assessment. We will try to understand the theoretical foundations of equity-based system and the adoption of risk-sharing paradigm in Islamic finance; we have also

---

[1]The original model based on risk and profit-sharing relationships can be referred to as "strongly" Islamic and the practical model, which resembles interest-based modes of transactions, is referred to as "weakly" Islamic (Mirakhor, 2010; The Kuala Lumpur Declaration, 2012; Askari *et al.*, 2012; Iqbal and Mirakhor, 2013; Alaabed *et al.*, 2015).

indicated their merits and their limits with respect to the analysis of recent and ongoing developments in the Islamic financial sector.

The major theoretical characteristics of Islamic banking model is the good risk match between the assets side and the liabilities side of a bank. A bank that collects demand deposits is not exposed to withdraw risk because it adopts the 100% reserves rule. Concerning investment deposits, the Islamic bank uses them to finance projects under the Mudharaba contract: the profits are distributed between bank and the investment account holders (IAHs) if the project succeeds; if not (loss), the bank is not exposed to this risk of borrower's defaults because the IAHs are considered as residual claimant. Islamic banks provide a great effort of selection and monitoring of the projects to reduce the probability of the recurrence of bad event (risk of losses); some of these risks may "disappear" through diversification. If despite this effort, these risks occur (the case of non-diversifiable risks), this does not lead to the banking failure because any shocks on assets side are passed on the liabilities side. In conventional banking system, effects of this sort led to banking crises. The question is, why in practice Islamic banks do not follow the risk-sharing strategy and try to protect their depositors from non-diversifiable risks?

Many economists charged competition from conventional banks and statutory regulation as the main reason responsible for the deviation behavior of Islamic banks from the original risk-sharing model. Without denying the importance of statutory regulation in banking or the detrimental effects of certain depositor behavior driven by profit goals, we are not convinced that this is the entire story. To understand the phenomenon, we need to overlook the fact that the lack of risk-sharing in Islamic banks is due to institutional and legal constraints. For example, The IAHs suffer the same consequences as a shareholder without having the same rights. they cannot sit on the board of directors, don't have any voting power, or the possibilities to sell their assets on the markets. In the *Mudharaba* contract, the entrepreneur has a measure of managerial independence. There is a *sharia* ruling that it is not permissible for the bank to interfere in the running of the work in order to administer the execution of the project. Given that the entrepreneur is not fully supervised, and his effort cannot be contracted, due to these constraints and undesirable features, PLS contract like Mudharaba is an inefficient risk-sharing mode and depositors are naturally averse to PLS contracts.

The remainder of this chapter is organized as follows: Section 2 describes framework of PLS (equity-based) financial system and risk-sharing paradigm. Section 3 describes the Islamic banking system in operation and compromised risk-sharing: the evolution to non-profit and loss sharing "Non-PLS" system, to debt-based system. Section 4 discusses an organizational framework for the Islamic banking industry: some proposals for effective and efficient risk sharing.

2.   Framework of Equity Oriented Financial System (EOFS) and Risk-Sharing Paradigm

The original model of Islamic finance tries to explain how a banking system could work without interest.[2] This theoretical model is an equity-based system in which different stake-holders share profits and losses of the projects.

2.1.   *Features of Islamic financial intermediation in equity-based financial system*

Islamic jurists treat interest (*ribaa*) as an act of exploitation and a form of injustice and its prohibition leads to justice and the respect of property rights. In Islamic jurisprudence, there are no gains or profits without risk. The interest is a gain obtained by the lender as provider of capital without taking the business risk, which is completely borne

---

[2]Until the late sixties, the developments of Islamic finance were mostly on the theoretical plane. The practical experimentation at large scale has started in the early 1970s by the creation of the first Islamic banks one in private sector (Dubai Islamic Bank) and another as a multilateral organization (Islamic Development Bank). For more details on the history and intellectual evolution of modern Islamic economics and finance, we can refer to Islahi (1997), Ahmad (2000), and Kahf (2005).

by the entrepreneur. The owner of capital must restitute his capital without any surplus. Therefore, the prohibition of interests poses the central question as to what replaces the interest rate mechanism in an Islamic framework? If the debt contract based on paying and receiving interest is prohibited, how do Islamic banks operate? The Islamic banking system has two alternative mechanisms of resources allocation and financial intermediation: the first is based on profit–loss sharing and the second involves modes which depend on fixed return (mark-up) (Table 1).

Table 1: Typical balance sheet of an Islamic bank.

Assets	Liabilities
Asset-backed transactions (*Murabaha, Ijara*, etc.)	Demand deposits (*Wadi'ah* with 100% reserve)
Mudharaba	Investment accounts (*Mudharaba* with low risk aversion)
Musharaka	Equity (participation in riskier investments)

The liabilities of an Islamic bank in equity-based system are divided into current accounts and investment accounts. Demand deposit accounts are setup on the principle of safekeeping without any interest paid to depositors. Bank provides safekeeping and liquidity facility into these accounts with management fees paid by the customers. The bank cannot utilize these accounts for financing activities. In fact, simply said, demand deposit is held by banks under the form of 100% reserve.[3]

Investment accounts are setup on the principle of risk keeping (*Mudharaba*) with return paid by the bank under profit and loss sharing mechanism. Depositors as owner of capital (Rabb elMal) provide capital and the bank (*El-mudharib*) provides expertise (his

---

[3]This is also the essence of the Chicago Plan, proposed in the aftermath of the great depression by leading American economists. The proposal advocates a 100% reserve against demand deposits and no deposit insurance for investment deposits (see Askri *et al.*, 2012; Benes and Kumof, 2012; Mirakhor *et al.*, 2012).

management skills into the business). The profit-sharing rate shall be determined and mutually agreed between the bank and the IAHs. In the event of loss, the IAHs bear all the financial losses and the banker as manager of funds loses his time and his work. It is the risk of capital loss by IAHs and the risk of wasted effort by the banker that entitle these two parties to a share in the profits. The bank as manager of funds (*El-mudharib*) utilizes the investment deposits under restricted or unrestricted forms. In restricted Mudharaba, IAHs stipulate certain conditions concerning the uses of their funds and the maturity date of the contract. Unrestricted *Mudharaba*, however, gave the banks greater flexibility in the management process and to use available funds. Simply said, investment deposits (particularly, under unrestricted form) can be considered as a long-term resource used to finance long-term, high-risk, and low-liquid assets. Theoretically, all the investment account holders accept the financial loss without creating the danger of a bank failure.

The assets of Islamic banks are divided into two categories: markup (fixed return)-based contract and equity-based contract. Markup-based contract are setup on the principle of trade of goods or service with profit margin charged by the bank under sales contract (*Murabaha*) mechanism. Banks sell or lease goods and receive fixed return. Simply said, debt associated with *Murabaha* financing are short-term, low-risk, and high-liquid assets held by banks.[4]

The equity-based assets are setup on the principle of risk keeping (*Mudharaba/Musharaka*) with uncertain return paid by the entrepreneur. Mudharaba (or PLS contract) can be considered as a mode of financing on partnership between two parties: the bank as delegated manager of investment account funds and the entrepreneur. The bank provides capital and the entrepreneur provides his management skills into the business. The profit-sharing rate shall be determined and mutually agreed between the bank and the entrepreneur, before the beginning of the project. In the event of loss, the bank bears all the financial losses and the entrepreneur manager loses his

---

[4]Unlike conventional debt, such debt is not marketable except at its nominal value.

time and his work. It is the risk of capital loss by bank and the risk of wasted effort by the entrepreneur that entitle these two parties to a share in the profits. This is the principle of Mudharaba. Simply said, *Mudharaba* financing are long-term, high-risk and low-liquid assets.

Musharaka is the second main equity-based contract under which a bank and its customers contribute jointly to finance a project. It may be left to the partners to decide the ratios of profit-sharing profit. However, loss must be borne in proportion to capital contribution.[5] In the context of business and trade, it means a joint enterprise in which all the partners share the profit or loss of the joint venture.[6]

2.2. Mechanism of risk management in equity-based financial system: No gain without risk

The equity-based financial system is based on risk-sharing as a mechanism of risk management rather than risk transfer/risk shifting, which is the chief characteristic of the debt-based financial system. In conventional finance, risk transfer constitutes a mechanism of risk management where the risk of a contract is passed by one of the parties to the contract to another. In this system, the axiom of self-interest implies that the economic agents stake risks because they can benefit from the potential positive outcome while passing on any potential low end of the risk-return distribution to someone less averse to risk.[7] An example is a bank deposit contract where the depositor passes the risk to the bank and does not bear the loss of capital. In turn, the bank passes the risk to a borrower who bears the credit risk. In Islamic finance, the axiom of takaful (cooperation between the contractual parties) implies that the outcome of the random event (profits or losses) must be borne collectively by a group of individuals or entities involved in a contract. This position

---

[5] It is this principle that has been mentioned in the famous maxim: "Profit is based on the agreement of the parties, but loss is always subject to the ratio of investment."

[6] For more details, see Taqi Usmani (1999).

[7] In equity arrangement (i.e. *Mudharaba* contract), the *ex post* profit and loss are *ex ante* risk-sharing. In debt arrangement, the *ex post* profit is *ex ante* risk-sharing, while, the *ex post* loss is *ex ante* risk transfer.

is summarized in two Islamic legal maxims: no gain without risk and earning commensurate with liability (respectively, the Arabic form of the maxims *al-gunm-bi-al-ghurm* and *al-kharaj-bi-Etthamen*).[8] These rules are applicable to both labor and capital factors. As no payment can labor unless it is applied to work, so no reward for capital should be allowed unless it is exposed to business risks. In financial transactions, the *Mudharaba* and the *Musharaka* contracts constitute the two financial instruments which best reflect the principle of risk-sharing. For example, in a Mudharaba contract, IAHs and banks accept to share the business risk with the entrepreneur in exchange for returns; in this arrangement, the risk is not transferred but shared among the three participants with their explicit knowledge and consent. When the bank realizes that there is a down side risk (losses), it resorts to share it with the entrepreneur rather than pass the risk to the debtor, since the potential profits are shared between the two parties. On the other hand, IAHs as risk sharers accept to share the losses with the bank, since they will be able to achieve higher returns in a reverse situation. More explicitly, in the case of profits, banks, IAHs, and entrepreneurs share this in pre-agreed proportions. In the reverse situation, all financial losses are borne by IAHs as the capital supplier and both bank and entrepreneur are penalized by receiving no return (wages or salary) for their expertise and management activities.

2.3. *Origins of the risk-sharing paradigm in Islamic financial system*

The risk-sharing business model is not only the way to manage risks by Islamic banks, but it represents the values which characterize Islamic banking operation.[9]

---

[8]which corresponds to idea of "skin in the game", suggested by Taleb (2018).

[9]The risk-sharing principle has been envisioned by conventional literature on the allocation of resources in decentralized economy governed by moral-ethical values, complete market, and contracts (Arrow and Debreu, 1954; Arrow and Hahn, 1971). But with time, some of these original principals and ideas of ideal-conventional financial system got diluted, creating a relatively different financial system, which we will refer to as the

What are the major reasons that explain the emergence of the risk-sharing model in Islamic finance? Why the choice of risk-sharing paradigm and not risk transfer or risk shift for Islamic finance? As for origins, there are several explanations put forth for the genesis of the risk-sharing model in the Islamic financial system.

2.3.1. Religion principles (shari'ah objectives: Islamic laws and values)

In Quran, verses 275, 276, 278, and 279 of Chapter 2 deal directly with the concept of risk-sharing. According to these verses, all financial transactions should be done by means of contracts of exchange (*al-Bay*) and should refrain from contracts that are based on interest (no *Ribaa*). The interpretation is clear: the establishment of justice is the main objective of shari'ah and the contracts based on interest lead to injustice. Thus, Islam discourages the believers of shari'ah to engage in this form of contracting, which is interest based. Islam has termed interest as an unjust instrument of financing because it can bring injustice either to the creditor or to the debtor (Usmani, 1999).

On the other hand, interest-based debt contract gives highest attention to the ability to repay loans. According to Dhaigude *et al.* (2015), Islam recommends engaging in contracts that involve dependence on future outcomes to decide on the claim on property rights. Quran not only teaches people to be patient "Allah is with those who are patient" (Chapter 8, verse 46) but also asks them to be ready to be tested with hardships and uncertainties (Chapter 2, verses 76 and 155). These along with a very high degree of impetus on the faithfulness of an individual to their contracts and covenants (Chapter 2, verse 172; Chapter 7, verses 172–173; Chapter 8, verse 32; Chapter 16, verses 91–92; Chapter 17, verse 34), forms the basis of human behavior.

---

conventional/practiced financial system, which prevails in today's world and is characterized by risk transfer and shift principles (Dhaigude *et al.*, 2015).

The risk-sharing hypothesis appears to be related to another influential hypothesis of the Islamic financial system, i.e. the hypothesis concerning no gain without risks or skin in the game.[10] The two Islamic legal maxims: *algunm bi-algurm* (no gain without risk) and *Alkharaj bi-etthamen* (revenue goes with liability) touch as well the concept of risk-sharing. Both stipulate that no rewards without risk. That is to say that the one who gets the benefit of something, must bear also the loss from it. These maxims lead to the profit loss sharing between the contractual parties who form a united group in the face of risks and have a stabilizing effect on the performance of firms. According to this argument, no gain without risk is distinctive in that it works as a mechanism of insurance between contractual parties. As PLS contracting forms the core of the arrangement between the contractual parties, they can be regarded as supporting this insurance mechanism by acting as a main form of contracting between different agents.

2.4.   *The strengths of PLS mechanism*

The PLS contract has several attractive features.

2.4.1.   *PLS mechanism and the resolution of agency problems and problems of asymmetric information: The self-discipline*

The moral hazard problem in PLS contract has been identified as one of the important factors hindering its use in Islamic banking practices. The moral hazard refers to a situation in which the entrepreneur or bank has relevant information that the depositor lacks about the level of the returns of the projects. The term refers to the problem created by asymmetric information after the transaction occurs. In general, moral hazard arises when the entrepreneur uses his superior information on firm performance to work against

---

[10]The term "skin in the game" implies taking risk and being invested in achieving an outcome.

the interest of banks and deposits (Habib, 2002). For example, in PLS contract, the entrepreneur has an incentive to cheat on the true level of profits or absorbs some of the project revenues through perquisites. Also, the bank has an incentive to underreport the income from *Mudharaba* operations. In the PLS contract, the moral hazard problem occurs when the bank's conduct changes after the receipt of the funds from the depositors. It takes the form of the principal–agent problem found by Jensen and Meckling (1976) in equity contracts. The bank acts as an agent using the funds provided by the depositor (the principal). The principal–agent problem arises when the bank misuses the funds, is slack about the selection and the monitoring of the entrepreneur, and underreports the income from Mudharaba operations.

Chapra (2002) and Mirakhor (2010) argue that agency problem is significantly reduced under risk-sharing Islamic finance through its emphasis on the no risk–no gain principle that ensures that IAHs and banks as risky assets holders, are motivated to monitor the activities of the firms. IAHs take high interest in the soundness of the bank as their investments are directly at risk and their returns are impacted by the results of the project (Calomiris, 1999; Distinguin *et al.*, 2013). Thus, Depositors, as investors, are not neutral and will have direct motivation to oversee bank funding on the asset side. In case of current deposit accounts, the agency problem is limited because the bank cannot use this account to finance the acquisitions of any assets.

On the other hand, the bank as delegated to monitor by the depositor has direct motivation to monitor entrepreneurs because its income depends on the outcome of the projects. When the project turns bad because bank managers do not monitor the entrepreneur very well, the bank will suffer and register losses and have everything to gain if the real monitoring is exerted. The presence of explicit risk sharing leads to an adequate and greater market discipline whereby the depositors are motivated to monitor the banks and the banks are incited to monitor the entrepreneurs. According to Chapra (2002), the PLS mechanism strongly motivates the depositors to be cautious in "choosing their bank and the bank management to be more careful in making their loans and investments. Without such risk sharing, the depositors may keep on receiving competitive rates of interest because the banks receive a predetermined higher rate. However, the quality of assets may not be good" and one day, there may be a revelation to the bank examiners about the poor quality of the bank's assets. It would be decided to dump these losses on bank's capital, deposit insurance, or the taxpayers.

We can also suppose a discipline mechanism based on the threat of IAHs to withdraw their saving funds or to refuse the renewing of the placements in investment account by IAHs (Beck *et al.*, 2013; Van Wijnbergen *et al.*, 2013; Abedifar *et al.*, 2013). The deposit market forces decide which Islamic banks survive and which fail. This decision is efficient if the return of deposits reflects all available information on banking results. Given this assumption, any deviation from the objective of maximizing the interest of depositors is reflected in the banking results. In other words, the banks pursuing an objective that maximize their interest to the detriment of depositors will be penalized by the withdrawal or non-renewal of deposits.[11] This decision is a strong incentive for bank managers to manage in accordance with the maximization of the wealth of depositors. This scheme of operation has many practical implications for banks in which depositors hold savings accounts with withdrawal (exit) possibilities or hold short-term investment accounts.

On the asset side, each Islamic bank is itself tied to the market forces via the no risk–no gain principle. Banks as holders of risky assets cannot demand the liquidation of the projects in the situation of losses beyond the control of the entrepreneur. Therefore, project withdrawal may take place and the entrepreneurs only bear losses when they are responsible or accountable for such losses. Moreover, the decision to cancel the project completely or partially may also happen during the project, especially when the entrepreneur is accused of major negligence. These disciplinary measures constitute

---

[11]The disciplinary withdrawal risk is also known as displaced commercial risk.

a strong incentive for firms' managers to manage in accordance with the maximization of the wealth of banks. Since they are concerned with both high and low-probability events, the payoff to banks for exercising very effective control is substantial.

2.4.2. *Absence of systemic risk*

Many authors suggest that Islamic finance based on risk-sharing principle is more volatile at the subsystem (individual bank or individual depositor) level and the risks of failure remain local.[12] At the system level, risk-sharing Islamic finance will be resilient and the risks of failure do not become systemic.

The profit shock undergone by entrepreneurs, will have a negative effect on the income of Islamic banks and the wealth of IAHs (local risk). Since the depositors' claims on banks are not guaranteed in nominal terms, the decreases of bank income will have a negative impact on the wealth of any depositor whose portfolio contains a significant amount of investment accounts. This structure may better resist the shocks to the asset side of the balance sheet because these shocks can be instantaneously absorbed by the liabilities side. This type of adjustment causes the stability of the banking system. In the case of conventional banking system, there exists a dichotomy between assets and liabilities and any shock that hits the assets side can generate instability.

2.4.3. *No interventionism*

The structure of the balance sheet of Islamic banks obviates the need of interventionism — like lender of last resort (LLOR), deposit insurance, or bailouts — aimed to prevent the collapse of the system. On the liability side, the demand deposit accounts are subject to cent per cent reserves and consequently the bank cannot utilize it for any of its own purposes; Theoretically, all the depositors of the

---

[12]Khan (1986) and Mirakhor and Krichene (2009) argue that equity-based finance is stable as assets and liabilities adjust to shocks; making the bank less likely to fall bankrupt and bank run least probable.

bank can simultaneously take out all their demand deposits from the bank without creating the danger of a bank run. Investment deposit accounts operate on a risk-sharing basis. The holders of these accounts cannot demand the repayment of their funds or any return in case of losses as these accounts are tied to the market forces via the no risk–no gain principle. Theoretically, this arrangement eliminates the danger of a bank default in case of losses. Under the conditions of risk-sharing, all investors are aware of the risks involved and must bear the consequences of their investment choices.

2.4.4. *PLS mechanism and positive asymmetry*

In the PLS contract, IAHs provide the funds, the banks provide the selection and the monitoring of the projects, and the entrepreneurs provide work; the three parties agree to the division of any profits made in advance. There exists a linearity between the rewards of the three parties and the performance of the project undertaken. An increase of the profit level leads to an increase of the rewards of each party. In some circumstances, linearity can be regarded as an efficient way to share the good state between all parties. It may provide a perfect alignment of interest between the bank and the entrepreneur, and hence induce appropriate incentive for the bank to select good investment projects and to monitor the entrepreneur, while the entrepreneur maximizes profits of the projects. If no profit is made, the financial loss is borne by the depositors and the bank and the entrepreneurs take no remuneration for their expertise and work. The losses of IAHs are limited to their capital, the losses of the banks are restricted to their selection and monitoring costs, and the losses of the entrepreneurs don't exceed the remuneration of their efforts (wages).

2.5. *The weakness of PLS mechanism: The lack of risk-sharing prerequisites and the failures of market discipline mechanism to allocate risk*

Despite the several attractive features, the PLS mechanism has many limits. Risk-sharing Islamic finance believes in self-regulation through the market discipline, which is designed to curtail bad behavior of banks and entrepreneurs. There are many fundamental limits or failures in market discipline strategy leading PLS contract to be an inefficient risk-sharing mode.

IAHs suffer the same consequences as a shareholder without having the same rights. IAHs reward is dependent of the realized outcome which is mainly dependent upon the effort level of the entrepreneur and his avoidance of perquisites. Therefore, they do not have the means to defend themselves in case of mismanagement; they cannot sit on the board of directors, don't have any voting power, or the possibilities to sell their assets on the markets. In *Mudharaba* contract, the entrepreneur has a measure of managerial independence. Given that the entrepreneur is not fully supervised, and his effort cannot be contracted, the bank, as delegated monitor, can withdraw from the project, especially when the entrepreneur is accused of major negligence. These undesirable features increase the discretionary power of the entrepreneur and put him in the position of sole owner–manager projects, without bearing the risk of financial losses.

- The bank must have the technical capability to evaluate the projects, to monitor the project execution, and in the situation of losses it must verify the causes because, according to *Mudharaba* rules, the entrepreneur will suffer the consequences if the bank proves that he has caused the losses.
- Too-big-to-fail and too-correlated-to-fail and a too-interlinked-to-fail financial system constitute obstacles to the good functioning of the deposit market discipline. The way the failure of a single bank, Lehman Brothers, threatened to bring down the entire economy illustrates the risk of being too interconnected-to-fail. These obstacles increase the discretionary power of the bank *vis-à-vis* of IAHs and puts the bank in the position of sole owner of capital, without bearing the risk of financial losses.
- **The myopia of deposit market discipline:** Myopia and short-sightedness of investment deposit market are the other concerning undesirable effects of market discipline. Depositors are not able to

assess the future profitability of certain types of investments. The bank can finance projects that prove profitable in the short term for depositors, while having negative repercussions on the firm's future. Since the market for depositors is short-sighted (myopia), it encourages banks to finance projects with short-term gains, not with the long-term returns. Companies engaged in long-term investments will not be financed. The threat of withdrawing or changing banks by depositors leads to poor allocation of resources. The banks, which fear being the target of a threat of withdrawal and the loss of market share, adopt a financing strategy that favors short-term considerations, to the detriment of the long-term goals. The bank managers will reduce the financing of projects requiring more research and development expenses, in order to allocate priority deposits to projects generating immediate cash flow. This practice is intended to ensure the depositors' satisfaction and not for rational considerations.

- **Public good nature of monitoring by depositors:** In PLS contract, depositors have an incentive to gather information to ascertain that the banks acted in the depositors' interests. Then, the depositor would have to bear considerable information costs and any gains that accrue to the single depositor as a result of his actions accrue to all depositors and shareholders. Thus, it is not in the interests of any depositor to devote much attention to the performance of a firm and to bear information costs. It is in his interest to be a free rider. Thus, depositors have certain rights to control banks, they do not individually have the incentive required to induce them to exercise those rights.

- **The structure of bank market:** While they do not have access to similar risk management tools, Islamic banks must compete with conventional financial intermediaries. The PLS mechanism is fragile and that competition from conventional banks can lead profit driven investors and good firms to switch from Islamic banks to conventional banks (displaced commercial risk, DCR).

- **Asymmetric risk of PLS contract:** The presence of asymmetric information between banks, entrepreneurs, and IAHs can lead to asymmetric risk because the results of the projects and the income from bank investments are driven by non-market forces (operational risks). The result of adverse selection and moral hazard is that Islamic banks are subject to asymmetric risk because the project fails not due to business risk but due to the discretionary behavior of the firm's manager. On the other hand, the result of asymmetric information between IAHs and banks is that depositors are subject to asymmetric risk because the project fails not due to business risk but due to the opportunist behavior of banks. Imperfect information means that *Mudharaba* market cannot work and develop well due to a distorted yield. IAHs can accept the performance risk of the entrepreneur if the bank fully assumes its delegated monitoring and financing role because they can benefit from positive upside opportunities; if it's not the case, IAHs undergo the performance risk of the entrepreneur and the risk associated with opportunism behavior of banks leading to a situation where the Islamic banking system ends up in a negatively asymmetric position where the downside losses of investment account outweigh the downside benefits. This very risk deposit contract is never held. It is dominated by the safe asset (current account or conventional saving deposits). The current account has a zero return but not subject to the uncertainty of the risky asset's value (fixed nominal value).

- **Lack of moral dimension:** No efficient risk-sharing without trust; the trust deficit.

Islam encourages risk-sharing to promote social solidarity. Sharing allows risk to be spread and thus lowered for individual participants (Mirakhor, 2012). The mutuality element in risk-sharing means high level of trust is required between transaction parties. With low trust, the success of risk-sharing depends on the observance of rule of law and the existing of legal institutions that protect property, shareholders, and depositors' rights, and enforce contracts. Arrow (1971) identified trust as a lubricant for the smooth functioning of an economy. He proposed, "it is possible that the process of exchange

requires or at least is greatly facilitated by the presence of several . . .
virtues (not only truth, but also trust, loyalty and justice in future
dealings). The virtue of truthfulness in fact contributes in a very
significant way to the efficiency of the economic system . . . ethical
behavior can be regarded as a socially desirable institution which
facilitates the achievement of economic efficiency in a broad sense"
(Arrow, 1971, pp. 345–346). For example, in an economy where trust
is very strong, simple contracts may be a surrogate for a complete
contract as the contracting parties' trust is so high that at the time of
contingency the terms and conditions of the contract may be reversed
without much problem.

According to Shaikh (2010), "Islamic values like justice, equality,
truth, trust, kindness, honesty, and responsibility are often discussed
in literature and seminars on Islamic economics; whereas the lack of
these values in practice is the major reason why preferable partici-
patory modes remain unusable."

These conditions of trust: loyalty and justice, are not respected in
most Muslim countries who operate Islamic banks. Islamicity index
for individual countries reveals an indisputable fact: Muslim countries are not the best representatives of underlying Islamic values,
especially when it comes to economics and economic justice. The
highest performers on the Islamicity index were the advanced countries like New Zeland, Luxembourg, Ireland; with the top Muslim
country, Malaysia, at rank 38 and the others like Kuwait at 48,
Bahrain at 64 (Askari *et al.*, 2012).

Due to these constraints and undesirable features, PLS contract
like *Mudharaba* is an inefficient risk-sharing mode and depositors have
a natural aversion for PLS contract. In other words, PLS contract
makes the financiers participate in the risks of business, but legal and
institutional obstacles prevent financiers to assess the risks more care-
fully and to monitor the borrowers. To overcome the problems associated with intermediation activity based on *Mudharaba* mode, Islamic
banks adopt an adjusted business model. They reduce the asset's
risk by choosing to finance the projects according to the *Murabaha*
mode and on the liability side they adopt a system of risk smoothing.

Thus, Islamic banking is farther from its origin model of PLS and moves more and more towards conventional finance practices.

3. The Islamic Banking System in Operation and Compromized Risk-sharing: The Evolution to Non-profit and Loss Sharing (Non-PLS System or Non-equity — Debt-based — system)

Principal idea: Islamic banking system smooths the profit shock rather than pass it on to depositors (application of debt-like conventional mechanism).

The ideal-Islamic financial system assumes a risk-sharing strategy in an economy that is governed by Islamic values. But in practice, some of these original principles and ideas of equity-based financial system got adjusted, creating a relatively different financial system, which we will refer to as Islamic/practical financial system, which prevails in today's Islamic world and is characterized by the risk smoothing principle.

3.1. *Islamic financial intermediation in practice*

The practice of Islamic financial intermediation differs from its conceptual foundations outlined in the first section in notably four aspects: income allocation policies, Islamic bank preference for liquidity, implementation of the risk-sharing principle, and governance rights granted to investment account holders.

3.1.1. *Liabilities*

The liabilities of a practical Islamic banking system are more oriented to debt instruments. Demand deposits accounts are considered as a free interest debt.[13] According to this principle, Islamic bank grants the nominal value of deposits and liquidity facility into these

---

[13] *Qard-al-Hassan* (generous loans, given on very easy terms with no expectations of returns).

accounts and in counterparties, it is the only one who benefits from
any output from the using of these funds. In fact, simply said, demand
deposits are held by banks under the fractional reserve rule. Investment accounts continue to be considered as a *Mudharaba* contract
with a mechanism of smoothing the profit shock rather than passing
it on to IAHs (adjusted Mudharaba contract).

In a competitive environment, Islamic banks are encouraged to
redistribute enough profits to avoid the flight of their customers to
the conventional banking sector. The rate of profit announced to the
owners of the investment accounts does not reflect what the bank is
able to offer. This forces Islamic banks to strengthen their capitalization, which they would normally not do if they strictly applied
the principle of PLS (pure model) and made the risks to be assumed
only by their IAHs.

3.1.2. *Assets*

On the assets side, the bank employs those funds collected from
depositors to finance essentially short-term, low-risk, asset-backed
transactions (*Murabaha, Ijara*, etc.). Bank uses directly the deposit
funds for real transactions without recourse to entrepreneurs or without investing in capital projects, and the remuneration of the bank is
directly related to these debt and quasi-debt instruments under the
form of markup and rents.[14]

In this new model of intermediation, Islamic banks continue to
finance projects with long-term instruments like Mudharaba and
Musharaka, but rarely.

In this form of intermediation, the principal of deposit accounts
and income are guaranteed and do not support risk (only, profit-
sharing and not losses). On the assets side and contrary to contracts

---

[14]The Murabaha contract is an Islamic alternative to bank credit; it involves three
actors: (i) the entrepreneur client who wishes to purchase a good, (ii) the Islamic bank
that buys the goods on request and according to the instructions of its customer (the
entrepreneur), and (iii) the seller of the good. The Islamic bank resells the property to
its customer with a profit margin with immediate or staggered payment. However, the
assets purchased remain the property of the bank until settlement of the last payment.

Assets	Liabilities
Asset-backed transactions or markup financing; non-profit loss sharing arrangements, non-PLS (*Murabaha*, *Ijara*, etc.)	Demand deposits (*qard-hacen*, with fractional reserves)
PLS arrangements: *Mudharaba* and *Musharaka*	Investment accounts (*Mudharaba*, with high risk aversion) Equity (with CAR)

based on the PLS principal, this model has a predetermined and fixed rate of return and is associated with collateral. If most depositors prove to be averse to risk, they will have the motivation to deposit their money in banks because the high level of risk related to direct trade is assumed by banks.

Bitar and Madiès (2013) demonstrate the dominant role of commercial operations (i.e. asset-backed transactions) which represent, on average, over the period 2000–2011, 90% of the activities of Islamic banks. The contracts of Moudharaba and Mousharaka constitute for the same period only 5% of the activities of the Islamic banks. It should be noted that the Murabaha contract, which accounts for 80% of the activities of Islamic banks, predominates in commercial operations.

3.2. What might be the factors behind the changes in the Islamic banking structure?

When the model of Islamic banks started in the Muslim countries, lending was oriented to financing the projects that sustain growth, industry, and development. However, in practice, asset-backed transactions soon became the primary banking activities. Still, Islamic bankers tried to make their financing secure, through collateral and assignment of ownership rights in case of default. Also, Islamic bankers tried to cover IAHs against profit shocks, through the holding of large reserves and appropriate capital. This activity is not intrinsically different from that of a conventional bank.

The change in the acceptable riskiness of Islamic bank activities can be traced to the origins of equity-based Islamic banking. Equity-based Islamic banking was both a different type of institution and a different concept from conventional banking activity. The theoretical framework of Islamic financial intermediation developed in the 20th century introduced a different philosophy of banking, since it involved financial resources to industry rather than being a simple lender and getting good guarantees. This implies making more risky investments and more risky placements for IAHs. the assessment of risk and the estimation of the risk return on a bank financing is one of the main functions of an equity-based banking system. Consequently, the necessary contracts will be much more elaborate, since issues related to risk aversion of depositors, moral hazard of entrepreneurs and banks, regulation rules of banks and competition of conventional banks come into play. The original PLS mechanism must be adjusted in order to allow Islamic banks to continue their activities which come closer and closer to commercial and debt-based banks and distance themselves from the original model of investment and equity-based banking.

Moreover, if you looked at it from the depositor's point of view, the increase in the uncertainty of the business environment for a specific industry should increase the proportion of depositors that change their PLS arrangements; in other words, changes in PLS deposits will be systematically related to changes in the uncertainty of the performance of the firm. This is even more plausible under a reasonable assumption of depositors' risk aversion, which the hypotheses of deposits contracts often make. A depositor as *rabb-el-mal* has the incentive to either change the existing PLS modes of investment or to free itself from any Islamic modes of investment when the expected return rate from a non-PLS placement or from the severance of an Islamic modes of investment becomes larger that the return rate obtained through the present PLS investment. Thus, we can expect those depositors that have relatively high risk aversion to show more tendencies to leave PLS placements than those that have been riskless. Second, as international financial markets grow, an investor's demand for financial investments will become more diversified and complex. Islamic banks must accommodate their customer's expanding demands for diversified financial placements. Thus, risk aversion depositors will, if not terminate their relationships with Islamic bank, tend to switch to Islamic banks providing diversified financial placements. In sum, both switching and termination of Islamic bank relationships should be positively correlated with a depositor's behavior against risk. Risk-sharing-based investment accounts are channeled into risk-sharing-based financing and risk-transfer-based investment accounts are channeled into risk-transfer-based financing.

3.2.1. *The competition from conventional banks — DCR risk and its management: The genesis of intertemporal smoothing and the implicit insurance contract in Islamic deposit market*

The bearing of losses by depositors in equity-based financial system has implications in the management of risks by Islamic banks, since competition of conventional banks is considered. In fact, when an Islamic bank mobilizes risky deposits in competition with liquid, fixed return and guaranteed deposits, it takes a displaced commercial risk (DCR). This is because, the return rate on an investment account, which depends on the return of the projects financed by Islamic banks, may decrease below the interest rate of the deposits granted by conventional banks. Still, IAHs bear the risk of capital losses (principal) if the return rate of the projects is negative. Even if no return and capital supplement are paid on investment account, the Islamic banks may face unexpected withdrawals, which will force them to seek more expensive sources of funds. Consequently, the Islamic banks will have to manage the displaced commercial risks due to the risk of capital losses and due to the spread between interest rate in conventional deposits market and return rate on investment account. It is interesting to note that DCR is peculiar to Islamic banks and its management has been introduced only recently in Islamic banks' management standard. The reason for this could presumably be the high-risk aversion of IAHs against the risk of capital losses, the volatility of return rate, and their need for liquid and low-risk placements.

3.2.2. *Assets-backed or markup operations or off-PLS operations*

In dual banking system, the competition from conventional banks made it necessary for Islamic banks to shift to less risky and short-term assets, which were better adapted to the needs of customers. To do so, Islamic banks offered more sophisticated financing techniques, such as Murabaha, Ijara, Salam, etc. From an income view point, none of these operations corresponds to random income for the banks, but only to predetermined fixed rate of return and are associated with collateral. Therefore, they have been considered as off-PLS operations.

The factors that have fostered the growth of off-PLS operations have different natures. Some are related to the Islamic banks' desire to increase their less risky income (fee income); others are linked to the demand of firms for more custom-made financial products.

Clearly, since many constraints have prevented Islamic banks to develop a know-how in managing business risk associated to PLS contract, it is only natural that they refuse to buy and sell risky assets like *Mudharaba* and orient their activity to short-term and less risky assets, even if these assets are not of type PLS. Islamic banks tried to hedge the risk associated to off-PLS operations (credit risk, DCR risk, and liquidity risk) through collateral, through insurance (deposit insurance), and through the assignment of rights.

In practical Islamic banking, there is a risk transfer mechanism expressed through "implicit insurance contract" regarding investment account return rate. Islamic banks are assumed to provide IAHs with insurance return rate that could contribute to stabilizing deposit contract.

The presence of a random-return investment instrument such as a *Mudharaba* increases the risks facing depositors and banks.

You must find assets *sharia* compliant with relatively low risk and a constant nominal return. It is, of course, conceivable that depositors would obtain the same utility in holding these assets as in holding some combination of cash and *Mudharaba* assets (investment account). This would require the constitution of cash reserves by IAHs at period of high return rate and use at reverse situations. IAHs will be forced to save a proportion of their return from investment account in order to avoid a decrease of wealth in a period of very low income.

a. Market economy and profit shocks

The market economy does not provide perfect insurance against profit shocks and does not lead to an efficient allocation of resources. The reason is that a complete contingent market cannot exist: the state of the project (i.e. the complete list of the projects with low and negative returns) is not observable by anyone. Thus, any individual may demand compensation even if his or her project realizes high returns. The following discussion will show how a financial intermediary can solve this problem.

b. Financial intermediation and profit shocks

In Islamic banking system, the bank is considered as an investor working on behalf of depositors. In this system, where savings are placed with banks according to the PLS principles, the depositors will be adversely affected by a sharp drop of firms' profits. Islamic banks can be considered as a "pool of reserve" that provides depositors in investment accounts with insurance against idiosyncratic business shocks that affect the income from their savings. If these shocks are not perfectly correlated, the total cash reserve needed by a bank increases less than the amount of reserves accumulated by banks. It's an implicit contingent contract between Islamic banks and IAH's: in situations of profit shocks, Islamic banks commit to compensate IAHs. More specifically, some fraction of share of IAHs from projects income can be used to constitute reserve and the rest can be used by IAHs to finance their consumption needs. In case of idiosyncratic shocks, the bank uses the reserve to smooth the income of IAHs. This contingent contract is optimal because the number of projects with profit shocks (i.e. the complete list of the projects with low return or realized losses) is observable by the bank and no IAHs will require an indemnity for reasons other than profit shocks. However, this arrangement is also the source of potential fragility of Islamic banks, if a higher number of projects more than anticipated by banks incur negative shocks. Moreover, this contingent contract is also the source of a potential expropriation by Islamic banks if buffer stock of reserve is constituted only from share of IAHs. The bank has incentives to inflate the amount of reserves to constitute a free cash flow used only for the interest of the banks. The position of banks leads to overinvestment in reserves, whereas optimality requires the holding of a level of reserves to hedge low-return rate or losses over time. The solution to this moral hazard is to require banks to allocate more or less of their income into these smoothing reserves. A second solution consists of setting return rates on investment accounts at the maximum level to eliminate any excess reserve. Thus, a threat of termination (withdrawal) by IAHs provides incentives for the bank to pay the fixed return rate.

In practice, Islamic banks try to smooth the profit shock rather than pass it on to depositors by using a profit reserve, which could lower the volatility for the depositors. They use different techniques to hedge against the uncertainty of the risky deposit's return by accumulating buffer stocks of reserve or income (storage technology). We distinguish four major profit smoothing techniques exerted by Islamic banks.

Finally, no discussion of risk-sharing would be complete without including the role of the insurance deposits. Indeed, IAHs (investment account holders) allow many risks such as changes in the value of liability and losses of the projects or banks. The PLS contracts do not allow the Islamic banks to protect IAHs, but protection by third party (the deposit insurer) is allowable and so also helps to share risks.

Table 2: List of the major profit smoothing techniques exerted by Islamic banks.

	PER	IRR	Hiba (Gift)	Bank's shareholders funds
Source	Mudaraba income	IAHs income	Bank income	Bank's shareholders funds
Stage of assignment	Before bank share is allocated	After bank share is allocated	After bank share is allocated	After bank share is allocated
Purpose	Profit stabilization/ smoothing	reserves against future losses	Profit stabilization/ Smoothing	Profit stabilization/ smoothing
Beneficiary	IAHs and banks	IAHs	IAHs	IAHs

4. An Organizational Framework for the Islamic Banking Industry: Towards Effective and Efficient Risk-sharing

Principal idea: Adequate corporate governance (control of capital) leads to effective and efficient risk-sharing.

This allows for the involvement of a wider section of entrepreneurs and investors in economic activities, so that people will eventually feel they are partners rather than spectators. In this system, Islamic finance with proper corporate governance allows depositors some influence on banks' investment decisions. The banks and financial institutions can also share the decision-making process as their representatives sit on the boards of directors of firms receiving funds.

4.1. *The necessary return to the original (orthodox) model — PLS*

The recurrence to the PLS-based financial intermediation is not an easy task. The difficulties involved in the changeover justifiably raise the question of why we should try to replace the actual non-PLS financial intermediation which has become highly sophisticated with effective system of prudential regulation and supervision. Is the case toward PLS-based system compelling and is there a strong rationale behind the transition?

So, it is necessary to show that the PLS financial system (*Mudharaba*) is superior to the non-PLS system (*Murabaha, Ijara,* etc.) based on efficiency, stability, and equity, three criteria used in evaluating any economic or financial system.

The function of a financial system is to make the best use of the financial resources (efficiency) to provide the best possible services (effects) in order to achieve the objectives of users as depositors and firms (efficiency) while maintaining its stability and in full respect of social justice by providing everyone equal opportunities of access to the financial services (equity).

Based on the criteria of equity or socio-economic justice and stability, the non-PLS-based system was always assumed to be inferior to the PLS system. However, it was superior according to the efficiency criterion. The persistent instability and crises of the international financial system have raised doubts about its superiority on the efficiency criterion.

4.2. *Vibrant stock markets*

The stock market model has particularly met with the favor of several economists. Thus, capital markets (stock markets) are represented in this literature as playing the most important role in risk allocation among different agents in the financial system. It must take a dominant position in the Islamic financial system based on the risk-sharing paradigm.

Several authors proposed reforms that would abolish the credit system and replace it by a stock-based investment system (Haque and Mirakhor, 1987; Khan and Mirakhor, 1989–1994; Mirakhor *et al.*, 2012–2013; Mirakhor and Krichene, 2013). The conditions of success are as follows:

• removing biases against equity finance;
• reducing transaction costs of stock market participation;

- minimizing speculative behavior;
- developing low cost-efficient secondary markets;
- restructuring the original model of financial intermediation by engaging in institutional reforms.

4.3. *Vibrant Islamic banks and the institutional reforms of corporate governance*

While capital (stock) markets are usually shown in economic school-books as playing the most important role in allocating risks among different agents, they have been quite insignificant in the Islamic countries. According to numerous authors, stock markets are almost non-existent in most Muslim counties; and where they exist, they are plagued with informational problems and governance issues (Askari *et al*, 2012; Mirakhor and Askari, 2010; Iqbal and Mirakhor, 2011; Chapra, 2000). Instead, banks must take the dominant position in the Islamic financial system. The financial intermediation model has particularly met with the favor of several economists. Thus, banks are represented in this literature as playing the most important role in risk allocating among different agents in the financial system. They must take a dominant position in the Islamic financial system based on risk sharing paradigm.

Several authors cite German and Japanese experiences as successful models of banking relationships. In Japan and Germany, there has been risk-sharing between banks and borrowing institutions through the main bank and Hausbank relationship.[15] We can draw on these two experiences to propose adequate reforms to strengthen risk sharing in Islamic financial system.

---

[15]The Hausbank system in Germany and the Mainbank system in Japan often use additional power by directly holding large shareholdings in client companies and by voting proxies on behalf of investors who leave their shares. For more details, one can refer to Patrick (1997), Miarka (1999), Aoki (2001), Hackethal (2004) and Frick and Lehmann (2005).

4.3.1. *Concentrated investment accounts holders*

In the case of commercial banks, the number of depositors is sufficiently large and there is enough anonymity between them that an effective control will not work. Here, the monitoring of banks' activities, considered as public good is not resolved: it is in the interest of each depositor to ensure that the bank on which it invests is performant, lest other depositors bear the cost of monitoring. Therefore, the public good of monitoring can be resolved for depositors by having a few investment accounts holders (IAHs), each of whom has enough share of bank deposits and has sufficiently great incentives for information acquisition and for exerting control of banks. This strategy has a cost: the limited diversification which these IAHs can achieve. Besides, the interests of these IAHs may well not coincide with those of small IAHs. Small depositors will continue as "free riders" on the efforts of the larger depositors. Presumably, for large IAHs to be willing to undertake this limited risk diversification, they must be compensated, for example, by allowing them to sit on the bank board of directors and take advantage of and high fees from this position.

4.3.2. *Concentrated equity ownership with Musharaka contract*

In the case of large commercial banks, the problem of control is not resolved due to the large number of shareholders and the subsequent free rider problem. Therefore, a few shareholders with enough stake in the bank have private incentives for controlling the manager of the bank and spend sufficient amount of time to acquire information. On the asset side, Islamic banks must take large positions in the firm, alongside investment account holders. The nature of *musharaka* contract enables them to do this and to focus their attention on information gathering on good and bad set of issues: those associated with the net worth of the firm in low and high return states. Since they are concerned with low and high probability events, and because the managerial incentives structure encourages managers to avoid bad events and to go towards good events, the payoff to Islamic banks exercising very effective control has no limit. There are points of concordance in the control mechanisms described in the preceding analysis. Depositors and shareholders are concerned with the high and the bottom part of the tail of the distribution of returns.

This new architecture of Islamic banking system constitutes a solution to public good of monitoring activity. The concentration of equity ownership and of IAHs lead to effective control of the bank's manager. It leads to compensate large depositors and shareholders and allows to coincide interests of class of large shareholders and IAHs with class of small shareholders and IAHs. Therefore, this solution is not without problems if the bank uses current accounts to finance the risky assets. In this case their current accounts are insured and might be liable to expose them to greater risks. If the bank adopts cent per cent reserve principle with current account, this proposal does not pose problems.

5.   Conclusion

This chapter investigates the evolution of the role of banks in allocating risks in an Islamic economy. The risk-sharing theories are typically presented in a setting in which financial intermediaries and depositors play an active monitoring role. This chapter constitutes an essay to understand the theoretical foundations of equity-based system and the adoption of risk-sharing paradigm in Islamic finance. The major theoretical characteristics of Islamic banking model are the good risk match between assets and liabilities of the banks.

In Mudharaba contract, there is a sharia rule stipulating that it is not allowed for the bank to interfere in the running of the work in order to administer the execution of the project. The entrepreneur is not fully supervised, and his effort cannot be contracted, and consequently the PLS contract (like *Mudharaba*) is an inefficient risk-sharing mode and depositors have a natural aversion for PLS contracts.

In addition, no discussion of risk sharing would be complete without including the role of the insurance deposits. Indeed, the IAHs allow many risks such as changes in the value of liability and losses of the project or banks. The PLS contracts do not allow the Islamic banks to protect the IAHs, but protection by third party (the deposit insurer) is allowable and therefore also helps to share risks.

Otherwise, adequate corporate governance leads to effective and efficient risk sharing. Islamic finance with appropriate corporate governance allows depositors some influence on banks investment decisions. The banks and financial institutions can also share the decision-making process as their representatives sit on the boards of directors of firms receiving funds.

Finally, the reforms require the eradication of the credit system and replacing it by a stock-based investment system. The conditions of success contain, among others, the removal of biases against equity finance, the reduction of transactions' costs of stock market participation, the minimization of speculative behaviors, and the development of cost-efficient secondary markets.

References

Abedifar, P., Molyneux, P. and Tarazi, A. (2013). Risk in Islamic banking, *Review of Finance*, 17(6), 2035–2096.
Adebola, S. S., Yusoff, W. S. W. and Dahalan, J. (2011). The impact of macroeconomic variables on Islamic banks financing in Malaysia, *Research Journal of Finance and Accounting*, 2(4).
Ahmad, K. (2000). Islamic finance and banking: The challenge and prospects, *Review of Islamic Economics*, 9, 57–82.
Alaabed, A., Masih, M., Mansur, A. and Abbas, M. (2015). Undermining shared prosperity? Risk shifting and Islamic banking, in paper presented at the *World Bank and Islamic Development Bank Inaugural Annual Symposium on Islamic Finance 2015*, Istanbul, Turkey.
Aoki, M. (2001). *Toward a Comparative Institutional Analysis*, MIT Press, Cambridge, MA.
Arrow, K. J. and Debreu, G. (1954). Existence of an equilibrium for a competitive economy, *Econometrica: Journal of the Econometric Society*, 265–290.
Askari, H., Iqbal, Z., Krichene, N. and Mirakhor, A. (2012). *Risk Sharing in Finance: The Islamic Finance Alternative*, Wiley, Singapore.
Beck, T., Demirgüç-Kunt, A. and Merrouche, O. (2013). Islamic vs. efficiency and stability, *Journal of Banking and Finance*, 37, 433–447.
Benes, J. and Kumhof, M. (2012). The Chicago plan revisited, IMF Working Paper WP/12/202.

Calomiris, C. W. (1999) Building an incentive-compatible safety net, *Journal of Banking and Finance*, 23, 1499–1519.

Chapra, M. U. (1985). *Towards a just Monetary System*, The Islamic Foundation, Leicester.

den Haan, W. (2010). Comparison of solutions to the incomplete markets model with aggregate uncertainty, *Journal of Economics Dynamics and Control*, 34(1), 4–27, doi: 10.1016/j.jedc.2008.12.010.

Dhaigude, A., Jawed, S., Tapar, A. and Tiwari, S. (2015). Risk-sharing in conventional and islamic finance: convergent and divergent, *The Academy of Management Review*, 11(3), 29–35.

Distinguin, I., Kouassi, T. and Tarazi, A. (2013). Interbank deposits and market discipline: Evidence from Central and Eastern Europe, *Journal of Comparative Economics*, 41(2), 544–560.

Elosegui, P. L. (2003). Aggregate risk, credit rationing, and capital accumulation, *Quarterly Journal of Economics and Finance*, 43(4), 668–696, doi: 10.1016/S1062-9769(03)00040-1.

Ergec, E. H. and Arslan, B. G. (2013). Impact of interest rates on Islamic and conventional banks: The case of Turkey, *Applied Economics*, 45(17), 2381–2388.

Frick, B. and Lehmann, E. (2005). Corporate governance in Germany: Ownership, codetermination and firm performance in a stakeholder economy, in H. Gospel and A. Pendleton (eds.), *Corporate Governance and Labour Management: An International Comparison*, Oxford University Press, Oxford.

Habib, A. (2002). Incentive-compatible profit sharingcontract: A theoretical treatment, in *Islamic Banking and Fnance, New Perspective on Profit-sharing and Risk*, Iqbal, M. and Llewellyn, D. T. (eds.), Edward Elgar, pp. 40–56.

Hackethal, A. (2004). German banks and banking structure, in J. P. Krahnen and R. H. Schmidt (eds.), *The German Financial System*, Oxford University Press, Oxford, pp.71–105.

Ibrahim, M. H. and Sukmana, R. (2011). Dynamics of Islamic financing in Malaysia: Causality and innovation accounting, *Journal of Asia-Pacific Business*, 12(1), 4–19.

Ibrahim, M. H. and Sufian, F. (2014). A Structural VAR analysis of Islamic Financing in Malaysia, *Studies in Economics and Finance*, 31(4), 371–386.

Islahi, A. A. (1997). *History of Economic Thought in Islam: A Bibliography*, Scientific Publishing Centre, KAAU, Jeddah.

Iqbal, Z. and Mirakhor, A. (2013). Economic Development and Islamic Finance, World Bank Publications, The World Bank, No. 15787.

Jovanovic, B. (1987). Micro shocks and aggregate risk, *Quarterly Journal of Economics*, 102(2), 395–410. CiteSeerX10.1.1.1011.1481. doi:10.2307/1885069. JSTOR1885069.

Kader, R. A. and Leong, Y. K. (2009). The impact of interest rate changes on Islamic bank financing, *International Review of Business Research Papers*, 5(3), 189–201.

Kahf, M. (2005). Islamic banks: The rise of a new power alliance of wealth and shariah scholarship, in Clement M. Henry and Rodney Wilson (eds.), *The Politics of Islamic Finance*, Oxford University Press, Karachi, pp. 17–36.

Kahf, M. and Khan, T. (1992). *Principles of Islamic Financing: A Survey*, IRTI, Jeddah.

Khan, M. S. (1986). Islamic Interest-Free Banking, IMF Staff Papers, March.

Kuala Lumpur Declaration (2012). Available from ISRA's website (20th September 2012).

Maginn, J., Tuttle, D., McLeavey, D. and Pinto, J. (2007). *Managing Investment Portfolios: A Dynamic Process*, John Wiley & Sons., Hoboken, New Jersey, pp. 231–245.

Mas-Colell, A., Whinston, M. and Green, J. (1995). *Microeconomic Theory*, Oxford University Press, New York, pp. 692–693.

Miarka, T. (1999). *Financial Intermediation and Deregulation, a Critical Analysis of Japanese Bank-Firm Relationships*. Physica-Verlag, Berlin.

Mirakhor, A. (2002). Hopes for the future of Islamic finance, *New Horizons*, 121, July–August, pp. 5–8.

Mirakhor, A. (2007). Islamic finance and globalization: A convergence? *Journal of Islamic Economics, Banking and Finance*, 3(2), 11–72.

Mirakhor, A. and Bacha, I. (2012). Islamic capital market and development, in Paper presented at *22nd Annual Conference on Monetary and Exchange Rate Policies: Banking Supervision and Prudential Policies*, May 2012.

Mirakhor, A. and Bacha, I. (2013). *The Islamic Capital Market: A Comparative Approach*, INCEIF and Wiley Finance.

Mirakhor, A. and Haneef, R. (2012). Islamic Finance Industry: Can it achieve its Ideals? in Presented at the *3rd Asia Pacific Regional Forum Conference of the International Bar Association (IBA)*, November 2012.

Mirakhor, A. and Shaukat, M. (2012a). Regime uncertainty: Interest rate based debt financing system, *The Journal of Islamic Business*, 2(2), 15–30.

Mirakhor, A. and Shaukat, M. (2012b). Survival of the interest rate based debt financing regime, *Journal of Economy and Money*, 6(2).

Mirakhor, A. and Shaukat, M. (2013). Islamic finance in a multipolar world: Traversing the complexities of a new world, *The Journal of Islamic Banking and Finance*, 31.

Mirakhor, A. (2002). *Hopes for the Future of Islamic Finance, New Horizons*, (121), London, U.K., IIBI.

Mirakhor, A. (2007). Islamic finance and globalization: A convergence? *Journal of Islamic Economics, Banking and Finance*, 3(2).

Mirakhor, A. (2009). Resilience and Stability of Islamic Finance. *New Horizon: Global Perspective on Islamic Banking and Insurance*. London, Institute of Islamic Banking and Insurance.

Mirakhor, A. (1993). Equilibrium in a non-interest open economy, *International Monetary Fund*, Working Paper, published in *Islamic Economics: Journal of King Abdulaziz University*, 5, 3–23.

Mirakhor, A. (2009). Islamic economics and finance: An institutional perspective, *IIUM Journal of Economics and Management*, 17(1).

Mirakhor, A. (2010). Whither Islamic Finance? Risk Sharing in an Age of Crises. Paper presented at the Inaugural Securities Commission Malaysia (SC) — Oxford Centre for Islamic Studies (OCIS) Roundtable, *Developing a Scientific Methodology on Shariah Governance for Positioning Islamic Finance Globally*, March 15.

Mirakhor, A. (2012). Shariah compliant macro-economic policy, Paper presented at *SisanaKijang*, Bank Negara Malaysia, November.

Mirakhor, A. and Krichene, N. (2008). The recent crisis: Lessons for Islamic finance, Islamic financial services board, 2nd public lecture on financial policy and stability, Kuala Lumpur, Malaysia.

Mirakhor, A. (2011a). Islamic Finance in the multi polar world, in Presented at the *Asian Institute Finance Distinguished Speaker Series*, Kuala Lumpur, 13 September.

Mirakhor, A. (2011b). Epistemological Foundation of Finance: Islamic and Conventional, in Keynote address presented at the *Foundations of Islamic Finance Conference Series*, Kuala Lumpur, March 8–10.

Mirakhor, A. (2011c). Risk Sharing and Public Policy, in Paper presented in the *5th International Islamic Capital Market Forum*, Security Commission of Malaysia, Kuala Lumpur, November 10th.

Mirakhor, A., Krichene, N. and Shaukat, M. (2012). Unsustainability of the regime of interest-based debt financing, *ISRA International Journal of Islamic Finance*, 4(2), 25–52.

Mirakhor, Abbas (1987). Analysis of Short-Term Asset Concentration in Islamic Banking, *IMF Working Paper*, 67(87), 1–28.

Mirakhor, A. and Hamid, I. S. (2009). *Islam and Development*, Global Scholarly Publications, New York.

Patrick, H. (1997). How the Japanese Financial System and Its Main Bank System Have Dealt with Generic Issues of Financial Development,

World Bank Mediterranean Development Forum Marrakesh, Morocco May 13.

Qureshi, A. I. (1946). *Islam and Theory of Interest*, Sheikh M. Ashraf, Lahore.

Shaikh, S. A. (2010). An ideal Islamic economic system: A gone case, MPRA Paper, No. 26701.

Seho, M., Alaaabed, A. and Masih, M. (2016). Risk-sharing financing of Islamic banks: Better shielded against interest rate risk? MPRA Paper No. 82558.

Shiller, R. (1995). Aggregate income risks and hedging mechanisms, *Quarterly Review of Economics and Finance*, 35(2), 119–152, CiteSeerX 10.1.1.143.9207. doi:10.1016/1062-9769(95)90018-7.

Siddiqi, M. N. (1967). *Bila Sudi Bankari* (Urdu) (Banking without Interest), Islamic Publications, Lahore, Revised version in English (1983), The Islamic Foundation, Leicester.

Taqi, U. M. (1999). The concept of Musharaka and its application as an islamic method of financing, *Arab Law Quarterly*, 14(3).

Van Wijnbergen, S. J. G., Zaheer, S. and Farooq, M. (2013). Capital Structure, Risk Shifting and Stability: Conventional and Islamic Banking, Tibergen Institute Discussion paper.

Zaher, S. Tarek and Kabir Hassan, M. (2001). A comparative literature survey of islamic finance and banking, *Financial Markets, Institutions and Instruments*, 10(4), November, University Salomon Center, Blackwell Publishers, New York.

Chapter 8

Commodity Markets' Asset Allocation with Robust Liquidity Risk Management Optimization Parameters

Mazin A. M. Al Janabi

Finance & Banking and Financial Engineering,
Tecnologico de Monterrey, EGADE Business School
Santa Fe Campus, Mexico City, Mexico
mazin.aljanabi@tec.mx, mazinaljanabi@gmail.com

1. Introduction and Overview

Recent years have witnessed the increasing role of investment funds in most commodity markets, and with a particular emphasis on commodity-dependent countries (Satyanarayan and Varangis, 1994). In the last two decades, commodity markets have played a crucial role as an alternative asset class for institutional investors and hence become an imperative risk diversification mechanism. Commodity assets, in addition to offering high-expected rates of return, also offer significant risk management benefits. Since commodity assets are customarily negatively correlated with each other and with other assets, they are fundamentally used in active and passive portfolio management (Claessens and Varangis, 1994).

In consequence, investment funds, traditionally dealing with financial markets, are nowadays spreading their assets holdings into commodity markets with the objective of achieving major risk/return benefits (Satyanarayan and Varangis, 1994). On the other hand, commodity markets may also be less liquid than other financial markets and as a result changes in supply and demand can have a strong impact on prices and volatility. In addition, the volatility of commodity prices has also been a cause of uncertainty in commodity-reliant countries, influencing producers, traders, and financial entities (Giot and Laurent, 2003). Consequently, the characteristics of these markets can make price transparency and the effective hedging of commodity risk much more difficult, and as a result suggest a thorough and rigorous treatment of commodity price risk management under the notion of adverse and illiquid market settings (Al Janabi, 2009). In this context, a growing need to incorporate the traditional financial risk management tools into the commodity market has become a fundamental need for market participants and financial institutions, and thus it is the focus of this chapter.

The significance of assessing the market risk of a portfolio of financial securities has long been acknowledged by academics and practitioners. In recent years, the growth of trading activities and instances of financial market upheavals has prompted new research underlining the necessity for market participants to develop reliable risk assessment methods. In measuring market risk, one technique advanced in the literature involves the use of value-at-risk (VaR) models that ascertain how much the value of a trading portfolio would plunge, in monetary terms, over a given period with a given probability because of changes in market prices. Nowadays, VaR is by far the most popular and most accepted risk measure among financial institutions. Although VaR is a very popular measure of market risk of financial trading portfolios, it is not a panacea for all risk assessments and has several drawbacks, limitations, and undesirable properties.

In spite of the increasing importance of commodity markets, there is very little published research in this respect, and particularly within the commodity trading risk management context. Given the general interest and acceptance of VaR within the financial risk management community, VaR has the ability of being an effective risk measure for energy and agricultural risk management as well. Therefore, it is imperative to gain an understanding of how standard VaR estimation techniques operate in the context of commodity prices.

In commodity markets, the measurement of volatility and management of related risks is relatively a new field of research and a few research papers deal with this particular timely topic. For instance, applying VaR models to measuring crude oil price volatility and associated risks is a field that is only starting to draw the attention of researchers. Nonetheless, commodity price volatility and dynamics have been studied, among others, in works of Giot and Laurent (2003) and Manfredo and Leuthold (1999, 2001).

Several agricultural risk management problems have been investigated within a multi-product context. These settings offer logical portfolios for probing the performance of alternative VaR estimation techniques under credible portfolio situations. To date, the performance of VaR techniques has not been rigorously tested on portfolios exposed to agricultural commodity price risk, although Manfredo and Leuthold (1999, 2001) represent an exception.

The dynamic nature of agriculture as well as the reduction of government programs creates a new risky environment in agriculture and, as such, agribusinesses are exposed to multifaceted market risks. With the growing use and interest in VaR, there appear to be several practical applications to agriculture as well as a greater need to assess and evaluate current methods of estimating volatility. The recent interest in VaR has created a new and additional motivation for accurate and meaningful measures of volatility and correlations (Manfredo and Leuthold, 1999).

Considering the growing interest in VaR and the variability of the market risk factors of the cattle feeding margin, Manfredo and Leuthold (2001) examine the application of VaR measures in the context of agricultural prices, using several alternative procedures (both parametric and full-valuation) in predicting large losses in the cattle feeding margin. In another relevant paper, Manfredo and Leuthold

(1999) review the various VaR estimation techniques and empirical findings and suggest potential extensions and applications of VaR in the context of agricultural risk management.

For commodity traders with both long- and short-selling trading positions, Giot and Laurent (2003) put forward VaR models relevant for commodity markets and particularly for short-term horizon. In a 5-year out-of-sample study on aluminum, copper, nickel, Brent crude oil, and WTI crude oil daily cash prices and cocoa nearby futures contracts, they assess the performance of the $RiskMetrics^{TM}$ (Morgan Guaranty Trust Company, 1994), skewed Student APARCH, and skewed student ARCH models.

Because UK arable farms face substantial price risk, White and Dawson (2005) estimate price risk for a representative UK arable farm using VaR methodology. To determine the distribution of commodity returns, two multivariate generalized auto-regressive conditional heteroscedasticity (GARCH) models, with t-distributed and normally distributed errors, and a $RiskMetrics^{TM}$ (Morgan Guaranty Trust Company, 1994) model are examined. Finally, Wilson and Nganje (2007) provide a case study on the application of VaR in bakery procurement. They illustrate the application of VaR to a bread baking company and demonstrate how it can be used by a commodity processor in reporting risk, evaluating risk reduction alternatives, and setting risk limits.

As indicated above, commodity prices are exposed to a variety of volatile market prices that can be and have been examined in a portfolio context. However, despite the rising impact of commodity markets, earlier research does not provide any broad methods for handling trading risk under illiquid and adverse market settings, and particularly within large commodities trading portfolios.

Indeed, the conventional VaR approach, employed by previous researches, to computing market risk of a portfolio, does not explicitly consider liquidity risk. Typical VaR models assess the worst change in mark-to-market portfolio value over a given time horizon but do not account for the actual trading risk of liquidation. Customary fine-tunings are made on an *ad hoc* basis. At most, the holding period (or liquidation horizon) over which the VaR number is calculated is adjusted to ensure the inclusion of liquidity risk. As a result, liquidity trading risk can be imprecisely factored into VaR assessments by assuring that the liquidation horizon is at a minimum larger than an orderly liquidation interval. Moreover, the same liquidation horizon is employed to all trading commodity asset classes, albeit some assets may be more liquid than others. Therefore, neglecting liquidity risk can lead to an underestimation of the overall market risk and misapplication of capital cushion for the safety and soundness of commodities dealers and markets.

To address the above deficiencies, this chapter examines the use of a liquidity-adjusted value-at-risk (L-VaR) measure in the context of commodity markets, under both normal and adverse market conditions,[1] using the modeling algorithms and optimization techniques of the Al Janabi model (Al Janabi, 2008; Madoroba and Kruger, 2014). As such, in this chapter, we characterize trading risk for diverse commodity products using a multivariate L-VaR approach that focuses on the modeling of optimum L-VaR under illiquid and severe market conditions. The overall objective of this chapter is to construct a large commodity portfolio, which includes several crude oil/energy spot prices as well as other common commodities, and to evaluate the risk characteristics of such a portfolio besides examining a robust

---

[1]Other literatures examined the issue of liquidity risk and particularly the use of L-VaR for the assessment of risk exposures in foreign exchange and stock market portfolios. For the sake of presenting this chapter in a manageable size, we decided not to include those studies within the literature review. However, for further details of previous approaches on asset liquidity risk and conventional L-VaR methods one can refer to Jarrow and Subramanian (1997), Almgren and Chriss (1999), Bangia *et al.* (2002), Berkowitz (2000), and Angelidis and Benos (2006). Furthermore, in their research paper, Madoroba and Kruger (2014) introduce a VaR model that incorporates intraday price movements on high–low spreads and adjusts for a trade impact measure, a novel sensitivity measure of price movements due to trading volumes. Furthermore, the authors compare and contrast 10 worldwide-recognized liquidity risk management models including the *Al Janabi model*, which is used in this chapter for commodity liquidly risk modeling and for the optimization of different commodities portfolios.

optimization algorithm for assessing efficient and coherent market portfolios.[2]

To this end, we discuss a general trading risk model that accounts for the characteristics of the series of commodity price returns — for example, fat tails (leptokurtosis), skewness, correlation factors, and liquidity horizons — and effectively forecasts the market risk within a short-to-medium-term time horizon. As such, our focus on a short-to-medium-term time horizon is coherent with the use of a pure risk management method in which a more fundamental economics model would be of little aid *vis-à-vis* short-to-medium-term risk estimations. Moreover, it is possible to justify and to handle (with reasonable accuracy) the issue of non-normality for cash commodities with the simple use of a parametric L-VaR method; along with the incorporation of a credible stress-testing approach under the notion of different correlation factors; as well as by supplementing the risk analysis with a realistic liquidity risk factor that takes into account real-world trading circumstances.

Considering the recent interest in L-VaR and the variability of the market risk factors of different commodities, the overall aim of this chapter is to examine L-VaR measures in the context of large commodity trading portfolios (of both long- and short-selling positions) and under the notion of different correlation factors and liquidity horizons. In particular, this chapter develops and tests L-VaR measures, using several alternative strategies in predicting large losses, with the aid of different liquidation horizons and under a predetermined confidence level. Thus, large commodity trading portfolios provide a practical case for testing L-VaR methodologies in the prospect of commodity prices, helping to establish the appropriateness of L-VaR as a viable and important risk management tool for commodity risk managers.

---

[2]In this chapter, the concept of coherent market portfolios refers to rational portfolios that are subject to meaningful financial and operational constraints. In this sense, coherent market portfolios do not lie on the efficient frontiers as defined by Markowitz (1959), and instead have logical and well-structured long/short asset allocation proportions.

This chapter makes the following contributions to the literature in this specific commodity risk management field. Firstly, it represents one of the limited number of research papers that empirically examine commodity trading risk management using actual data of different commodity markets, which hitherto has been an under researched empirical area.

Secondly, unlike most empirical studies in this field, this study employs a comprehensive and real-world trading risk management model that considers risk analysis under normal, adverse, and illiquid market conditions by focusing on L-VaR rather than the standard VaR approach. As such, this chapter extends prior attempts by explicitly modeling the liquidation of commodity trading portfolios with a pertinent stochastic stationary process, over the holding period, with the aid of an appropriate scaling of the multiple-assets' L-VaR matrix. The principal advantage of employing such a model is the ability to capture a full picture of possible loss scenarios of actual commodity trading portfolios. The key methodological contribution is a different and less conservative liquidity-scaling factor than the conventional root-t multiplier. Indeed, the traditional root-t rule overestimates asset liquidity risk in almost all asset allocation cases since it does not consider real-world circumstances in which traders can liquidate small portions of their trading portfolios on a daily basis; but rather it assumes that the whole trading position can be sold completely in the last trading day. Indeed, in real financial market operations, liquidation occurs during the holding period and thus scaling the holding period to account for orderly liquidation can be justified if one allows the assets to be liquidated throughout the holding period. This latter attribute is the key aspect of our proposed asset liquidity model.

Thirdly, in this chapter we discuss a robust approach to optimal and coherent portfolios selection, within an L-VaR framework. To this end, a novel L-VaR optimization algorithm technique is introduced to allocate commodity assets by minimizing L-VaR subject to imposing financially and operationally meaningful constraints. The focus on L-VaR as the appropriate measure of portfolio risk allows risk managers and portfolio managers to assign the desired liquidity horizon and to allocate long and short-trading assets according to realistic market trading conditions. Another contribution of the chapter is to provide a new approach to estimating the portfolio managers optimal risk parameters. Accordingly, a robust optimization algorithm process is introduced to calculate risk tolerance in the L-VaR asset allocation model and to determine efficient and coherent portfolios subject to the imposition of fundamental operational and financial constraints.

The rest of the chapter proceeds as follows: Section 2 lays out the salient features and derives the necessary quantitative infrastructure of the Al Janabi model and the L-VaR technique. Section 3 examines the overall results of the different empirical tests and discusses the process and infrastructure that support large-scale quantitative-based investing and the role of an optimization engine in this process. This section also discusses the construction of efficient and coherent portfolios. Section 4 remarks on conclusions.

2. Theoretical Foundation of Al Janabi Model and L-VaR for Commodity Price Risk Management

2.1. *Commodity trading risk management with a broad parametric VaR approach*

To estimate VaR using the variance/covariance (also known as the parametric, analytical, and delta-neutral) method, the volatility of each risk factor is extracted from a predefined historical observation period. The potential effect of each component of the portfolio on the overall portfolio value is then worked out. These effects are then aggregated across the whole portfolio using the correlations between the risk factors (which are, again, extracted from the historical observation period) to give the overall VaR value of the portfolio with a given confidence level. As such, for a single trading position the absolute value of VaR can be defined in monetary terms as follows

(Al Janabi, 2009, 2012):

$$\text{VaR}_i = |(\mu_i - \alpha * \sigma_i)[MTM\ Commodity_i]|$$
$$\approx |\alpha * \sigma_i[MTM\ Commodity_i]|, \qquad (1)$$

where μ_i is the expected return of the commodity, α is the confidence level (or in other words, the standard normal variant at confidence level α), and σ_i is the forecasted standard deviation (or conditional volatility) of the return of the commodity that constitutes the single position. The *MTM Commodity$_i$* is the mark-to-market value of the commodity trading asset and indicates the monetary amount of investment in commodity i. Without loss of generality, we can assume that the expected value of daily returns μ_i is close to zero. As such, though Equation (1) includes some simplifying assumptions, it is routinely used by researchers and practitioners in the commodity markets for the estimation of VaR for a single trading position.

Trading risk in the presence of multiple risk factors is determined by the combined effect of individual risks. The extent of the total risk is determined not only by the magnitudes of the individual risks but also by their correlations. Portfolio effects are crucial in risk management not only for large diversified portfolios but also for individual instruments that depend on several risk factors. For multiple assets or portfolio of assets, VaR is a function of each individual security's risk and the correlation factor $[\rho_{i,j}]$ between the returns on the individual securities as follows:

$$\text{VaR}_P = \sqrt{\sum_{i=1}^{n}\sum_{j=1}^{n} \text{VaR}_i\, \text{VaR}_j \rho_{i,j}} = \sqrt{|\text{VaR}|^T |\rho|\, |\text{VaR}|}. \qquad (2)$$

This formula is a general one for the calculation of VaR for any portfolio regardless of the number of securities. It should be noted that the second term of this formula is presented in terms of vectors and matrix-algebra — a useful form to avoid mathematical complexity, as more and more securities are added. This approach can simplify the programming process and permits easy incorporation of short-selling positions in market risk management process. This means, that in order to calculate VaR (of a portfolio of any number of securities), we need to first create a vector $|\text{VaR}|$ of individual VaR positions — i.e. an explicitly n-rows-and-one-column $(n * 1)$ vector, such as

$$|\text{VaR}| = \begin{bmatrix} \text{VaR}_1 \\ \text{VaR}_2 \\ \cdots \\ \text{VaR}_n \end{bmatrix}. \tag{2a}$$

Second, we need to construct a transpose vector $|\text{VaR}|^T$ of individual VaR positions — that is, an $(1 * n)$ vector, and hence the superscript T indicates transpose of the vector:

$$|\text{VaR}|^T = [\text{VaR}_1 \quad \text{VaR}_2 \quad \cdots \quad \text{VaR}_n]. \tag{2b}$$

Finally, we ought to build a matrix $|\rho|$ of all correlation factors (ρ) — i.e. an $(n * n)$ matrix in the following form:

$$|\rho| = \begin{bmatrix} 1 & \rho_{1,2} & \rho_{1,3} & \cdots & \rho_{1,n} \\ \rho_{2,1} & 1 & \rho_{2,3} & \cdots & \rho_{2,n} \\ \rho_{3,1} & \rho_{3,2} & 1 & \cdots & \rho_{3,n} \\ \cdots & \cdots & \cdots & \cdots & \cdots \\ \rho_{n,1} & \rho_{n,2} & \rho_{n,3} & \cdots & 1 \end{bmatrix}. \tag{2c}$$

2.2. *Modeling commodity liquidity trading risk in VaR framework*

Asset liquidity is a key risk factor, which until lately, has not been appropriately dealt with by risk models. Illiquid trading positions can add considerably to losses and can give negative signals to traders due to the higher expected returns they entail. The concept of liquidity trading risk is immensely important for using VaR accurately and recent upheavals in financial markets confirm the need for laborious treatment and assimilation of liquidity trading risk into VaR models.

In fact, if returns are independent and they can have any elliptical multivariate distribution, then it is possible to convert the VaR horizon parameter from daily to any t-day horizon. The variance of a t-day return should be t times the variance of a 1-day return or $\sigma^2 = f(t)$. Thus, in terms of standard deviation (or volatility), $\sigma = f(\sqrt{t})$ and the daily VaR number [VaR (1-day)] can be adjusted for any horizon as

$$\text{VaR}(t\text{-day}) = \text{VaR}(1\text{-day})\sqrt{t}. \tag{3}$$

The above formula was proposed and used by J. P. Morgan in their earlier *RiskMetrics*^{TM} method (Morgan Guaranty Trust Company, 1994). This methodology implicitly assumes that liquidation occurs in one block sale at the end of the holding period and that there is one holding period for all assets, regardless of their inherent trading liquidity structure. Unfortunately, the latter approach does not consider real-life trading situations, where traders can liquidate (or re-balance) small portions of their trading portfolios on a daily basis. The assumption of a given holding period for orderly liquidation inevitably implies that assets' liquidation occurs during the holding period. Accordingly, scaling the holding period to account for orderly liquidation can be justified if one allows the assets to be liquidated throughout the holding period.

In this chapter, we discuss a different re-engineered approach for calculating a closed-form parametric VaR with explicit treatment of liquidity trading risk. The essence of the model relies on the assumption of a stochastic stationary process and some rules of thumb, which can be of crucial value for more accurate overall trading risk assessment during market stress periods when liquidity dries up. To this end, a practical framework of a methodology (within a simplified mathematical approach) is examined in what follows with the purpose of incorporating and calculating illiquid assets horizon VaR, detailed along these lines.[3]

---

[3]The mathematical approach presented herein is largely drawn from the Al Janabi (2008, 2009, 2012) research papers.

In order to take into account the full illiquidity of assets (that is, the required unwinding period to liquidate an asset) we define the following:

σ_{adj}^2 = variance of the illiquid trading position;

σ_{adj} = liquidity risk factor or standard deviation of the illiquid position,

t = number of liquidation days (t days to liquidate the entire asset fully).

The proposed approach assumes that the trading position is closed out linearly over t days and hence it uses the logical assumption that the losses due to illiquid trading positions over t days are the sum of losses over the individual trading days. Moreover, we can assume with reasonable accuracy that asset returns and losses due to illiquid trading positions are independent and identically distributed (*iid*) and serially uncorrelated day-to-day along the liquidation horizon and that the variance of losses due to liquidity risk over t days is the sum of the variance (σ_i^2, for all $i = 1, 2, \ldots, t$) of losses on the individual days, thus:

$$\sigma_{\text{adj}}^2 = (\sigma_1^2 + \sigma_2^2 + \sigma_3^2 + \cdots + \sigma_{t-2}^2 + \sigma_{t-1}^2 + \sigma_t^2). \tag{4}$$

In fact, the square root-t approach (Equation (3)) is a simplified special case of Equation (4) under the assumption that the daily variances of losses throughout the holding period are all the same as first day variance, σ_1^2, thus, $\sigma_{\text{adj}}^2 = (\sigma_1^2 + \sigma_1^2 + \sigma_1^2 + \cdots + \sigma_1^2) = t\sigma_1^2$. As discussed above, the square root-t equation overestimates asset liquidity risk since it does not consider that traders can liquidate small portions of their trading portfolios on a daily basis and then the whole trading position can be sold completely on the last trading day. Indeed, in real financial market operations, liquidation occurs during the holding period and thus scaling the holding period to account for orderly liquidation can be justified if one allows the assets to be liquidated throughout the holding period. As such, for this special linear liquidation case and under the assumption that the variance of losses of the first trading day decreases linearly each day (as a function of t), we can derive from Equation (4) the following:

$$
\sigma_{\text{adj}}^2 = \left(\left(\frac{t}{t}\right)^2 \sigma_1^2 + \left(\frac{t-1}{t}\right)^2 \sigma_1^2 + \left(\frac{t-2}{t}\right)^2 \sigma_1^2 + \cdots + \left(\frac{3}{t}\right)^2 \sigma_1^2 \right.
$$
$$
\left. + \left(\frac{2}{t}\right)^2 \sigma_1^2 + \left(\frac{1}{t}\right)^2 \sigma_1^2 \right). \tag{5}
$$

Evidently, the additional liquidity risk factor depends only on the number of days needed to sell an illiquid position linearly. In the general case of t days, the variance of the liquidity risk factor is given by the following functional expression of t:

$$
\sigma_{\text{adj}}^2 = \sigma_1^2 \left(\left(\frac{t}{t}\right)^2 + \left(\frac{t-1}{t}\right)^2 + \left(\frac{t-2}{t}\right)^2 + \cdots + \left(\frac{3}{t}\right)^2 \right.
$$
$$
\left. + \left(\frac{2}{t}\right)^2 + \left(\frac{1}{t}\right)^2 \right), \tag{6}
$$

or $\sigma_{\text{adj}}^2 = \sigma_1^2 \left(\dfrac{1}{t^2} \{ (t)^2 + (t-1)^2 + (t-2)^2 \right.$
$$
\left. + \cdots + (3)^2 + (2)^2 + (1)^2 \} \right). \tag{7}
$$

To calculate the sum of the squares, it is convenient to use a short-cut approach. From mathematical infinite-series, the following relationship can be obtained:

$$
(t)^2 + (t-1)^2 + (t-2)^2 + \cdots + (3)^2 + (2)^2 + (1)^2
$$
$$
= \frac{t(t+1)(2t+1)}{6}. \tag{8}
$$

Hence, after substituting Equation (8) into Equation (6), the following can be achieved:

$$
\sigma_{\text{adj}}^2 = \sigma_1^2 \left[\frac{1}{t^2} \{ (t)^2 + (t-1)^2 + (t-2)^2 + \cdots + (3)^2 + (2)^2 + (1)^2 \} \right],
$$
$$
\text{or } \sigma_{\text{adj}}^2 = \sigma_1^2 \left(\frac{(2t+1)(t+1)}{6t} \right). \tag{9}
$$

Accordingly, from Equation (9) the liquidity risk factor can be expressed in terms of volatility (or standard deviation) as

$$\sigma_{\text{adj}} = \sigma_1 \left\{ \sqrt{\frac{1}{t^2}[(t)^2 + (t-1)^2 + (t-2)^2 + \cdots + (3)^2 + (2)^2 + (1)^2]} \right\},$$

$$\text{or } \sigma_{\text{adj}} = \sigma_1 \left\{ \sqrt{\frac{(2t+1)(t+1)}{6t}} \right\}. \tag{10}$$

The final result of Equation (10) is of course a function of time and not the square root of time as employed by some financial market's participants based on the *RiskMetrics*[TM] methodologies. The above approach can also be used to calculate L-VaR for any time horizon. Likewise, in order to perform the calculation of L-VaR under illiquid market conditions, it is possible to use the liquidity factor of equation (10) and define the following:

$$L\text{-VaR}_{\text{adj}} = \text{VaR} \sqrt{\frac{(2t+1)(t+1)}{6t}}, \tag{11}$$

where VaR is the value-at-risk under liquid market conditions (as defined formerly in Equation (1)), and L-VaR$_{\text{adj}}$ is the value-at-risk under illiquid market conditions. The latter equation indicates that L-VaR$_{\text{adj}} \gg$ VaR, and for the special case when the number of days to liquidate the entire assets is one trading day, then L-VaR$_{\text{adj}} = $ VaR. Consequently, the difference between L-VaR$_{\text{adj}}$ and VaR should be equal to the residual market risk due to the illiquidity of any asset under illiquid market conditions.

The above mathematical formulas can be applied for the calculation of L-VaR for each trading position and for the entire portfolio. In order to calculate the L-VaR for the full trading portfolio under illiquid market conditions (L-VaR$_{P_{\text{adj}}}$), the above mathematical formulation can be extended, with the aid of Equation (2), into a matrix-algebra form to yield the following:

$$L\text{-VaR}_{P_{\text{adj}}} = \sqrt{|L\text{-VaR}_{\text{adj}}|^T |\rho| |L\text{-VaR}_{\text{adj}}|}. \tag{12}$$

The above mathematical structure (in the form of two vectors and a matrix, $|\text{L-VaR}_{\text{adj}}|$, $|\text{L-VaR}_{\text{adj}}|^T$, and $|\rho|$) can facilitate the programming process so that the trading risk manager can specify different liquidation horizons for the whole portfolio and/or for each individual trading commodity according to the necessary number of days to liquidate the entire asset completely. The latter can be achieved by specifying an overall benchmark liquidation period to liquidate the entire constituents of the portfolio fully. In fact, the number of liquidation days (t) necessary to liquidate the entire commodity assets fully is related to the choice of the liquidity threshold; however, the size of this threshold is likely to change under severe market conditions. Indeed, the choice of the liquidation horizon can be estimated from the total trading position size and the daily trading volume that can be unwound into the market without significantly disrupting commodity market prices.

3. A Rational Empirical Relevance — Analysis of Large Commodity Portfolios[4]

For the purpose of this chapter and in order to examine various L-VaR estimation alternatives for commodity price risk management, price return series are needed. Returns are constructed from cash (or spot) prices of 25 different commodities, in addition to an "All Commodities Index". The sample portfolio of commodities is included in Table 1 and their classification is along these lines: energy sector (seven commodities with main focus on crude oil), metal sector (nine commodities), agriculture sector (seven commodities), and miscellaneous sectors (two commodities).

Moreover, in this chapter price returns are defined as $R_{i,t} = \ln(P_{i,t}) - \ln(P_{i,t-1})$, where $R_{i,t}$ is the monthly return of commodity i, ln is the natural logarithm, $P_{i,t}$ is the current month price of commodity i, and $P_{i,t-1}$ is the previous month price. Furthermore,

---

[4] *Note and disclaimer:* All empirical testing results, including tables and figures, are produced and designed by the author using an in-house built software.

for this particular study we have chosen a confidence interval of 95% (or 97.5% with "one-tailed" loss side) and several liquidation time horizons to compute L-VaR.[5] The historical database of average monthly commodity prices is obtained from the International Financial Statistics Browser (http://imfStatistics.org) of the International Monetary Fund (IMF). The analysis of data and discussions of relevant empirical findings are organized and explained as follows.

3.1. *Datasets, statistical analysis, and testing for asymmetric distributions*

In this section, analysis of the particular risk of each commodity (monthly and annual volatilities), the commodity relationships with respect to the benchmark index (that is, All Commodities Index), and finally a test of normality are performed on the large portfolio of commodities. To investigate the statistical properties of the data, we have computed the log returns of each series. Table 1 illustrates the monthly volatility of each commodity under normal and severe (adverse) market conditions.[6] Severe market volatilities are calculated by implementing an empirical distribution of past returns for all commodity assets' time series. As such, the maximum negative returns (losses), which are witnessed in the historical time series, are selected for this purpose. Indeed, this downside risk approach can aid in overcoming some of the limitations of the normality assumption in the parametric L-VaR method and can provide a better analysis of L-VaR, especially under severe and illiquid market settings.

From Table 1 it is apparent that the commodity with the highest volatility is gasoline (under normal market conditions), whereas coffee has demonstrated the highest volatility under severe market

---

[5]The commodities database time series span from 1987 to 2007, providing 20 years (240 monthly observations) of relevant price returns for estimation and in-sample testing. The dataset includes certain severe events during the latest subprime financial crisis.

[6]In this chapter, severe or crisis market conditions refer to unexpected extreme adverse market situations at which losses could be several-fold larger than losses under normal market situations. Stress-testing technique is usually used to estimate the impact of unusual and severe events.

Table 1: Risk analysis data: Volatility under normal and crisis market conditions and sensitivity factors.

Commodity name	Monthly volatility (normal market), %	Monthly volatility (crisis market), %	Annual volatility (normal market), %	Annual volatility (adverse market), %	Sensitivity factors, %
Petroleum: Average Crude Price	8.1	24.6	28.1	85.2	1.72
Petroleum: Dubai	8.5	30.6	29.3	106.1	1.65
Petroleum: West Texas Intermediate	7.7	20.6	26.6	71.5	1.63
Petroleum: UK Brent	8.8	25.2	30.4	87.2	1.88
Gasoline	10.4	25.4	36.0	88.0	1.97
Natural Gas	5.8	20.6	20.0	71.2	0.14
Coal	4.0	13.5	13.9	46.9	0.26
Gold	3.3	12.5	11.3	43.2	0.18
Silver	5.4	21.6	18.7	75.0	0.18
Copper	6.2	20.0	21.5	69.2	0.48
Zinc	6.1	24.9	21.3	86.4	0.34
Lead	6.3	23.8	21.9	82.3	0.15
Aluminium	5.8	32.6	20.0	113.1	0.31
Nickel	8.9	22.2	30.7	76.9	0.54
Iron Ore	4.4	12.9	15.2	44.7	0.18
Phosphate Rock	2.3	21.7	8.1	75.2	0.01
Wheat	5.1	15.1	17.7	52.3	0.08
Cotton	4.9	12.6	17.0	43.5	0.14
Sugar	2.1	11.0	7.3	38.2	−0.05
Maize	5.3	25.2	18.4	87.2	−0.08
Tobacco	1.8	4.9	6.2	16.8	0.01
Coffee	8.0	37.1	27.6	128.6	0.04
Tea	7.7	23.6	26.8	81.8	0.11
Rubber	6.0	18.1	20.8	62.7	0.37
Wool	4.7	16.5	16.4	57.3	−0.02
All Commodities Index	3.6	12.3	12.5	42.5	1.00

conditions. Annualized volatilities are depicted in Table 1, too; and this is performed by adjusting (multiplying) the monthly volatilities with the square root of 12. An interesting outcome of the study of sensitivity factors (beta factors for systematic risk) is the manner in which the results are varied across the sample commodities as indicated in Table 1. Gasoline appears to have the highest sensitivity factor (1.97) *vis-à-vis* the All Commodities Index (that is, the highest systematic risk) and both tobacco and phosphate rock seem to have the lowest beta factor (0.01).

To take into account the distributional anomalies of asset returns, tests of normality (symmetry) are performed on the sample commodities. In the first study, the measurements of skewness and kurtosis are achieved on the sample commodities. The results are depicted in Table 2.

In general, we can deduce that almost all commodities show asymmetric behavior (between both positive and negative values). Moreover, kurtosis studies show similar patterns of abnormality (i.e. peaked/flat distributions). At the furthest extent, iron ore shows the greatest positive skewness (8.29) which is combined with a high Kurtosis — peakedness of (96.83). Some commodities, such as lead, show a close relationship to normality (Skewness of 0.20 and kurtosis of 3.11). As evidenced in Table 2, the above results of general departure from normality are also confirmed with the Jarque–Bera (JB) test. The JB statistic is calculated in the following manner:

$$JB = n/6 \lfloor S^2 + (K-3)^2/4 \rfloor \approx \chi^2(2), \qquad (13)$$

where S is the skewness, K is the kurtosis, and n is the number of observations. The JB statistic ressembles approximately a Chi-squared distribution $[\chi^2(2)]$ with 2 degrees of freedom. The 95% and 99% points of the Chi-squared distribution with 2 degrees of freedom are 5.99 and 9.21, respectively, thus, the lower the JB statistics, the more likely a distribution is normal. Nonetheless, the JB test shows an obvious general deviation from normality and, thus, rejects the null hypothesis that the actual commodity portfolio's time series returns are normally distributed.

The interesting outcome of this empirical analysis suggests the necessity of combining L-VaR calculations — which assumes normal distributions of returns — with other methods such as stress-testing and scenario analysis to get a detailed picture of other remaining

Table 2: Risk analysis data: Descriptive statistics, Skewness, Kurtosis, and JB test.

Commodity name	Maximum (%)	Minimum (%)	Median (%)	Arithmetic mean (%)	Skewness (%)	Kurtosis	JB-statistics
Petroleum: Average Crude Price	45.7	−24.6	0.8	0.5	0.50	3.73	15**
Petroleum: Dubai	52.1	−30.6	0.9	0.5	0.55	6.08	107**
Petroleum: West Texas Intermediate	39.1	−20.6	0.8	0.5	0.36	2.17	12**
Petroleum: UK Brent	46.6	−25.2	0.4	0.5	0.43	2.82	8*
Gasoline	36.4	−25.4	1.1	0.5	0.09	0.40	68**
Natural Gas	40.5	−20.6	0.0	0.6	1.77	12.26	978**
Coal	15.9	−13.5	0.0	0.4	0.29	2.69	4
Gold	16.2	−12.5	−0.1	0.2	0.59	3.16	14**
Silver	19.7	−21.6	−0.2	0.2	0.04	2.30	5
Copper	24.8	−20.0	0.7	0.6	0.39	2.02	16**
Zinc	23.4	−24.9	0.4	0.6	−0.11	1.84	14**
Lead	30.7	−23.8	0.0	0.5	0.20	3.11	2
Aluminium	18.0	−32.6	0.1	0.3	−0.67	4.85	52**
Nickel	58.1	−22.2	−0.1	1.0	1.34	6.85	219**
Iron Ore	53.9	−12.9	0.0	0.5	8.29	96.83	90413**
Phosphate Rock	15.0	−21.7	0.0	0.2	−1.02	46.43	18828**
Wheat	15.9	−15.1	0.0	0.2	0.18	0.80	50**
Cotton	16.3	−12.6	−0.2	−0.1	0.31	0.86	50**
Sugar	9.8	−11.0	0.0	0.0	−0.11	5.93	86**
Maize	28.7	−25.2	0.4	0.3	0.01	5.40	57**
Tobacco	5.5	−4.9	0.1	0.0	0.00	0.24	76**
Coffee	29.1	−37.1	−0.5	0.0	−0.17	4.43	21**
Tea	21.5	−23.6	0.1	0.1	−0.14	0.52	62**
Rubber	19.6	−18.1	0.2	0.4	0.31	1.33	31**
Wool	19.9	−16.5	−0.2	0.2	0.49	2.63	11**
All Commodities Index	10.0	−12.3	0.0	0.4	−0.29	1.31	32**

Note: * and ** denote statistical significance at the 0.05 and 0.01 levels, respectively.

risks (fat tails in the probability distribution) that cannot be captured with the simple assumption of normality. In this chapter, we implement a stress-testing strategy in which severe market volatilities (as discussed earlier) are combined with various unwinding liquidity horizons under the notion of different correlation factors. The effects of the latter are of paramount importance (especially under severe market settings) as assets tend to be more correlated and perhaps correlation factors under some circumstances have a propensity of switching signs.

To conclude, Tables 3 and 4 demonstrate the liquidity holding horizons and commodity specific liquidity-adjusted risk factors (under both normal and severe market settings), while Table 5 depicts a matrix of empirical correlation factors that are used next for the estimation of L-VaR. The objective here is to establish the

Table 3: Risk analysis data: Liquidity holding horizon and L-VaR factors (normal market condition).

Commodity name	Liquidity holding horizon (in months)	Monthly volatility (%)	Liquidity-adjusted monthly volatility (%)	Commodity specific liquidity-adjusted risk factors (%)
Petroleum: Average Crude Price	1.2	8.1	8.3	16.5
Petroleum: Dubai	1.2	8.5	8.6	17.2
Petroleum: West Texas Intermediate	1.2	7.7	7.8	15.7
Petroleum: UK Brent	1.2	8.8	8.9	17.9
Gasoline	1.3	10.4	10.7	21.4
Natural Gas	1.4	5.8	6.0	12.0
Coal	1.5	4.0	4.2	8.4
Gold	1.2	3.3	3.3	6.6
Silver	1.5	5.4	5.7	11.4
Copper	1.7	6.2	6.7	13.4
Zinc	2.0	6.1	6.9	13.7
Lead	2.5	6.3	7.5	15.0
Aluminium	1.5	5.8	6.1	12.2
Nickel	2.5	8.9	10.5	21.0
Iron Ore	1.8	4.4	4.8	9.6
Phosphate Rock	3.0	2.3	2.9	5.8
Wheat	1.5	5.1	5.4	10.8
Cotton	1.8	4.9	5.4	10.7
Sugar	1.7	2.1	2.3	4.5
Maize	2.0	5.3	5.9	11.9
Tobacco	3.0	1.8	2.2	4.4
Coffee	1.6	8.0	8.5	17.0
Tea	1.7	7.7	8.3	16.7
Rubber	3.0	6.0	7.5	14.9
Wool	2.0	4.7	5.3	10.6

Table 4: Risk analysis data: Liquidity holding horizon and liquidity-adjusted VaR factors (severe market condition).

Commodity name	Liquidity holding horizon (in months)	Monthly volatility (%)	Liquidity-adjusted monthly volatility (%)	Commodity specific liquidity-adjusted risk factors (%)
Petroleum: Average Crude Price	1.2	24.6	25.1	50.1
Petroleum: Dubai	1.2	30.6	31.2	62.4
Petroleum: West Texas Intermediate	1.2	20.6	21.0	42.1
Petroleum: UK Brent	1.2	25.2	25.7	51.3
Gasoline	1.3	25.4	26.2	52.3
Natural Gas	1.4	20.6	21.4	42.9
Coal	1.5	13.5	14.3	28.6
Gold	1.2	12.5	12.7	25.4
Silver	1.5	21.6	22.8	45.6
Copper	1.7	20.0	21.5	43.1
Zinc	2.0	24.9	27.9	55.8
Lead	2.5	23.8	28.1	56.2
Aluminium	1.5	32.6	34.4	68.8
Nickel	2.5	22.2	26.3	52.5
Iron Ore	1.8	12.9	14.1	28.2
Phosphate Rock	3.0	21.7	27.1	54.1
Wheat	1.5	15.1	15.9	31.8
Cotton	1.8	12.6	13.7	27.4
Sugar	1.7	11.0	11.9	23.8
Maize	2.0	25.2	28.1	56.3
Tobacco	3.0	4.9	6.1	12.1
Coffee	1.6	37.1	39.6	79.2
Tea	1.7	23.6	25.5	51.0
Rubber	3.0	18.1	22.6	45.1
Wool	2.0	16.5	18.5	37.0

necessary quantitative infrastructures for advanced risk management analysis that will follow shortly.

The empirical correlation matrix is an essential aspect along with volatility matrices for the creation of L-VaR and stress-testing calculations for commodity market risk management processes and procedures. Contrary to general belief, our analysis indicates that in the long run there are very small and/or negative correlations between the various commodity markets. The result of Table 5 confirms several well-known facts in the commodity markets, such as the high

Table 5: Risk analysis data: Correlation matrix for a diverse portfolio of commodities.

Commodity name	Petroleum: Average Crude Price	Petroleum: Dubai	Petroleum: WTI	Petroleum: UK Brent	Gasoline	Natural gas	Coal	Gold	Silver	Copper	Zinc	Lead	Aluminium	Nickel	Iron ore	Phosphate rock	Wheat	Cotton	Sugar	Maize	Tobacco	Coffee	Tea	Rubber	Wool	All commodities index
Petroleum: Average Crude Price	100%																									
Petroleum: Dubai	97%	100%																								
Petroleum: WTI	98%	92%	100%																							
Petroleum: UK Brent	99%	94%	95%	100%																						
Gasoline	73%	67%	75%	72%	100%																					
Natural Gas	-5%	-8%	-2%	-5%	-2%	100%																				
Coal	11%	7%	14%	10%	17%	3%	100%																			
Gold	21%	19%	20%	21%	6%	3%	16%	100%																		
Silver	7%	5%	8%	8%	6%	-2%	11%	57%	100%																	
Copper	18%	17%	17%	18%	11%	5%	22%	27%	16%	100%																
Zinc	4%	4%	4%	3%	7%	3%	12%	14%	21%	45%	100%															
Lead	3%	3%	4%	2%	-4%	-11%	14%	22%	20%	36%	44%	100%														
Aluminium	22%	22%	21%	22%	13%	3%	13%	20%	24%	41%	37%	29%	100%													
Nickel	15%	14%	14%	17%	11%	-2%	21%	24%	21%	38%	40%	34%	44%	100%												
Iron Ore	10%	8%	11%	10%	16%	23%	11%	0%	-4%	1%	7%	2%	-2%	0%	100%											
Phosphate Rock	3%	3%	3%	4%	9%	-13%	1%	-7%	-1%	-13%	6%	-4%	0%	1%	22%	100%										
Wheat	-7%	-7%	-6%	-6%	2%	-3%	9%	8%	8%	9%	7%	1%	5%	1%	-2%	-5%	100%									
Cotton	0%	-1%	2%	0%	7%	7%	2%	-5%	-1%	8%	8%	11%	8%	9%	6%	-6%	-4%	100%								
Sugar	-6%	-4%	-6%	-8%	-2%	6%	10%	-5%	0%	0%	-5%	8%	-9%	-7%	8%	-3%	12%	17%	100%							
Maize	-18%	-18%	-16%	-20%	-6%	-4%	18%	8%	15%	-1%	12%	5%	7%	5%	0%	6%	48%	15%	9%	100%						
Tobacco	7%	10%	6%	6%	0%	-18%	-3%	-7%	-1%	6%	8%	9%	-14%	-5%	3%	12%	0%	-8%	-3%	2%	100%					
Coffee	2%	-1%	3%	2%	7%	6%	8%	-2%	7%	8%	0%	3%	-3%	7%	0%	-1%	7%	-2%	-3%	3%	0%	100%				
Tea	6%	3%	9%	5%	1%	5%	8%	2%	-8%	3%	4%	1%	-1%	-5%	13%	3%	8%	11%	-9%	-10%	-12%	6%	100%			
Rubber	20%	21%	19%	19%	16%	-3%	19%	24%	10%	13%	-1%	-7%	20%	18%	0%	0%	11%	19%	-4%	10%	-13%	6%	7%	100%		
Wool	-3%	-1%	-3%	-4%	7%	7%	13%	9%	10%	5%	7%	3%	15%	10%	5%	1%	-4%	4%	-1%	5%	-7%	7%	1%	7%	100%	
All Commodities index	77%	71%	77%	78%	69%	9%	24%	20%	12%	28%	20%	9%	20%	22%	15%	1%	6%	10%	-8%	-6%	2%	2%	5%	23%	-2%	100%

relationships between energy sector commodities, with the exception of natural gas and coal. In general, it seems that the energy sector, with the exclusion of natural gas and coal, is the dominate sector and therefore has the biggest effect (and correlation relationship) on the All Commodities Index.

3.2. *Examination of commodity markets risk management with L-VaR*

In order to illustrate the linkage between the theoretical constructs of L-VaR and its practical application and value as a tool for commodity risk management, the following hypothetical examples with full case studies are presented. These case studies parallel descriptions of L-VaR often found in the finance literature where portfolios of interest rate, equities, or currencies are the norm. These case studies also help in understanding the methods used in determining the performance of alternative L-VaR estimation procedures in the context of commodity trading risk management.

Using the definition of L-VaR in Section 3 and under the assumption that a given commodity portfolio has both long- and short-selling trading positions, Table 6 illustrates L-VaR at the one-tailed 97.5% level of confidence over the upcoming 1-month period. In this first full case study, the total portfolio value is USD10,000,000, with different asset allocation percentage and 1-month liquidity horizon — that is, 1 month to unwind all commodity trading positions. Furthermore, Table 6 illustrates the effects of stress testing (that is, L-VaR under severe market conditions) and the impact of different correlation factors on monthly L-VaR estimations. The L-VaR report depicts also monthly volatilities, in addition to their respective sensitivity factors *vis-à-vis* the All Commodities Index. Adverse (or severe) market monthly volatilities are calculated and illustrated in the report, too. These monthly severe volatilities represent the maximum negative returns (losses), which are perceived in the historical time series, for all commodities under consideration.

The L-VaR results are calculated under normal and severe market conditions by considering four different correlation factors

Table 6: Commodity trading risk management and control report.

Commodity Name	Market Value in USD	Asset Allocation Percentage	Liquidity Holding Horizon	Monthly Volatility (Normal)	Monthly Volatility (Severe)	Sensitivity Factors
Petroleum:Average Crude Price	$ 3,000,000	30.0%	1.0	8.11%	24.60%	1.72
Petroleum:Dubai	$ 6,000,000	60.0%	1.0	8.46%	30.62%	1.65
Petroleum:West Texas Intermediate	2,000,000	20.0%	1.0	7.68%	20.64%	1.63
Petroleum:UK Brent	3,000,000	30.0%	1.0	8.78%	25.18%	1.88
Gasoline	(2,000,000)	-20.0%	1.0	10.40%	25.40%	1.97
Natural Gas	(1,000,000)	-10.0%	1.0	5.76%	20.57%	0.14
Coal	(1,000,000)	-10.0%	1.0	4.00%	13.54%	0.26
Gold	(3,000,000)	-30.0%	1.0	3.25%	12.48%	0.18
Silver	(1,000,000)	-10.0%	1.0	5.40%	21.65%	0.18
Copper	1,000,000	10.0%	1.0	6.21%	19.96%	0.48
Zinc	1,000,000	10.0%	1.0	6.14%	24.94%	0.34
Lead	1,000,000	10.0%	1.0	6.33%	23.76%	0.15
Aluminium	1,000,000	10.0%	1.0	5.78%	32.64%	0.31
Nickel	1,000,000	10.0%	1.0	8.86%	22.19%	0.54
Iron Ore	2,000,000	20.0%	1.0	4.37%	12.91%	0.18
Phosphate Rock	1,000,000	10.0%	1.0	2.33%	21.71%	0.01
Wheat	(1,000,000)	-10.0%	1.0	5.12%	15.11%	0.08
Cotton	(1,000,000)	-10.0%	1.0	4.91%	12.56%	0.14
Sugar	(1,000,000)	-10.0%	1.0	2.10%	11.03%	-0.05
Maize	(1,000,000)	-10.0%	1.0	5.32%	25.18%	-0.08
Tobacco	(1,000,000)	-10.0%	1.0	1.78%	4.86%	0.01
Coffee	(2,000,000)	-20.0%	1.0	7.96%	37.11%	0.04
Tea	1,000,000	10.0%	1.0	7.73%	23.62%	0.11
Rubber	1,000,000	10.0%	1.0	5.99%	18.09%	0.37
Wool	1,000,000	10.0%	1.0	4.72%	16.53%	-0.02
All Commodities Index	$ -	0.0%	1.0	3.62%	12.26%	1.00
Total Portfolio Value in USD	$ 10,000,000	100%				

Monthly Liquidity-Adjusted Value-at-Risk (L-VaR) in USD — Normal Market Conditions

Correlation = Empirical	Correlation = 1	Correlation = 0	Correlation = -1
2,228,671	1,975,109	1,479,635	691,075
22.29%	19.75%	14.80%	6.91%

Diversification Effects

$ (253,562)	-11.38%

Monthly Liquidity-Adjusted Value-at-Risk (L-VaR) in USD — Severe (Crisis) Market Conditions

Correlation = Empirical	Correlation = 1	Correlation = 0	Correlation = -1
7,555,895	6,333,949	5,051,325	3,303,462
75.56%	63.34%	50.51%	33.03%

Diversification Effects

$ (1,221,946)	-16.17%

Overall Sensitivity Factor: Portfolio of Commodities

2.139

(+1, 0, −1, and empirical correlations between the various risk factors). Under correlation +1, the assumption is for 100% positive relationship between all risk factors (risk positions) at all times, whereas for the zero-correlation case, there is no relationship between all risk positions. While the −1 correlation case assumes 100% negative relationship, the empirical correlation case considers the actual empirical correlation factors between all positions and it is calculated via a variance/covariance matrix. Therefore, with 97.5% confidence, the actual commodity portfolio should expect to realize no greater than a USD2,228,671 decrease in the value over a 1-month period. In other words, the loss of USD2,228,671 is one that a commodity portfolio should realize only 2.5% of the time. If the actual loss exceeds the L-VaR estimate, then this would be considered a violation of the estimate. From a risk management perspective, the L-VaR estimate of USD2,228,671 is a valuable piece of information. Since every commodity trading business has different characteristics and tolerances toward risk, the commodity risk manager must examine the L-VaR estimate relative to the overall position of the entire business. Simply put, can the firm tolerate or even survive such a rare event — a loss of USD2,228,671 (or a 22.3% of total portfolio value)? This question is not only important to the commodity trading unit but also to financial institutions who lend money to these firms. The inability of a commodity trading unit to absorb large losses may jeopardize their ability to make principal and interest payments. Therefore, various risk management strategies could be examined in the context of how they might affect the L-VaR estimate. Presumably, risk management strategies, such as the use of futures and options contracts in hedging possible fluctuations in commodity prices, should reduce the L-VaR appraisal. In other words, those extreme losses in commodity trading, that would normally occur only 2.5% of the time, should be smaller with the incorporation of some type of risk management strategy. Furthermore, the degree of risk-diversification (namely, the effects of diversified L-VaR) of this hypothetical commodity trading portfolio can also be deduced simply as the difference in the values of the two greatest L-VaRs — that is the L-VaR of unity correlation case versus the L-VaR of empirical correlation case (USD−253,562 or −11.38% for the normal market condition case). However, it is appealing to note here that for this particular case, L-VaR under correlation +1 is less than L-VaR under empirical correlation case due to the impact of shorting (i.e. short-selling) some commodity positions. In addition, the overall sensitivity factor (beta factor) of this long/short commodity portfolio is indicated in this report as +2.139, or in other words, the total commodity portfolio value, with actual asset allocation ratios, is riskier than the benchmark index (All Commodities Index).

Finally, since the variations in L-VaR are mainly related to the ways in which the assets are allocated in addition to the liquidation horizon, it is instructive to examine the way in which L-VaR figures are influenced by changes in such parameters. All else equal, and under the assumption of normal and severe market conditions, Table 7 illustrates the nonlinear alterations to L-VaR figures when the liquidation periods are increased in line with the liquidity holding horizons and commodity specific liquidity-adjusted risk factors of Tables 3 and 4, respectively. Indeed the results of Tables 3 and 4 are essential inputs for the L-VaR engine to demonstrate the impact of liquidity holding horizons and commodity specific liquidity-adjusted risk factors on the overall L-VaR figures. For the sake of simplifying the L-VaR optimization algorithm, it should be noted that in this study the liquidation horizons (defined in Tables 3 and 4), under normal and severe market settings, are kept the same for both events and the variables that we decided to stress-test are merely limited to the monthly volatilities under both settings.

3.3.   *Optimization of efficient and coherent portfolios for commodity markets using L-VaR method*

One of the basic problems of applied finance is the optimal selection of assets, with the aim of maximizing future returns and constraining risk by appropriate measures. To this end, Markowitz (1959) illustrated that, for a given level of risk, one can identify certain groups of equity securities that maximize expected return. He considered

Table 7: Commodity trading risk management and control report.

Commodity Name	Market Value in USD	Asset Allocation Percentage	Liquidity Holding Horizon	Monthly Volatility (Normal)	Monthly Volatility (Severe)	Sensitivity Factors
Petroleum:Average Crude Price	$ 3,000,000	30.0%	1.2	8.11%	24.60%	1.72
Petroleum:Dubai	$ 6,000,000	60.0%	1.2	8.46%	30.62%	1.65
Petroleum:West Texas Intermediate	$ 2,000,000	20.0%	1.2	7.68%	20.64%	1.63
Petroleum:UK Brent	$ 3,000,000	30.0%	1.2	8.78%	25.18%	1.88
Gasoline	$ (2,000,000)	-20.0%	1.3	10.40%	25.40%	1.97
Natural Gas	$ (1,000,000)	-10.0%	1.4	5.76%	20.57%	0.14
Coal	$ (1,000,000)	-10.0%	1.5	4.00%	13.54%	0.26
Gold	$ (3,000,000)	-30.0%	1.2	3.25%	12.48%	0.18
Silver	$ (1,000,000)	-10.0%	1.5	5.40%	21.65%	0.18
Copper	$ 1,000,000	10.0%	1.7	6.21%	19.96%	0.48
Zinc	$ 1,000,000	10.0%	2.0	6.14%	24.94%	0.34
Lead	$ 1,000,000	10.0%	2.5	6.33%	23.76%	0.15
Aluminium	$ 1,000,000	10.0%	1.5	5.78%	32.64%	0.31
Nickel	$ 1,000,000	10.0%	2.5	8.86%	22.19%	0.54
Iron Ore	$ 2,000,000	20.0%	1.8	4.37%	12.91%	0.18
Phosphate Rock	$ 1,000,000	10.0%	3.0	2.33%	21.71%	0.01
Wheat	$ (1,000,000)	-10.0%	1.5	5.12%	15.11%	0.08
Cotton	$ (1,000,000)	-10.0%	1.8	4.91%	12.56%	0.14
Sugar	$ (1,000,000)	-10.0%	1.7	2.10%	11.03%	-0.05
Maize	$ (1,000,000)	-10.0%	2.0	5.32%	25.18%	-0.08
Tobacco	$ (1,000,000)	-10.0%	3.0	1.78%	4.86%	0.01
Coffee	$ (2,000,000)	-20.0%	1.6	7.96%	37.11%	0.04
Tea	$ 1,000,000	10.0%	1.7	7.73%	23.62%	0.11
Rubber	$ 1,000,000	10.0%	3.0	5.99%	18.09%	0.37
Wool	$ 1,000,000	10.0%	2.0	4.72%	16.53%	-0.02
All Commodities Index	$ -	0.0%	1.0	3.62%	12.26%	1.00
Total Portfolio Value in USD	$ 10,000,000	100%				

Monthly Liquidity-Adjusted Value-at-Risk (L-VaR) in USD
Normal Market Conditions

Correlation = Empirical	Correlation = 1	Correlation = 0	Correlation = -1
2,300,071	2,095,117	1,528,778	533,672
23.00%	20.95%	15.29%	5.34%

Diversification Effects

$ (204,954)	-8.91%

Monthly Liquidity-Adjusted Value-at-Risk (L-VaR) in USD
Severe (Crisis) Market Conditions

Correlation = Empirical	Correlation = 1	Correlation = 0	Correlation = -1
7,814,212	6,753,398	5,231,602	3,021,742
78.14%	67.53%	52.32%	30.22%

Diversification Effects

$ (1,060,814)	-13.58%

Overall Sensitivity Factor: Portfolio of Commodities

2.139

these optimum portfolios as "efficient" and referred to a continuum of such portfolios in dimensions of expected return and standard deviation as the efficient frontier. Accordingly, for asset allocation purposes, portfolio managers should choose portfolios located along the efficient frontier. Consequently, over a period of six decades a wide body of knowledge has been accumulated about the performance, strengths, and weaknesses of this approach when applied to equity portfolios. However, much less is known about portfolio optimization techniques in commodity markets and particularly under illiquid and adverse market conditions.

In this chapter, we look at the optimization problem from a different realistic operational angle. In view of that, the optimization problem formulated by finding the portfolio that minimizes L-VaR, with expected returns, trading volumes, and liquidation horizons, is constrained according to the requirements of the portfolio manager. As such, the focus in this research study is on the forecast of risk measure, rather than on expected returns for two reasons: first, several studies have analyzed the forecasts of expected returns in the context of mean–variance optimization (see, for instance, Best and Grauer, 1991). The common opinion is that expected returns are not easy to forecast, and that the optimization process is very sensitive to these variations. Second, there exists a general notion that L-VaR, in a wide sense, is simpler to assess than expected returns from historical data.

Essentially, our approach is a robust enhancement of the traditional Markowitz mean–variance approach, where the original risk measure, variance, is replaced by L-VaR. The task is attained here by minimizing L-VaR$_{P_{\mathrm{adj}}}$, while requiring minimum expected returns subject to the imposition of some meaningful operational and financial constraints. Thus, by considering different expected returns, we can generate an efficient L-VaR frontier. Alternatively, we can also maximize returns while not allowing for large risks. For the purpose of this research study, the optimization problem is formulated as follows:

From Equation (11), we can define liquidation horizon factor (LHF$_i$) for each trading asset as

$$\text{LHF}_i = \sqrt{\frac{(2t_i + 1)(t_i + 1)}{6t_i}}. \tag{14}$$

To compute efficient and coherent portfolios, we solve for the following nonlinear quadratic programming objective function:

$$\text{Minimize}: \text{L-VaR}_{P_{\text{adj}}} = \sqrt{|\text{L-VaR}_{\text{adj}}|^T \, |\rho| \, |\text{L-VaR}_{\text{adj}}|}. \tag{15}$$

Subject to the following financial and operational budget constraints as specified by the portfolio manager:

$$\sum_{i=1}^{n} R_i x_i = R_P; \; l_i \le x_i \le u_i, \quad i = 1, 2, \ldots, n, \tag{16}$$

$$\sum_{i=1}^{n} x_i = 1.0; \; l_i \le x_i \le u_i, \quad i = 1, 2, \ldots, n, \tag{17}$$

$$|\text{LHF}| \ge 1.0; \; \forall_i, \quad i = 1, 2, \ldots, n, \tag{18}$$

$$\sum_{i=1}^{n} V_i = V_P, \quad i = 1, 2, \ldots, n. \tag{19}$$

Here, R_P and V_P denote the target portfolio mean return and total portfolio volume, respectively, and x_i the weight or percentage asset allocation for each asset. The values l_i and $u_i, i = 1, 2, \ldots, n$ denote the lower and upper constraints for the portfolio weights x_i. If we choose $l_i = 0, i = 1, 2, \ldots, n$, then we have the situation where no short-selling is allowed. Moreover, $|\text{LHF}|$ indicates an $(n * 1)$ vector of the individual liquidity horizon of each commodity for all $i = 1, 2, \ldots, n$. The rationality behind imposing the above constraints is to comply with current regulations which enforce capital requirements on investment companies, proportional to VaR and/or L-VaR of a trading portfolio besides other operational limits (for instance, volume trading limits).

For the sake of solving the above optimization enigma, a software package is programmed for the purpose of creating realistic commodity trading portfolios and consequently for carrying out L-VaR's optimization (of both efficient and coherent portfolios) under normal and extreme illiquid market conditions. To this end, Figures 1 and 2 provide evidence of the empirical L-VaR efficient frontier (under normal and severe market settings) defined using a 97.5% confidence level.

As mentioned above, the optimal portfolio selection is performed by relaxing the short-sales constraint, for the different commodity assets. On the other hand, efficient portfolios cannot always be attained (e.g. short-selling without realistic lower boundaries on x_i) in the day-to-day real-world portfolio management operations and, hence, the portfolio manager should establish proactive coherent portfolios under more realistic and restricted budget constraints, detailed as follows:

- $\sum$ (energy commodities volume) = USD 15 million between long and short-selling trading positions.
- Trading volume in any energy commodity should be between $[-7, +7]$ million USD.

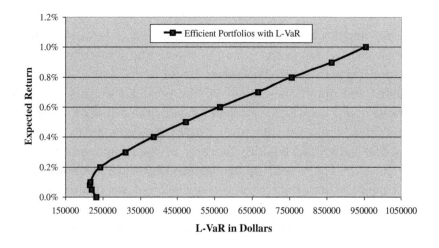

Figure 1: Efficient portfolios with L-VaR under normal market conditions.

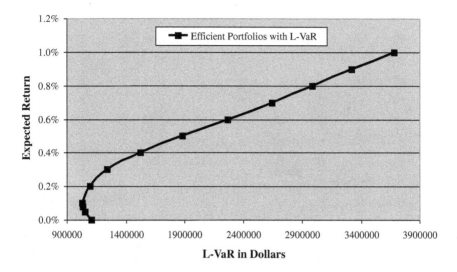

Figure 2: Efficient portfolios with L-VaR under adverse market conditions.

- Trading volume in any metal commodity should be between [−2, +2] million USD.
- Trading volume in any agriculture commodity should be between [−1, +1] million USD.
- Trading volume in any miscellaneous commodity should be between [−0.5, +0.5] million USD.

Now the weights are allowed to take negative or positive values, however, since arbitrarily high or low percentages have no financial sense, we determined to introduce lower and upper boundaries for the weights and in accordance with reasonable trading practices. Furthermore, for comparison purposes and since the endeavor in this chapter is to minimize L-VaR subject to specific expected returns, we decide to plot L-VaR versus expected returns and not the reverse, as is commonly done in the portfolio management literature. Accordingly, it is interesting to note here that the three benchmark portfolios (coherent portfolios [1], [2], and [3]) do not lie on the efficient frontier as indicated in Figures 3 and 4, respectively. This is because real-world considerations make it unlikely that a trading portfolio will behave exactly as theory predicts. Imperfections such as restriction on long

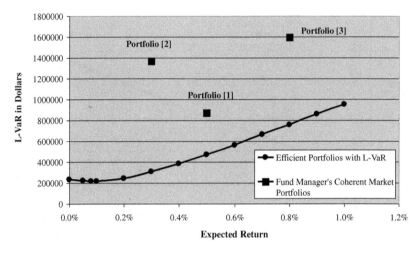

Figure 3: Efficient and coherent portfolios under normal market conditions (long and short trading positions).

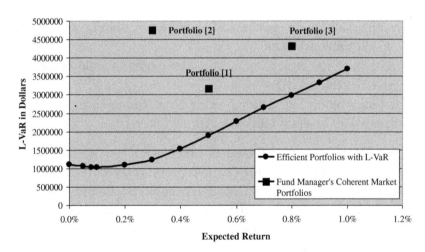

Figure 4: Efficient and coherent portfolios under adverse market conditions (long and short trading positions).

and short-trading positions, total trading volume, and liquidation horizons make it unlikely to create an efficient trading portfolio.

Moreover, it is important to note here that incorporating the effects of non-normality into the portfolio manager's portfolio

Table 8: Fund manager's coherent market portfolio [1].

Commodity name	Liquidation period (in months)	Market value in USD	Asset allocation per commodity
Petroleum: Average Crude Price	1.2	$ (7,000,000)	−70%
Petroleum: Dubai	1.2	$ 5,315,759	53%
Petroleum: West Texas Intermediate	1.2	$ 2,959,700	30%
Petroleum: UK Brent	1.2	$ 1,661,370	17%
Gasoline	1.3	$ (272,763)	−3%
Natural Gas	1.4	$ 5,335,934	53%
Coal	1.5	$ 7,000,000	70%
Gold	1.2	$ (2,000,000)	−20%
Silver	1.5	$ 399,380	4%
Copper	1.7	$ (1,135,090)	−11%
Zinc	2	$ (104,590)	−1%
Lead	2.5	$ 707,628	7%
Aluminium	1.5	$ (805,003)	−8%
Nickel	2.5	$ (286,493)	−3%
Iron Ore	1.8	$ (2,000,000)	−20%
Phosphate Rock	3	$ 1,631,085	16%
Wheat	1.5	$ 588,184	6%
Cotton	1.8	$ 168,754	2%
Sugar	1.7	$ (1,000,000)	−10%
Maize	2	$ (275,080)	−3%
Tobacco	3	$ 930,815	9%
Coffee	1.6	$ (368,496)	−4%
Tea	1.7	$ (453,263)	−5%
Rubber	3	$ (500,000)	−5%
Wool	2	$ (497,831)	−5%

Correlation Factor	L-VaR (Normal)	L-VaR (Severe)	Expected Return
Empirical	872,005	3,163,942	0.50%
1.0	1,069,335	4,209,277	Sensitivity Factor
0.0	1,840,019	6,109,964	0.51
−1.0	2,372,312	7,546,212	

decision causes a great change in the resulting optimal portfolio allocation (e.g. coherent portfolio [2] tends to be more riskier under adverse market conditions than portfolio [3] and vice-versa under normal market setting). Thus, the portfolio manager should apply active strategies in order to earn excess returns. These considerations are especially relevant for individual portfolio managers who

Table 9: Fund manager's coherent market portfolio [2].

Commodity name	Liquidation period (in months)	Market value in USD	Asset allocation per commodity
Petroleum: Average Crude Price	1.2	$ (3,000,000)	−30%
Petroleum: Dubai	1.2	$ (1,000,000)	−10%
Petroleum: West Texas Intermediate	1.2	$ 3,000,000	30%
Petroleum: UK Brent	1.2	$ 2,000,000	20%
Gasoline	1.3	$ 1,000,000	10%
Natural Gas	1.4	$ 7,000,000	70%
Coal	1.5	$ 6,000,000	60%
Gold	1.2	$ (2,000,000)	−20%
Silver	1.5	$ (2,000,000)	−20%
Copper	1.7	$ (1,000,000)	−10%
Zinc	2	$ (1,000,000)	−10%
Lead	2.5	$ (1,000,000)	−10%
Aluminium	1.5	$ (1,000,000)	−10%
Nickel	2.5	$ (2,000,000)	−20%
Iron Ore	1.8	$ 2,000,000	20%
Phosphate Rock	3	$ 1,000,000	10%
Wheat	1.5	$ 500,000	5%
Cotton	1.8	$ 200,000	2%
Sugar	1.7	$ 1,000,000	10%
Maize	2	$ (300,000)	−3%
Tobacco	3	$ 1,000,000	10%
Coffee	1.6	$ 1,000,000	10%
Tea	1.7	$ (400,000)	−4%
Rubber	3	$ (500,000)	−5%
Wool	2	$ (500,000)	−5%
Correlation Factor	L-VaR (normal)	L-VaR (severe)	Expected return
Empirical	1,366,869	4,754,694	0.30%
1.0	751,248	2,373,646	Sensitivity factor
0.0	1,429,041	4,741,863	0.35
−1.0	1,876,151	6,271,868	

may spread their trading positions across a few securities. Nevertheless, the elegance and compelling logic of the theory prompt attempts to apply the theory even though practitioners recognize the variance between the simplifying assumptions of the theory and the realities of the world.

In order to illustrate the composition of coherent portfolios [1], [2], and [3], Tables 8–10 point out the asset allocation weights for

Table 10: Fund manager's coherent market portfolio [3].

Commodity name	Liquidation period (in months)	Market value in USD	Asset allocation per commodity
Petroleum: Average Crude Price	1.2	$ (1,000,000)	−10%
Petroleum: Dubai	1.2	$ (2,000,000)	−20%
Petroleum: West Texas Intermediate	1.2	$ 5,000,000	50%
Petroleum: UK Brent	1.2	$ 4,000,000	40%
Gasoline	1.3	$ 2,000,000	20%
Natural Gas	1.4	$ 1,000,000	10%
Coal	1.5	$ 6,000,000	60%
Gold	1.2	$ (2,000,000)	−20%
Silver	1.5	$ (2,000,000)	−20%
Copper	1.7	$ (300,000)	−3%
Zinc	2	$ 1,000,000	10%
Lead	2.5	$ (1,000,000)	−10%
Aluminium	1.5	$ (2,000,000)	−20%
Nickel	2.5	$ 2,000,000	20%
Iron Ore	1.8	$ 2,000,000	20%
Phosphate Rock	3	$ (1,000,000)	−10%
Wheat	1.5	$ 1,000,000	10%
Cotton	1.8	$ -	0%
Sugar	1.7	$ 1,000,000	10%
Maize	2	$ (300,000)	−3%
Tobacco	3	$ (1,000,000)	−10%
Coffee	1.6	$ (1,000,000)	−10%
Tea	1.7	$ (400,000)	−4%
Rubber	3	$ (500,000)	−5%
Wool	2	$ (500,000)	−5%
Correlation factor	L-VaR (normal)	L-VaR (severe)	Expected return
Empirical	1,595,564	4,320,607	0.80
1.0	1,647,492	2,597,313	Sensitivity factor
0.0	1,473,626	4,579,007	1.62
−1.0	1,276,290	5,931,995	

all 25 different classes of commodity assets in all the periods considered. Similarly, the three tables depict L-VaR for normal and severe market settings and under the assumption of four different correlation factors. In this way, portfolio managers should employ risk measures which allow them to take decisions which would produce a risk budget lower than a specific target. In this line of reasoning, under adverse market conditions, L-VaR is calculated by implementing downside volatilities only (i.e. maximum negative asset returns throughout the sampling period). Thus, this analysis is substantially a robust generalization of the Markowitz analysis that permits one to determine the asymmetric aspect of risk. In any case, the benefit of portfolio optimization critically depends on how accurately the implemented L-VaR risk measure is forecasted.

4.   Concluding Remarks

This chapter is an attempt to examine the performance of L-VaR measures in the framework of a diverse commodity portfolio. To date, all known empirical studies examining the performance of alternative VaR measures have been conducted in the framework of portfolios containing foreign exchange, interest rate, or equity data with portfolios often developed arbitrarily. The commodities selected for this research project provide a realistic alternative portfolio, as well as new data, for studying existing techniques of L-VaR estimation. The empirical results reported in this chapter also provide an incentive for further research in the area of L-VaR and commodity markets price risk management.

In fact, one of the basic problems of applied finance is the optimal selection of assets, with the aim of maximizing future returns and constraining risk by appropriate measures. In this chapter, we examine how to determine the optimal portfolio choice for a commodity portfolio manager under normal and adverse distributional assumptions. We then provide a new portfolio optimization technique using L-VaR as a risk measure.

This chapter extends previous approaches to optimization problems with L-VaR constraints. In particular, the suggested approach can be used for minimizing L-VaR under several budget constraints. Furthermore, multiple L-VaR constraints with various unwinding liquidation periods and correlation factors can be used to shape the profit/loss distribution. In this research study, the optimization problem is formulated by finding a set of portfolios that minimize L-VaR subject to given expected returns, trading volume, and liquidity horizons. To this end, the L-VaR's risk function is constrained by a downside risk measure in addition to several operational and financial constraints such as total volume, long and short-trading positions, and liquidity unwinding periods. Our model is an enhancement of the conventional Markowitz mean–variance approach, where the original risk measure, variance, is replaced by L-VaR and by guaranteeing minimum expected returns under different liquidation horizons. This approach can aid in solving some of the real-world trading dilemmas under adverse market conditions: when liquidity dries up; correlations factors switch signs; and the incorporation of non-normal distribution of asset returns in the risk measurement process.

This chapter shows that the performance of efficient and coherent portfolios depends on the expected returns, individual VaR positions, liquidity horizons of each trading asset, and the set of portfolio weights. The empirical findings indicate that the risk tolerance in the L-VaR framework is time-varying and closely related to the selection of the unwinding liquidity horizons, expected returns, in addition to the impact of the determined correlation factors of the portfolio. Moreover, in this work, the relative performance of the L-VaR selection model is compared in a dynamic asset allocation framework. The objective of the dynamic asset allocation is to find the optimum assets mix by minimizing L-VaR subject to the application of several proactive real-world operational and financial constraints.

The empirical results indicate that our innovative portfolio optimization approach, with the incorporation of L-VaR method, performs better than the standard mean–variance VaR model in terms of the optimal portfolio's selection as well as in determining the portfolio managers' coherent portfolios. The empirical findings are persistent over the entire commodities markets' sample period and robust across alternative investment horizons.

References

Al Janabi, M. A. M. (2012), Optimal commodity asset allocation with a coherent market risk modeling, *Review of Financial Economics*, 21(3), 131–140.

Al Janabi, M. A. M. (2009). Commodity price risk management: Valuation of large trading portfolios under adverse and illiquid market settings, *Journal of Derivatives & Hedge Funds*, 15(1), 15–50.

Al Janabi, M. A. M. (2008). Integrating liquidity risk factor into a parametric value at risk Method, *Journal of Trading*, 3(3), 76–87.

Almgren, R. and Chriss, N. (1999). Optimal execution of portfolio transaction, Working Paper, Department of Mathematics, The University of Chicago.

Angelidis, T. and Benos, A. (2006), Liquidity adjusted value-at-risk based on the components of the bid-ask spread, *Applied Financial Economics*, 16(11), 835–851.

Bangia, A., Diebold, F., Schuermann, T. and Stroughair, J. (2002). Modeling liquidity risk with implications for traditional market risk measurement and management, in Figlewski, S. and Levich, R. M. (eds.), *Risk Management: The State of the Art*, Vol. 8, The New York University Salomon Center Series on Financial Markets and Institutions, pp. 3–13.

Berkowitz, J. (2000). Incorporating liquidity risk into VAR models, Working Paper, Graduate School of Management, University of California, Irvine.

Best, M. J. and Grauer, R. R. (1991). On the sensitivity of mean-variance-efficient portfolios to changes in asset means: Some analytical and computational results, *Review of Financial Studies*, 4, 315–342.

Claessens, S. and Varangis, P. (1994). Commodity risk management in developing countries, in Papaioannou, M. and Tsetsekos, G. (eds.), *Derivative Instruments and Hedging Strategies for Emerging Capital Markets*, Dow Jones Irwin, Illinois.

Giot, P. and Laurent, S. (2003). Market risk in commodity markets: A VaR approach, *Energy Economics*, 25(5), 435–457.

International Financial Statistics Browser (XXXX). International Monetary Fund (IMF), Available at: http://imfStatistics.org.

Jarrow, R. and Subramanian, A. (1997). Mopping up liquidity, *Risk*, 10(12), 170–173.

Madoroba, S. B. W. and Kruger, J. W. (2014). Liquidity effects on value-at-risk limits: Construction of a new VaR model, *Journal of Risk Model Validation*, 8, 19–46.

Manfredo, M. and Leuthold, R. (2001). Market risk and the cattle feeding margin: An application of value-at-risk, *Agribusiness: An International Journal*, 17(3), 333–353.

Manfredo, M. and Leuthold, R. (1999). Value-at-risk analysis: A review and the potential for agricultural applications, *Review of Agricultural Economics*, 21(1), 99–111.

Markowitz, H. (1959). *Portfolio Selection: Efficient Diversification of Investments*, John Wiley, New York.

Morgan Guaranty Trust Company (1994). *RiskMetrics-Technical Document*, Morgan Guaranty Trust Company, Global Research, New York.

Satyanarayan, S. and Varangis, P. (1994). An efficient frontier for international portfolios with commodity assets, Policy Research Working Paper, WPS 1266, The World Bank, International Economics Department, International Trade Division, Washington, DC.

White, B. and Dawson, P. J. (2005). Measuring price risk on UK arable farms, *Journal of Agricultural Economics*, 56(2), 239–252.

Wilson, W. W. and Nganje, W. E. (2007). Value-at-risk in bakery procurement, *Review of Agricultural Economics*, 29(3), 581–595.

Chapter 9

Comovements and Integration in African Stock Markets

El Mehdi Ferrouhi

Faculty of Law, Economics, and Social Sciences.
Ibn Tofail University. Kénitra, Morocco
elmehdiferrouhi@gmail.com

1. Introduction

Recent financial crises and shocks showed that many stock markets around the world comove, e.g., their variations and movements are correlated. A significant increase in comovements is considered as contagion while a continued market correlation at high levels is considered to be interdependence (Forbes and Rigobon, 2002). The impact of stock exchanges comovements was fatal for many investors whose portfolios have suffered severe damage and loss.

Various studies investigated stock exchanges comovements in Europe, Asia, Latin America, and at the international level. Thus, in Europe, Scheicher (2001) studied integration of stock markets in Hungary, Poland, and the Czech Republic and found limited interactions in returns and low correlations between these markets. Bhar and Hamori (2008) studied comovement among four European equity markets and found evidence of integration among these markets. Johnson and Soenen (2009) analyzed the comovement among European Union (EU) equity markets between 1980 and 2006.

237

Results obtained show a negative relationship among European markets. Dunis, Sermpinis, and Karampelia (2013) investigated comovement and integration among five members of the European Monetary Union (Cyprus, Estonia, Malta, Slovakia, and Slovenia) and the euro area. Results obtained show a high degree of integration for Malta and Slovenia and also for Cyprus and Slovakia.

Regarding comovement of Asian stock exchanges, Jang and Saul (2002) analyzed the comovement among the Asian markets using Johansen cointegration test and found evidence of short-term and long-term cointegration among these markets. Chiang *et al.* (2007) analyzed correlation among nine Asian daily stock-return data series for the period 1990–2003 and we identify two phases of the Asian crisis. The authors found that the first period is characterized by increase in correlation (contagion) while the second shows a continued high correlation (herding). Majid *et al.* (2009) explored market comovements among five ASEAN stock markets (Malaysia, Thailand, Indonesia, the Philippines, and Singapore) and found that the stock markets in the ASEAN region were cointegrated both during the pre- and post-1997 financial crisis.

Arouri *et al.* (2010) studied comovements of Latin American stock markets using dynamic conditional correlation GARCH model. The authors found a changing cross-market comovement over time.

Other studies focussed on comovement among international stock exchanges. Thus, Engsted and Tanggaard (2004) investigated comovements among US and UK stock returns for the period 1918–1999 and found evidence of high comovements correlated over the period of the study. Hoque (2007) analyzed dynamics of stock price movements of the stock market of Bangladesh with those of the US, Japan, and India, using Johansen and Juselius multivariate cointegration approach. Results obtained show evidence of cointegration among these markets. Morana and Betreatti (2008) investigated integration and comovement among stock markets of the US, the UK, Germany, and Japan for the period 1973–2004 and found a progressive integration of the four stock markets and increasing comovements in prices, returns, volatilities, and correlations. Graham and Nikkinen (2011) used wavelet analysis to examine the short-term and long-term comovement of international stock markets. Results show that the comovement of Finland and the emerging market regions is confined to long-term fluctuations. Results also find evidence of comovement between Finland and the developed regions in Europe, the Pacific, and North America. Qadan and Yagil (2015) studied international comovements of both real economic activity and financial activity for the period 1980–2010. Results show that the United States and the G7 countries are not symmetrically cointegrated with respect to the GDP.

Lee and Yu (2018) examined comovements in stock returns between Korea, China, Japan, and the US for the period 2003–2016 and found that the comovements of the Korean stock returns with those of the US and Japan became smaller after the global financial crisis. In contrast, the comovement in stock returns between Korea and China became larger after the crisis.

The countries used in this study are considered as the main economies in Africa. Indeed, according to MSCI, Egypt and South Africa are classified as emerging markets, while Kenya, Mauritius, Morocco, Nigeria, Tunisia, and WAEMU (The West African Economic and Monetary Union) are considered as frontier markets. In the same list, we find in the standalone market indexes Botswana, Ghana, and Zimbabwe. According to Bloomberg, in the top 20 emerging markets, we find Morocco (19), South Africa (15), Zambia (14), and Namibia (13). According to a recent ranking of African Stock markets, the eight Top Stock Exchanges in Africa are, respectively, those of South Africa, Nigeria, Morocco, Kenya, Ghana, Egypt, and Tunisia.

This chapter aims to define short-term and long-term comovements of major African stock markets using Granger-causality and Johansen cointegration test. We use daily stock price indices for the period January 1, 2012–December 31, 2018, and stock exchanges investigated are those of Egypt (Egyptian Stock Exchange 30 Index), Kenya (Nairobi Stock Exchange 20 Share Index), Mauritius (Stock Exchange of Mauritius Index), Morocco (Moroccan All Shares

Index), Namibia (Namibia Stock exchange Overall Index), Nigeria (Nigeria Stock Exchange 30), South Africa (FTSE South Africa), and Tunisia (Tunisia Stock Exchange Index).

This chapter is organized as follows. Methodology and data used are presented in Section 2. Results obtained are presented in Section 3, while Section 4 offers conclusions.

2.   Methodology and Data

This chapter aims to define short-term and long-term comovements of African stock markets. To do this, we first conduct Granger-causality that indicates short-term integration among markets. We then use Johansen cointegration test (Johansen, 1988), which demonstrates the stable long-term equilibrium relations between variables and which requires, as a *sine qua non* condition, the integration of the studied variables in the same order (Ferrouhi, 2017). Johansen cointegration test uses the following equation:

$$\Delta Z_t = \prod Z_{t-1} + \sum_{i=1}^{p-1} \Gamma_i \Delta_{t-i} + \mu_0 + \mu_1 t + \nu_t,$$

where Z_t is the column vector of p-variables, Π and Γ are coefficients matrices to test μ_i are column vectors of constant terms and trend coefficients, and vt is the Gaussian error of dimension p. To define time series order of integration, we use the widely used unit root tests augmented Dickey Fuller (Dickey and Fuller, 1981) and Phillips Perron (1988).

Regarding data, we use daily stock price indices for the period January 1, 2012–December 31, 2018. Stock prices indices are in local currency and we use daily closing prices for each stock market. We select all African stock markets and retained stock markets whose data are available for the last 6 years. We obtained eight stock markets, which are the major African stock markets. Obtained stock indices are those of Egypt (Egyptian Stock Exchange 30 Index), Kenya (Nairobi Stock Exchange 20 Share Index), Mauritius

Table 1: Main African stock markets and indices for the period of the study.

Number	Country	Stock exchange	Stock index	Ticker
1	Egypt	Egyptian Exchange	Egyptian Stock Exchange 30 Index	EGX 30
2	Kenya	Nairobi Securities Exchange	Nairobi Stock Exchange 20 Share Index	NSE20
3	Mauritius	Stock Exchange of Mauritius	Stock Exchange of Mauritius Index	SEMDEX
4	Morocco	Casablanca Stock Exchange	Moroccan All Shares Index	MASI
5	Namibia	Namibia Stock Exchange	Namibia Stock exchange Overall Index	OVRLNM
6	Nigeria	Nigerian Stock Exchange	Nigeria Stock Exchange All Shares	NGSE
7	South Africa	JSE Limited	FTSE South Africa	INVSAF 40
8	Tunisia	Bourse de Tunis	Tunisia Stock Exchange Index	TUNINDEX

(Stock Exchange of Mauritius Index), Morocco (Moroccan All Shares Index), Namibia (Namibia Stock exchange Overall Index), Nigeria (Nigeria Stock Exchange 30), South Africa (FTSE South Africa), and Tunisia (Tunisia Stock Exchange Index). Data were obtained from investing.com database. Table 1 lists selected stock markets and relative information of each stock market. Thus, column 2 shows countries, column 3 stock markets while columns 4 and 5 present stock indices retained and their tickers.

When data were unavailable, e.g., due to national holidays, the selected days were deleted from all stock markets so we could retain data for the same days for the entire time series, which will allow us to avoid skewing of our series because of the mismatching between days in each time series.

Figures 1–8 represent the evolution of African indices for the period January 1, 2012–December 31, 2018. We remark that NSE20, SEMDEX, MADEX, and NGSE were volatile during this period while EGX30, OVRLNM, FTSE South Africa, and TUNINDEX were volatile with a growing trend. Thus, the Kenyan index NSE20 was instable and volatile as it decreased from January 2012 to November

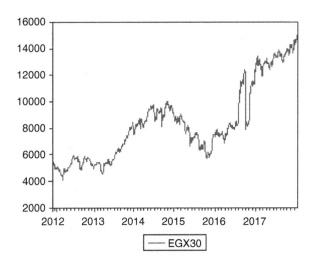

Figure 1: Evolution of EGX between January 1, 2012 and December 31, 2018.

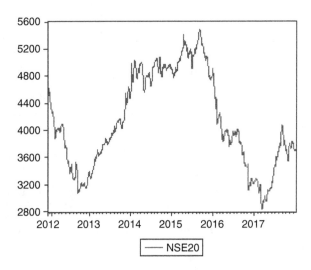

Figure 2: Evolution of NSE20 between January 1, 2012 and December 31, 2018.

2013, and then increased from December 2013 to September 2016, followed by a fall of this index from October 2016 to December 2018. The Mauritian index SEMDEX is also characterized by its volatility as it didn't follow a trend for the overall period of the study. The

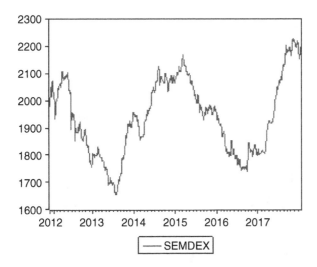

Figure 3: Evolution of SEMDEX between January 1, 2012 and December 31, 2018.

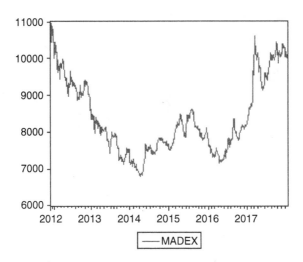

Figure 4: Evolution of MADEX between January 1, 2012 and December 31, 2018.

Moroccan index MADEX is characterized by a downward trend until 2015, followed by an increasing one. Nigeria Stock Exchange Index is characterized by a first period of increase, from January 2012 to January 2015, followed by a decreasing period until December 2016, then

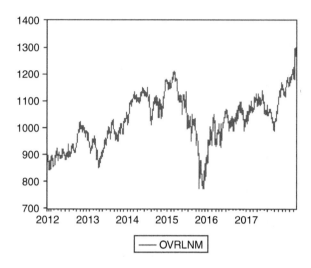

Figure 5: Evolution of OVRLNM between January 1, 2012 and December 31, 2018.

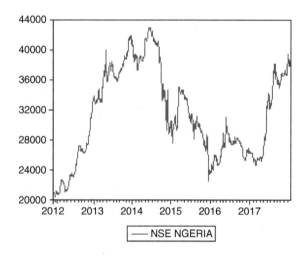

Figure 6: Evolution of NGSE between January 1, 2012 and December 31, 2018.

a last increasing trend. The Egyptian index EGX30 had an increasing trend for the overall period. We also remark that three trends characterize this index: a growing trend from January 2012 to November 2015, followed by a decreasing one from December 2015 to October 2016. The last period from October 2016 to December 2018 is

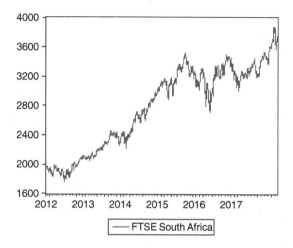

Figure 7: Evolution of FTSE SA between January 1, 2012 and December 31, 2018.

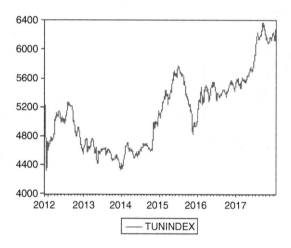

Figure 8: Evolution of TUNINDEX between January 1, 2012 and December 31, 2018.

characterized by an increasing trend. The Namibian index OVTLNM was also volatile, but in general followed an increasing trend. FTSE South Africa and TUNINDEX in general followed an increasing trend.

Table 2 represents descriptive statistics of 1,326 daily index data of African stock markets. Regarding standard variation, we

Table 2: Descriptive statistics for the main African stock indices.

Country	Egypt	Kenya	Mauritius	Morocco
Index	EGX 30	NSE 20	SEMDEX	MADEX
Observations	1326	1326	1326	1326
Mean	8382.36	4130.39	1940.20	8384.63
Median	7981.20	3992.92	1936.21	8090.43
St.variation	2273.38	607.81	118.55	848.88
Max	15019.14	5499.64	2229.99	10965.49
Min	4031.60	2824.32	1654.81	6782.18
Skewness	0.66	0.13	0.06	0.62
Kurtosis	2.36	1.75	2.02	2.20
Jarque–Bera	118.77	89.78	53.65	120.12
Probability	0.00	0.00	0.00	0.00
Country	Namibia	Nigeria	South Africa	Tunisia
Index	OVRLNM	NGSE	FTSE SA	TUNINDEX
Observations	1326	1326	1326	1326
Mean	1025.14	31416.63	2782.32	5145.65
Median	1028.28	30447.52	2956.50	5131.97
St.variation	78.89	5263.76	505.13	433.90
Max	1299.70	43039.42	3879.85	6376.08
Min	771.41	20329.62	1756.31	4321.23
Skewness	−0.13	0.11	−0.27	0.42
Kurtosis	2.47	1.87	1.66	2.30
Jarque–Bera	19.39	73.85	115.11	66.90
Probability	0.00	0.00	0.00	0.00

Source: Based on author's calculation.

remark that the OVRLNM was the less volatile stock index. For the eight African stock indices, time series are not normally distributed (Skewness and kurtosis, respectively, differed from 0 and 3), so we can apply our test to these time series.

3.   Results

Comovements between every two African stock indices are represented using the correlation matrix (Table 3). Thus, we remark that the EGX30 is positively correlated to OVLNM and FTSE South Africa (0.74), TUNINDEX (0.66), SEMDEX (0.35), MADEX (0.24), and NGSE (0.20) and negatively correlated to NSE20 (−0.19). The Kenyan index NSE20 is positively correlated to OVRLNM (0.39)

Table 3: Correlation matrix.

	EGX30	NSE20	SEMDEX	MADEX	OVRLNM	NGSE	FTSE SA	TUNINDEX
EGX30	1.00	−0.19	0.35	0.24	0.74	0.20	0.74	0.66
NSE20	−0.19	1.00	0.39	−0.49	0.09	0.32	0.16	−0.23
SEMDEX	0.35	0.39	1.00	0.39	0.35	0.09	0.28	0.39
MADE0	0.24	−0.49	0.39	1.00	−0.10	−0.39	−0.02	0.50
OVRLNM	0.74	0.09	0.35	−0.10	1.00	0.43	0.52	0.32
NGSE	0.20	0.32	0.09	−0.39	0.43	1.00	0.04	−0.27
FTSE SA	0.74	0.16	0.28	−0.02	0.52	0.04	1.00	0.74
TUNINDEX	0.66	−0.23	0.39	0.50	0.32	−0.2	0.74	1.00

and NGSE (0.32) and negatively correlated to MADEX (−0.49), TUNINDEX (−0.23), and EGX (−0.19). However, NSE20 is neither significantly correlated to FTSE South Africa nor OVRLNM. The Mauritian index SEMDEX is significantly correlated to NSE20, MADEX, TUNINDEX (0.39), OVRLNM, EGX30 (0.35), and FTSE South Africa (0.28). SEMDEX and NGSE are not significantly correlated (0.09). MADEX is positively correlated to TUNINDEX (0.50), SEMDEX (0.39), and EGX30 (0.24) while it is negatively correlated to NSE20 (−0.49) and NGSE (−0.39). However, MADEX is neither significantly correlated to OVRLNM nor to FTSE South Africa. OVRLNM is positively correlated to EGX30 (0.74), FTSE South Africa (0.52), NGSE (0.43), SEMDEX (0.35), and TUNINDEX (0.32). The Namibian index is neither significantly correlated to MADEX nor to NSE20. NGSE is positively correlated to OVRLNM (0.43), NSE20 (0.32), and EGX30 (0.20). NGSE is negatively correlated to MADEX (−0.39), TUNINDEX (−0.27), while there is no significant correlation with SEMDEX and FTSE South Africa. FTSE South Africa is positively correlated to EGX30, TUNINDEX (0.74), OVRLNM (0.52), SEMDEX (0.28), and NSE20 (0.16). The South African index has no significant correlation with NGSE and MADEX. TUNINDEX is positively correlated to FTSE South Africa (0.74), EGX30 (0.66), MADEX (0.50), SEMDEX (0.39), and OVRLNM (0.32) and negatively correlated to NSE20 (−0.23) and NGSE (−0.27).

We remark that EGX30 and SEMDEX are highly correlated to all African stock indices except, respectively, to NSE20 and NGSE.

Also, the Moroccan index MADEX is negatively correlated with the Kenyan, Namibian, Nigerian, and South African ones. From a geographical point of view, we remark that North African stock markets (Egypt, Morocco, and Tunisia) are correlated. Also, Austral African countries (Mauritius, Namibia, and South Africa) are highly correlated.

Thus, as a very low or negative correlation coefficient implies a reduction of the systematic risk and as we remark the existence of high correlations between African stock indices, we can say that investors who invest in the Kenyan, the Moroccan, and the Nigerian stock exchanges can reduce the level of systematic risk.

Table 4 presents results of unit root tests augmented Dickey Fuller and Phillip–Perron. Thus, we present test statistics for each variable using both tests (∗ means that variables are statistically representative at the 1% level). We note that the null hypothesis for both tests is the existence of a unit root which means that our time series are non-stationary. According to obtained results, all variables are non-stationary at level and stationary at first difference. Thus, our time series are integrated as the same order (first order) I (1). Thus, Granger-causality test and Johansen cointegration test can be conducted.

Table 5 presents the results of Granger causality test for African markets. Thus, we reject the null hypothesis of no Granger causality

Table 4: Augmented Dickey Fuller and Phillips–Perron Unit root tests.

	ADF		PP	
	At level	First difference	At level	First difference
EGX 30	−2.100862	−32.71343*	−2.049585	−32.71939*
NSE 20	−1.188374	−21.06625*	−1.118812	−30.50509*
SEMDEX	−0.851707	−30.68660*	−0.972055	−0.972055*
MADEX	−1.671121	−34.32751*	−1.725830	−34.32475*
OVRLNM	−2.511246	−35.83961*	−2.167300	−2.167300*
NGSE	−1.714455	−27.66429*	−1.669368	−27.33907*
FTSE SA	−3.257633	−37.54039*	−3.070764	−37.87433*
TUNINDEX	−2.449480	−27.13632*	−2.329708	−27.32887*

Note: Variables statistically representative at the * 1% level.

Table 5: Granger-causality test.

Null hypothesis	F-statistic	Probability	Null hypothesis	F-statistic	Probability
NSE20 does not Granger Cause EGX30	0.69727	0.49813	OVRLNM does not Granger Cause SEMDEX	3.49867	0.03052
EGX30 does not Granger Cause NSE20	0.80570	0.44699	SEMDEX does not Granger Cause OVRLNM	0.41123	0.66292
SEMDEX does not Granger Cause EGX30	0.35026	0.70457	NGSE does not Granger Cause SEMDEX	2.97019	0.05164
EGX30 does not Granger Cause SEMDEX	5.66532	0.00355	SEMDEX does not Granger Cause NGSE	0.50886	0.60130
MADEX does not Granger Cause EGX30	1.53001	0.21692	FTSE_SA does not Granger Cause SEMDEX	1.24276	0.28893
EGX30 does not Granger Cause MADEX	6.15754	0.00218	SEMDEX does not Granger Cause FTSE_SA	0.40294	0.66843
OVRLNM does not Granger Cause EGX30	2.79979	0.06118	TUNINDEX does not Granger Cause SEMDEX	0.06845	0.93384
EGX30 does not Granger Cause OVRLNM	4.32897	0.01337	SEMDEX does not Granger Cause TUNINDEX	2.04020	0.13041
NGSE does not Granger Cause EGX30	0.16617	0.84692	OVRLNM does not Granger Cause MADEX	4.19059	0.01534
EGX30 does not Granger Cause NGSE	0.25760	0.77295	MADEX does not Granger Cause OVRLNM	0.05053	0.95073
FTSE_SA does not Granger Cause EGX30	0.50788	0.60189	NGSE does not Granger Cause MADEX	0.03282	0.96772
EGX30 does not Granger Cause FTSE_SA	3.58674	0.02796	MADEX does not Granger Cause NGSE	1.22343	0.29455
TUNINDEX does not Granger Cause EGX30	0.06417	0.93785	FTSE_SA does not Granger Cause MADEX	2.96831	0.05173
EGX30 does not Granger Cause TUNINDEX	4.14800	0.01600	MADEX does not Granger Cause FTSE_SA	0.13125	0.87701
SEMDEX does not Granger Cause NSE20	0.47305	0.62320	TUNINDEX does not Granger Cause MADEX	5.40886	0.00458
NSE20 does not Granger Cause SEMDEX	0.74849	0.47328	MADEX does not Granger Cause TUNINDEX	0.17474	0.83969
MADEX does not Granger Cause NSE20	2.06128	0.12770	NGSE does not Granger Cause OVRLNM	0.76777	0.46425

(*Continued*)

Table 5: (*Continued*)

Null hypothesis	F-statistic	Probability	Null hypothesis	F-statistic	Probability
NSE20 does not Granger Cause MADEX	1.31695	0.26830	OVRLNM does not Granger Cause NGSE	0.16058	0.85167
OVRLNM does not Granger Cause NSE20	2.22751	0.10820	FTSE_SA does not Granger Cause OVRLNM	1.11057	0.32968
NSE20 does not Granger Cause OVRLNM	0.28309	0.75350	OVRLNM does not Granger Cause FTSE_SA	2.89243	0.05579
NGSE does not Granger Cause NSE20	10.5515	0.00002	TUNINDEX does not Granger Cause OVRLNM	0.29532	0.74434
NSE20 does not Granger Cause NGSE	3.26931	0.03834	OVRLNM does not Granger Cause TUNINDEX	4.13278	0.01625
FTSE_SA does not Granger Cause NSE20	0.94557	0.38872	FTSE_SA does not Granger Cause NGSE	0.56511	0.56843
NSE20 does not Granger Cause FTSE_SA	0.09904	0.90571	NGSE does not Granger Cause FTSE_SA	1.54922	0.21280
TUNINDEX does not Granger Cause NSE20	0.56528	0.56834	TUNINDEX does not Granger Cause NGSE	0.08366	0.91975
NSE20 does not Granger Cause TUNINDEX	0.16593	0.84712	NGSE does not Granger Cause TUNINDEX	0.04364	0.95730
MADEX does not Granger Cause SEMDEX	0.55957	0.57159	TUNINDEX does not Granger Cause FTSE_SA	1.93471	0.14488
SEMDEX does not Granger Cause MADEX	1.16580	0.31199	FTSE_SA does not Granger Cause TUNINDEX	2.50071	0.08242

from EGX30 to SEMDEX, MADEX, and TUNINDEX at 1% and to FTSE South Africa at 5%. Regarding relationship between OVRLNM and EGX30, we found Granger causality in both directions at 5% (from OVRLNM to EGX30) and 1% (from EGX30 to OVRLNM). Also, results of relationship between NGSE and NSE20 show the existence of Granger causality in both directions at 5% (from NGSE to NSE20) and at 1% (from NSE20 to NGSE). Regarding relationships of OVRLNM with other stock indices, we reject the null hypothesis of Granger causality with SEMDEX and FTSE South Africa (at 5%), MADEX and TUNINDEX (at 1%). We also found

Granger causality in both directions with EGX30, from OVRLNM to EGX30 (at 5%) and from EGX30 to OVRLNM (at 1%). The null hypothesis of no Granger-causality is rejected from NGSE to SEMDEX (at 5%) and from TUNINDEX to MADEX (at 1%). We also reject the null hypothesis of Granger-causality from FTSE South Africa to MADEX (at 5%) and to TUNINDEX (at 10%).

Thus, the Moroccan stock index MADEX depends on EGX30, TUNINDEX, FTSE South Africa, and OVRLNM. The Mauritius index SEMDEX depends on EGX30, OVRLNM, and NGSE. The Tunisian index TUNINDEX depends on EGX30, OVRLNM, and FTSE South Africa while the South African index FTSE South Africa depends on EGX30 and OVRLNM. The Kenyan index NSE20 and the Nigerian one are interdependent. Also, the Egyptian stock index EGX30 and the Namibian one OVRLNM are interdependent. Granger-causality results confirm precedent results. Regarding short-term integration we can say that MADEX is short-term integrated with EGX30, TUNINDEX, FTSE South Africa, and OVRLNM. Also, SEMDEX is short-term integrated with EGX30, OVRLNM, and NGSE. TUNINDEX is short-term integrated with EGX30, OVRLNM, and FTSE South Africa. FTSE South Africa is short-term integrated with EGX30 and OVRLNM. NSE20 and NGSE are short-term integrated. EGX30 and OVRLNM are short-term integrated. Thus, investors who invest in integrated stock markets can benefit from good performances in case of price indices' increases at short term.

According to unit root tests, all variables used in this chapter are integrated at the same order I(1). Thus, Johansen cointegration test can be applied to these variables. We note that before the application of Johansen cointegration test, we have to determine the optimal length of VAR model. Thus, we use Akaïke Information Criterion and the Schwarz Criterion. According to Kasri and Kassim (2009), the optimal lag length proposed is 1.

Tables 6 and 7 present results of Johansen cointegration tests (Trace statistic and Max-Eigen statistic). For both, we reject the null hypothesis of no cointegration at the 5% level. Thus, Table 6

Table 6: Johansen cointegration test (trace statistic).

Hypothesized no. of CE(s)	Eigenvalue	Trace statistic	0.05 critical value	Prob.**
None*	0.028701	163.9286	159.5297	0.0281
At most 1	0.024781	125.3726	125.6154	0.0517
At most 2	0.021171	92.14866	95.75366	0.0863
At most 3	0.019450	63.81703	69.81889	0.1372

Note: * is 90% and ** is 95%.

Table 7: Johansen cointegration test (max eigen statistic).

Hypothesized no. of CE(s)	Eigenvalue	Max-Eigen statistic	0.05 critical value	Prob.**
None*	0.028701	50.55603	49.36261	0.0456
At most 1	0.024781	33.22395	46.23142	0.5766
At most 2	0.021171	28.33163	40.07757	0.5383
At most 3	0.019450	26.00493	33.87687	0.3204

Note: * is 90% and ** is 95%.

shows the existence of a cointegration vector in "Trace Statistic", as the 163.9286 value exceeds the critical value 159.5297 at 5%. Table 7 shows the existence of a cointegration vector in "Max-Eigen Statistic", 50.55603 as the value exceeds the critical value 49.36261 at 5%. It indicates the existence of one cointegration equation. Thus, there is cointegration among African stock markets.

Results of long-term relationships that exist between all African stock indices during the period 2012–2018 are presented in Table 8. Results show that the Egyptian index EGX30, the Kenyan index NSE, the Moroccan index MADEX, and the Namibian one OVRLNM comove and are positively cointegrated while markets of Mauritius SEMDEX, Nigeria NGSE, and South Africa FTSE South Africa are negatively cointegrated.

These results imply the existence of cointegration and a long-term relationship between the variables. Thus, investments in African stock markets can benefit investors because they are cointegrated in the long term. Thus, while the markets of Egypt, Kenya, Morocco,

Table 8: Long-term relationships between African stock indices.

EGX30	NSE20	SEMDEX	MADEX	OVRLNM	NGSE	FTSE SA	TUNINDEX
1.00	25.45	−100.84	10.50	14.93	−0.43	−21.17	18.15
0.04	1.00	−3.96	0.41	0.59	−0.02	−0.83	0.71
−0.01	−0.25	1.00	−0.10	−0.15	0.00	0.21	−0.18
0.10	2.43	−9.61	1.00	1.42	−0.04	−2.02	1.73
0.07	1.71	−6.75	0.70	1.00	−0.03	−1.42	1.22
−2.34	−59.58	236.04	−24.57	−34.95	1.00	49.55	−42.48
−0.05	−1.20	4.76	−0.50	−0.71	0.02	1.00	−0.86
0.06	1.40	−5.56	0.58	0.82	−0.02	−1.17	1.00

and Namibia vary in the same direction, the market indices of Mauritius, Nigeria, and South Africa vary in the opposite direction.

4. Conclusion

Recent financial crises and shocks showed that many stock markets around the world comove, e.g., their variations and movements are correlated. Authors that studied comovements in international stock exchanges found contradictory results.

In this chapter, we investigated short-term and long-term comovements of major African stock markets (Egypt, Kenya, Mauritius, Morocco, Namibia, Nigeria, South Africa, and Tunisia) using Granger-causality and Johansen cointegration test for the period January 1, 2012–December 31, 2018.

Regarding bilateral correlations between African stock markets, we found that investors in the Kenyan, the Moroccan, and the Nigerian stock exchanges are less exposed to systematic risk. Thus, they can benefit from good performances in case of price indices' increases, in these markets, at short term. At long term, results obtained show that African stock markets are cointegrated and comove at long term. However, we found that markets of Egypt, Kenya, Morocco, and Namibia comove positively while those of Mauritius, Nigeria, and South Africa comove negatively.

References

Afkinsider (2016). 8 Top Stock Exchanges In Africa, https://afkinsider.co
m/120492/8-top-stock-exchanges-in-africa/. Last accessed on March
18, 2018.

Al Asad Bin Hoque, H. (2007). Co-movement of Bangladesh stock market with other markets: Cointegration and error correction approach,
Managerial Finance, 33(10), 810–820.

Bhar, R. and Hamori, S. (2008). A new approach to analyzing comovement in European equity markets, *Studies in Economics and Finance*,
25(1), 4–20.

Bloomberg (2013). The Top 20 Emerging Markets, https://www.bloomb
erg.com/news/photo-essays/2013-01-31/the-top-20-emerging-mar
kets/. Last accessed on March 18, 2018.

Chiang, T. C., Jeon, B. N. and Li, H. (2007). Dynamic correlation analysis of financial contagion: Evidence from Asian markets, *Journal of
International Money and finance*, 26(7), 1206–1228.

Dickey, D. A. and Fuller, W. A. (1981). Likelihood ratio statistics for autoregressive time series with a unit root, *Econometrica: Journal of the
Econometric Society*, 49(4), 1057–1072.

Dunis, C., Sermpinis, G. and Ferenia Karampelia, M. (2013). Stock market
linkages among new EMU members and the euro area: Implications
for financial integration and portfolio diversification, *Studies in Economics and Finance*, 30(4), 370–388.

El Hedi Arouri, M., Bellalah, M. and Nguyen, D. K. (2010). The comovements in international stock markets: New evidence from Latin
American emerging countries, *Applied Economics Letters*, 17(13),
1323–1328.

Engsted, T. and Tanggaard, C. (2004). The comovement of US
and UK stock markets, *European Financial Management*, 10(4),
593–607.

Ferrouhi, E. M. (2017). Determinants of bank performance in a developing country: Evidence from Morocco, *Organizations & Markets in
Emerging Economies*, 8(1).

Forbes, K. J. and Rigobon, R. (2002). No contagion, only interdependence:
Measuring stock market comovements, *The Journal of Finance*, 57(5),
2223–2261.

Graham, M. and Nikkinen, J. (2011). Co-movement of the Finnish and
international stock markets: A wavelet analysis, *The European Journal of Finance*, 17(5–6), 409–425.

Jang, H. and Sul, W. (2002). The Asian financial crisis and the co-movement
of Asian stock markets, *Journal of Asian Economics*, 13(1), 94–104.

Johansen, S. (1988). Statistical analysis of cointegration vectors, *Journal of Economic Dynamics and Control*, 12(2–3), 231–254.

Johnson, R. and Soenen, L. (2009). European economic integration and stock market co-movement with Germany, *Multinational Business Review*, 17(3), 205–228.

Kasri, R. A. and Kassim, S. H. (2009). Empirical determinants of saving in the Islamic Banks: Evidence from Indonesia, *Journal of King Abdulaziz University, Islamic Economics*, 22(2), 181–201.

Lee, J. and Yu, B. K. (2018). *What Drives the Stock Market Comovements between Korea and China, Japan and the US?* (No. 2018-2). Economic Research Institute, Bank of Korea.

Morana, C. and Beltratti, A. (2008). Comovements in international stock markets, *Journal of International Financial Markets, Institutions and Money*, 18(1), 31–45.

MSCI (2018). Market cap indexes, https://www.msci.com/market-cap-we ighted-indexes/. Last accessed on March 18, 2018.

Phillips, P. C. and Perron, P. (1988). Testing for a unit root in time series regression, *Biometrika*, 75(2), 335–346.

Qadan, M. and Yagil, J. (2015). Are international economic and financial co-movements characterized by asymmetric co-integration? *Review of Accounting and Finance*, 14(4), 398–412.

Scheicher, M. (2001). The comovements of stock markets in Hungary, Poland and the Czech Republic, *International Journal of Finance & Economics*, 6(1), 27–39.

Shabri Abd. Majid, M., Kameel Mydin Meera, A., Azmi Omar, M. and Abdul Aziz, H. (2009). Dynamic linkages among ASEAN-5 emerging stock markets, *International Journal of Emerging Markets*, 4(2), 160–184.

Chapter 10

Interdependence or Contagion in Equity Markets? Evidence from Past Crises

Olfa Kaabia

*INSEEC U., INSSEC School of Business and
Economics Paris, France*

okaabia@inseec.com

1. Introduction

The last three decades have been marked by numerous financial crises: the European Exchange Rate Mechanism (ERM) crisis in 1992–1993, the Asian crisis in 1997–1998, the dot-com crisis in 2000, the subprime mortgages crisis in 2007, followed by the global financial crisis in 2009 (GFC).

During those crises, contagion was observed when a local crisis originating in a particular nation spreads out, in a very severe and unexpected way, to other countries, sometimes very distant. An illustration of this phenomenon is the transmission of turmoil from Hong Kong to Mexico and Chile in 1997. A second illustration is the subprime crisis that spreads out across advanced and emerging countries. Even if it initially had its origin in the US in a relatively small segment of the lending market, it affects worldwide equity markets. Hence, it is interesting to revisit the debate about the presence and sources of "contagion" in equity markets.

The discussion of the cross-markets transmission mechanism is well established and documented in the literature; however, there is some misunderstanding between some concepts such as comovements, interdependence, and contagion. Unfortunately, the definition of contagion is still not unanimous among the economists.[1] A widely cited definition of contagion is "when an extreme negative event in one country affects others" (Forbes, 2013). Pericoli and Sbracia (2003) exposed five academic definitions that continue to be widely used in the literature. Along with the various studies on different crises, the literature can bring to light two main distinctions: "pure contagion" (known as true contagion, shift-contagion, or even market-based contagion) and interdependencies (also called spillovers and fundamentals). More precisely, interdependence is defined as the relationship that exists between asset classes on average over the sample period; whereas, contagion is defined as a change in the transmission mechanism between assets in crisis periods. Consequently, it seems more useful to restrict the term of contagion to those situations where the extent and magnitude to which a local shock is transmitted internationally exceeds what was expected *ex ante*.

An important question is whether this increase in comovements of global financial markets during past crises provides evidence of contagion. In this chapter, we attempt addressing this issue in the literature. Hence, has there been contagion in OECD equity markets during the Asian crisis, the ERM, or even the GFC? If so, did contagion primarily emanate from the USA or from a specific region?

The novelty of our analysis is to distinguish clearly between the calm and the turbulent period when studying the increase of the unexpected returns, inspired by the Bekaert *et al.* (2005, 2011) model. We develop a different procedure by adding two dummy variables to consider both turmoil and calm periods. Thus, we consider that the comovements unexplained by fundamentals are signs of contagion.

---

[1]For more details, see, among others, Rigobon (1999), Forbes and Rigobon (2000, 2002), Jang and Sul (2002), Claessens *et al.* (2002), and Corestti *et al.* (2005).

We focus on the changes in the dynamics of the conditional correlation of stock market returns of 16 OECD countries.

Dealing with a three-factor model with time-varying betas, we extract the unexpected returns of 17 OECD stock markets in three regions: Europe, Asia-Pacific, and North America. To this proposition, we estimate time-varying betas using rolling regressions and test the appropriate GARCH-type model to capture the (a)symmetries in volatility,[2] which is highly desirable when the topics of contagion and interdependence are studied. Once extracted, the residual correlations are introduced in a panel model by adding dummy variables to account for both tranquil and crisis periods to test contagion.

Our analysis is particularly relevant in focusing on a country's vulnerability to externally originated shocks from local, regional, and the US risks, both in tranquil and crisis periods.

Our study is useful for both investors and policymakers to counter the negative impacts during calm and crisis periods. In fact, if OECD equity markets are contagious, economic policy should focus on structural reforms ensuring a stable domestic market, in order to limit, even stop, the amplification of shocks between stock markets since it is well known that the dynamics of international stock markets share common features, and influence one another. Moreover, distincting between interdependency and contagion has important implications for researchers, investors, and policymakers. Since investors use correlations as input for portfolio diversification and selection, if the correlations are estimated in times of tranquility and used in the crisis periods, this could generate unpredictable consequences. Similarly, policymakers need to distinguish the transmission of shocks to domestic economies between tranquil and crisis period. Decision-making (policy responses and contingency plans) during the crisis period, on the basis of the study of the transmission of shocks during the tranquil period, could yield serious consequences for the

---

[2]Inspired by the results of Bakshi *et al.* (1997), Bekaert and Harvey (1997), and Ng (2000), we model the error terms using a type-GARCH model in order to well characterize the stylized facts of the variance in the OECD stock returns.

domestic economies. Our work relates to the growing literature on global financial crises and, to the best of our knowledge, no paper in the contagion literature has proposed such a methodology to test and model contagion effects in OECD equity markets.

The main results of our study are as follows:

First, cross-sectional patterns exist both in regional and the US market correlations with OECD equity markets, however, differences in vulnerability are reported. Indeed, the idiosyncratic residuals are better correlated with the US even in a tranquil period.

Second, the hypothesis of no contagion over the entire period, for the US, can be rejected for most of the OECD markets with different magnitudes. The additional correlation of the country's idiosyncratic shocks with the US during the GFC period is positive denoting that residuals have become more correlated during that crisis.

Third, European countries such as Germany, the UK, the Netherlands, Spain, and Italy are most significantly affected by the ERM crisis. And during the Asian crisis, there is no regional contagion.

Fourth, contagion effects are not strongly related to high levels of global integration.

The rest of the chapter is structured as follows: Section 2 exposes the literature review. Section 3 presents the theoretical framework. Section 4 describes the empirical study. Section 5 deals with the results and interpretations. Section 6 draws appropriate conclusions.

2.   Literature Review

A high number of theoretical and empirical studies deal with the notions of market linkages and excess comovements in stock market prices. The results of these studies are hybrids and do not lead to convincing conclusions. It is difficult to precisely pin down what should be considered "normal" or "in excess" (Rigobon, 2016).

Mainly, studies tackle the issue of market contagion and specifically asset markets. Bekaert *et al.* (2005) develop a model to identify economic fundamentals (such as the systematic sources of risk) from the residual correlations, which are used to test directly the existence and dynamics of contagion. They find no evidence in favor of contagion during the Mexican crisis, but show that the Asian crisis was characterized by large movements of contagion. Dungey *et al.* (2007)[3] study contagion in Asia and Australia and get similar results. Chiang *et al.* (2007) use a dynamic conditional correlation GARCH model to test contagion between nine Asian stock returns from 1990 to 2003. They use dummy variables to delimit their sample in three periods, and for each period, they observe the correlation dynamic between selected stock markets. More recently, there is a growing body of empirical literature testing for financial contagion during the GFC. In that sense, Longstaff and Ang (2011) study the exposure of sovereigns to systemic shocks, in the US and EU and find that sovereign risk is strongly and negatively correlated with stock market indexes. Bekaert *et al.* (2011) analyze contagion across different portfolios of 55 countries' equity markets during the 2007–2009 financial crisis. Using a CAPM, they find systematic and substantial contagion from domestic equity markets to individual domestic equity portfolios, with its severity inversely related to the quality of countries' economic fundamentals. Therefore, they conclude that investors focus substantially more on country-specific characteristics (idiosyncratic risks) during the crisis period.

Guo *et al.* (2011) and Longstaff (2010) study the cross-asset contagion between several asset classes in the US market. Kenourgios *et al.* (2011) deal with the contagion in the BRIC emerging equity markets. Johansson (2011) examines equity market movements in East Asia and Europe during the GFC. Neaime (2012) examined the impact of the GFC in the MENA region, he found a higher correlation with the US stock market during the crisis.

Hau and Lai (2012) show that stocks with a high share of equity funds ownership performed relatively well during the GFC, whereas stocks with ownership link to funds that were heavily affected

---

[3]The authors propose a synthesis of theoretical and empirical works on international financial contagion.

by portfolio losses in financial stocks severely underperform. Beltratti and Stulz (2012) investigate whether the variation in the cross-section of stock returns of large banks across the world during the crisis is related to bank-level governance, country-level governance, country-level regulation, as well as to bank balance sheet and profitability characteristics before the GFC. Calomiris *et al.* (2012) show that credit supply shocks, global demand shocks, and selling pressures in the equity market had a significant negative effect on individual stock returns during the GFC but had no such effects during other crises.

Almeida *et al.* (2012) find that firms with large portions of long-term debt maturing at the time of the GFC reduced investment significantly more than similar firms that did not need to refinance their debt during the crisis.

Beirne and Gieck (2014) assess interdependence and contagion across three asset classes (bonds, stocks, and currencies) for over 60 economies during the period 1998–2011, concluding that in times of financial crisis, US equity shocks lead to risk aversion by investors in equities and currencies globally. Caporale *et al.* (2014) examine the linkages between stock market prices and exchange rates in six advanced economies, finding evidence of uni-directional Granger causality from stock returns to exchange rate changes in the US and the UK, from exchange rate changes to stock returns in Canada, and bi-directional causality in the Euro area and Switzerland.

The literature review identifies a necessity to conduct further research on the topic as the issue is lacking the requisite evidence. By construction, the tested models cannot, in general, clearly distinguish between interdependence and contagion in global and regional stock markets.[4]

3.   Theoretical Framework

This section outlines the models we estimate, contrasts the concepts of correlation versus contagion, and explains the estimation process.

---

[4]See King and Wadhwani (1990).

3.1.   Model to capture unexpected returns

We assume that the PPP is verified[5] and built on the results of Bekaert and Harvey (2005, 2011) by retaining a three-factor model based on the capital assets pricing model (CAPM) framework. Our model simultaneously considers local sources in addition to global and regional risk factors.

In addition, we assume that the portfolio of the US market is a good benchmark of the global market within a portfolio of the regional market and local sources of risks as follows:

$$\Re_{i,t} = \delta'_i Z_{i,t-1} + \beta^{\mathrm{US}}_{i,t-1} \Re_{\mathrm{US},t-1} + \beta^{\mathrm{reg}}_{i,t-1} \Re_{\mathrm{reg},t-1}$$

$$+ \beta^{\mathrm{US}}_{i,t-1} e_{\mathrm{US},t} + \beta^{\mathrm{reg}}_{i,t-1} e_{\mathrm{reg},t} + e_{i,t}, \tag{1}$$

$$e_{i,t}|\Omega_{t-1} \sim N(0, \sigma^2_{i,t}), \tag{2}$$

where the conditional expected excess returns for the country i, the US, and regional markets are, respectively, $\Re_{i,t} = E(R_{i,t}/\Omega_{t-1}) - R_{f,t}$; $\Re_{\mathrm{US},t-1} = E((R_{\mathrm{US},t}/\Omega_{t-1}) - R_{f,t})$, and $\Re_{\mathrm{reg},t-1} = E((R_{\mathrm{reg},t}/\Omega_{t-1}) - R_{f,t})$ that are expressed in US dollars with $R_{i,t}$, $R_{\mathrm{US},t}$ and $R_{\mathrm{reg},t}$, correspondingly, being the returns in US dollars of the market i, the US and the regional markets.

Ω_{t-1} includes all the information available at the time $t-1$. $R_{f,t}$ is the risk-free rate. $e_{\mathrm{US},t}$ and $e_{\mathrm{reg},t}$ are, respectively, the unanticipated returns of the global market and the regional one. $e_{i,t}$ is the residual of the estimated model for the market i; $Z_{i,t-1}$ is the set of local information variables available until the date $t-1$, including a constant, and δ_i is the vector of coefficients to be estimated. Also, $\beta^{\mathrm{US}}_{i,t-1}$ and $\beta^{\mathrm{reg}}_{i,t-1}$ are the sensitivities of the market i to the US market and the regional one.

To account for the stylized fact that the variance of the idiosyncratic return shock of the market i is conditional and asymmetric,

---

[5]This is a simplifying assumption. We agree as Adler and Dumas (1983), Carrieri *et al.* (2007), and Tai (2007) that there are deviations from Purchasing Power Parity (PPP), and variations in consumption baskets across geographies. Therefore, if PPP is not verified, any investment in a foreign asset is a combination of an investment in the performance of the foreign asset and an investment in the performance of the domestic currency relative to the foreign currency.

we assume that the error term of Equation (2) is modeled using a DCC–GJR–GARCH (1,1) process.[6] The latest captures any asymmetric effects in volatility and assumes that bad and good news have different effects on volatility: negative shocks are supposed to have a higher effect on stock return volatility compared to positive ones of the same scale. Moreover, Dungey and Zhumabekova (2001), and Corsetti *et al.* (2012) point out mis-specification issues and suggest using dynamic conditional correlation GARCH models when studying contagion.

Therefore, the DCC–GJR–GARCH (1,1) model specified is

$$H_t = D_t R_t D_t',$$
$$D_t = \text{diag}(\sqrt{h_{11,t}}, \sqrt{h_{22,t}}, \ldots, \sqrt{h_{n,n,t}}), \tag{3}$$
$$R_t = (1 - \theta_1 - \theta_2)R + \theta_1 \Psi_{t-1} + \theta_2 R_{t-1},$$

where H_t is the variance matrix and D_t is a diagonal matrix of conditional standard deviations for each of the return series, obtained from estimating a univariate GJR–GARCH[7] process of Glosten *et al.* (1993) in the equation of variance expressed as

$$h_{ii,t} = w_i + \alpha \varepsilon_{ii,t-1}^2 + \beta_i h_{ii,t-1} + \gamma_i I_{i,t} \varepsilon_{ii,t-1}^2. \tag{4}$$

The persistence is measured by the coefficients α_i and β_i, and $I_{i,t}$ is an indicator function capturing asymmetry in the estimate of the coefficient γ_i. For instance, a negative value of γ_i implies that negative residuals increase the variance more than positive residuals.

R is a symmetric $N \times N$ positive definite parameter matrix of dynamic conditional correlations in which θ_1 and θ_2 are non-negative parameters satisfying $\theta_1 + \theta_2 < 1$. It is specified as Tse and Tsui (2002) GARCH model with Ψ_{t-1} as the $N \times N$ correlation matrix of ε_τ for $\tau = t - M, t - M + 1, \ldots, t - 1$.

---

[6]The multivariate framework is more relevant than the bivariate one when considering the dynamic interactions and capturing the comovements between the international returns (see Glosten *et al.*, 1993; Bekaert *et al.*, 2005).

[7]This model gives better statistical results than the DCC–GARCH one.

Its i, jth element is given by

$$\Psi_{ij,t-1} = \frac{\sum_{m=1}^{M} u_{i,t-m}, u_{j,t-m}}{\sqrt{\left(\sum_{m=1}^{M} u_{i,t-m}^2\right)\left(\sum_{m=1}^{M} u_{j,t-m}^2\right)}}, \tag{5}$$

where $u_{i,t} = \frac{\varepsilon_{i,t}}{\sqrt{h_{ii,t}}}$. The matrix Ψ_{t-1} can be expressed as $\Psi_{t-1} = B_{t-1}^{-1} L_{t-1} L'_{t-1} B_{t-1}^{-1}$ in which $L_{t-1} = (u_{t-1}, \ldots, u_{t-M})$ is an $N \times M$ matrix and B_{t-1} is an $N \times N$ diagonal matrix with the ith diagonal element given by $[\sum_{h=1}^{M} u_{i,t-h}^2]^{1/2}$ and $u_t = (u_{1,t}, u_{2,t}, \ldots, u_{N,t})'$.

A necessary condition to measure the positivity of Ψ_{t-1}, and therefore that of R_t is $M \geq N$. Then, R_t is itself a correlation matrix if R_{t-1} is also a correlation matrix ($\rho_{ii} = 1$).

Moreover, Equation (1) can decompose the return of the market i into an expected return and an unexpected one. More clearly, the expected return is given by

$$E[\Re_{i,t-1}|\Omega_{t-1}] = \delta'_i Z_{i,t-1} + \beta_{i,t-1}^{\text{US}} \Re_{\text{US},t-1} + \beta_{i,t-1}^{\text{reg}} \Re_{\text{reg},t-1}. \tag{6}$$

Thus, the unexpected portion of the market return is driven not only by shocks from the local market but also by two foreign shocks originating in the US and the regional risks given by

$$\varepsilon_{i,t} = \beta_{i,t-1}^{\text{US}} e_{\text{US},t} + \beta_{i,t-1}^{\text{reg}} e_{\text{reg},t} + e_{i,t}. \tag{7}$$

Also, following Bekaert *et al.* (2005, 2011), we conduct an analysis of the total variance in each of the studied markets.

The expressions are derived by assuming that local shocks are uncorrelated across countries and that they similarly do not correlate with the US and regional markets.

Therefore, the variance of the market i is given by

$$h_{i,t} = E(\varepsilon_{i,t}^2|\Omega_{t-1}) = (\beta_{i,t-1}^{\text{US}})^2 \sigma_{\text{US},t}^2 + (\beta_{i,t-1}^{\text{reg}})^2 \sigma_{\text{reg},t}^2 + \sigma_{i,t}^2. \tag{8}$$

Besides, we focus on the time variation and cross-sectional patterns, both in the US and regional market correlations of the market i that are given by

$$\rho_{i,\text{us},t} = \frac{\beta_{i,t-1}^{\text{us}}\sigma_{\text{us},t}}{\sqrt{h_{i,t}}},$$

$$\rho_{i,\text{reg},t} = \frac{\beta_{i,t-1}^{\text{us}}\beta_{\text{reg},t-1}^{\text{us}}\sigma_{\text{us},t}^2 + \beta_{\text{reg},t-1}^{\text{us}}\sigma_{\text{reg},t}^2}{\sqrt{h_{i,t}h_{\text{reg},t}}},$$

$\quad$ (9)

where $h_{\text{reg},t} = (\beta_{\text{reg},t-1}^{\text{us}})^2\sigma_{\text{us},t}^2 + \sigma_{\text{reg},t}^2$ is the conditional variance of the regional market return.

Additionally, we analyze the shares of the total variance explained respectively by the global market (VR_i^{US}), and the regional one (VR_i^{reg}), computed as follows:

$$VR_{i,t}^{\text{US}} = \frac{(\beta_{i,t-1}^{\text{US}})^2\sigma_{\text{US},t}^2}{h_{i,t}},$$

$$VR_{i,t}^{\text{reg}} = \frac{(\beta_{i,t-1}^{\text{reg}})^2\sigma_{\text{reg},t}^2}{h_{i,t}}.$$

$\quad$ (10)

Those variance ratios are proportional to the increase of the "factor"[8] variances.

This preliminary analysis is to investigate when returns are excessive as a precondition for detecting contagion effects.

3.2. *Model to test contagion*

In order to test contagious effects, we concentrate on measuring the correlation of the model's idiosyncratic shocks or unexpected returns in normal and crisis periods.

We retain that significant increases in residual correlations are signs of contagion. These residual correlations are obviously corrected for heteroscedasticity as suggested by Forbes and Rigobon (2002).

---

[8]USA or regional.

Our tests involve the time-series cross-section regression model

$$\widehat{e}_{i,t} = \gamma_i + \delta_{i,t}\widehat{e}_{\text{US},t} + \beta_{i,t}\widehat{e}_{\text{reg},t} + u_{i,t}, \qquad (11)$$

$$\begin{aligned} \delta_{i,t} &= p_1 D_{i,t}^{1,1} + q_1 D_{i,t}^{1,2}, \\ \beta_{i,t} &= p_2 D_{i,t}^{2,1} + q_2 D_{i,t}^{2,2}, \end{aligned} \qquad (12)$$

where $\widehat{e}_{i,t}$, $\widehat{e}_{\text{US},t}$, and $\widehat{e}_{\text{reg},t}$ are the estimated idiosyncratic return shocks of the markets i, the US, and regional, respectively.[9] $D_{i,t}^{1,1}$, $D_{i,t}^{1,2}$, $D_{i,t}^{2,1}$, and $D_{i,t}^{2,2}$ are dummy variables. More specifically, $D_{i,t}^{1,1}$ and $D_{i,t}^{2,1}$ denote tranquil periods, respectively, in the US and regional markets and take a value of one during tranquil periods and zero otherwise. Whereas, $D_{i,t}^{1,2}$ and $D_{i,t}^{2,2}$ represent turmoil periods both in the US and regional markets, and so take the value of one during turbulent periods and that of zero otherwise.

By adding tranquil versus crisis dummies, we distinguish the change in the time-varying beta coefficients during tranquil versus crisis periods. If there is evidence for such a change, this suggests signs of contagion effects; we call this phenomenon contagion.

Unlike Bekaert *et al.* (2005, 2011), we add two dummy variables to consider both turmoil and calm periods. Bekaert *et al.* (2005, 2011) assume that the coefficient p accounts for the additional correlation in the whole period and that q reflects the excess of correlation during the crisis period. Consequently, additional residual correlations in crisis period are considered twice in p and q estimations. Thus, we assume that such estimations of the panel model lead to a redundancy in the parameter estimation. To avoid, we propose to correct this estimation redundancy by testing the contagion separately both in calm and crisis periods.

Our model has the advantage of first, taking into account both turmoil and calm periods, and second, considering simultaneously the US and regional risk factors. That being said, we are more interested

---

[9]We assume that the regional and international contagion effects are not correlated in Equation (11).

in studying the time-series patterns during crisis periods than in tranquil periods. The hypothesis of contagion would be supported if the model's idiosyncratic shocks exhibit significant correlations during calm/crisis periods. Thus, the test of significance of the parameter $q_i \forall i = 1, 2$ can be interpreted as a test of contagion in times of crisis.

And the test of significance of the parameters p_1 and p_2 can be interpreted as a test of contagion over tranquil periods for the US/regional markets.

4. Empirical Study

4.1. *Data*

Our dataset includes monthly stock market indices for 17 OECD countries[10]: S&P 500 (USA), TSX (Canada), Helsinki General (Finland), CAC 40 (France), DAX 30 (Germany), ISEQ (Ireland), Milan MIB (Italy), AEX (Netherlands), Madrid General Index (Spain), KFX Copenhagen (Denmark), Oslo Stock Exchange (Norway), Stockholm Index (Sweden), Zurich Swiss Market Index (Switzerland), FTSE 100 (United Kingdom), All Ordinaries Index (Australia), Nikkei 225 (Japan), and New Zealand Stock Exchange 50 (New-Zealand). Our sample covers the period from January 1, 1990 to January 11, 2013.

Our dataset is drawn from Datastream and Morgan Stanley Capital International (MSCI). Each stock market index is taken with a dividend reinvestment and for each country, we compute the growth rates.[11]

We divide the included OECD countries in three regions: North America (the US and Canada), Europe (Finland, Norway, Sweden, Denmark, Ireland, the UK, France, the Netherlands, Germany, Switzerland, Italy, and Spain), and Asia-Pacific (Japan,

---

[10]The selection of these countries is based on their size (in terms of gross domestic product, GDP) and their economic/market structure.

[11]Stock return, $r_{i,t}$, is computed as the logarithmic difference of closing stock price index, $P_{i,t}$ as follows: $r_{i,t} = \log(p_{i,t}/p_{i,t-1}) \times 100$.

Australia, and New Zealand). Thus, for each region we construct our own indices.

So, we compute a stock market index by region as the geometric mean of stock returns weighted by the stock market capitalization of each member country.

When the market i is studied, the regional index used is equal to the weighted average of all regional markets except that of the market i as follows:

$$R^i_{\text{reg},t} = \frac{\sum^n_{i \neq l} \alpha_{l,t} R_{l,t}}{\sum^n_{i \neq l} \alpha_{l,t}}, \tag{13}$$

where n is the number of markets in the region reg and α is the market capitalization.

We first transform the series into returns and then subtract from them the Eurodollar rate at one month (the risk-free rate) in order to get the excess returns. All data are expressed in US dollars.

Equity returns are the basis for our analysis as they incorporate all available information on the expected future profitability of companies in a country, and therefore capture even expected changes in real indicators.

Besides and as to capture the local sources, we include the dividend yield of the local market portfolio, inflation, and real effective exchange rate indices in our database.

These monthly data are extracted from Datastream, Federal Reserve Bank of Saint Louis, and Financial Statistics of the Federal Reserve Board for the same sample period.

4.2. *Statistical properties*

The statistical properties for the return series are summarized in Table 1.

It appears that Finland has the highest monthly returns of 30.5% followed by Sweden and Italy with, respectively, 24.87% and 21.03%. However, Norway has the lowest returns with -31.21%.

Table 1: Return series descriptive statistics.

Stock returns	Mean	Median	Maximum	Minimum	Std Dev	Skewness	Kurtosis	Jarque-Bera	Corr with the US	LM ARCH
S&P 500	0.0058	0.0113	0.1441	-0.1879	0.0467	-0.7679	5.1381	76.8098 [0.0000]	—	2094.664 [0.0000]
TSX	0.0055	0.0112	0.1366	-0.2178	0.0491	-0.8836	5.6347	111.5521 [0.0000]	0.7581	2524.420 [0.0000]
DAX 30	0.0039	0.0097	0.1264	-0.1721	0.0565	-0.7239	3.6330	27.6754 [0.0000]	0.7502	1717.540 [0.0000]
All Ordinaries Index	0.0044	0.0088	0.0979	-0.1408	0.0412	-0.4863	3.2424	11.1355 [0.0038]	0.7014	2977.530 [0.0000]
KFX Copenhagen	0.0065	0.0100	0.1778	-0.2089	0.0550	-0.6623	4.2482	36.7153 [0.0000]	0.6508	2730.840 [0.0000]
Helsonki General	0.0059	0.0064	0.3050	-0.3050	0.0899	-0.1550	3.9711	11.5174 [0.0032]	0.5920	s53.373 [0.0000]
Madrid General Index	0.0034	0.0076	0.1503	-0.1656	0.0555	-0.5402	3.4424	15.1076 [0.0005]	0.7506	2181.422 [0.0000]
CAC 40	0.0034	0.0076	0.1503	-0.1656	0.0555	-0.5402	3.4424	15.1076 [0.0005]	0.7506	2171.242 [0.0000]
FTSE 100	0.0039	0.0098	0.1192	-0.1463	0.0451	-0.5234	3.8179	19.5583 [0.0001]	0.8057	1719.859 [0.0000]
Milan MIB	0.0008	0.0008	0.2103	-0.1807	0.0645	0.0530	3.5618	3.6225 [0.1635]	0.6090	1980.872 [0.0000]
Stockholm Index	0.0063	0.0144	0.2487	-0.1850	0.0685	-0.2893	3.6164	7.9225 [0.0190]	0.6577	2304.311 [0.0000]
Zurich Swiss Market Index	0.0051	0.0129	0.1825	-0.2028	0.0480	-0.8209	5.5834	103.8454 [0.0000]	0.7177	2316.242 [0.0000]
New Zealand Stock Exchange 50	0.0013	0.0039	0.1440	-0.1922	0.0450	-0.3840	4.3138	25.6673 [0.0000]	0.5185	2081.190 [0.0000]
Oslo Stock Index	0.0058	0.0159	0.1658	-0.3121	0.0698	-1.1197	5.8562	146.0017 [0.0000]	0.6589	2242.252 [0.0000]
AEX	0.0034	0.0100	0.1138	-0.2558	0.0560	-1.2546	6.1808	181.9162 [0.0000]	0.7816	1911.685 [0.0000]
Nikkei 225	-0.0041	-0.0011	0.1745	-0.2443	0.0592	-0.3770	4.6396	36.0943 [0.0000]	0.4742	413.0745 [0.0000]
ISEQ	0.0032	0.0148	0.1809	-0.2820	0.0673	-1.0031	5.3738	107.0630 [0.0000]	0.7035	2877.816 [0.0000]

Notes: We report the basic statistics of sample data over the period from 01/01/1990 to 01/05/2012. LM ARCH refers to the Lagrange Multiplier test for conditional heteroscedasticity to residuals with $q = 5$. The associated probabilities are reported in brackets.

Finland experiences the highest risk level of 8.99% followed by Norway and Sweden, respectively, with 6.89% and 6.85%. The Australian market appears to be the least risky with 4.12%.

Skewness is negative in most cases, indicating that the tail on the left side is longer than the right one. For Kurtosis, the values exceed 3 denoting the non-normality of the return series, which is confirmed by the Jarque–Bera test statistic (JB) that strongly rejects the hypothesis of normality, except for Italy.

Moreover, we report the unconditional correlations between the US market, and the considered OECD stock returns. We can see that cross-market correlation of the US and the OECD equity returns are positive and high indicating that the OECD equity markets move closely and are not disconnected from the US stock market.

We also perform the Engle (1982) LM ARCH test to further analyze the distributional characteristics of stock return series. This test provides a clear indication of the ARCH effects in the return series.

Overall, the equity market returns' distributions are typically non-normal and display volatility clustering (time-varying heteroscedasticity/GARCH effects) and fat tails (leptokurtosis).

The stylized facts of the equity returns justify our choice of using GARCH processes to model their conditional volatility.

4.3. *Specification tests and the model estimation*

As a preliminary analysis and since we find the existence of GARCH effects in the statistical properties, a special focus on the GARCH models fitting the asset return series is made to determine if an asymmetric model is required, or whether a symmetric GARCH model is sufficient.[12]

---

[12]There are two main categories: symmetric (GARCH) or asymmetric models (EGARCH and GJR–GARCH). In the first category, the conditional variance only depends on the magnitude, and not on the sign of the asset, reflecting that volatility increases more after negative shocks than after positive ones of the same magnitude. In other words, bad news generates higher volatility whereas good news lowers the volatility. In the second category, these characteristics are more or less captured in the asymmetric models.

We follow Engle and Ng (1993) by applying tests for asymmetry in volatility, known as sign bias tests, applied to the residuals and based on the significance of $\phi_{1,i}$ for each market i as follows:

$$\hat{e}_{i,t}^2 = \phi_{0,i} + \phi_{1,i} S_{i,t-1}^- + \zeta_{i,t}, \tag{14}$$

where

$$S_{i,t-1}^- = \begin{cases} 1 & \text{if } \hat{e}_{i,t-1} < 0 \\ 0 & \text{otherwise,} \end{cases}$$

and $\zeta_{i,t}$ is an independent and identically distributed error term.

If $\phi_{1,i}$ is statistically significant, it implies that positive and negative shocks to $\hat{e}_{i,t-1}$ impact differently upon the conditional variance.

We carry out this test[13] and find evidence of asymmetric volatility in all return series. Thus, volatility process is modeling using a GJR fr model.

Besides, we pay attention to the robustness of the parameters' estimation in the three-factor model. The normality hypothesis is strongly rejected in our data, so we use a quasi-maximum likelihood estimation (QMLE) method.

First, the simplex algorithm is applied to initialize the process. Then, the estimation of the unknown parameters is carried out with a hill-climbing method using the algorithm BHHH[14] or BFGS[15] developed respectively by Berndt *et al.* (1974) and Broyden (1970).

The idea is that the simplex algorithm is used to refine initial estimates before using one of the derivative-based methods (BHHH or BFGS), which are more sensitive to the choice of initial estimates.

This preliminary check is done to ensure the robustness and the convergence of the estimation.

To sum up, our estimation process is carried out in three stages:

Firstly, we estimate, conditional on Ω_{t-1}, the vector of unknown parameters $\theta_{\mathrm{US}} = [\delta_{\mathrm{US}}', \alpha_{\mathrm{US}}, \beta_{\mathrm{US}}, \gamma_{\mathrm{US}}, \gamma_{\mathrm{US}}]'$ in the system from Equations (1) to (4) for the US market.

---

[13] The results are available on request.
[14] Referring to the Berndt, Hausman, Hall, and Hall.
[15] Referring to the Broyden, Fletcher, Goldfarb, and Shanno.

Secondly, based on the US estimates of stage 1, we examine the model for the different regions: Conditional on Ω_{t-1} and $\Re_{\text{US},t}$, we estimate the density function of the different regional market's returns that depend on $[\theta'_{\text{US}}, \theta'_{\text{reg}}]'$; and where $\theta'_{\text{reg}} = [\delta'_{\text{reg}}, \alpha_{\text{reg}}, \beta_{\text{reg}}, \gamma_{\text{reg}}]$ is a vector of unknown parameters obtained by maximizing the likelihood function for the regional market returns in the system from Equations (1) to (4).

Thirdly, we estimate the system from Equations (1) to (4) in a multivariate setting[16] for all markets, conditioning on the US and regional markets model estimations.

Before carrying out the panel regressions, we also, perform panel unit root tests in three stages to ensure that the idiosyncratic return shocks are stationary. The results are summarized in Table 2.

We start by applying the first-generation tests, along the lines of Im *et al.* (2003) and Maddala and Wu (1999). Then, the second-generation panel unit root tests, referring to Moon and Perron (2004), Choi (2002), and Pesaran (2003). Finally, Carrion-i-Silvestre (2005), a third-generation panel unit root test is used for taking into account the hypothesis of structural breaks in addition to that of the interdependencies.

Given the results, we conclude after the first two tests (without dependencies and structural breaks of Im *et al.* (2003) and Maddala and Wu (1999)), that our model series are stationary. When applying the tests of second and third generations, the assumption of stationarity is also confirmed. This denotes that the first-generation tests themselves are sufficiently robust to take into account the existence of interdependencies and structural breaks in our data. All the tests lead to rejecting the presence of unit roots. This is a necessary condition in our panel analysis.

---

[16] In a previous work, we followed Bekaert *et al.* (2005) and estimated of the second and third steps in a univariate setting. However, a multivariate framework seems to be more realistic when considering relationships between return series.

Table 2: Unit root tests.[a]

Tests	Statistic	e_i	e_{reg}
First-generation tests			
Im *et al.* (2003)	W_{tbar}	−56,078	−66,692
		(0.00)	(0.00)
	Z_{tbar}	−53,477	−63,288
		(0.00)	(0.00)
Maddala and Wu (1999)	P_{MW}	138,155	147,365
		(<0.01)	(<0.01)
	Z_{MW}	13,962	14,420
		(0.00)	(0.00)
Second-generation tests			
Moon and Perron (2004)	t_a	−493,325	−618,293
		(0.00)	(0.00)
	t_b	−42,345	−55,266
		(0.00)	(0.00)
	t_a^*	−488,097	−620,079
		(0.00)	(0.00)
	t_b^*	−42,420	−55,757
		(0.00)	(0.00)
Choi (2002)	P_m	31,798	32,841
		(0.00)	(0.00)
	Z	−14,403	−14,876
		(0.00)	(0.00)
	L^*	−19,666	−20,311
		(0.00)	(0.00)
Pesaran (2003)	$CIPS^*$	−5,834	−6,143
		(0.01)	(0.01)
Moon and Perron (2004)	t_a	−493,325	−618,293
		(0.00)	(0.00)
	t_b	−42,345	−55,266
		(0.00)	(0.00)
	t_a^*	−488,097	−620,079
		(0.00)	(0.00)
	t_b^*	−42,420	−55,757
		(0.00)	(0.00)
Choi (2002)	P_m	31,798	32,841
		(0.00)	(0.00)
	Z	−14,403	−14,876
		(0.00)	(0.00)
	L^*	−19,666	−20,311
		(0.00)	(0.00)
Pesaran (2003)	$CIPS^*$	−5,834	−6,143
		(0.01)	(0.01)
Third-generation test			
		0.719	0.712
Carrion-i-Silvestre (2005)	$LM(\lambda)$	(0.236)	(0.238)
		[4.079]	[3.808]

Note: [a]We consider the tests for a model with a trend. Numbers in parentheses are the standard deviations, and the associated probabilities are reported in brackets.

5.   Results

5.1.   *Cross-patterns comovements during the whole period*

We report in Table 3 the average betas, correlations, and variance ratios for all countries. We remind that our ICAPM produces time-varying betas, correlations, and variance ratios, but we only report the sample average of these conditional variables.

This analysis highlights interdependencies' levels between equity markets within the region and thus the consequences of decisions taken by governments and investors.

While correlation coefficients between world markets (Hamao *et al.*, 1990; Tse, 2000), spillovers in means, and spillovers in variances (Edwards, 1998; Forbes and Rigobon, 2002; McAleer and Nam, 2005) have been established, we concentrate on OECD equity markets. Our main interest is to track the stability of the OECD equity markets.

First, let us focus on the estimated coefficients $\hat{\beta}_i^{us}$ and $\hat{\beta}_i^{reg}$ that measure the OECD equity markets' sensitivities to global and regional risks, respectively.

For Canada, which represents with the US the North American region, the beta with respect to the US market is positive, of 0.717. In the whole sample, Canada has the highest beta' value. This denotes that the closest country to the US is the most sensitive one.

If we move to the Asian equity markets, the betas with respect to the US market factor are positive and significant, too, varying between 0.404 and 0.592, respectively, for New Zealand and Japan, denoting that the Asian region is sensitive to what happens in the US.

The betas with respect to the Asian-Pacific region factor are also positive and significant, varying between 0.270 to 1.004, respectively, for Japan and New Zealand. This indicates that Japan and New Zealand may be impacted both by the US and regional markets. Therefore, the US and the Asian-pacific factors do account in the Asian return shocks.

Table 3: Betas, correlations, and variance ratios.

Country	$\hat{\beta}_i^{\text{us}}$	$\hat{\beta}_i^{\text{reg}}$	$V\hat{R}_i^{\text{us}}$	$V\hat{R}_i^{\text{reg}}$	$\hat{\rho}_i^{\text{us}}$	$\hat{\rho}_i^{\text{reg}}$
		North American Region				
Canada	0.717	0.756	0.348	—	0.574	—
	(0.051)	(0.047)	(0.167)	—	(0.137)	—
		Asian-Pacific Region				
Japan	0.592	1.004	0.121	0.005	0.325	0.242
	(0.101)	(0.001)	(0.100)	(0.003)	(0.124)	(0.066)
Australia	0.503	0.288	0.283	0.016	0.511	−0.509
	(0.113)	(0.09)	(0.165)	(0.006)	(0.149)	(0.199)
New Zealand	0.404	0.270	0.238	0.011	0.469	0.121
	(0.130)	(0.107)	(0.142)	(0.008)	(0.133)	(0.043)
		European Region				
UK	0.636	0.874	0.005	0.972	0.007	0.142
	(0.042)	(0.030)	(0.000)	(0.009)	(0.002)	(0.039)
Norway	0.816	1.166	0.002	0.005	0.045	0.084
	(0.112)	(0.095)	(0.003)	(0.005)	(0.021)	(0.038)
Sweden	0.864	1.353	0.002	0.018	0.043	0.163
	(0.162)	(0.153)	(0.003)	(0.009)	(0.020)	(0.045)
Switzerland	0.553	0.752	0.002	0.007	0.039	0.079
	(0.068)	(0.060)	(0.002)	(0.007)	(0.019)	(0.031)
Denmark	0.574	0.875	0.002	0.013	0.040	0.021
	(0.102)	(0.080)	(0.002)	(0.009)	(0.019)	(0.020)
Finland	0.911	1.221	0.002	0.009	0.046	0.093
	(0.233)	(0.285)	(0.002)	(0.006)	(0.019)	(0.028)
France	0.185	0.883	0.001	0.026	0.017	0.174
	(0.139)	(0.115)	(0.000)	(0.024)	(0.008)	(0.051)
Germany	0.724	0.940	0.002	0.019	0.041	0.162
	(0.125)	(0.146)	(0.002)	(0.011)	(0.018)	(0.057)
Spain	0.702	0.964	0.002	0.024	0.042	0.172
	(0.076)	(0.078)	(0.002)	(0.015)	(0.019)	(0.050)
Ireland	0.825	0.818	0.001	0.029	0.030	0.214
	(0.189)	(0.216)	(0.001)	(0.013)	(0.009)	(0.072)
Italy	0.677	1.108	0.001	0.027	0.035	0.210
	(0.123)	(0.131)	(0.001)	(0.017)	(0.015)	(0.076)
Netherlands	0.716	0.868	0.002	0.031	0.045	0.203
	(0.071)	(0.081)	(0.003)	(0.013)	(0.021)	(0.055)

Note: Numbers in parentheses are the standard deviations.

Concerning the European region, the betas with respect to the US market are positive and relatively high, ranging from 0.185 for France to 0.911 for Finland. Betas with respect to the regional market (the European index) are positive and highest, reaching 1.353 for Sweden for instance.

Second, we analyze the correlations and variances ratios.

For Canada, the correlation with the US market is positive, significant, and the highest. The relative proportion of conditional return variance that is accounted for by the US is also the highest one.

Moreover, the results for the Asian-Pacific markets' correlations are more pronounced with the US than with the regional factor. For instance, Australia is the most correlated with the US (51.1%) and surprisingly negatively correlated with the Asian region, with −50.9%.

Japan is more positively correlated with the US market (32.5%) than with the Asian-Pacific region, with 24.2%. The same feature is true for New Zealand with a correlation of 46.9% and 12.1% with the US and regional factors, respectively.

Our results confirm those of other empirical studies. For example, Ratanapakon and Sharma (2002) and Lim *et al.* (2003) showed that Asian markets are partially integrated regionally. Also, Siklos and Ng (2001) showed the existence of strong interdependencies between the Asian and the US markets.

Still in the Asian-Pacific region, the amount of variance explained by the US market is more pronounced than the one explained by the Asian-Pacific region. To give some values, 12.1%, 28.3%, and 23.8% are the conditional return variances, respectively, for Japan, Australia, and New Zealand and can be attributed to US shocks.

In contrast, the amounts of variance of those countries explained by the Asian-Pacific region are very low at, respectively, 0.5%, 1.6%, and 1.1%. Surprisingly, the regional factor does not account for very much of the total variation of return shocks in Asia.

If we move to the European region, the correlations with respect to the US market are significant and positive, although, very low (not exceeding 0.5%). The correlations with the regional market (the European index) are low, but, in all cases, larger than the ones with the US market and more pronounced for some countries than others. For instance, for Ireland, the correlation is 21.4%, while it is 2.1% for Denmark. Fratzscher (2002) and Hardouvelis *et al.* (2006) showed an increase in European market integration. This increase in correlations over time may result from increased volatility and/or any change in cross-country linkages. Forbes and Rigobon (2002) show that higher volatility in one country's stock market will automatically increase the unconditional correlation in returns with another country. If volatility in one country increases, even if the transmission mechanism between the two countries is constant, a larger share of the return in the second country will be driven by the larger, idiosyncratic shocks in the first country.

The relative proportion of conditional return variance that is accounted for by the US is low because of the higher idiosyncratic volatility of these markets. This finding is in line with the one of Bekaert *et al.* (2005).

The fraction of the return shock variance explained by the US factor is small, ranging from 0.5% to 1%. The regional market does not explain a large amount of total shock variance, with the exception being of the UK (97.20%).

These results on betas, correlations, and variance ratios give us a taste about the behavior of OECD equity markets towards the global and regional risks and are in line with what we would expect, given the relatively idiosyncratic nature of the markets.

According to our findings, we, first, remark that the country-specific beta parameter (β_i^{us} or β_i^{reg}) is positive, denoting that higher volatility in the US market or regional one may affect the market i.

Second, we notice that the return volatility of the market i is positively related to the conditional variances of the US and regional markets with differences across countries. There appear to be potential asymmetric effects in the US or regional markets that induce asymmetry in the conditional return volatility of any equity market.

However, these cross-patterns capture comovements between markets during crises as well as normal events. Therefore, although the results in this section document trends in interdependencies over time, they do not necessarily denote the existence of contagion. So after investigating patterns in regional and global factors, we move to test contagion effects. We consider three crises: the Asian crisis, the ERM crisis, and the subprime-global financial one.

5.2. Contagion effects

The correlation detected in the previous section itself is not evidence of contagion.

We are interested in the time-series patterns during calm/turmoil events.

To study contagion effects, we use a panel regression of the country's idiosyncratic shocks onto a country-specific constant, and both global and regional residuals whose slope coefficients are allowed to change both in calm and turbulent periods.

We estimate the model described by Equations (11) and (12), using panel data for each group of countries. We consider three groups: North America, Asia-Pacific, and Europe, and test the significance of parameters p_i and q_i $\forall i = 1, 2$.

Significant increases in correlations between residuals are signs of contagion. We test the existence of contagion during three specific periods: the ERM (1992:07–1993:12), the Asian crisis (1997:04–1998:10), and the subprime/GFC (2007:07–2013:11).

For clearness, $D_{i,t}^{1,1}$ and $D_{i,t}^{1,2}$ denote, respectively, tranquil, time and subprime crisis in the US market. While $D_{i,t}^{2,1}$ and $D_{i,t}^{2,2}$ represent both calm and turmoil periods in the different regional markets. The coefficients q_1 and q_2 measure the increase in residuals' correlations of the different OECD equity markets, respectively, with the benchmark (USA) and regional markets during crisis periods. While the coefficients p_1 and p_2 account for the correlation of the additional residuals of the OECD equity markets, respectively, with the benchmark (USA) and regional markets during calm times. Therefore, test for the existence of contagion over the entire period for the US market (respectively, for the region) amounts to testing the null hypothesis of joint coefficients p_i and q_i, $H_0 : p_1 = q_1 = 0$ (respectively, $H_0 : p_2 = q_2 = 0$).

Moreover, understanding the channels through which shocks are transmitted across countries (global or regional factors risks) is the key issue for policymakers hoping to mitigate any negative effects.

The baseline tests of contagion from the panel model are reported in Table 4.

Table 4: Cross-section analysis of OECD idiosyncratic shocks.

Country	Coefficients					Wald test	
	p_1	q_1	p_2	q_2	Constant	$p_1 = q_1 = 0$	$p_2 = q_2 = 0$
USA and Regional Return Residuals							
North America	0.0046 (0.0490)	0.2071 (0.1415)	—	—	-0.010* (0.002)	2.043 [0.874]	—
Europe	-0.0655 (0.0446)	0.1618* (0.0296)	-0.0155 (0.132)	-0.0642** (0.0303)	-0.022* (0.001)	25.987 [<0.001]	0.833 [0.825]
UK	0.0789 (0.062)	0.1503* (0.0243)	-0.1076** (0.061)	0.4489* (0.2117)	-0.024* (0.0028)	6.286 [0.043]	79.49 [<0.001]
Norway	0.0865 (0.1208)	0.1141 (0.0803)	-0.1950*** (0.0995)	0.0397 (0.3088)	-0.025* (0.0036)	2.827 [0.243]	0.854 [0.836]
Sweden	-0.1042 (0.123)	0.0720 (0.082)	-0.0966 (0.1025)	0.9778* (0.3175)	-0.021* (0.0037)	20.09 [<0.001]	2.523 [0.772]
Switzerland	-0.0161 (0.1015)	-0.0265* (0.0028)	-0.1466*** (0.0819)	-0.1976 (0.2606)	-0.026* (0.0028)	26.456 [<0.001]	2.063 [0.84]
Denmark	0.1379 (0.1071)	0.1285*** (0.0712)	-0.2950* (0.08)	0.2471 (0.2404)	-0.024* (0.0031)	38.833 [<0.001]	1.489 [0.472]
Finland	0.0152 (0.1575)	0.1140 (0.1047)	-0.2091 (0.1801)	0.9780*** (0.5877)	-0.018* (0.005)	79.459 [<0.001]	3.526 [0.832]
France	0.0585 (0.0841)	0.1445* (0.0437)	0.0321 (0.4635)	0.0761 (0.0923)	-0.020* (0.004)	20.011 [0.002]	2.341 [0.93]
Germany	0.1214* (0.038)	0.1515* (0.0701)	-0.2403* (0.0779)	0.0901*** (0.049)	-0.020* (0.003)	26.456 [<0.001]	38.586 [<0.001]
Spain	0.0853 (0.1051)	0.1363 (0.0696)	-0.0882 (0.1122)	0.0418*** (0.0229)	-0.021* (0.003)	4.749 [0.093]	0.211 [0.004]
Ireland	0.3824* (0.07)	0.5862* (0.1048)	-0.3032* (0.1022)	0.1284 (0.4207)	-0.025* (0.003)	2.827 [0.243]	2.365 [0.812]
Italy	0.1234 (0.1210)	0.1395*** (0.0804)	-0.2131** (0.1013)	0.7851** (0.3611)	-0.022* (0.003)	14.703 [0.095]	65.256 [<0.001]
Netherlands	0.1873* (0.0654)	0.2348* (0.0986)	-0.2689* (0.0693)	0.0570 (0.3015)	-0.021* (0.003)	0.309 [0.857]	47.258 [<0.001]
Asia-Pacific	-0.0687 (0.0746)	0.1395* (0.0494)	-0.0188 (0.1252)	0.0493 (0.0409)	-0.007* (<0.001)	6.484 [0.039]	3.241 [0.666]
Japan	0.2852* (0.0751)	0.2912** (0.1144)	0.0692 (0.1336)	0.1522 (0.3827)	0.0003 (0.003)	11.29 [0.004]	0.510 [0.91]
Australia	0.0803*** (0.0486)	0.1047* (0.073)	-0.1332 (0.1482)	0.1266 (0.4528)	-0.014* (0.002)	1.306 [0.52]	4.521 [0.882]
New Zealand	-0.0743 (0.0613)	-0.2418* (0.091)	-0.0389 (0.2573)	0.191 (0.49)	-0.013* (0.003)	0.422 [0.81]	3.634 [0.689]

Notes: Numbers in parentheses are the standard deviations and the ones in brackets are Wald-test *p*-values.
* significative to 1%, ** significative to 5%, *** significative to 10%.

We start by the p_1 coefficient that measures the additional correlation of the OECD country's idiosyncratic shocks with the US idiosyncratic shocks during the US normal period. p_1 is positive, with exceptions of Sweden, Switzerland, and New Zealand, suggesting that the idiosyncratic residuals are better correlated with the US even in a tranquil period. This confirms that the US retains its place of world's leader.

The correlation with respect to the US is significantly higher for most European countries, but with different magnitudes. Differences in vulnerability to contagion, especially in the Eurozone, are reported.

For instance, in Europe, the correlation with the US for Ireland is the highest one with 0.3824, followed by that of Japan with 0.2852, for the Asian-Pacific region. This is due to the relation of the financial institutions with the US. It is well known that international companies like Apple, Amazon, and eBay are notable Irish companies that have subsidiaries in the US. Toyota, Fujifilm, and Panasonic are examples of very famous Japanese companies.

Moreover, the coefficient q_1, measuring the additional correlation of the country's idiosyncratic shocks with the US during the subprime/GFC period, is positive, indicating that residuals have become more correlated during the subprime crisis. The highest increase is that of Ireland with 0.5862, followed by that of Japan with 0.2912. This coefficient is negative only for Switzerland and New Zealand.

The hypothesis of no contagion over the entire period, $H_0 : p_1 = q_1 = 0$, for the US, can be rejected for most of the OECD markets. Instead, this hypothesis is strongly rejected for Europe, exceptions being of Ireland and Norway, and New Zealand and Australia, when considering the Asian-Pacific region. Only Japan seems to be significantly impacted by the subprime/GFC. However, for Canada, this hypothesis is accepted denoting that even though Canada is the nearest country to the US, it has not been affected by the subprime and the GFCs. So, contagion effects from the US on OECD markets exist both in calm and turbulent times; however, contagion is higher in a crisis period than in a calm one.

For the coefficient p_2, in eight out of twelve European equity markets, the correlation with the regional residuals is significant. This suggests that, even in a calm period, any idiosyncratic shock in the European region is transmitted to most of its countries. However, this is not the case for the Asian-Pacific countries.

Focusing on the coefficient q_2, we find that the correlation jumps highly especially during the ERM crisis for Finland and Sweden with, respectively, 0.978 and 0.9778, followed by Italy with 0.7851. Besides, the UK reaches a significant and important value of 0.4489. However, for the Asian crisis, the correlations with the Asian region are insignificant indicating no contagion during the Asian crisis for Japan, Australia, and New Zealand.

So, signs of transmission effects exist between the European Union and the US (Manasse and Zavalloni, 2012).

Besides, we carry out the joint Wald test to determine whether $H_0 : p_2 = q_2 = 0$ denotes regional overall contagion or not?

During the Asian crisis, the joint Wald test $p_2 = q_2 = 0$ is not rejected at the level of 5%. This indicates that there is no regional contagion during the Asian crisis. This may be an unexpected result, but may be explained by the fact that we include in the Asian-Pacific region only Australia, Japan, and New Zealand. However, this finding was confirmed by Forbes and Rigobon (2001) who conclude that only interdependencies exist. Also, in Europe, the joint test suggests that the UK, Germany, Spain, Italy, and the Netherlands are significantly impacted by the ERM crisis.

Our results have important implications both for researchers and market players interested in high levels of interdependencies in global equity markets.

6. Conclusion

This chapter studies interdependencies and contagion across OECD countries during different past crises, proposing an empirical approach. We consider that the comovements are explained by the common sources of risk, economic fundamentals, to focus on cross-patterns. Therefore, we consider a dynamic three-factor model, including local, global, and regional factors allowing to extract the idiosyncratic shocks used when making contagion analysis. Hence, the idiosyncratic comovements allow to test potential contagion effects. Using a panel model, contagion is tested as a significant excess correlation, both in the US and regional factors, among the residuals during normal and crisis periods.

We are interested in the case of three main past crises: the Asian crisis, the ERM one, and the subprime/GFC. Our framework allows for testing time-varying expected returns and time-varying risk loadings for OECD equity markets, both in crisis and non-crisis periods.

Our exploratory results suggest that: first, the idiosyncratic residuals are better correlated with the US, even in a tranquil period. This confirms that the US retains its place as world's leader.

Second, the additional correlation of the country's idiosyncratic shocks with the US during the subprime/GFC period is positive, denoting that residuals have become more correlated during the subprime crisis.

Third, the hypothesis of no contagion over the entire period, for the US, can be rejected for most OECD markets. Besides, in Europe, Germany, the UK, the Netherlands, Spain, and Italy are significantly impacted by the ERM crisis. However, during the Asian crisis, there is no regional contagion during the Asian crisis.

Our results are in line with those of Dungey and Martin (2001), Bekaert *et al.* (2005), Hsien-Yi (2012), and Bouaziz *et al.* (2012).

References

Acharya, Viral V., Drechsler, I. and Schnabl, P. (2011). A Pyrrhic victory? — Bank Bailouts and Sovereign Credit Risk, NBER Working Paper No. 17136, National Bureau of Economic Research.

Adler, M. and Dumas, B. (1983). International portfolio selection and corporation finance: A synthesis, *Journal of Finance*, 38, 925–984.

Allen, F., Babus, A. and Carletti, E. (2012). Asset commonality, debt maturity and systemic risk, *Journal of Financial Economics*, 104(3), 519–534.

Allen, F. and Carletti, E. (2006). Credit risk transfer and contagion, *Journal of Monetary Economics*, 53, 89–111.

Almeida, H., Campello, M., Laranjeira, B. and Weisbenner, S. (2012). Corporate debt maturity and the real effects of the 2007 credit crisis, *Critical Finance Review*, 1, 3–58.

Bagliano, F. C. and Morana, C. (2012). The great recession: US dynamics and spillovers to the world economy, *Journal of Banking and Finance*, 36(1), 1–13.

Bekaert, G. and Harvey, C. R. (1997). Emerging equity market volatility, *Journal of Financial Economics*, 43, 29–77.

Bekaert, G., Harvey, C. R. and Ng, A. (2005). Market integration and contagion, *Journal of Business*, 78(1), 39–69.

Bekaert, G. and Wu, G. (2000). Asymmetric volatility and risk in equity markets, *Review of Financial Studies*, 13, 1–42.

Bekaert, G., Ehrmann, M., Fratzscher, M. and Mehl, A. J. (2011). Global crises and equity market contagion, NBER Working Papers 17121, National Bureau of Economic Research, Inc.

Beltratti, A. and Stulz, R. M. (2012). The credit crisis around the globe: Why did some banks perform better? *Journal of Financial Economics*, 105, 1–17.

Berndt, E. R., Hall, B. H. and Hausman, J. A. (1974). Estimation and inference in nonlinear structural mosdels, *Annals of Economic and Social Measurement*, 3, 653–666.

Billio, M. and Pelizzon, L. (2003). Volatility and shocks spillover before and after EMU in european stock markets, *Journal of Multinational Financial Management*, 13, 323–340.

Bollerslev, T. (1986). Generalized autoregressive conditional heteroskedasticity, *Journal of Econometrics*, 31, 307–327.

Bollerslev, T. and Wooldridge, J. M. (1992). Quasi-maximum likelihood estimation and inference in dynamic models with time-varying covariances, *Econometric Reviews*, 1, 143–173.

Bouaziz, M., Selmi, N. and Boujelbene, Y. (2012). Contagion effect of the subprime financial crisis: Evidence of DCC multivariate GARCH models, *European Journal of Economics, Finance and Administrative Sciences*, (44), ISSN 1450-2275.

Boyer, B. H., Gibson, M. S. and Loretan, M. (1999). Pitfalls in Tests for Changes in International Finance, Discussion Papers, No. 597, Board of Governors of the Federal Reserve Board.

Beirne, J. and Gieck J. (2014). Interdependence and contagion in global asset markets, *Review of International Economics*, 22, 639–659.

Broyden, C. G. (1970). The convergence of single-rank quasi-Newton methods, *Mathematical Computation*, 24, 365–382.

Calomiris, C., Love, I. and Martinez Peria, M. S. (2012). Stock returns' sensitivities to crisis shocks: Evidence from developed and emerging markets, *Journal of International Money and Finance*, 31, 743–765.

Carrieri, F., Errunza, V. and Hogan, K. (2007). Characterizing world market integration through time, *Journal of Financial and Quantitative Analysis*, 42, 915–941.

Carrion-i-Silverstre, J. L. (2005). Health care expenditure and GDP: are they broken stationary? *Journal of Health Economics*, 24(5), 939–854.

Carrasco, M. and Chen, X. (1999). B-mixing and moment properties of various GARCH, stochastic volatility and ACD models, *London School of Economics*, Working Paper.

Chiang, T. C., Jeon, B. N. and Li, H. (2007). Dynamic correlation analysis of financial contagion: Evidence from Asian markets, *Journal of International Money and Finance*, 26(7), 1206–1228.

Choi, I. (2002). Combination Unit Root Tests for Cross-Sectionally Correlated Panels, Mimeo, Hong Kong University of Science and Technology.

Chen, N. and Zhang, F. (1997). Correlations, trades and stock returns of the Pacific rim markets, *Pacific Basin Finance Journal*, 5, 559–77.

Claessen, S. and Forbes, K. (2001). *International Financial Contagion*, Kluwer Academic Publisher.

Claessens, S., Djankov, S., Fan, J. and Lang, L. (2002). Disentangling the incentive and entrenchment effects of large shareholdings, *Journal of Finance*, 57, 2741–2771.

Corsetti, G., Kuester, K., Meier, A. and Muller, G. J. (2012). Sovereign risk, fiscal policy, and macroeconomic stability, IMF Working Paper 12/33.

Corsetti, F., Pericoli, M. and Sbracia, M. (2005). Some contagion, some interdependence: More pitfalls in tests for financial contagion, *Journal of International Money and Finance*, 24(8), 1177–1199.

Diebold, F. and Yilmaz, Y. (2012). Better to given than to receive: Predictive Directional measurement of volatility spillovers, *International Journal of Forecasting*, 28, 57–66.

Dumas, B. and Solnik, B. (1995). The world price of foreign exchange risk, *Journal of Finance*, 50, 445–479.

Dungey, M. and Zhumabekova, D. (2001). Testing for contagion using correlation: some words of caution, Pacific Basin Working Paper Series, Working Paper No. PB01-09.

Dungey, M., Fry, R. A., Gonzalez-Hermisillo, B. and Martin, V. L. (2003). Empirical modelling of contagion: A review of methodologies, Mimeo, ANU and CERF.

Dungey, M. and Martin, V. L. (2007). Unravelling financial market linkages during crises, *Journal of Applied Econometrics*, 22, 89–119.

Dungey, M., Milunovich, G. and Thorp, S. (2010). Unobservable shocks as carriers of contagion, *Journal of Banking and Finance*, 34, 1008–1021.

Dungey, M., Fry, R., Gonzalez-Hermosillo, B. and Martin, V. (2011). *Transmission of Financial Crises: A Latent Factor Approach*, Oxford University Press, New York.

Edwards, S. (1998). Interest rate volatility, contagion and convergence: An empirical investigation of the cases of Argentina, Chile and Mexico, *Journal of Applied Economics*, 1(1), 55–86.

Engle, R. (1982). Autoregressive conditional heteroskedasticity with estimates of the variance of United Kingdom inflation, *Econometrica*, 50, 987–1007.

Engle, R. F. and Ng, V. K. (1993). Time-varying volatility and the dynamic behavior of the term structure, *Journal of Money, Credit and Banking*, 25(3), 336–49.

Eichengreen, B., Rose, A. K. and Wyplosz, C. (1996). Contagious currency crises. Scandinavian, *Journal of Economics*, 98(4), 463–484.

Eichengreen, B., Mody, A., Nedeljkovic, M. and Sarno, L. (2012). How the subprime crisis went global: Evidence from bank credit default swap spreads, *Journal of International Money and Finance*, 31, 1299–1318.

Ehrmann, M. and Fratzscher, M. (2003). Interdependence between the Euro area and the USA: what role for EMU? in *Proceedings, Board of Governors of the Federal Reserve System (US)*.

Favero, C. and Giavazzi, F. (2002). Is the international propagation of financial shocks nonlinear? Evidence from the ERM, *Journal of International Economics*, 57, 231–246.

Forbes, K. (2012). The "Big C": Identifying Contagion, NBER Working Papers 18465, National Bureau of Economic Research, Inc.

Forbes, K. and Rigobon, R. (2002). No contagion, only interdependence: Measuring stock market comovements, *Journal of Finance*, 57(5), 2223–2261.

Forbes, K. and Rigobon, R. (2000). Contagion in Latin America: Definitions, measurement, and policy Implications, *Economica*, 1(2), 1–46.

Forni, M., Hallin, M., Lippi, M. and Reichlin, L. (2003). Do financial variables help forecasting inflation and real activity in the euro area? *Journal of Monetary Economics*, 50, 1243–1255.

Frankel, J. and Saravelos, G. (2010). Are leading indicators of financial crises useful for assessing country vulnerability? Evidence from the 2008–09 global crisis, NBER Working Paper 16047.

Fratzscher, M. (2002). Financial market integration in Europe: On the effect of EMU on stock markets, *International Journal of Finance and Economics*, 7(3), 165–194.

Fratzscher, M. (2003). On currency crises and contagion, *International Journal of Finance and Economics*, 8(2), 109–129.

Glick, R. and Rose, A. K. (1999). Contagion and trade: Why are currency crises regional, *Journal of International Money and Finance*, 18(4), 603–618.

Glosten, L. R., Jaganathan, R. and Runkle, D. E. (1993). On the relation between the expected value and the volatility of the nominal excess return on stocks, *Journal of Finance*, 48, 1779–1801.

Gourieroux, C. and Monfort, A. (1989). *Statistics and Econometric Models*, vol. 1, Cambridge University Press, Cambridge.

Guo, F., Chen, C. R. and Huang, Y. S. (2011). Markets contagion during financial crisis: A regime-switching approach, *International Review of Economics and Finance*, 20, 95–109.

Greenwood, R., Landier, A. and Thesmar, D. (2011). Vulnerable banks, TSE Working Paper 11-280, Toulouse School of Economics, November.

Hamao, Y. R., Masulis, R. W. and Ng, V. K. (1990). Correlations in price changes and volatility across international stock markets, *Review of Financial Studies*, 3, 281–307.

Hau, H., and Lai, S. (2012). The role of equity funds in the financial crisis propagation, CEPR Discussion Paper 8819, Centre for Economic Policy Research.

Hardouvelis, G. M. and Priestley, D. (2006). EMU and stock market integration, *Journal of Business*, 79, 365–392.

Hsien-Yi, L. (2012). Contagion in international stock markets during the sub prime mortgage crisis, *International Journal of Economics and Financial Issues, Econjournals*, 2(1), 41–53.

Im, K. S., Pesaran, M. H. and Shin, Y. (2003). Testing for unit roots in heterogeneous panels, *Journal of Econometrics*, 115(1), 53–74.

Jang, H. and Sul, W. (2002). The Asian financial crisis and the comovement of Asian stock markets, *Journal of Asian Economics*, 13, 94–104.

Jarque, C. M. and Bera, A. K. (1987). A test for normality of observations and regression residuals, *International Statistical Review*, 55, 163–172.

Johansson, A. C. (2011). Financial markets in east asia and europe during the global financial crisis, *The World Economy*, 2011, 1088–1105.

Kaabia, O. and Abid, I. (2013), Theoretical channels of international transmission during the subprime crisis to OECD countries: A FAVAR model under bayesian framework, *Journal of Applied Business Research*, 29(2), 443–460.

Kaminsky, G. and Reinhart, C. (2001). On crises, contagion and confusion, *Journal of International Economics*, 51(1), 145–168.

Kenourgios, D., Samitas, A. and Paltalidis, N. (2011). Financial crises and stock market contagion in a multivariate time-varying asymmetric framework, *Journal of International Financial Markets, Institutions and Money*, 21, 92–106.

King, M. and Wadhwani, S. (1990). Transmission of volatility between stock markets, *Review of Financial Studies*, 3, 5–33.

King M, Sentana, E. and Wadhwani S. (1994). Volatility and links between national stock markets, *Econometrica*, 62, 901–933.

Lim, K., Lee, H. and Liew, K. (2003). International diversification benefits in Asian stock markets: A revisit, Mimeo, Lebuan School of International Business and Finance, Universiti Malasya Sabbah y Faculty of Economics and Management, University Putera Malaysia.

Longin, F. and Solnik, B. (1995). Is the international correlation of equity returns constant: 1960–1990? *Journal of International Money and Finance*, February, 3–26.

Longstaff, F. A. (2010). The subprime credit crisis and contagion in financial markets, *Journal of Financial Economics*, 97, 436–450.

Longstaff, F. A. and Ang, A. (2011). Systemic sovereign credit risk: Lessons from the USA and Europe, NBER Working Paper 16892, National Bureau of Economic Research, Inc.

Maddala, G. S. and Wu, S. (1999). A comparative study of unit root tests with panel data and a new simple test, *Oxford Bulletin of Economics and Statistics*, special issue, 631–652.

Manasse, P. and Zavalloni, L. (2012). Sovereign contagion in Europe: Evidence from the CDS market, DSE Working Paper No. 863.

McAleer, M. and Nam, J. C. (2005). Testing for contagion in asian exchange rates, *Mathematics and Computers in Simulation*, 68, 519–527.

Mishkin, F. (2011). Over the cliff: From the subprime to the global financial crisis, *Journal of Economic Perspectives*, 25, 49–70.

Moon, H. R. and Perron, B. (2004). Testing for a unit root in panels with dynamic factors, *Journal of Econometrics*, 122, 81–126.

Moussalli, C. B. (2007). Financial crises, panic and contagion: Evidence from a cross-country comparison using two time frames, *Business and Public Affairs*, 1(2), 1–17.

Nagayasu, J. (2000). Currency crisis and contagion: Evidence from exchange rates and sectoral stock indices of the Philippines and Thailand, Working Paper No. 00/39, IMF.

Neaime, S. (2012). The global financial crisis, financial linkages and correlations in returns and volatilities in emerging MENA stock markets, *Emerging Markets Review*, 268–282.

Ng, A. (2000). Volatility spillover effects from Japan and the US to the Pacific Basin, *Journal of International Money and Finance*, 19, 207–233.

Pesaran, H. M. (2003). A simple panel unit root test in the presence of cross section dependence, Mimeo, University of Southern California.

Pesaran, M. H. and Pick, A. (2007). Econometric issues in the analysis of contagion, *Journal of Economics Dynamics and Control*, 31(4), 1245–1277.

Phylaktis, K. and Xia, L. (2006). Sources of firms' industry and country effects in emerging markets, *Journal of International Money and Finance*, 25, 459–475.

Pindyck, R. S. and Rotemberg, J. J. (1990). The excess co-movement of commodity prices, *Economic Journal*, 100, 1173–1189.

Pindyck, R. S. and Rotemberg, J. J. (1983). Dynamic factor demands and the effects of energy price shocks, *American Economic Review*, 73, 1066–1079.

Rose, A. and Spiegel, M. (2010). Cross-country causes and consequences of the 2008 crisis: International linkages and American exposure, *Pacific Economic Review*, 15, 340–363.

Rose, A. and Spiegel, M. (2011). Cross-country causes and consequences of the crisis: An update, *European Economic Review*, 55, 309–324.

Ratanapakon, O. and Sharma, S. (2002). Interrelationships among regional stock indices, *Review of Financial Economics*, 11, 91–108.

Rigobon, R. (1999). On the measurement of the international propagation of shocks, Working Paper 7354, National Bureau of Economic Research, Cambridge, MA.

Shin, H. S. (2012). Global banking glut and loan risk premium, *IMF Economic Review*, 60(2), 155–192.

Siklos, P. L. and Ng, P. (2001). Integration among Asia-Pacific and international stock markets: Common stochastic trends and regime shifts, *Pacific Economic Review*, 6, 89–110.

Tai, C. (2007). Market integration and currency risk in Asian emerging markets, *Research in International Business and Finance*, 21(1), 98–117.

Taylor, S. J. (1986). *Modeling Financial Time Series*, John Wiley and Sons, Chichester, UK.

Tong, H. and Wei, S-J. (2010). The misfortune of non-financial firms in a financial crisis: Disentangling finance and demand shocks, in *Wealth, Financial Intermediation and the Real Economy*, National Bureau of Economic Research.

Tong, H. and Wei, S.-J. (2011). The composition matters: Capital inflows and liquidity crunch during a global economic crisis, *Review of Financial Studies*, 24, 2023–2052.

Tse, Y. K. (2000). A test for constant correlations in a multivariate GARCH model, *Journal of Econometrics*, 98(1), 107–127.

Tse, Y. K. and Tsui, A. K. C. (2002). A multivariate generalized autoregressive conditional heteroscedasticity model with time-varying correlations, *Journal of Business & Economic Statistics*, 20(3), 351–362.

Van Wincoop, E. (2011). International financial contagion through leveraged financial institutions, NBER Working Paper No. 17686, National Bureau of Economic Research.

Chapter 11

Impact of Contagion on Proxy-Hedging in Jet-Fuel Markets[*]

Dominique Guegan[†,§], Marius-Cristian Frunza[‡,§]
and Rostislav Haliplii[†,§]

[†]*Paris-1 Sorbonne, 106 bd de l'Hopital, 75013, Paris, France*
[‡]*Ural Federal University (UrFU), 620002, 19 Mira street,
Ekaterinburg, Russia*
[§]*LABEX ReFi, 79 av de la Republique, 75011 Paris, France*

1. Introduction

An extensive literature covers the economy of oil markets, but less attention is given to the oil distillates and particularly to the jet-fuel market. The lack of efficiency in oil and middle distillates markets was pointed previously by the academic literature Balbás *et al.* (2008), Kanamura *et al.* (2010) and Roncoroni *et al.* (2015). Oil distillates markets are by their nature dependent on the oil market behavior, but also are exposed to specific risks linked to the changes in the supply/demand equilibrium for those products. Therefore in this research we intend to explore the modeling based on non-Gaussian distribution, volatility clustering and regime switching. Furthermore, we address the problem of contagion between the fuel-related

---

[*]Paper presented at the 2017 IPAG conference in Nice, France.

291

markets and focus on benchmarking the densities of these markets over various periods of time.

The main motivation, however, behind this study is to address the challenges faced by a company trading illiquid refined products such as jet fuel and providing it with optimal solutions with regards to their proxy-hedging. Nascimento and Powell (2008) modeled the jet-fuel price using two-factor model to allow mean-reversion in the short term and proposed oil future contracts for tackling the hedging problem. Adams and Gerner (2012) investigated the effect of the maturity on the cross-hedging performance of jet-fuel within an Error Correction model. They evaluated the performance of several oil forwards contracts including WTI, Brent, Gasoil and heating oil to manage jet-fuel spot price exposure. Their results highlight that the standard approach in the literature to use crude oil as a cross-hedge for jet-fuel is not optimal for time horizons of three months or less. By contrast, for short-hedging horizons their results indicate that gasoil forwards contracts represent the highest cross-hedging efficiency for jet-fuel spot price exposure, while for maturities of more than 3 months, the predominance of gasoil diminishes in comparison to WTI and Brent.

Clark *et al.* (2003) have attempted to test for the most effective cross-hedging instrument for the Singapore jet-fuel spot market, using regression techniques. Their research concludes that for the period February 1997 to August 2001, Heating Oil Futures contract gives best in sample results. Nevertheless, after correcting for serial correlation, their out of sample results proved to be weak for all regression models and ambiguous with respect to the heating oil contract.

This paper aims to enrich the scarce literature on the economics of oil distillates and attempts to estimate a good model capturing the dynamics of jet-fuel futures. In contrast to level forecasting regression and cointegration models used in previously mentioned papers, our research provides a different approach for testing proxy-hedging based on density forecasting. The main finding of this paper is that a trader exposed to jet-fuel price risk might think he has different hedging alternatives in term of markets, where in reality from a risk management perspective, the alternatives could exhibit a similar behavior in term of density forecasting capability. The contagion between markets reduces considerably the range of possible options for a hedger. Also the contagion effect can create basis risk management issues, especially in times of high volatility and scarce liquidity. The paper is organized as follows: Section 2 explores the econometric features of oil middle distillates refined products (including gasoil and jet fuel). Section 3 explains the challenges of jet-fuel proxy-hedging as well as the associated basis risk. Section 4 assesses the density forecasting methodologies (including probability forecasting Gneiting Test (Gneiting and Ranjan, 2011)). Section 5 presents the results of the ability of more liquid traded products such as Brent Crude and Gasoil returns to forecast density the jet fuel market. Section 6 concludes.

2.   Econometric Modeling of the Singapore Jet-Fuel and Related Oil Distillates

The first part of this research is dedicated to the econometric study of the Singapore jet fuel and related oil distillates prices. Our aim is not to find the "true" model that would explain the behavior of these commodities, but to propose a benchmark from different models commonly used to describe financial assets. Based on the historical time series, few models are estimated with the objectives to capture volatility clustering. Clustering in volatility is another ubiquitous feature observed in returns. Few models from the GARCH universe allow to capture this phenomena emphasizing the various particularities of the return series. Thus, we explore the following models:

- Models without volatility clustering, but with non-Gaussian innovations (NIG, t-student, asymmetric student).
- Models with volatility clustering and Gaussian innovations (GARCH, EGARCH, IGARCH, GJR-GARCH, APARCH).
- Models with volatility clustering and non-Gaussian innovations.
- Markov regime switching GARCH models.

2.1. *Dataset presentation*

As emphasized earlier, the final goal of this chapter is to assess the risk of a refinery or airline company that hedges its exposure to illiquid petroleum products such as jet-fuel. There are two primary futures contracts which are commonly used for jet-fuel-hedging: brent crude and gasoil. These contracts serve as the primary benchmarks across the world. In addition, there are many other contracts (futures, crack futures, swaps and options) available for jet-fuel-hedging, most of which are tied to one of the major, global trading hubs of Singapore, US Gulf Coast (Houston/New Orleans) and NW Europe/ARA (Amsterdam, Rotterdam and Antwerp).

For this purpose, we consider ICE Brent Crude, ICE Low Sulphur Gasoil and Singapore 50ppm Gasoil Futures for our proxy analysis. We also consider the Singapore Jet Kerosene (Platts) versus Gasoil (Platts) Futures differential (called Regrade), often used in jet-fuel-hedging. As for the jet fuel, there are three reference futures contracts for each geographical hub: Platts CIF NWE, USGC Jet 54 and Singapore Jet FOB. For our analysis, we consider the jet fuel contract traded in Singapore. Figure 1[1] presents the evolution of the above-mentioned front month futures contract quoted in USD/barrel.

Table 1 synthesizes the summary statistics over the considered dataset. ICE brent and ICE Low Sulphur Gasoil exhibit a higher volatility compared to the other three series. We notice that compared to the highly liquid Brent and LS Gasoil futures, Singapore Jet Fuel/Kerosene, Singapore Gasoil and Regrade exhibit a considerably higher kurtosis values which implies the need of heavy tailed distributions for modeling purposes.

Figures 3, 8, 10, 12 and 14 show the historical prices for Brent, LS Gasoil, Jet Kerosene and Regrade futures for the most liquid maturities of the curve.

---

[1]The ICE Low Sulphur Gasoil contract, quoted in USD per metric tones on the exchange, has been converted here to USD/bbl using a scale conversion factor of 7.45 used in the industry.

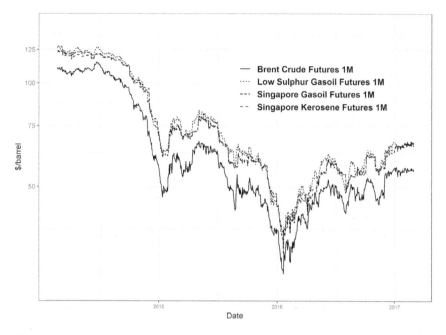

Figure 1: Evolution of the front month futures of Singapore Jet Kerosene, ICE Brent Crude, ICE Low Sulphur Gasoil and Singapore 50ppm Gasoil (USD/bbl).

Table 1: Summary statistics.

Underlying	Mean	Volatility	Skewness	Kurtosis
Regrade	−0.003	0.287	0.803	34.157
Singapore Gasoil	−0.001	0.289	−0.374	15.039
Singapore Kerosene	−0.001	0.265	−0.338	22.417
ICE Brent	−0.001	0.390	0.248	5.134
ICE LS gasoil	−0.001	0.328	0.597	6.862

Note: ICE brent and ICE Low Sulphur Gasoil exhibit a higher volatility compared to the other three series. Regrade and Singapore Kerosene have a more pronounced Kurtosis.

2.2. Generalized hyperbolic models

A recent modeling technique introduced here permits both skewness and kurtosis in the assets returns. Indeed, these features are not accounted for in the previous modelings. Following the works of Eberlein and Prause (2002) and Barndorff-Nielsen (1977) done on financial assets, we calibrate the class of Generalized Hyperbolic distributions to our data sets. This very flexible class of distributions (definition recalled in Appendix A) is able to capture heavy tails and asymmetry. It is characterized by five parameters with a parameter which permits very specific shapes. The four other parameters are linked in an easy way with the first four moments of the distribution.

2.2.1. *Distributions fit results*

In the view of hedging in illiquid markets we begin to fit the best model in term of AIC(BIC). In order to add leptokurtic distribution shapes of our datasets and overpass the limitations of using the classic Gaussian modeling framework, we consider the following set of candidate distributions: t-student, asymmetric student (ASTD) and normal inverse Gaussian (NIG), which retained our attention for their capability to take in account heavy tails. The results of the statistical estimation are provided in Tables 2–6. The 95% confidence intervals are compute through bootstrap approaches. The fittings are compared based upon the Bayesian information criterion (BIC).[2] NIG and Student distributions exhibit the best fits for the jet-fuel returns as well as for the proxy-hedging candidates.

Table 2: Distribution fitting for ICE brent front month futures returns.

Gaussian		Student		ASTD		NIG	
Parameter	Value	Parameter	Value	Parameter	Value	Parameter	Value
μ	0.000	μ	-0.001	μ	0.000	μ	-0.000
	[0.000 0.000]		[0.000 0.000]		[0.000 0.000]		[0.000 0.000]
σ	0.025	σ	0.026	σ	0.026	α	0.025
	[0.023, 0.026]		[0.024, 0.027]		[0.024, 0.027]		[0.023, 0.026]
		ν	3.529	β	1.071	β	0.115
			[3.4, 3.6]		[1.061, 1.081]		[0.11, 0.12]
				ν	3.550	δ	0.676
					[3.440, 3.660]		[0.442, 0.852]
BIC	-1724.58		-1760.64		-1724.82		-1764.04

Note: NIG and student distribution exhibit the best fits in regards of the BIC criteria.

---

[2]In our formalism the higher the absolute value of the BIC, the better the fit is.

Table 3: Distribution fitting for ICE LS Gasoil front month futures daily returns.

Gaussian		Student		ASTD		NIG	
Para-meter	Value	Para-meter	Value	Para-meter	Value	Para-meter	Value
μ	−0.000	μ	−0.001	μ	−0.001	μ	0.000
	[−0.230, 0.220]		[−0.203, 0.323]		[−0.101, 0.14]		[−0.120, 0.122]
σ	0.021	σ	0.028	σ	0.028	α	0.021
	[0.019, 0.023]		[0.024, 0.033]		[0.025, 0.032]		[0.019, 0.022]
		ν	2.468	β	1.001	β	0.064
			[2.325, 2.514]		[0.952, 1.053]		[0.042, 0.086]
				ν	2.469	δ	0.349
					[2.221, 2.66]		[0.247, 0.424]
BIC	−1856.41		−1922.24		−1880.75		−1923.88

Note: NIG and student distributions exhibit the best fits in regards of the BIC criteria.

Table 4: Distribution fitting for Singapore jet-fuel/kerosene front month futures daily return.

Gaussian		Student		ASTD		NIG	
Parameter	Value	Parameter	Value	Parameter	Value	Parameter	Value
μ	−0.000	μ	0.000	μ	−0.000	μ	0.000
	[−0.210, 0.215]		[−0.213, 0.223]		[−0.11, 0.12]		[−0.110, 0.132]
σ	0.017	σ	0.066	σ	0.066	α	0.012
	[0.014, 0.023]		[0.028, 0.088]		[0.038, 0.091]		[0.002, 0.021]
		ν	2.010	β	0.938	β	−0.112
			[1.968, 2.13]		[0.842, 1.201]		[−0.154, −0.049]
				ν	2.010	δ	0.100
					[1.840, 1.260]		[0.042, 0.152]
BIC	−2011.99		−2260.43		−2192.86		−2245.14

Note: Student and NIG distributions exhibit the best fits in regards of the BIC criteria.

Table 5: Distribution fitting for Singapore Gasoil front month futures returns.

Gaussian		Student		ASTD		NIG	
Parameter	Value	Parameter	Value	Parameter	Value	Parameter	Value
μ	0.000	μ	0.000	μ	−0.000	μ	0.000
	[−0.20, 0.205]		[−0.23, 0.22]		[−0.112, 0.122]		[−0.110, 0.101]
σ	0.018	σ	0.082	σ	0.082	α	0.015
	[0.015, 0.021]		[0.059, 0.118]		[0.041, 0.128]		[0.09, 0.021]
		ν	2.010	β	0.958	β	−0.079
			[1.64, 2.48]		[0.847, 1.131]		[−0.104, −0.045]
				ν	2.010	δ	0.100
					[1.740, 2.460]		[0.042, 0.152]
BIC	−1949.60		−2151.21		−2082.55		−2141.86

Note: Student and NIG distributions exhibit the best fits in regards of the BIC criteria.

Table 6: Distribution fitting for regrade front month futures returns.

Gaussian		Student		ASTD		NIG	
Parameter	Value	Parameter	Value	Parameter	Value	Parameter	Value
μ	−0.000	μ	−0.003	μ	−0.005	μ	−0.001
	[−0.22,		[−0.28,		[−0.112,		[−0.10,
	0.205]		0.2]		0.122]		0.111]
σ	0.287	σ	0.911	σ	0.911	α	0.181
	[0.265, 0.312]		[0.88, 1.08]		[0.85, 1.02]		[0.184, 0.221]
		ν	2.010	β	0.983	β	0.038
			[1.842,		[0.652,		[0.018,
			2.268]		1.201]		0.054]
				ν	2.010	δ	0.100
					[1.540, 2.560]		[0.042, 0.152]
BIC	128.943		−177.201		−117.776		−156.712

Note: Student and NIG distributions exhibit the best fits in regards of the BIC criteria.

2.3. *Volatility models*

Typical Gaussian flat volatility failed to provide with conspicuous valuations for contingencies and also underestimated the risk measures. The dynamic volatility models add value also for testing hedging strategies as, the traditional flat volatiles model tend to underestimate the clustering effect. Thus, for this purpose we consider the GARCH-type models. The GARCH process introduced by Bollerslev (1987) and its different variations have gained increasing prominence for modeling financial asset over the last decade. The GARCH process presents three particular features compared to other modelings. First it assumes that the present conditional variances is linearly linked to the past conditional variances and to past market squared return. Second for an accurate calibration GARCH requires large datasets. Third the models transfers through volatility pastern the risk premium of the underlings price. The classic GARCH framework bring obviously significant improvements in term of econometric description compared to the classic Gaussian model, and yet Bollerslev's GARCH remains still under an assumption of normally distributed innovations.

Further under the framework described by Bollerslev (1987), ϵ_t follows a GARCH(1,1) process is

$$\epsilon_t | \phi_{t-1} \propto N(0, h_t) \ or \ z_t \propto N(0,1), \tag{1}$$

$$h_t = \alpha_0 + \alpha_1 \cdot \epsilon_{t-1}^2 + \beta_1 \cdot h_{t-1}, \qquad (2)$$

where ϕ_t is the corresponding σ-algebra generated by the previous an present information; The unconditional variance is $h_0 = \frac{\alpha_0}{(1-\alpha_1-\beta_1)}$. GARCH model assumes that the conditional variance is a linear function of past squared disturbances and the past conditional variance, genuinely making h_t ϕ_t-predictable.

Generalizing the above given definition a GARCH(p,q) follows:

$$h_t = \alpha_0 + \alpha_1 \epsilon_{t-1}^2 + \cdots + \alpha_q \epsilon_{t-q}^2 + \beta_1 h_{t-1} + \cdots + \beta_p h_{t-p}^2$$

$$= \alpha_0 + \sum_{i=1}^{q} \alpha_i \epsilon_{t-i}^2 + \sum_{i=1}^{p} \beta_i h_{t-i},$$

where $p \geq 0$, $q \geq 0$, $\alpha_0 > 0$, $\alpha_i > 0$, $i = 1, \dots, q$; $\beta_i \geq 0$, $i = 1, \dots, p$. and $\sum_{i=1}^{q} \alpha_i + \sum_{i=1}^{p} \beta_i < 1.$[3]

In order to mitigate the existence of significant kurtosis and skewness effects assets returns returns an extension of the GARCH model could be the introduction of non-Gaussian (Generalized Hyperbolic) innovations, with the parametrization introduced in the previous section:

$$z_t \propto GH(\lambda; \alpha; \beta; \mu; \delta) \text{ or,} \qquad (3)$$

$$\epsilon_t | \phi_{t-1} \propto GH\left(\lambda; \frac{\alpha}{\sqrt{h_t}}; \frac{\beta}{\sqrt{h_t}}; \mu\sqrt{h_t}; \delta\sqrt{h_t}\right), \qquad (4)$$

$$h_t = \alpha_0 + \alpha_1 \cdot \epsilon_{t-1} + \beta_1 \cdot h_{t-1}. \qquad (5)$$

GARCH diffusion presents in term of pricing three particular features compared to other modelings. First, the GARCH derivatives prices depends of risk premium embedded in the underlying asset. Second, the GARCH pricing model is non-Markovian and is an interesting alternative for markets with serial dependency. Third,

---

[3]For insuring the covariance stationarity of the GARCH(p,q) it is imposed that the persistence is inferior to the unity

the GARCH models might explain some valuation biases of out-of the money options, associated with classic models.

We estimated through max-likelihood method the volatility models presented above. Table 7 exhibits the results of fitting of GARCH-type model with normal, Student and NIG innovations for Singapore Jet-Fuel daily returns. The models with NIG innovation show a superior fitting performance in terms of BIC/AIC. APARCH model fits better than the rest of the GARCH family for all three innovation types. The APARCH with NIG innovations and with a power factor (δ) of 0.94 exhibits the best features, underlining the leverage effects in volatility.

2.3.1. *Markov regime switching GARCH models*

Despite adding value for modeling assets with leptokurtoic behavior single regime GARCH models, fail to capture time of a transition between a low risk and high risk regime. An alternative was introduced by Haas *et al.* (2004) with the switching regime GARCH model detailed in the below formula.

$$h_t = \begin{cases} \alpha_0^1 + \alpha_1^1 \cdot \epsilon_{t-1}^2 + \beta_1^1 \cdot h_{t-1}; \\ \alpha_0^2 + \alpha_1^2 \cdot \epsilon_{t-1}^2 + \beta_1^2 \cdot h_{t-1}. \end{cases} \tag{6}$$

Middle distillates markets are particularly concerned by this feature due to the variation in liquidity. Thus, one volatility regime can correspond to thin liquidity conditions while another to appropriate levels of liquidity.

The results of fitting the switching GARCH model for the underlyings studied in this paper are exhibited in Table 8. The occurrence of two distinct states with statistically significant probability of transition is confirmed for Singapore Gasoil and Regrade. The particularity of these two underlyings is the fact that they trade on thinner liquidity than the other three markets considered in this study. This finding confirms our initial assumption and is a valuable learning when testing the risk related to proxy hedging.

Table 7: Fitting of GARCH-type model with normal, student and NIG innovations for Singapore Jet-Fuel daily returns.

Model	Param.	Normal Est.	Normal Std. error	Normal p-val	Param.	STD Est.	STD Std. error	STD p-val	Param.	NIG Est.	NIG Std. error	NIG p-val
GARCH	ω	0.000	0.000	0.000	ω	0.000	0.000	0.007	ω	0.000	0.000	0.001
	α_1	0.002	0.000	0.000	α_1	0.347	0.061	0.000	α_1	0.307	0.055	0.000
	β_1	0.994	0.000	0.000	β_1	0.652	0.064	0.000	β_1	0.692	0.043	0.000
					ν	2.314	0.074	0.000	α	−0.228	0.047	0.000
									β	0.055	0.009	0.000
BIC/AIC	−5.351	−5.333			−6.714	−6.690			−6.770	−6.739		
EGARCH	ω	−0.040	0.004	0.000	ω	−0.904	0.265	0.001	ω	−0.642	0.201	0.001
	α_1	−0.061	0.018	0.001	α_1	−0.004	0.040	0.911	α_1	−0.005	0.066	−0.937
	β_1	0.994	0.000	0.000	β_1	0.895	0.027	0.000	β_1	0.907	0.026	0.000
	γ_1	0.033	0.013	0.011	γ_1	0.558	0.057	0.000	γ_1	0.886	0.259	0.001
					ν	2.100	0.037	0.000	α	−0.264	0.049	0.000
									β	0.010	0.006	0.079
BIC/AIC	−5.424	−5.399			−6.677	−6.646			−6.776	−6.740		
IGARCH	ω	0.000	0.000	0.900	ω	0.000	0.000	0.000	ω	0.000	0.000	0.000
	α_1	0.000	0.001	0.995	α_1	0.348	0.042	0.000	α_1	0.308	0.039	0.000
	β_1	1.000			β_1				β_1	0.692		
					ν	2.313	0.040	0.000	α	−0.229	0.046	0.000
									β	0.055	0.008	0.000
	−5.355	−5.343			−6.717	−6.698			−6.773	−6.748		

(*Continued*)

Table 7: (Continued)

Model		Normal				STD				NIG		
	Param.	Est.	Std. error	p-val	Param.	Est.	Std. error	p-val	Param.	Est.	Std. error	p-val
gjrGARCH	ω	0.000	0.000	0.010	ω	0.000	0.000	0.071	ω	0.000	0.000	0.001
	α_1	0.000	0.005	1.000	α_1	0.314	0.089	0.000	α_1	0.274	0.066	0.000
	β_1	0.980	0.002	0.000	β_1	0.649	0.098	0.000	β_1	0.690	0.044	0.000
	γ_1	0.032	0.010	0.001	γ_1	0.073	0.127	0.566	γ_1	0.081	0.109	0.459
					ν	2.318	0.097	0.000	α	-0.231	0.047	0.000
									β	0.055	0.009	0.000
	-5.406	-5.382			-6.712	-6.681			-6.768	-6.731		
APARCH	ω	0.001	0.000	0.000	ω	0.000	0.000	0.520	ω	0.003	0.005	0.573
	α_1	0.007	0.002	0.001	α_1	1.000	0.335	0.003	α_1	1.000	0.229	0.000
	β_1	0.991	0.000	0.000	β_1	0.636	0.040	0.000	β_1	0.670	0.054	0.000
	γ_1	1.000	0.001	0.000	γ_1	0.093	0.080	0.245	γ_1	0.081	0.109	0.455
	δ	0.432	0.038	0.000	δ	1.646	0.319	0.000	δ	0.939	0.365	0.010
					ν	2.128	0.053	0.000	α	-0.302	0.049	0.000
									β	0.014	0.006	0.016
	-5.538	-5.507			-6.748	-6.711			-6.833	-6.790		

Table 8: Switching Regime GARCH models fitting for ICE Brent, ICE Low Sulphur Gasoil, Singapore Gasoil, Jet Fuel/Kerosene and Regrade.

	State1			State2				
	α_{01}	α_{11}	β_1	α_{02}	α_{12}	β_2	P_1	P_2
Regrade	0.0008	0.1677	0.3855	0.1053	0.0266	0.7489	0.8670	0.8546
Sing GO	0.0001	0.0001	0.0001	0.0001	0.0001	0.9484	0.9532	0.2853
Kerosene	0.0001	0.0423	0.0001	0.0008	0.0001	0.7934	0.9442	0.9145
Brent	0.0001	0.2862	0.5219	0.0005	0.0016	0.8411	0.9673	1.0000
LSGO	0.0001	0.0004	0.0001	0.0001	0.0863	0.7308	0.9946	0.0000

3. Proxy-Hedging

In an incomplete financial market, it is hardly ever possible to find the hedging instrument that perfectly mirrors a given price risk. Most of refiners and airline companies attempt to hedge around 80% of their jet-fuel exposure Adams and Gerner (2012). In large part, they do this by purchasing futures contracts on crude oil, the feedstock for producing jet fuel, or other oil derivative products such as heating oil, used in USA, and gasoil in Europe. The regional prices of these commodities with jet fuel are correlated in the long run, however in the short term, price comovements are asynchronous. This erratic relationship defines the basis risk, which is the financial risk occurred when the chosen "proxy-hedge" does not entirely offset the price risk of the main underlying asset (Kamara and Siegel, 1987; Ankirchner and Imkeller, 2011).

This is clearly seen from the 1 Month rolling correlation plot in Figure 2, which shows that despite the "obviously" highly correlated dynamics of the spot prices exhibited earlier in Figure 1, there exists basis risk when hedging in oil markets and this is mainly explained by product, location and time factors.

Another representation of the basis risk is exhibited in Figure 3 which shows the evolution of the price difference between Singapore Gasoil and Jet Kerosene, known also as Regrade. All this is to show that even when a proxy instrument appears to be a highly corre-lated instrument, the basis risk associated with it undermines the

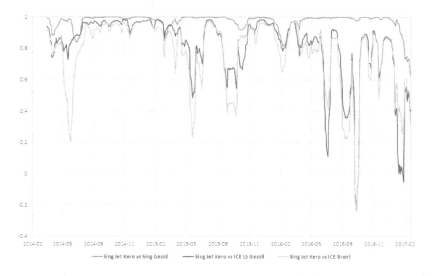

Figure 2: 1M rolling correlation of front month futures.

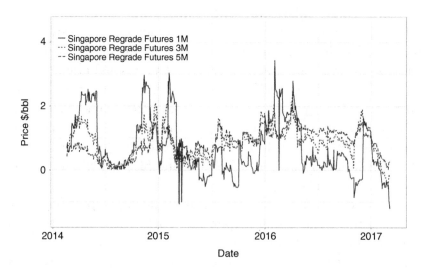

Figure 3: Evolution of Singapore regrade futures price.

effectiveness of the proxy-hedge as it exacerbates the cash flow
volatility that the hedge is designed to reduce.

A major challenge in "proxy-hedging" (Viken and Thorsrud,
2014) consists in finding the proxy instrument which minimizes basis

risk and hedge volatility. As such, an Asian company willing to cover its long jet-fuel exposure has the following options:

- *Jet-Fuel direct hedge*: Sell Singapore Jet Kerosene Futures or first line swap.
- *Crude "proxy hedge"*: Sell ICE Brent Crude Futures or first line swap.
- *Gasoil "proxy hedge"*: Sell ICE LS Gasoil or Singapore 0.5% Gasoil Futures.
- *Basis risk "slice & dice proxy hedge"*: Hedge jet fuel price components opportunistically (Firstly hedge crude oil component, secondly Brent/Gasoil crack, and lastly Regrade).

Companies exposed to jet-fuel price risk prefer to hedge their exposure using crude oil or Gasoil contracts even if jet fuel future contracts are also available because the liquidity on jet fuel is very thin. Figure 3 exhibits volumes of the considered dataset on a logarithmic scale. We notice that ICE Brent Crude oil and LS Gasoil futures are significantly more liquid than the Singapore Kerosene and Gasoil 0.5% futures. If jet fuel contracts were available at the same 'cost' as crude oil contracts, then clearly this would be a better alternative.

As such, if an Asian airline company wants to cover its jet-fuel price risk, since the volumes exchanged on this market are thin, it might use one of the "proxy-hedge" options described earlier. However, choosing the right one means making a trade-off between liquidity and basis.

The current literature focuses mainly on the risks related to level forecasting when using a proxy-hedge, but ignores completely the density forecasting. The main issue with proxy-hedging is the fact that markets have different depth. On one hand, a shock in the Brent market might not be fully reflected in the jet-fuel market. On the other hand, a small variation in the Brent Market might generate a shock in the jet-fuel market due to difference in liquidity. The basis risk of proxy-hedge using both plain or derivatives-based strategies is

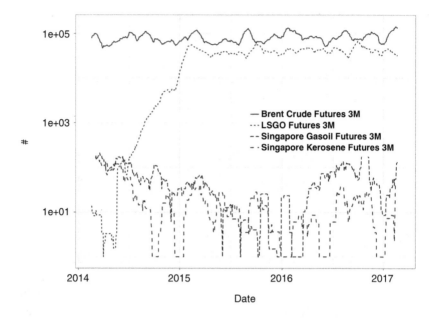

Figure 4: ICE Brent, ICE LS Gasoil, Singapore Gasoil and Jet Fuel Futures liquidity.

generated also by the differences in the distribution features thereby underlying the need of testing the density forecasting ability.

For testing the proxy-hedging with Brent, gasoil or regrade, a trader exposed to jet-fuel price risk should assess the density forecasting capacity of an econometric risk model. Thus a model estimated on Brent or Gasoil returns should be tested in terms of density forecasting on the jet-fuel prices. Furthermore these test would be a good indicator of how the proxy hedging is affected by contagion, mainly in periods were regime switches are observed.

4.   Forecasting Densities

4.1.   *Gneiting test*

This section describes the technique for reaching the main goal of this paper, the testing in terms of density forecasting of proxy-hedging strategies. In a recent paper, Gneiting and Ranjan (2011) proposed a test that develops the weighting approach of Amisano and Giacomini (2007) but avoids counter intuitive inferences. We use this test for assessing the density forecasting in proxy-hedging.

Gneiting's test aims to built a proper score with the respect of the above definition based on appropriately weighted versions of the continuous ranked probability score (CPRS). For any density function f(y) with a cumulative distribution function $F(z) = \int_{-\infty}^{z} f(y)dy$ the continuous ranked probability score is then defined as

$$CPRS(F, y) = \int_{-\infty}^{\infty} PS(F(r), 1(y \leq r))dr, \tag{7}$$

where

$$PS(F(r), 1(y \leq r)) = (1(y \leq r) - F(r))^2 \tag{8}$$

is the Brier probability score for the probability forecast $F_t(r) = \int_{-\infty}^{r} f(y)dy$ of the event $y \leq r$.

The weighted probability score described by Matheson and Winkler (1976) and Gneiting and Raftery (2007) is written as

$$S^w(f, y) = -\int_{-\infty}^{\infty} PS(F(r), 1(y \leq r)) \cdot w_r(r)dr$$

$$= -\int_{-\infty}^{\infty} (1(y \leq r) - F(r))^2 \cdot w_r(r)dr, \tag{9}$$

where the weighting function $w_r(r)$ applies to the forms presented in Equation (7). In a discrete form the above score can be approximated by assuming an I steps equidistant discretization of a target region with the boundaries y_l, y_u

$$S_f^w(f, y) = \frac{y_u - y_l}{I - 1} \sum_{i=1}^{I} w(y_i)PS(F(y_i), I(y \leq y_i)), \tag{10}$$

$y_i = y_l + i\frac{y_u - y_l}{I}$. The test based on the following statistic which is leveraged from the Amisano–Giacomini test

$$Z_n = \frac{E(S_f^w(f, y) - S_f^w(g, y))}{\widehat{\omega}_n}, \tag{11}$$

where

$$E_t(S_f^w(f,y)) = \frac{1}{n-k+1} \sum_{t=m}^{m+n-k} S(f_{t+k}, y_{t+k}), \qquad (12)$$

$$E_t(S_f^w(g,y)) = \frac{1}{n-k+1} \sum_{t=m}^{m+n-k} S(g_{t+k}, y_{t+k}), \qquad (13)$$

and $\widehat{\omega_n}$ is an estimate of $\text{var}(\sqrt{n}(E_t(S_f^w(f,y)) - E_t(S_g^w(g,y)))$.

5. Backtesting Results of Proxy-Hedging

Density forecasting techniques provide with insightful information for risk assessment purposes especially in the commodities markets dominated by non-Gaussian behavior and volatility clustering (Frunza and Guégan, 2013).

Thus, based on the specifications of the Gneiting test presented above we built a testing process for the proxy-hedging strategies. The full dataset contains the daily prices of Jetfuel, ICE Brent, ICE gasoil or Singapore Gasoil between 01/01/2014 and 01/03/2017. The testing process has the following steps:

(1) A model (M1) is estimated on the daily returns of the proxy (ICE Brent, ICE gasoil or Singapore Gasoil). The data set contains a (*out of sample*) the first 250 consecutive days of the considered full sample.

(2) A model (M2) is estimated on the daily returns of the jet-fuel prices. The data set (*in sample*) contains a window of 250 consecutive days, which starts immediately after the end of the out of sample dataset.

(3) The Gneiting test score is computed for comparing the model M1 estimated *out of sample* on the proxy with model M2 estimated on the actual *in sample* jet-fuel returns.

(4) The *out of sample* window is rolled over with one day and same is for the *in sample* window. Steps 1–3 are repeated until the end of the full sample.

(5) A time series of Gneiting test scores is built.

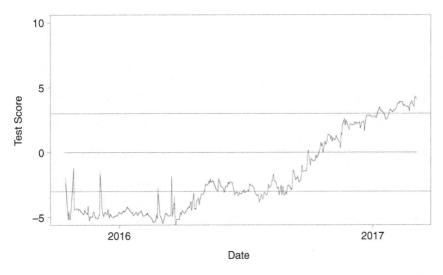

Figure 5: Evolution of the Gneiting test score for NIG model with Singapore Gasoil. The horizontal solid lines are the boundaries out of which test's null hypothesis is rejected.

The previous sections underlined that NIG distribution exhibits good fitting features for all the underlying studied in this chapter. Therefore, we will consider the NIG model for both *out of sample* and *in sample*. Therefore, the test score will assess the power of the density fitted on the proxy to forecast the jet-fuel distribution feature.

Figure 5 shows the evolution of the testing Score for NIG model, where as the proxy-hedge is realized with Singapore Gasoil. Until July 2016 the score rejects at 99% confidence level the null hypothesis that the model fitted on the proxy is similar to the model fitted on the jet fuel and in fact the proxy provides with better results. After July 2016 the score enter in the confidence region thereby not rejecting the null hypothesis. Towards 2017 the NIG model fitted on proxy losses gradually from its forecasting capacity but remains close to the confidence region.

Figure 6 shows the evolution of the testing Score for NIG model, where as the proxy-hedge is realized with ICE Low Sulphur Gasoil. Until July 2016 the score does not rejects at 99% confidence level the null hypothesis that the model fitted on the proxy is similar to the

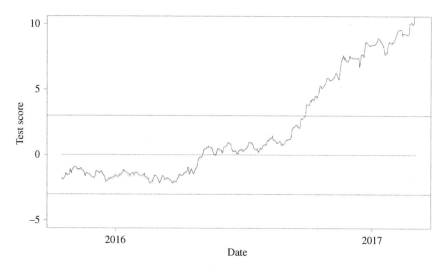

Figure 6: Evolution of the Gneiting test score for NIG model and ICE low Sulphur Gasoil. The horizontal solid lines are the boundaries out of which test's null hypothesis is rejected.

model fitted on the jet-fuel. After July 2016 the NIG model fitted on Low Sulphur Gasoil proxy has lost its forecasting capacity and became inappropriate.

Figure 7 shows the evolution of the testing Score for NIG model, where as the proxy-hedge is realized with ICE Brent. Until July 2016 the score does not rejects at 99% confidence level the null hypothesis that the model fitted on the proxy is similar to the model fitted on the jet fuel. After July 2016 the NIG model fitted on Brent returns has lost massively its forecasting ability and became inappropriate.

The three charts (Figures 5–7) and of the testing scores exhibit a positive trend after July 2016 due to the fact that the NIG model losses its forecasting capability in terms of density. The forecasting test specified above is implemented over rolling windows, hence the newer data is included in the test gradually. Thus the test score does not have a jump in 2016 but shows a continuous trend. Moreover the contagion of market coupling related to the extreme events, contributes to the stability of the hedging process with proxies. Nevertheless if the contagion of market decoupling persists during regime

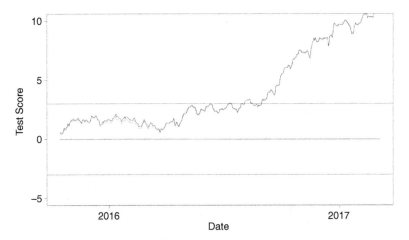

Figure 7: Evolution of the Gneiting test score for NIG model with ICE Brent. The horizontal solid lines are the boundaries out of which test's null hypothesis is rejected.

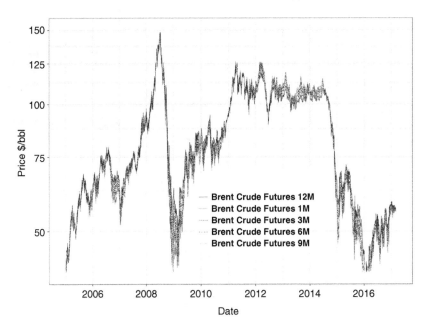

Figure 8: Evolution of Brent Crude Futures price listed on ICE for the following maturities: 1M, 3M, 6M, 9M and 12M.

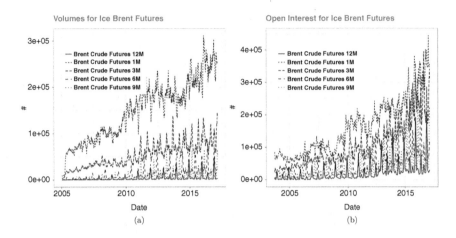

Figure 9: (a) Volume Ice Brent Futures. (b) Open Interest for Ice Brent Futures.

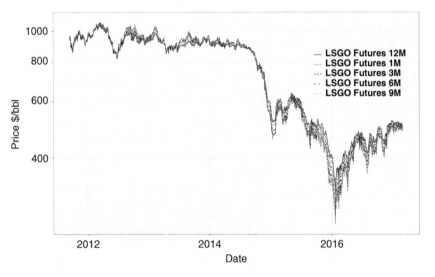

Figure 10: Evolution of Low Sulphur Gasoil Futures price listed on ICE for the following maturities: 1M, 3M, 6M, 9M and 12M.

changes, the hedging can became less stable especially in condition of high volatility. Interestingly in the studied case the contagion effect diminishes concomitantly the interdependence for all four markets after July 2016, Brent, Jetfuel, Sigapore and Ice Gasoil, thereby

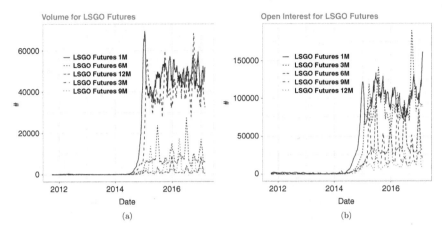

Figure 11: (a) Volume for ICE Low Sulphur Gasoil Futures. (b) Open Interest for ICE Low Sulphur Gasoil Futures.

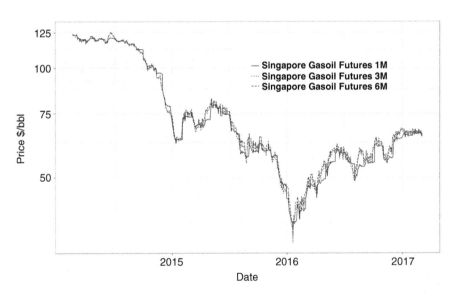

Figure 12: Evolution of Gasoil 0.5% (Platts) Futures price listed on Singapore exchange for the following maturities: 1M, 3M and 6M.

leaving the hedger with very limited options in terms of basis risk management.

The Singapore and London gasoil markets are different in term of returns time series, but have structural similarities in term of density

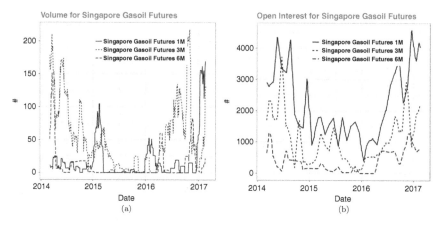

Figure 13: (a) Volume for Singapore Gasoil 0.5% (Platts) Futures. (b) Open Interest for Singapore Gasoil 0.5% (Platts) Futures.

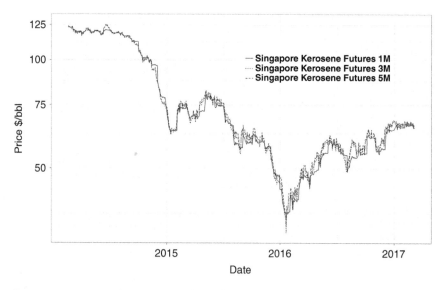

Figure 14: Evolution of Jet Kerosene (Platts) Futures price listed on Singapore exchange for the following maturities: 1M, 3M and 5M.

features. Thus a trader (ie. airliner) could be tempted to interpret that he has different hedging alternatives in term of markets, but from a risk management perspective, the three studied alternatives exhibit a similar behavior. Changes in behavioral regimes can alter

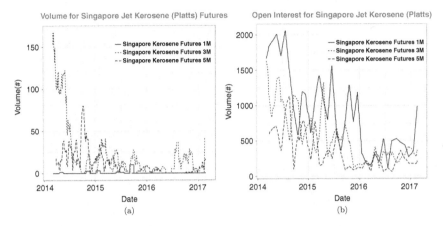

Figure 15: (a) Volume for Singapore Jet Kerosene (Platts) futures. (b) Open interest for Singapore Jet Kerosene (Platts) futures.

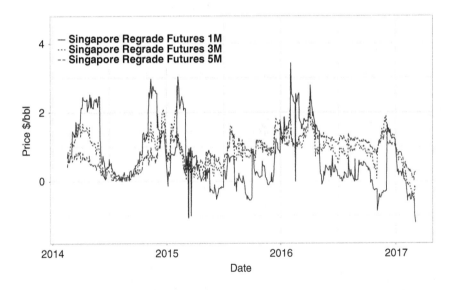

Figure 16: Evolution of Singapore regrade futures prices.

the proxy-hedging process especially due to the fact that contagion impact the coupling and the decoupling of the four markets in similar ways.

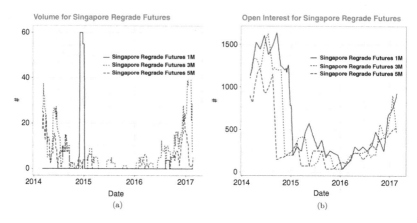

Figure 17: (a) Volume Singapore regrade futures. (b) Open interest for Singapore regrade futures.

6. Conclusions

This paper explores the topic of proxy hedging in middle distillates market with a focus on jet-fuel. The research addresses the problem of a refinery or an airline company that hedges its jet fuel price risk with proxy instruments including Brent futures and gasoil futures. The problem is studied in two steps: first the various econometric models with fat tails and volatility clustering are explored in relation with the returns of daily time series and second the proxy hedging is test based on density forecasts methods using the results for the first step.

The results from the first part show that NIG distribution, APARCH specifications of the volatility dynamics capture in an appropriate manner the behavior of jet fuel, brent and gasoil prices. Also GARCH switching regimes models are good candidates for analyzing the markets that might exhibit thin liquidity.

The second part shows that the NIG model fitted on the Singapore Gasoil as proxy has the best density forecasting abilities from the considered choices. The main finding of this paper is that a trader exposed to jet fuel price risk might think he has different hedging alternatives in term of markets, where in reality from a risk management perspective, the alternatives could exhibit a similar behavior in term of density forecasting capability. Contagion impacts negatively the proxy-hedging especially when the behavior of jet-fuel and its proxy-hedging are decoupling at the same time, thereby leaving the trader with limited options.

A future direction for our research is the consideration of transaction costs in the Gneiting test score function, as trading future contracts usually involves brokerage fees and liquidity across different product maturities. This leads to addressing the problem of dimensionality, as it would be necessary to consider a technique such as approximate dynamic programming to produce a hedging policy that reflects such costs.

Appendix A

A.1. *Generalized hyperbolic distributions*

This brief review of the Generalized Hyperbolic distribution functions focuses on the Normal Inverse Gaussian function. The generic form of a Generalized Hyperbolic model is:

$$
f(x; \lambda; \chi; \psi; \mu; \sigma; \gamma) = \frac{(\sqrt{\psi\chi})^{-\lambda}\psi^{\lambda}\left(\psi + \frac{\gamma^2}{\sigma^2}\right)^{0.5-\lambda}}{\sqrt{2\pi}\sigma K_{\lambda}(\sqrt{\psi\chi})}
$$

$$
\times \frac{K_{\lambda-0.5}\left(\sqrt{\left(\chi + \frac{(x-\mu)^2}{\sigma^2}\right)\left(\psi + \frac{\gamma^2}{\sigma^2}\right)}\right) e^{\frac{\gamma(x-\mu)}{\sigma^2}}}{\left(\sqrt{\left(\chi + \frac{(x-\mu)^2}{\sigma^2}\right)\left(\psi + \frac{\gamma^2}{\sigma^2}\right)}\right)^{\lambda-0.5}},
$$

where $K_{\lambda}(x)$ is the modified Bessel function of the third kind:

$$
K_{\lambda}(x) = \frac{1}{2}\int_0^{\infty} y^{\lambda-1} e^{-\frac{x}{2}(y+y^{-1})} dy. \tag{A.1}
$$

With properly chosen parameters, this distribution reduces to the following distributions:

(1) $\lambda = 1$: hyperbolic distribution,
(2) $\lambda = -1/2$: NIG distribution,

(3) $\lambda = 1$ and $\xi \to 0$: Normal distribution,
(4) $\lambda = 1$ and $\xi \to 1$: Symmetric and asymmetric Laplace distribution,
(5) $\lambda = 1$ and $\chi \to \pm\xi$: Inverse Gaussian distribution,
(6) $\lambda = 1$ and $|\chi| \to 1$: Exponential distribution,
(7) $-\infty < \lambda < -2$: Asymmetric Student,
(8) $-\infty < \lambda < -2$ and $\beta = 0$: Symmetric Student,
(9) $\gamma = 0$ and $0 < \lambda < \infty$: Asymmetric Normal Gamma distribution.

Among the Generalized Hyperbolic family, the Normal Inverse Gaussian distribution can be obtained by setting $\lambda = -\frac{1}{2}$ in the previous equation. Thus:

$$f\left(x; -\frac{1}{2}; \chi; \psi; \mu; \sigma; \gamma\right) = \frac{\chi^{\frac{1}{2}}\left(\psi + \frac{\gamma^2}{\sigma^2}\right)}{\pi\sigma e^{\sqrt{-\psi\chi}}}$$

$$\times \frac{K_1\left(\sqrt{\left(\chi + \frac{(x-\mu)^2}{\sigma^2}\right)\left(\psi + \frac{\gamma^2}{\sigma^2}\right)}\right) e^{\frac{\gamma(x-\mu)}{\sigma^2}}}{\left(\sqrt{\left(\chi + \frac{(x-\mu)^2}{\sigma^2}\right)\left(\psi + \frac{\gamma^2}{\sigma^2}\right)}\right)}.$$

By changing the variables of the previous equation $c = \frac{1}{\sigma^2}$; $\beta = \frac{\gamma}{\sigma^2}$; $\delta = \sqrt{\frac{\chi}{c}}$; $\alpha = \sqrt{\frac{\psi}{\sigma^2} + \beta^2}$ we obtain a more popular representation, and the density of the $NIG(\alpha,\beta,\mu,\delta)$ distribution is equal to:

$$f_{NIG}(x; \alpha; \beta; \mu; \delta) = \frac{\delta\alpha \cdot exp(\delta\gamma + \beta(x - \mu))}{\pi \cdot \sqrt{\delta^2 + (x - \mu)^2}} K_1(\alpha\sqrt{\delta^2 + (x - \mu)^2}).$$

The moments (mean, variance, skewness and kurtosis) are, respectively, equal to:

$$E(X) = \mu + \delta\frac{\beta}{\gamma},$$

$$V(X) = \delta\frac{\alpha^2}{\gamma^3},$$

$$S(X) = 3\frac{\beta}{\alpha \cdot \sqrt{\delta\gamma}},$$

$$E(X) = 3 + 3(1 + 4(\frac{\beta}{\alpha})^2)\frac{1}{\delta\gamma}.$$

Thus, the NIG distribution allows for behavior characterized by heavy tails and strong asymmetries, depending on the parameters α, β and δ.

A.2.   GARCH models

Few popular variations of the GARCH model include:

- *The integrated GARCH (IGARCH) model* The integrated GARCH model (Engle and Bollerslev, 1986) assumes that the persistence is one. Omitted structural breaks should be assessed before using an IGARCH model.

$$\epsilon_t | \phi_{t-1} \propto N(0, h_t) \ or \ z_t \propto N(0, 1), \tag{A.2}$$

$$h_t = \alpha_0 + (1 - \beta_1) \cdot \epsilon_{t-1}^2 + \beta_1 \cdot h_{t-1}. \tag{A.3}$$

- *The Glosten–Jagannathan–Runkle (GJR–GARCH) model* introduced by Glosten *et al.* (1993) adds asymmetry in the volatility process:

$$h_t = \alpha_0 + (\alpha_1 + c \cdot I_{t-1}) \cdot \epsilon_{t-1}^2 + \beta_1 \cdot h_{t-1}, \tag{A.4}$$

where

$$I_{t-1} = \begin{cases} 0 & \epsilon_{t-1} \geq 0 \\ 1 & \epsilon_{t-1} < 0. \end{cases}$$

- *The exponential GARCH (EGARCH) model* introduced by Nelson (1991) aims to capture asymmetric reaction of volatility to the positive and negative information about the market. Volatility of the

EGARCH model, which is measured by the conditional variance is an explicit multiplicative function of lagged innovations.

$$\log h_t = \alpha_t + \sum_{i=1}^{\infty} \beta_i g(Z_{t-k}), \qquad (A.5)$$

where the function g is defined as $g(Z_t) = \theta Z_t + \gamma(|Z_t| - E|Z_t|)$, $g(Z_t)$ having a zero mean $E[g(Z_t)] = 0$. No restriction are imposed in this version of the GARCH model. EGARCH can also assess whether the shocks in variance are persistent or not.

- *The Asymmetric Power GARCH model (APARCH)* introduced by (Ding *et al.*, 1993) accounts for leverage effect and also the fact that the sample autocorrelation of absolute returns is higher than that of squared returns (Reider, 2009).

$$h_t^{0.5 \cdot \zeta} = \alpha_0 + \sum_{i=1}^{q} \alpha_i (|\epsilon_{t-i}^{\zeta}| - \gamma_i \cdot \epsilon_{t-i})^{\zeta} + \sum_{i=1}^{p} \beta_i h_{t-i}^{0.5 \cdot \zeta}. \qquad (A.6)$$

It can be notice that Equation (A.6) with $\zeta=2$ and $\gamma_i = 0$ matches the classic GARCH model with Gaussian innovations.

References

Adams, Z. and Gerner, M. (2012). Cross hedging jet-fuel price exposure, *Energy Economics*, 34(5), 1301–1309.

Amisano, G. and Giacomini, R. (2007). Comparing density forecasts via weighted likelihood ratio tests, *Journal of Business & Economic Statistics*, 25(2), 177–190.

Ankirchner, S. and Imkeller, P. (2011). Hedging with residual risk: A bsde approach, in *Seminar on Stochastic Analysis, Random Fields and Applications VI*, (Springer), pp. 311–325.

Balbás, A., Downarowicz, A. and Gil-Bazo, J. (2008). Price inefficiencies in commodities-linked derivatives markets: A model-free analysis, Available at SSRN 1304085.

Barndorff-Nielsen, O. (1977). Exponentially decreasing distributions for the logarithm of particle size, *Proceedings of the Royal Society of London. A. Mathematical and Physical Sciences*, 353(1674), 401–419.

Bollerslev, T. (1987). A conditionally heteroskedastic time series model for speculative prices and rates of return, *The Review of Economics and Statistics*, 69, 542–547.

Clark, E., Tan, M. and Tunaru, R. (2003). Cross hedging jet fuel on the singapore spot market, *International Journal of Banking and Finance*, 1(2), 1.

Ding, Z., Granger, C. W. and Engle, R. F. (1993). A long memory property of stock market returns and a new model, *Journal of Empirical Finance*, 1(1), 83–106.

Eberlein, E. and Prause, K. (2002). The generalized hyperbolic model: Financial derivatives and risk measures, in *Mathematical Finance Bachelier Congress 2000*, Springer, pp. 245–267.

Engle, R. F. and Bollerslev, T. (1986). Modelling the persistence of conditional variances, *Econometric Reviews*, 5(1), 1–50.

Frunza, M.-C. and Guégan, D. (2013). Risk assessment for a structured product specific to the co2 emission permits market, *The Journal of Alternative Investments*, 15(3), 72–91.

Glosten, L. R., Jagannathan, R. and Runkle, D. E. (1993). On the relation between the expected value and the volatility of the nominal excess return on stocks, *The Journal of Finance*, 48(5), 1779–1801.

Gneiting, T. and Raftery, A. E. (2007). Strictly proper scoring rules, prediction, and estimation, *Journal of the American Statistical Association*, 102(477), 359–378.

Gneiting, T. and Ranjan, R. (2011). Comparing density forecasts using threshold-and quantile-weighted scoring rules, *Journal of Business & Economic Statistics*, 29, 3.

Haas, M., Mittnik, S. and Paolella, M. S. (2004). A new approach to markov-switching garch models, *Journal of Financial Econometrics*, 2(4), 493–530.

Kamara, A. and Siegel, A. F. (1987). Optimal hedging in futures markets with multiple delivery specifications, *The Journal of Finance*, 42(4), 1007–1021.

Kanamura, T., Rachev, S. T. and Fabozzi, F. J. (2010). A profit model for spread trading with an application to energy futures, *The Journal of Trading*, 5(1), 48–62.

Matheson, J. E. and Winkler, R. L. (1976). Scoring rules for continuous probability distributions, *Management Science*, 22(10), 1087–1096.

Nascimento, J. and Powell, W. (2008). An optimal solution to a general dynamic jet fuel hedging problem, Department of Operations Research and Financial Engineering.

Nelson, D. B. (1991). Conditional heteroskedasticity in asset returns: A new approach, *Econometrica: Journal of the Econometric Society*, 1, 347–370.

Reider, R. (2009). *Volatility forecasting i: Garch Models*, New York.

Roncoroni, A., Fusai, G. and Cummins, M. (2015). *Handbook of Multi-commodity Markets and Products: Structuring, Trading and Risk Management*, John Wiley & Sons.

Viken, C. and Thorsrud, M. S. (2014). Proxy hedging of commodities. Student thesis, Copehagen business school, https://studenttheses.cbs.dk/handle/10417/4750.

Index

A

A-DCC, 86, 92, 97–98, 100, 102, 104, 112
ADF, 17–18, 32–33, 54–55, 147, 150
ad hoc sample splitting, 52
adverse market conditions, 201, 212, 227–228, 231, 233
African markets, 248
African stock indices, long-term relationships between, 253
African stock markets, 241
    comovements of, 237–240
    daily index data of, 245–246
    descriptive statistics for, 246
    integration in, 237–240
    methodology and data, 240–246
    results, 246–253
agricultural prices, 199
agricultural risk management problems, 199–200
agriculture, dynamic nature of, 199
AIC, 63, 99, 147, 150, 296, 300
Akaike information criterion (*see also* AIC), 63
Al Janabi model, 204
    and L-VaR, 204–211
All Commodities Index, 211, 214, 219
Amisano–Giacomini test, 307
annualized volatilities, 213

application specific Integrated Circuit, 13
APARCH, 200, 293, 300, 320
ARCH, 38, 42, 64, 97, 100, 139, 200, 271
ASEAN stock markets, 238
Asian crisis, 257, 282
Asian economic crisis, 86, 89
Asian equity markets, 275
Asian-Pacific markets' correlations, 277
Asian return shocks, 275
Asian stock exchanges, comovement of, 238
assets, 180–187
    liquidity risk, 208
    markets, 260–261
    returns, distributional anomalies of, 214
ASTD, 296–298
asymmetric student (*see also* ASTD), 296
asymmetric behavior, 214
asymmetric-causality tests, 121, 123–127
asymmetric DCC (*see also* A-DCC), 86, 97, 100
    correlation, 102
    estimation results, 100
    method, 97–98
    of SP industry, 103–104

asymmetric distributions, testing for, 212–219
asymmetric impulse responses, 126–128
asymmetric information, problems of, 170–173
Asymmetric Power GARCH model (*see also* APARCH), 320
augmented Dickey–Fuller (*see also* ADF), 17, 32, 54
    unit root test, 147
auto-correlation, 7, 63–64, 100
    in Bitcoin–USD rates, 10
auto-regressive conditional heteroscedasticity (*see also* ARCH), 64, 200

B

Bai–Perron multiple break-point test results, 106–107
Baltic Dry Index (*see also* BDI), 48, 54
    changes in, 74
    predictive ability of, 74
    to stock returns, 72
banking
    problems, 32
    system, stability of, 173
banking sector, impacts of derivatives on, 133–135
    derivative usage of companies, 135–140
    Turkish (*see* Turkish banks)
bank-level governance, 262
bank market, structure of, 176
Bayesian Information criteria (*see also* BIC), 8
BDI, 48–49, 54, 56, 74–75
behavioral asymmetry, 13
betas, 275–276
BIC, 8, 296, 298, 300
bidirectional causality, 51
    from exchange rate returns, 65
bi-directional causality, 65, 128, 262
biofuels, 28–29, 39

Bitcoin, 1–4
    bubbles, 20
    currencies, 5–7
    econometric models, 7–12
    hedging capabilities of, 4
    and market efficiency, 12–16
    market price evolution, 3
    particularity of, 5
    price, 4
    rush, 18–22
    testing for bubbles, 16–18
    transactions, 15
    volatility, 4
Bitcoins–USD daily returns, 7–8, 15
Bitcoin–USD rates
    autocorrelation in, 10
    daily returns, 20
    volatility of, 9
blockchain, 5
Brent
    Crude Futures price, 311–312
    oil price changes, 63
Brent Market, 305
BRIC emerging equity markets, 261
bubbles
    corresponding timing of, 20
    detection tests on Bitcoin prices, 19
    formation and propagation of, 20
    testing for, 4, 16–18, 22
budget constraints, 225–226, 232
business risk, 164, 168, 177, 184
    efficient allocation of, 162

C

calm periods, 267
capital assets pricing model (CAPM) framework, 263
capital contribution, 167
causality, 49
    analysis methods, 146
    concept of, 61–62
    dynamics of, 53
    evidence of, 65
    testing for, 62–63

causality tests
 p-values of, 67–68
 results, 73
CBOE, 27, 31
CFSI, 86–87, 93–95, 103, 106–114
Chicago Board Options Exchange
 (*see also* CBOE), 27
China/Chinese
 economic growth, 37–38
 equity market, 37
 equity options, 28, 41
 industrial sectors in, 39
 metal market, 27
 oil consumption in, 37
 oil import dependency, 27
 stock markets, 29, 31, 38
 strategic oil reserves system,
  39
 volatility index, 27, 41
Chi-squared distribution, 214
Chow test, 65
Cleveland Financial Stress Index (*see*
 also CFSI), 86
 innovations in, 108
clustering in volatility, 10–11, 293
coherent portfolios
 composition of, 229–231
 efficient and, 204, 225–226, 228,
  233
 proactive, 226
 selection, 203
cointegration, existence of, 252–253
commodities, 91
 financialization of, 84, 91
 market risk management
  processes, 217
 portfolio of, 217–218
 risk management, 203
 time series dynamics of, 56
 trading portfolios, 202
 trading risk management,
  219–220, 222–223
commodity-dependent countries,
 197
Commodity Futures Trading
 Commission, 84

commodity markets, 85, 110, 198,
 217–218
 diversification advantages of, 90
 financialization of, 48, 50
 importance of, 198–199
 institutional investors in, 91
 portfolio optimization techniques
  in, 224
 spillover to, 91
 spot prices in, 53
commodity markets' asset allocation
 Al Janabi model and L-VaR,
  204–211
 large commodity portfolios,
  211–232
 overview, 197–204
commodity portfolios, 211–212
 datasets, statistical analysis, and
  testing for asymmetric
  distributions, 212–219
 L-VaR method, 219–232
commodity prices, 60, 200
 prospect of, 202
 returns, 202
 risk management, 198, 204–211
 volatility, 199
communication networks,
 development of, 140–141
comovements, 237, 246, 258
 of African stock markets, 240
 of Asian stock exchanges, 238
 of international stock markets,
  239
 in stock returns, 239
conditional heteroscedasticity, 64
conditional return variance, 277
 relative proportion of, 278
conditional volatility, 271
consumer price index (*see also* CPI),
 125
consumer prices, 121–123, 127
contagion, 90, 258, 262
 baseline tests of, 279
 correlation *vs.*, 262
 definition of, 258
 effects, 260, 279–282

existence and dynamics of, 261
hypothesis of, 268
interdependency and, 259
model to, 266–268
movements of, 261
signs of, 266
continuous development, 141
continuous ranked probability score, 307
contracts, 169
conventional banking
  competition from, 183–184
  sector, 180
  system, 163
copper prices, 57–58, 73
  to stock returns, 70
correlations, 275–276
  asymmetric timevarying nature of, 91
  vs. contagion, 262
  matrix, 246–247
  unconditional, 271
country-level governance, 262
covariance matrix stability, 64
covenants, 169
CPI, 124–125
creditworthiness of banks, 8
cross-correlations among variables, 60–61
cross-country linkages, 277–278
cross-market correlation, 271
cross-markets transmission
  mechanism, 258
cross-patterns comovements, 275–278
cross-sectional patterns, 260
crude, 294
  proxy hedge, 305
cryptocurrency, 1–2, 5–6, 9, 12, 20
currency exchange rate, 134
CUSUM of squares plots, 65–66

D

Data Envelopment Analysis, 139
datasets, 212–219
DCC model, 98

DCR, 176, 183–184
debt-based financial system, 167
debt-based system, 162
deposit accounts
  demand, 165, 179–180
  principal of, 180
depositors, 165–166, 171, 175–176
  detriment of, 172
  market for, 175–176
  public good nature of
    monitoring by, 176
  wealth of, 172
deposits
  guarantee scheme, 9
  market discipline, 175–176
  non-renewal of, 172
derivative-based methods, 272
derivative products, 134–141, 144, 148–149
  usage of, 148
derivatives, 149
  concept of, 141
  definition and historic root of, 141
  forward commitments, 142
  future commitments, 142–143
  general information about, 144–145
  options, 143
  purposes of, 143–144
  studies focused on, 136–138
  swap, 143
  types of, 141
descriptive statistics, 7, 31–32, 60, 95–96, 215
DigiCash Inc., 2
digital commodity, 6
digital currencies, 5
displaced commercial risk (*see also* DCR), 176, 183
distributed digital currency, 2
distributions of returns, 214
diversification, 83–84
domestic economies, 259
domestic market, 259
dual banking system, 161–162, 184

dynamic conditional correlations, 264
dynamic volatility models, 298–303

E

eCash, 2
econometric methodology, 122
economic theory, 162
effective and efficient risk-sharing, 187
  PLS, 187–188
  vibrant stock markets, 188–191
efficiency tests, 21
EGX30, 247–248
Egyptian index EGX30, 244
empirical analysis, 56, 214
empirical correlation matrix, 217
empirical mode decomposition, 4
energy price uncertainty, 27–28
energy sector commodities, 219
equities and oil, 83–87
  A-DCC method, 97–99
  data, 92–97
  generalized impulse responses,
    99–100
  Granger-causality results,
    99–100
  literature review, 87–92
  results, 100–112
equity-based assets, 166
equity-based contract, 167
equity-based Islamic banking, 182
equity-based system, 162–164
equity contract, context of, 162
equity index return distributions,
  60
equity markets, 25–26, 47–50, 74, 91,
  257–260, 275
  capture unexpected returns,
    263–266
  contagion effects, 279–282
  cross-patterns comovements
    during whole period, 275–278
  data, 53–61, 268–269
  econometric methodology, 61–63
  empirical study, 269–271
  literature review, 50–53, 260–262

model to test contagion, 266–268
movements, 261
results and discussion, 63–75
specification tests and model
  estimation, 271–274
statistical properties, 269–271
theoretical framework, 262–263
variables, 53–61
equity returns, 269
  for Saudi Arabia, 49
  stylized facts of, 271
  for United Arab Emirates, 49
  variables, 93
equity shocks, 262
error correction model, 292
estimation process, 272
Ethereum prices, 21–22
European currency, 8
European equity markets, 282
European Exchange Rate Mechanism
  crisis, 257
European market integration,
  277–278
European Union equity markets,
  237–238
Eurozone crisis, 8
exchange rate returns, 60, 75
  bidirectional causality from, 65
exponential GARCH (EGARCH)
  models, 97, 319–320
extreme value theory, 30

F

final prediction error (*see also* FPE),
  147, 150
finance, fundamental arguments of, 83
financial assets, 293
financial contagion, 261
financial crisis, 6
financial distress, 91
financial intermediation, 185
financial investors, participation of,
  91
financialization, 50
  of commodity markets, 48, 91

financial losses, 166, 168, 174–175
financial performance of companies, 139
financial securities, portfolio of, 198
financial stocks, 261–262
Financial Times Stock Exchange Index, 4
Finland, 271
forecasting densities, 306–308
foreign exchange rates, 51
forex markets, 7
FPE, 99, 147, 150
Framework of Equity Oriented Financial System
    equity-based financial system, 164–168
    origins of, 168–170
    religion principles, 169–170
funds
    expensive sources of, 183
    manager's coherent market portfolio, 228–231

G

GARCH models, 8, 200, 238, 259, 261, 264, 271–272, 299–303, 319–320
gasoil, 292, 294, 305–306
generalized auto-regressive conditional heteroscedasticity (*see also* GARCH) models, 200
    definition, 299
    derivatives prices, 299
    fit parameters, 11
    methodologies, 29, 86
    process, 271, 298–299
generalized hyperbolic distributions, 295–296, 317–319
    distributions fit results, 296–298
generalized hyperbolic models, 295–298
generalized impulse responses (*see also* GIRs), 99, 103, 105, 112, 123
    result summary, 111
    of RHO, 108

GFC, 87, 90–91, 257–260, 262, 279, 281, 283
GIRs, 99–100, 105, 110
GJR–GARCH process, 264
global economic activity, 74
global economy, 122
global financial crisis (*see also* GFC), 87, 90–91, 257–260, 262, 279, 281, 283
global financial markets, comovements of, 258
global market, 263, 265–266
global oil market, 37–38
global stock markets, 262
Glosten–Jagannathan–Runkle (GJR–GARCH) model, 319
Gneiting test, 293, 306–309
    for NIG model, 310–311
    specifications of, 308
gold prices, 57–58, 61, 67–68
Granger causality test, 48, 50, 62–63, 107, 110, 239, 248–250
    method, 99
    results, 99–100, 106, 109

H

Hammurabi Law, 141
Hannan-Quinn (*see also* HQ), 147, 150
HE, 41–42
Hedge ratios, 40–41
hedging, 141
    strategies, 41
hedging effectiveness (*see also* HE), 41–42
heteroscedasticity and auto-correlation consistent standard errors, 64
HQ, 99, 147, 150
hypothesis, 260, 281

I

IAHs, 163, 166, 168, 171, 174–175, 181, 185–186, 191
ICE Brent Crude, 296

ICE Low Sulphur Gasoil, 296, 309, 313

ICE LS Gasoil, 297

illiquidity of assets, 208

illiquid market conditions, 210

illiquid petroleum products, 293

illiquid trading positions, 206, 208

imperfections, 227–228

individual portfolio managers, 229–230

individual risks, 205

industrial metal commodity, 94

inflation, oil prices on, 122

institutional investors, 197

insurance
    mechanism of, 170
    policy, 134

integrated GARCH model, 319

interdependence, 258, 262

interdependency, 275
    and contagion, 259

interest-based debt contract, 169

interest rate shock, 128

intermediation, model of, 180

International Financial Statistics Browser, 212

International Monetary Fund, 212

international oil market, 29
    volatility index, 37

international oil prices, 29–30, 39

international stock markets, comovement of, 239

interventionism, 173–174

investment account funds, 166

investment account holders (*see also* IAHs), 163, 166, 179, 186
    losses of, 174
    risky placements for, 182
    share of, 186
    threat of, 172

investment accounts, 165

investment deposits, 166
    accounts, 174

market, shortsightedness of, 175–176

investment funds, 197–198

investors, 12–13

Islamic banking
    acceptable riskiness of, 182
    assets of, 166
    balance sheet of, 164–165
    income of, 173
    model of, 181
    theoretical characteristics of, 163
    theory and practice of, 162

Islamic economy, 161

Islamic finance, risk-sharing paradigm in, 162–163

Islamic financial intermediation, 162, 164–168

Islamic financial system, 161–164, 168–169
    banking structure, 181–187
    effective and efficient risk-sharing, 187–191
    influential hypothesis of, 170
    non-profit and loss sharing, 179–181
    PLS, 170–179, 187–188
    religion principles, 169–170
    vibrant stock markets, 188–191

Islamic jurisprudence, 164–165

J

Jarque–Bera (JB) test, 214–215, 271

jet-fuel direct hedge, 305

jet-fuel markets, 291–293
    cross-hedging performance of, 292
    econometric modeling of Singapore, 293–303
    forecasting densities, gneiting test, 306–308
    proxy-hedging, 303–306, 308–316

jet-fuel price risk, 292–293

jet-fuel proxy-hedging, challenges of,
        293
Jet Kerosene, 294, 303
        evolution of, 314
Johansen cointegration tests,
        238–240, 251–252

K

kurtosis, 295
        coefficient, 60–61
        measurements of, 214
Kwiatkowski–Phillips–Schmidt–Shin
        (KPSS) test, 32–33

L

LHF, 225
liabilities, 179–181
like lender of last resort (*see also*
        LLOR), 173
liquidation, 207–208, 228
        horizons, 211
        of projects, 172
liquidation horizon factor (*see also*
        LHF), 225
liquidity, 216–217, 305–306
        risk, 201, 206, 209–210
        threshold, 211
        variation in, 300
liquidity-adjusted value-at-risk (*see
        also* L-VaR), 201
        asset allocation model, 204
        commodity markets, 219–232
        definition of, 219
        efficient frontier, 226
        efficient portfolios with, 226–227
        of empirical correlation case,
                221–222
        essential inputs for, 222
        estimation procedures, 219
        factors, 216–217
        method, 212, 219–232
        optimization, 203–204, 222,
                226
        parallel descriptions of, 219
        parametric, 202

risk factors, 216
        technique, 204
        theoretical constructs of, 219
        variations in, 222
LLOR, 173
LM ARCH test, 271
London gasoil markets, 313–314
long-term interest rate, 93–94
low sulphur gasoil futures price, 312
L-VaR, 201, 231–232

M

MADEX, 243–244, 248, 252
managerial independence, 163–164,
        175
market
        comovements, 238
        correlation, 237
        coupling, contagion of, 310–311
        discipline strategy, 175
        economy, 185
        hypothesis, 14
        linkages, 260
        risk management process,
                205–206
Markowitz analysis, 222–223, 232
Markowitz mean–variance approach,
        224
max-likelihood method, 300
mean square prediction error, 62
mean–variance optimization, 224
metal prices, changes of, 27
Mexican crisis, 261
mining, 12–13
        capacity, 14–15
mismanagement, case of, 175
model estimation, 271–274
modified Wald test, 99
moral dimension, lack of, 177
MSCI, 54, 56, 59–60, 63, 67–73, 75
        time series dynamics of, 59
Mudharaba, 166, 184–185
        contract, 163–164, 180
        market, 177
        mode, 178–179

operations, 171
    principle of, 167
Musharaka contracts, 168, 190–191
myopia, 175–176

N

negative correlation coefficient,
    248
net profits/total equity, 145–146
NGSE, evolution of, 244
NIG, 296, 300, 309–310, 316,
    318–319
Nigeria Stock Exchange Index,
    243–244
non-Gaussian behavior, 308
non-Gaussian distribution, 291
nonlinear quadratic programming
    objective function, 225
non-normality, issue of, 203
Non-PLS system, 164
normal inverse Gaussian (*see also*
    NIG), 296, 318
    distribution, 309
    innovations, 300
    model, 310
normality, 212
    limitations of, 212
    simple assumption of, 215
    tests of, 214
normal market conditions, 227–228
NSE20, evolution of, 242
Nyblom test, 64

O

OECD
    equity markets, 275, 278–279
    equity returns, 271
    idiosyncratic shocks, 279–281
    markets, 281
off-balance accounts, 144–145
oil and equity markets, 25–29
    data, 31–33
    economic implications of results,
        40–41

review of related literature,
    29–31
spillover effects, 36–40
VAR–AGARCH approach, 35
VAR–GARCH approach, 34–35
oil dependency, 39–40
oil derivative products, 303
oil distillates markets, 291
oil exporting countries, 53
oil markets, 25–26, 40, 47–48
    economy of, 291
    information, 48
    uncertainty in, 26
oil prices, 26, 38, 57–58, 85–86, 88,
    122–123
    changes, evidence of, 74
    changes to stock returns, 71
    and consumer prices, 121–122
    data and the estimation results,
        125–129
    index, 125
    on inflation, 122
    literature review, 122–123
    methodology, 123–125
    movements, predictive power of,
        49
    shocks of, 30–31, 124, 126–127
    time series dynamics of, 56
    uncertainty, 28–30
    use of, 50
    variations in, 26
    volatility, 39
oil volatility index (*see also* OVX),
    26, 34, 41
    shocks, 28, 31
    stationary for, 33
one-step-ahead forecast, 63
optimization algorithm technique,
    203–204
optimum portfolio weights, 40
over-the-counter markets, 141
OVRLNM, 244–246
    evolution of, 244
OVTLNM, 245
OVX, 26, 28, 31–33, 36, 38

P

panel regressions, 273
parametrization, 299
peer-to-peer network, 5
perquisites, avoidance of, 175
persistence in returns, 7, 10–11, 264
Phillips–Perron (PP) test, 20, 32–33
PLS, 164, 187–188
    assets-backed or markup
        operations, 184–187
    contract, 170, 176–178
    moral hazard problem in,
        170–171
    principle of, 180
    strengths of mechanism, 170–174
    weakness of mechanism, 174–179
portfolios
    allocation, 229
    diversification, 29, 42, 87, 259
    effects, 205
    efficient and coherent, 227–228
    management, 197, 227
    managers, 225, 228–229, 231
    optimum weights, 40–41
price discovery, 13
price spillovers, 88–89
principal–agent problem, 171
profitability
    effect of, 140
    of Turkish banks, 149
profit-sharing rate, 165–166
profit shocks, 185–186
profit smoothing techniques, 186–187
property rights, 164
proxy-hedging, 292, 303–306
    backtesting results of, 308–316
    challenges of, 293
Purchasing Power Parity, 263
pure contagion, 258

Q

Quandt–Andrews breakpoint test, 65
quasi-maximum likelihood estimation
    method, 272

R

regional markets, 263, 275–276
    correlations, 265–266
    returns, 265–266, 273
regional risks, 265
    factors, 267–268
regional stock markets, 262
regrade, 294, 300, 303, 305–306
    front month futures returns,
        298
regression methodology, 138
remuneration of bank, 180
repercussions, 122
requisite evidence, 262
residual correlations, 260–261, 266
return of commodity, 211
return series descriptive statistics,
    269–270
return shock variance, 278
return volatility, 278
risk allocation/hedging, 144
    theories of, 162
risk analysis data, 213, 217–218
risk management, 29, 134, 139
    benefits, 197
    derivatives on, 138
    method, 203
    perspectives, 221, 292–293, 314
    purposes, derivatives for, 135
    strategies, 83–87, 221
RiskMetrics^{TM} methodologies, 207,
    210
risk–no gain principle, 172, 174
risk-return distribution, 167
risk-sharing, 167, 187
    concept of, 169
    hypothesis, 170
    PLS, 187–188
    prerequisites, 174–179
    principle, 173
    strategy, 163
    vibrant stock markets, 188–191
risks, local sources of, 263
risks, transfer, 162
rolling correlation plot, 303–304

S

Schwarz (SC), 147, 150
self-regulation, 174–175
SEMDEX, 242–243, 247–248, 252
serial dependency, 299–300
shocks, transmission of, 259–260
short-hedging horizons, 292
short-term interest rates, 93–94
sign bias tests, 272
silver prices, 57–58, 61
    changes, 67–69
Singapore
    gasoil markets, 313–314
    global trading hubs of, 294
    Jet-Fuel daily returns, 300
    regrade futures prices, 304, 315
Singapore Gasoil, 300, 303, 314
    front month futures returns, 297
Singapore jet-fuel, 293
    dataset presentation, 294–295
    econometric modeling of,
      293–303
    generalized hyperbolic models,
      295–298
    spot market, 292
    volatility models, 298–303
Singapore Jet Kerosene, 294–295, 315
skewness, 215, 271, 295
    measurements of, 214
social solidarity, 177
solar energy, 39
sovereign debt, 32
specification tests, 271–274
speculation, 144
spillover effects, 36–40
statistical analysis, 212–219
statutory regulation, importance of,
  163
stochastic stationary process, 207
stock markets, 26, 238–239, 268
    returns, 51
stock returns
    copper price changes to, 70
    exchange rate changes to, 67
    gold price changes to, 68

    oil price changes to, 71
    predictive ability for, 48
    silver price changes to, 69
    unidirectional causality from, 51
stress-testing strategy, 215
structural vector auto-regression
  model, 30
symmetric causality tests, 126
symmetric test results, 125
synthetic commodity, 6
systematic risk, 248
systematic theoretical assessment, 162
systemic risk, absence of, 173
systemic shocks, 261

T

test of significance, 268
three-factor model, 259
    parameters' estimation in, 272
time-series cross-section regression
  model, 267
Toda–Yamamoto-causality analysis,
  135, 146–148
traditional financial assets, 84–85
transmission, signs of, 282
TUNINDEX, 245
    evolution of, 245
Turkish banks
    analysis results, 147–149
    dataset and scope, 145–146
    derivatives for, 138, 140–141,
      143–145
    profitability of, 134–135, 139,
      145–146, 149
    Toda–Yamamoto causality
      analysis, 146–147
    type of, 142–143
turmoil, 267
    transmission of, 257
type of derivatives, 142–143

U

UK, arable farms, 200
uncertainty transmission, 31
unconditional correlations, 271

unidirectional causality, 51, 65
unit root tests, 33, 248, 251, 273–274
USD/EUR exchange rate, 92, 94–95
US equity returns, 86

V

value-at-risk (VaR) models, 62, 198
    in bakery procurement, 200
    calculation of, 205
    commodity liquidity trading
      risk, 206–211
    covariance matrix of, 63–64
    diagnostic tests, 64
    estimation techniques, 199–200
    general interest and acceptance
      of, 199
    model and maximum
      cointegration level, 146
    parameters, 64
    residuals of, 63–64
    typical, 200
    value of, 204–205
VAR, 48, 51, 62–65, 75, 99–100, 103,
    106, 112, 146–148, 150, 198–201,
    204–207, 210
VAR–AGARCH approach, 35–36
VAR–AGARCH models, 37, 40–42
VAR–GARCH approach, 34–35
VAR–GARCH models, 36, 38, 40
variables' notations and sources, 92
variance/covariance matrix, 221
variance, equation of, 264
variance ratios, 275–276
vector auto-regression (*see also* VAR)
    analysis, 147
    model, 48

vibrant Islamic banks, 189–190
    concentrated equity ownership
      with Musharaka contract,
      190–191
vibrant stock markets, 188–191
volatility, 39, 277–278
    annualized, 213
    asymmetry in, 263, 272, 319
    Bitcoin, 4, 9
    clustering in, 10–11, 271, 308
    of commodity prices, 198
    in market, 133–134
    measurement of, 199
    models, 298–303
    in oil prices, 84
    process, 272
    spillover, 28
    terms of, 210
    transmission, 26, 28, 89
Volume Singapore regrade futures,
    316
VXFXI, 31–33, 36, 38
    introduction of, 26

W

Wald test, 99
West Texas Intermediate (*see also*
    WTI), 75, 93
    crude oil daily cash prices, 200
    oil prices, 51–52, 75
WTI, 51, 75, 93, 112, 200, 292

Z

zero-correlation case, 221

CPSIA information can be obtained
at www.ICGtesting.com
Printed in the USA
BVHW040826050520
578090BV00008B/9

9 789811 210235